SUKKOT

סכות

FEAST OF TABERNACLES

Rabbi Jim Appel

APPOINTED TIMES SERIES

סכות
SUKKOT
FEAST OF TABERNACLES

Rabbi Jim Appel

סכות Sukkot, Feast of Tabernacles
Appointed Times Series
Copyright © 2023, 2024 by Rabbi James Appel

All rights reserved. No part of this book may be reproduced, stored in a retrieval system or transmitted in any way by any means—electronic, mechanical, photocopy, recording or otherwise—without the prior permission of the copyright holder, except for short excerpts accredited to the author, per the USA copyright law.

Printed in the USA
ISBN 978-1-941173-565

1. Jewish Holidays 2. Messianic Judaism 3. Spiritual Growth

Published by
Olive Press Messianic and Christian Publisher
www.olivepresspublisher.org
olivepressbooks@gmail.com

Our prayer at Olive Press is that we may help make the Word of Adonai fully known, that it spread rapidly and be glorified everywhere. We hope our books help open people's eyes so they will turn from darkness to Light and from the power of the adversary to God and to trust in ישוע Yeshua (Jesus),. (From II Thess.. 3:1; Col.. 1:25; Acts 26:18,15 NRSV and CJB.) May this book in particular reveal more deep meaning in the Jewish roots of our faith.

Front cover images: iStockphoto (artist, Chameleonseye), Gograph.com (artist, Pixelchaos). Used by permission. Sukkah image, copyright © 2023 by Rabbi Jim Appel, all rights reserved.

To honor Him, all pronouns referring to Adonai are capitalized, satan's names are not. Scriptures quotes are left as they are because of copyright laws.

All New Covenant (Testament) Scripture, unless otherwise indicated, and those elsewhere marked CJB, are taken from the *Complete Jewish Bible*. Copyright © 1998 by David H. Stern. Published by Jewish New Testament Publications, Inc. All rights reserved.

All Tanakh (Old Testament) Scripture, unless otherwise indicated, and those elsewhere marked TLV, are taken from the Tree of Life Translation of the Bible. Copyright © 2015 by The Messianic Jewish Family Bible Society.

Scriptures marked:

NASB are taken from the *New American Standard Bible* Copyright © 1960, 1962, 1968, 1971, 1972, 1973, 1975, 1977, 1995 by The Lockman Foundation, La Habra, California. All rights reserved.

NIV are taken from the Holy Bible, *New International Version*. Copyright © 1973, 1978, 1984 by International Bible Society. All rights reserved.

NKJV are taken from the *New King James Version*. Copyright © 1982 by Thomas Nelson, Inc. All rights reserved.

NLT are taken from the Holy Bible, New Living Translation, copyright ©1996, 2004, 2007 by Tyndale House Foundation. Used by permission of Tyndale House Publishers, Inc., Carol Stream, Illinois 60188. All rights reserved.

NRSV are taken from the *New Revised Standard Version* of the Bible, copyright © 1989 National Council of the Churches of Christ in the USA. Used by permission. All rights reserved.

Hag Pesakh, Passover (2019)

*Yom HaBikkurim, Firstfruits,
Resurrection Day* (2020)

Counting the Omer,
(2022)

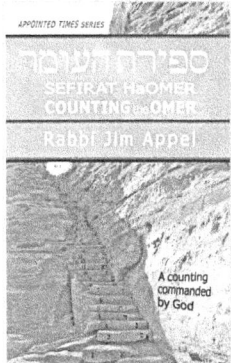

The
Appointed Time Series
by
Rabbi Jim Appel
(with the year they were published)

*Shavuot,
Pentecost,
Feast of Weeks*
(2023)

*Rosh Hashanah, Yom Teruah,
The Day of Sounding the Shofar* (2011)

Yom Kippur, The Day of Atonement
(2016)

*Sukkot, Feast
of Tabernacles* (2023)

Other books by Rabbi Jim Appel:

Messianic Judaism Class Teacher Book, Student Book, and five *Answer Books.*

I dedicate this book to

ישוע

Yeshua
who saved me.

Table Of Contents

Hebrew Terms					10
INTRODUCTION: SUKKOT THEMES			11
SECTION 1 THE SUKKAH			19
1. Life in the Sukkah			20
2. Sukkot Fellowship			39
3. Spending Time in Your Sukkah			54

SECTION 2 THE LULAV			73
4. Trees in Israel			74
5. The Mystery of the Etz Tamar (Palm Tree)   79
6. The Mystery of the Etrog and Lulav		86
7. We Are Lulavs!			102

SECTION 3 THE GREAT DAY and MORE MYSTERIES   109
8. Hoshana Rabbah			110
9. The Water Drawing Ceremony			114
10. The Mystery of Sh'mini Atzeret—
    The Eighth Day Assembly			127
11. The Mystery of the Sukkot Sacrifices		132

SECTION 4   Z'MAN SIMKHATENU, THE TIME
            OF OUR REJOICING			139
12. This is the Time of our Rejoicing		140
13. Born a King and Priest			160
14. Connected By Light			171

SECTION 5 PROPHETIC   183
15. Sukkot Themes in Prophecies about the Future   184
16. The Battle and Thousand Year Reign   192
17. Before and After the Millennial Reign   199
18. A Special History Tour of Israel   214
19. Jerusalem Jubilee   231
20. The Stranger, the Survey, the Sale,
       the Deed, and Possession   247

SECTION 6 SIMCHAT TORAH   253
21. Honoring God's Word on Simchat Torah   254
22. Josiah's Legacy   271
23 The Power of the Parashot   290
24. Stumbling Stone   301
25. How the Torah Spoke to Me   310
26. Torah vs Legalism   327
27. The Torah on Relationships   336
       Relationship Destroyers   337
       Relationship Restorers   341
28. Rightly Dividing the Word   352
       Nine Techniques for Rightly
              Dividing the Word   359
29. Biblical Meditation, *Hagah*   370
       Eight Ways to Meditate   375
30. Applying Biblical Meditation   383

9

Hebrew Terms:

יֵשׁוּעַ **Yeshua** *Yeh-shoo-ah* - Jesus' original Hebrew Name, which basically means Salvation and is pronounced and spelled almost exactly the same as the Hebrew word for salvation.

יְשׁוּעָה.**Yeshuah** *Yeh-shoo-ah* -salvation

מוֹעֵד **Moad** *moh-odd* - Hebrew for Appointed Time, referring to a Biblical Holiday

מוֹעֲדִים **Moadim** *moh-ah-deem* - plural of Moad

סֻכָּה **sukkah** *sooh-kah*- temporary dwelling *[Rhymes with "took a" as in "I took a day off."]*

סֻכּוֹת **Sukkot** *soo-koht*- Feast of Tabernacles, plural of sukkah [also spelled סוכות]

לוּלָב **lulav** *loo-lahv*- the branches commanded to be waved during Sukkot

אֶתְרוֹג **etrog** *eh-trawg*- citron, the special fruit waved with the lulav

שַׁבָּת **Shabbat** *shah-baht* - the Sabbath day of rest, the seventh day of the week which begins Friday evening and ends Saturday evening, also a rest day commanded during a Moad

בְּרִית חֲדָשָׁה **Brit Khadashah** (also spelled B'rit Hadashah or Hadasha or Chadasha) *B'reet Khah-d'-shah* (The **kh** is a **gutteral sound**.) - **New Covenant** (sometimes referring to the Covenant itself; sometimes to the whole New Testament.)

רוּחַ **Ruakh** (also spelled Ruach) *roo-ahkh* (gutteral sound) - Spirit

רוּחַ הַקֹּדֶשׁ **Ruakh HaKodesh** - the Holy Spirit

מָשִׁיחַ **Mashiakh** (also spelled Meshiach) *Muh-shee-akh* - Messiah

הַמָּשִׁיחַ **haMashiakh** ha-*Muh-shee-akh* - the Messiah

שַׁבָּתוֹת **Shabbatot** *shah-bah-toht* plural of Shabbat - Sabbaths

פָּרָשָׁה **parashah** *par-a-shah* or *par-shah* - portion (plural: parashot, *par-a-shoht* or *par-shoht*), the weekly section of the Torah read each week by observant Jews the world over.

הַשָּׂטָן **ha-satan** - the adversary (satan)

INTRODUCTION
SUKKOT THEMES

Sukkot (Feast of Tabernacles) is a Biblical Holiday that comes in the fall just four days after Yom Kippur (the day of Atonement). The Hebrew word for a Biblical *holiday* is **Moad**. The **New American Standard** version calls these days **Appointed Times**, which is a great term for them because these are appointments that God has made to meet with us.

Sukkot is a wonderful week long Moad that God appointed to be celebrated with rejoicing outside in what is called a sukkah, which we will learn all about in this book. First let me explain the word itself. *Sukkah* is singular for one sukkah. *Sukkot* is plural for more than one sukkah and is also the name of this Appointed Time. A sukkah (*booth* in some translations) is a temporary, portable shelter or dwelling.

Sukkot is the last Moad of the Biblical year. In the spring there's the Pesakh (Passover) week that includes the seven days of Unleavened Bread and Firstfruits (Resurrection Day). In the Summer there's Shavuot (Pentecost), and in the Fall we have Rosh Hashanah/Yom Teruah (Feast of Trumpets) then Yom Kippur ten days later, and the Sukkot week starts four days after that. It is seven days long, but there's also an eighth day. (We will look into that mystery in chapter 10.) On the first and eighth days, we are to have a Shabbat rest and a holy convocation (a worship meeting).

God has a purpose for each Moad. For Sukkot, He has a couple of purposes and several themes.

I am always so amazed when I think about all the different ways the themes of this whole Moad are connected and woven into so many other places in the Bible. Someone told me once that they just don't "get" Tabernacles, that they don't see how it connects. After I did a teaching on all the connections, another person sent me a note saying that she really appreciated how I connected the Old Covenant with the New Covenant.

We will just touch on the Sukkot themes here and introduce you to the overall picture as an introduction, and then in the chapters, we will go into more depth. It is really awesome how deeply woven into Scripture all these themes are. You will see Scriptures that you probably had no idea had any connection to Sukkot, but they do, and I think it will bless you.

God gives instructions in the Bible for each Moad. Non-Biblical holidays like Thanksgiving and Christmas can easily become something unintended because there are no Scriptures telling us how to celebrate them. For celebrating Sukkot, God gave us very detailed instructions and commandments to follow. Let's look at the first set:

> Leviticus 23:33--43 ADONAI *spoke to Moses saying: 34 "Speak to Bnei-Yisrael* [sons of Israel], *and say, On the fifteenth day of this seventh month is the Feast of Sukkot, for seven days to* ADONAI. *35 On the first day there is to be a holy convocation—you are to do no laborious work. 36 For seven days you are to bring an offering by fire to* ADONAI. *The eighth day will be a holy convocation to you, and you are to bring an offering by fire to* ADONAI. *It is a solemn assembly—you should do no laborious work. ... 39 So ...when you have gathered in the fruits of the land, you are to keep the Feast of* ADONAI *for seven days. The first day is to be a Shabbat rest, and the eighth day will also be a Shabbat rest. 40 On the first day you are to take choice fruit of trees, branches of palm trees, boughs of leafy trees, and willows of the brook, and rejoice before* ADONAI *your God for seven days. 41 You are to celebrate it as a festival to* ADONAI *for seven days in the year. It is a statute forever throughout your generations.... 42 You are to live in sukkot for seven days. All the native-born in Israel are to live in sukkot* (booths), *43 so that your generations may know that I had Bnei-Yisrael to dwell in sukkot when I brought them out of the land of Egypt. I am* ADONAI *your God."*

THE SUKKAH: Do you see the reason for Sukkot that God gives there at the end? The sukkah is to **remind us** that **our ancestors had to live in sukkot** for forty years wandering in the desert when they came out of bondage in Egypt on their way to the Promised Land. So that's the **first Sukkot theme.**

The **second very major theme** is **the presence of God.** Think about how amazing it was that during that time they were in the presence of a physical manifestation of God! What was that? Yes, it was the pillar of fire at night and the pillar of cloud by day. So when people crawled out of their tents early in the mornings, they'd say, "There's the fire of God." If it was later in the morning, they would've seen the cloud of God.

I want you to realize like I did one year that this was a unique period in human history. There never was a time before or since when people could just look out the door and say, "Oh! There's God!" Right? I mean, that was pretty awesome that for forty years that pillar of fire and cloud—the presence of God—was there.

The Tabernacle itself was like a giant sukkah. It was temporary and portable. And what was the purpose of the Tabernacle? It was for God's presence to dwell there. Again, it's the **theme of the presence of God**. That brings in also the need for atonement because the Holy God could not dwell in amongst the people without atonement. God told Moses that if He came down, His holiness would consume the sinful people unless atonement was made (Ex. 33:3). That's why on Yom Kippur every year, atonement was made. It was to enable the manifest presence of the Holy God to dwell for another year amongst the people as the cloud and fire.

The **third major theme** of Sukkot is seen in the **construction of the sukkah**. Traditionally, it is intentionally made in a very special way. Do you know what that is? Yes, **flimsy**. It's not supposed to be made with concrete blocks or bricks or two-by-fours. It's a flimsy structure with a roof of branches, so you can see the stars at night. The front cover photo is of our sukkah from a few years ago with the sun streaming through the latticework in the morning. It was really beautiful, but if there was a high wind, it would blow over. If there's rain, everything inside gets wet. But notice it's commanded to those "in Israel" which is more of a desert land, so they don't have to worry much about rain that time of year. (More on that in chapter 2.) One Sukkot when a few of us gathered in our congregation's sukkah to pray, it started to rain. We had umbrellas, and we sat out there and kept praying, but soon our feet got wet. The flimsiness is supposed to remind us of our dependence on God, that even though we might live in strong buildings made of concrete, stone, brick, steel, and wood, He is still Adonai Yireh, the Lord our provider.

The Israelites had to depend on God for many other things besides just their dwelling places. What were some of those things? He fed them quail and Manna. They drank water from the Rock. Health—they didn't get sick. What else? Their clothes and shoes didn't wear out! And He protected them! We are to remember and understand that God supplied **all** our ancestors' needs supernaturally in the desert for forty years. They should have perished, but God took care of them. And He gave us a special set-apart week, so we have time to celebrate and thank Him for providing for them and to remember and be thankful that He is providing and taking care of us.

So traditionally, the sukkah has to be flimsy, but what did it really have to be for the Israelites? What else did the Lord provide for them in the desert? Guidance! When He wanted them to move, the pillar of cloud moved and they followed it. Right? This shows me the real reason for living in a sukkah. What do you think it is? It had to be **portable** for traveling! The **fourth theme** is about **following God**. That's what this is all about. Their dwellings had to be portable, not flimsy. Right? Now portable dwellings must, of course, also be somewhat flimsy, but the biggest thing is they had to be portable. Why? So they could follow the cloud. God had a journey in store for them. They were going on an extended camping trip led by this pillar of cloud and fire. They had to be able to tear down and pack up at a moment's notice, and then set up again at the next stop. Their dwellings weren't like our modern tents today, which are awesome. They were probably more like ancient nomads tents held up by poles with skins and cloth around them, wind and waterproofing them. But they could be easily taken down, so the people could follow God.

The sukkah being portable is totally contrary to Jewish tradition. So why the tradition that says flimsy? Well, the only thing I could think of is that camping for recreation is really a relatively recent development that started like in the late 1950s. Before that nobody went camping. Right? And it's not a Jewish thing. Of all the Orthodox Jewish people I know, I've never met one that goes camping. So we're still with the flimsy sukkot. Okay? But not with the camping. However, in this book, along with the sukkah being flimsy, we are also going to make note of the need for it to be temporary and portable.

The **fifth theme** is **ushpizin**, which means *guests*, honored guests. When we are sitting out in our sukkah, we welcome the honored patriarchs—Abraham one day, Isaac the next day—in our minds. It's not like we are expecting them to be there. It is like we do for Elijah, setting a place for him at the Seder. The thing about these honored guests, which is another spiritual lesson, is that all of them were wanderers, following God. None of them had a permanent dwelling. So there's that theme again to remember that we are wanderers. So **needing to be hospitable to other wanderers** who come to us, is **a very strong theme** also.

So those first five themes are all related to the sukkah. There's much more to learn about the sukkah in Section 1. But first let's look at other Sukkot themes.

LULAV: The **sixth theme** is **waving the Lulav** in the sukkah. The Lulav is the traditional name for the branches and fruit the Lord commands us to wave during Sukkot:

> Leviticus 23:40 *On the first day you are to take choice fruit of trees, branches of palm trees, boughs of leafy trees, and willows of the brook, and rejoice before ADONAI your God for seven days.*

In Section 2, we will learn how this Lulav commandment is traditionally obeyed and will look into what God is illustrating and what He wants us to learn through it.

HARVEST FESTIVAL: Sukkot is a harvest celebration. The **seventh theme** is to **be thankful for the harvest**.

> Deuteronomy 16:13-15 *You are to keep the Feast of Sukkot for seven days, after gathering in the produce from your threshing floor and winepress.*

This theme applies to many things in our lives as we will learn throughout this book.

PRAYER FOR RAIN: The **eighth theme is praying for rain**. While the Temple was still standing, the Sukkot harvest festival became a time of prayer for rain for the coming year because as the people were thanking God for the harvest for this year, their minds automatically went to the next harvest, and they prayed for rain for the next year. We need to understand that in Israel the climate is very dry. They only get rain at particular times of the year. If they don't get it, the crops don't grow. So this is why the prayer for rain is such an important thing. So even today in synagogues all over the world, there are still prayers for rain being said. More on this in chapter 8.

WATER DRAWING CEREMONY: The **ninth theme is rain symbolizing salvation**. There's a wonderful verse in Isaiah about water that is sung during Sukkot:

> Isaiah 12:3 *With joy you will draw water from the wells of salvation.*

So Jewish people have kind of spiritualized the prayers for rain to be also prayers for spiritual rain. They are praying for the Spirit of God to come down and to bring salvation. That became the Great Hoshana (Hosanna) prayer. In Temple times while singing this and praying and rejoicing, the kohanim (priests) conducted a daily water drawing ceremony that culminated in a huge celebration on the last day called the Great Day. In chapters 8 and 9, we will find out much more about that and the amazing significance of what Yeshua did on this day.

Z'MAN SIMKHATENU: The **tenth theme** of Sukkot is **rejoicing**! Why? Because God commands it!

> Leviticus 23:40b *...and **rejoice** before Adonai your God for seven days*
> Deuteronomy 16:15 *Seven days you will feast to Adonai your God ... and you will be **completely filled with joy**.*

We call Sukkot "Z'man simkhatenu," which means the "time of our rejoicing." Chapter 12 is all about that!

PILGRIMAGE FEAST is the **eleventh theme**. Sukkot is one of the three pilgrimage Moadim when all males are com-

SUKKOT THEMES 17

manded to celebrate in Jerusalem and bring an offering to the Lord. Pesakh (Passover) and Shavuot (Pentecost) are the other two pilgrimage Appointed Times.

> Deuteronomy 16:16-17 *Three times a year all your males are to appear before ADONAI your God in the place He chooses—at the Feast of Matzot, the Feast of Shavuot, and the Feast of Sukkot. No one should appear before ADONAI empty-handed— 17 the gift of each man's hand according to the blessing ADONAI your God has given you.*

YESHUA'S BIRTH is the **twelfth theme**. Many Messianic rabbis, including me, have concluded that Yeshua was probably born on Sukkot. It makes a lot of sense because Yeshua was God coming in human form to dwell temporarily among men. Temporary dwellings are what this holiday is all about. In Section 4, we will look into how we have deduced Yeshua's time of birth based on Scripture. Then we will learn more about His birth that will make our hearts rejoice!

MILLENNIAL REIGN: The **thirteenth theme** is about the **final battles** of defeating the enemy's armies, and the **fourteenth theme** is Yeshua's **Millennial Reign**. The Prophet Zechariah tells us that this Millennial Kingdom will begin on Sukkot. It will be an amazing **new beginning**, which is the **fifteenth Sukkot theme**. That's when Yeshua will come to earth to reign for a thousand years, and people from all nations will come to Jerusalem to worship Him:

> Zechariah 14:16 *Then all the survivors from all the nations that attacked Jerusalem will go up from year to year to worship the King, ADONAI-Tzva'ot, and to celebrate Sukkot.*

See Section 5 for more on those final battles and the Millennial Reign. In 2013, during Sukkot, people from all nations came to Jerusalem and marched as a prophetic demonstration of what will happen in the millennium. The celebrations were so amazing!

SIMCHAT TORAH: The **sixteenth theme** is **celebrating the Word of God**, which we do on **Simchat Torah** the day after Sukkot. Section 6 that contains the last ten chapters of this book is itself a celebration of God's Word. It's all about learning how to dig in and receive the marvelous, miraculous treasure that His Word is for our lives.

So those are some of the themes associated with Sukkot that are woven in throughout Scripture. We will delve more into them and into many other things in this book. I hope you will be so blessed that your cup will run over. Let's learn all about this Moad, this Appointed Time of Sukkot, and let's rejoice together as we learn!

Section 1

THE SUKKAH

Moad Blessing:

בָּרוּךְ אַתָּה יי אֱלֹהֵינוּ מֶלֶךְ הָעוֹלָם
שֶׁהֶחֱיָנוּ וְקִיְּמָנוּ וְהִגִּיעָנוּ לַזְּמַן הַזֶּה

Barukh atah, ADONAI Eloheinu, Melekh ha'olam, shehekheyanu, v'kiy'manu, v'higiyanu la'zman hazeh.

Blessed are You, LORD our God, King of the universe, who has kept us alive, sustained us, and brought us to this season.

CHAPTER 1

LIFE IN THE SUKKAH

Sukkot is kind of an outdoor-sy holiday. In this chapter, I want to focus on living outdoors in your sukkah. So let's dig in here and understand why God wants us to do this, and what we're supposed to get out of it.

> Lev. 23:42-43 *You are to live in sukkot for seven days. All the native-born in Israel are to live in sukkot, 43 so that your generations may know that I had Bnei-Yisrael to dwell in sukkot when I brought them out of the land of Egypt. I am ADONAI your God.*

So what struck me here, because I grew up outside of Israel, is that the command is not to just build a sukkah and spend a little time in it. Do you see what the command is? *"Live in sukkot for seven days."* But notice that the command is to the citizens **in** Israel. The way this has always been interpreted is it means Jewish people living in the Land of Israel must live in their sukkot, but Jewish people in the diaspora, scattered all around the world, are not necessarily required to live in the sukkah. I believe the reason for that is because it's still very nice weather, sometimes still in the 80s, in Jerusalem at the time of Sukkot, which occurs in the fall. But in colder climates, when Sukkot comes in September or October, it's not very pleasant outside to be living in a sukkah.

Think of people in the far north like St. Petersburg in Russia or northern Canada, or Alaska, for example. Our congregation always builds a beautiful sukkah out in the yard of our

1. LIFE IN THE SUKKAH

building. Every year, I love spending some time out there in the mornings when I come in, and also having lunch out there. But it's too cold to sleep there, and when it rains, we get wet! Israel is a desert land. It hardly rains there at all except during the early and latter rains, neither of which are during Sukkot. So I'm thankful that people outside of Israel are not required to live in their sukkot (plural for *sukkah)*. We can just spend as much time as possible in them, as the weather allows. So this is the grace of God upon us.

So why would God want the people, the Israelis especially, to live in a sukkah every year, and not just for a day, but for a whole week? As I began to pray about this, my whole way of thinking about Sukkot changed because it suddenly struck me that this is the most difficult instructions of His Appointed Times to keep. It's much easier to fast for a day, than to live outside for seven days. It's easier to not eat leaven for seven days than to live in a sukkah for seven days. So I began to realize that there is more to this than just rejoicing. Why did He want us to live outdoors for seven days?

First notice that it says "*so that your generations may know...*" So this is similar to Passover. God wants our children after us to ask, "Why are you doing this?" Then we can teach them again that after the deliverance from Egypt, the plagues, and the destruction of the Egyptian army, our ancestors lived in these tent-like temporary dwellings while God led them in the wilderness and provided manna for food, water from the rock, and protected them. But it wasn't just temporary. It was forty years that they had to live in sukkot.

That's one reason, but I was led to Deut. 8 where God, through Moses, actually explains to us something else very important that we're supposed to get out of living in the sukkah. It is a whole different perspective on this. Here's what He says:

> Deuteronomy 8:1-2 *You are to take care to do the whole mitzvah that I am commanding you today, so that you may live and multiply and go in and possess the land that ADONAI swore to your fathers. 2 You are to remember all the way that ADONAI your God has led you these 40 years in the wilderness—in*

order to humble you, to test you, to know what was in your heart, whether you would keep His mitzvot or not.

He tells us we are to remember everything about the way we were led, humbled, and tested in the desert those forty years. So I was praying and asking, why? Well, there are a ton of lessons that the people of Israel learned while they were wandering in the desert—discipling lessons, and we are to live in the sukkah for seven days to help us learn those lessons. So now, if your mind works like my mind, it's like, what's the connection? The next verse tells us:

Deuteronomy 8:3 (CJB)   *He **humbled you**, allowing you to become hungry and then fed you....*

Here's what I saw, and maybe you have seen this in your own life, too. God understands that there is a powerful relationship between humility and the ability to learn, and a strong relationship between humility and the ability to apply what we have learned to our lives. In other words, it takes humility to be doers of what we've learned. Do you realize that? You see, a person must be humble enough to say they need help or to acknowledge that they lack something in order to receive that help or that knowledge. Otherwise it just goes in one ear and out the other. We have to be humble to be teachable. So, what the Lord is saying here is that the people of Israel were humbled through those years of living in sukkot in the desert.

How were they humbled? Well, this verse tells us the first way He humbled them was by hunger. They were unable to buy any food or gather it or hunt it. So they were unable to feed their families.

Now let me tell you that the meaning of Biblical humility is not understood very well. According to the Bible, humility means living with the understanding of your dependence on God, and with your understanding that whatever God calls you to do, you can do, but you've got to do it with His help. That's the meaning of Biblical humility.

So this was the idea. They began to be humbled by being hungry. Then verse 3 goes on to show the lesson:

1. LIFE IN THE SUKKAH

Deuteronomy 8:3b *... then He fed you manna—which neither you nor your fathers had known ...*

So God rescued them from hunger by sending the manna down from Heaven. The rest of verse 3 tells us why:

Deut. 8:3c *...—in order to make you understand that man does not live by bread alone but by every word that comes from the mouth of ADONAI.*

So do you see the lesson there? God will provide our food when we follow His leading. He will be our source of provision. And we need more than just physical food. That's actually the main lesson. This is interesting because this statement is the first thing recorded in the New Covenant that Yeshua said. He said it when He was confronting ha-satan. It has profound spiritual application because God's Word is our true source of nourishment. Our spirits need this sustenance. The lesson is that He will nourish us spiritually by His Word as long as we are going where He wants us to go.

So what's this got to do with living in a sukkah? Well, I now believe that God commands us to live in a sukkah to help us remember these lessons. How would it do that? Well, the sukkah is intentionally made to be flimsy. It doesn't provide the protection of a house. It doesn't protect us from sun or heat or cold. It reminds me of going camping. My wife and I used to do quite a bit of camping with our kids. And when I was thinking about this, it came back to me of a time when we went camping at a camp meeting at Elim Fellowship, a Bible college in Lima, New York.

We had this nice tent and the first night at about 2 am we started to get wet, and we couldn't stop it. Our two kids were little at the time. So we quickly packed up, took them out of the tent, and went home to get a good night's sleep, and came back the next day. That was humbling.

If you really were meant to live out in a sukkah for seven days, I mean to stay in it and never go in your house, just think about what it would be like. In our climate, you would get wet and cold when it rained. But think about how hard it would be to do things like make a meal, or to even get water. In the morning when you got up, it would be kind of difficult to shave or brush your teeth. You would have no electricity unless you had a long extension cord, I guess, but you would have no water, so don't even think about putting on your make up out there or doing your hair. How about if you had to use the bathroom? I can't even figure out how you would do that. And if it was in your front yard, you would be vulnerable to unwanted visitors. People would just be walking up and saying, "Hey, how are you today?" Welcoming visitors is a Sukkot theme, but these days they could be intruders! So life for a week of really living in the sukkah, I began to realize, would not be pleasant. It would be a chore. It would be inconvenient, uncomfortable, and even annoying to have to live there, especially when you actually have a warm, comfortable house with nice warm beds, running water, and a stove and oven to cook in just a few feet away. But imagine how humbling it would be. We'd have to live without running water, without a shower, without a toilet, without TV, without the internet! Oy vey! I was going to say cell phones, but people would probably get someone to charge their phones for them, or have an extension cord, and have it out there.

However, as you can see in the movie, *Ushpizin*,[1] even strictly observant Jewish people eat in their sukkot, but they cook the food in their house and bring it out to the sukkah. The men sleep in their sukkot, but go inside to shower, etc. The Orthodox and Hasidim believe the requirement to sleep in the sukkah applies only to the men. So the women are nicely off the hook.

So I began to see, and I hope you can see also, that living for a week in the sukkah was designed by God to humble us. That's really what this was all about. And to soften our proud hearts. Why? So we would be open to learning and applying the lessons our forefathers learned while they lived in sukkot for forty years.

So I believe that was the purpose. But what if you can't live in a sukkah for a week for some reason? What if you haven't

---

1 *Ushpizin*, a film written by Shuli Rand, directed and produced by Gidi Dar, about Sukkot in the Ultra Orthodox community. It starred Rand, and his wife, Michal, who had never acted before. Israeli film, Gilgamesh Productions, 2004.

got a yard or a porch or a garage to build one in. And as I said, in a cold climate, it would be really tough to actually live in a sukkah for a week. (That's why some north country people create a "pseudo" sukkah inside their houses.)

Rabbi Sha'ul (Apostle Paul) was writing to mostly non-Jewish people in Corinth, and they probably weren't going to live in a sukkah for a week. Listen to what he said about this learning:

> I Corinthians 10:6 *Now these things took place as prefigurative historical events* [He's talking about the 40 years in the desert], *warning us not to set our hearts on evil things as they did.*

So what Paul is saying here is that even if you can't live in a sukkah, there's great value in learning the history of that wandering in the desert. We can learn lessons from God if we are open to it, without living in a sukkah. If we will humble ourselves and say, "I do want to learn." But we have to humble ourselves to receive and apply those lessons.

So I'm just going to pray right now for each of us because I want to quickly go through what those lessons are. I want to pray that we will receive them. Can you agree with me in prayer?

Prayer: Father, we're in a nice, dry place. We thank You for it. But we humble ourselves right now and say, "We need to learn. We need to be able to apply the lessons that You taught our forefathers in the desert, so we humble ourselves and ask that You would teach us from these." In Yeshua's Name. Amein

So we're going to go on in Deuteronomy 8. We already learned part of the **first lesson**: **He will provide food.**

> Deut. 8:4 *Neither did your clothing wear out on you, nor did your foot swell these 40 years.*

So while camping in the desert, they had no place to buy or make clothing, but their clothes didn't wear out. That was an amazing thing. You see, it's humbling in the sense that, "We're depending on God here." And their feet didn't get tired or swollen from all of that hiking. God supplied their needs supernaturally.

So **lesson one is God will provide all of our basic needs when we follow Him: shelter, clothing, food.**

> Deut. 8:6 *So you are to keep the mitzvot of ADONAI your God—to walk in His ways and to fear Him.*

Here's **the second lesson. Fear the Lord and walk in His ways.** We understand that it means "reverence, respect" because the Scripture tells us it is the beginning of wisdom.

In verse 7-9, Moses describes the well watered, fertile land with great mineral wealth that they're going to come into.

> Deut. 8:10 *So you will eat and be full, and you will bless ADONAI your God for the good land He has given you.*

So we have **the third lesson there. God will provide abundantly for all your needs when you obey Him, and we are to respond by blessing Him, being thankful for His provision.**

> Deut. 8:11 *Take care that you do not forget ADONAI your God by not keeping His mitzvot, ordinances and statutes that I am commanding you today.*

Here's where it becomes really interesting.

> Deut. 8:12-14 *12 Otherwise, when you have eaten and are full and have built good houses and lived in them, 13 and when your herds and flocks multiply, and silver and gold multiplies for you and all that is yours multiplies, 14 then your heart will be haughty and you will forget ADONAI your God. He brought you out from the land of Egypt, from the house of slavery.*

> Deut. 8:14 (CJB) *you will become proud-hearted. Forgetting ADONAI your God—who brought you out of the land of Egypt, where you lived as slaves;*

This, I think, is probably the **key lesson**, one of the most important. Once they had settled in the land, built houses, had herds, and mined the gold, there was this danger that they would forget where it all came from. A spirit of pride would attempt to gain power over them. Pride is iniquity, which is in our nature. It's our flesh, our old man, our inclination to sin. We have an inclination toward the sin of pride. We have to fight against that inclination in order to become humble.

So, in their pride, they would forget that it was the Lord who freed them from being slaves in Egypt and brought them into the Promised Land because of His grace, not because of their own abilities.

So what's **the fourth lesson** here? **When things are going well, be on guard against pride.** Remember, all we have that's ours is because of God's grace.

> Deut. 8:15 *He led you through the great and terrible wilderness—fiery* [CJB: poisonous] *serpents and scorpions, and thirsty ground where there was no water. He brought forth water for you from the flinty rock.*

Here Moses reminds us of more discipling lessons: lack of water, and, He provided water for them; and dangerous snakes and scorpions, and He protected them. This would be a great danger living in a sukkah! But in my area in upstate New York, the most dangerous creature would only be mosquitoes. *smile*

This reminds me of another really interesting experience my wife and I had when we lived in California. We went backpacking up in the mountains around Santa Barbara, and the first night we kept walking a little too long so that it was getting dark by the time we decided to find a place to camp. We found this clearing and, even though it was dark, we were able to set up the tent and get something to eat and get to bed. When we woke up in the morning and got out of the tent, we saw there wasn't any grass. It was just bare ground, and there were all these little holes all around. All of a sudden the revelation came that we were in the middle of a snake-infested clearing. We got out of there real fast. That was a little worse than mosquitoes. But that was in the warm south, not in the cold north.

The **fifth lesson** here is: when we are following the Lord, **we will be protected from dangerous beasts** and **animals** that might be out there. (We weren't following the Lord at that time, but I'm so thankful that He still protected us.)

> Deut. 8:16 *He fed you in the wilderness with manna that your fathers did not know, in order to afflict you and test you, to do you good in the end.*

That is such a powerful, theological statement right there. It's the **sixth lesson. God will humble us and test us. Why? To do us good in the end.** So often we lose sight of that. "I'm going through these trials. Why, O Lord?" God will do good for us in the end. That's why.

> Deut. 8:17 *You may say in your heart, 'My power and the might of my hand has made me this wealth.'*

There's that pride rising up again.

> Deut 8:18 *Rather you are to remember ADONAI your God, for it is He who gives you power to make wealth, in order to establish His covenant that He swore to your fathers—as it is this day.*

So, this **seventh lesson** is one we mention many times when we are taking up an offering. **Our ability to earn wealth is what? It's a gift from God! Why?** To establish His Covenant. What does that mean? It means to build His Kingdom here on earth. It means to spread His Kingdom. That's why He gives us the power to make wealth.

> Deut. 8:19a *Now if you do forget ADONAI your God, and go after other gods and serve them and worship them....*

Here's that pride coming back in. Notice also that there's another lesson here. If your pride begins to make you think it's your own strength, what will you do? You will forget the Lord your God and follow other gods and serve and worship them. So that's the **eighth lesson: forgetting God's grace leads to idolatry, worshiping other gods.**

> Deut. 8:19b-20 *... I solemnly warn you today that you will certainly perish. 20 Like the nations ADONAI makes perish before you, so you will perish, since you would not listen to the voice of ADONAI your God.*

So there's the end result: **if we become proud, forget God's grace, and become idolaters, our end will be the same as the nations that God drove out** before our forefathers, the Hittites, Jebusites, Hivites, and Canaanites, all those.

So, that's a bunch of lessons, right? Eight of them. So I thought it might be a little tough for us to remember them all, so I listed them here. Then we will look at some other lessons that weren't covered in Deuteronomy 8. Here are the eight:

1. God will provide all of our basic needs when we follow Him: shelter, clothing, food.
2. Fear/reverence/respect the Lord and walk in His ways.
3. God will provide abundantly for all our needs when we obey Him, and we are to respond by blessing Him and being thankful for His provision.
4. When things are going well, be on guard against pride.
5. When we are following the Lord, we will be protected from dangerous beasts and animals.
6. God will humble us and test us. Why? To do us good in the end.
7. Our ability to earn wealth is a gift from God to establish His Covenant, to build and spread His Kingdom here on earth.
8. Forgetting God and His grace leads to idolatry—worshiping other gods.

Now we have more lessons beyond those eight. In I Cor. 10 when Paul gives us this exhortation to learn these lessons, he actually lists three more. Here's **lesson nine**:

> I Corinthians 10:8 *And let us not engage in sexual immorality, as some of them did, with the consequence that 23,000 died in a single day.*
>
> Numbers 25:1-3, 8-9 *While Israel was staying in Shittim, the people began to have immoral sexual relations with women from Moab. 2 Then they invited the people to the sacrifices of their gods, so the people were eating, and bowing down before their gods. 3 When Israel became bound to Baal of Peor, the anger of ADONAI grew hot against Israel. ... 8 ... Then the plague among Bnei-Yisrael was stopped. 9 However, 24,000 were dead because of the plague!*

Lesson nine is very clear: **keep yourselves from sexual immorality.** That was the incident with the Moabite women. Here's **lesson ten**:

> I Corinthians 10:9 *And let us not put the Messiah to the test, as some of them did, and were destroyed by snakes.*
>
> Numbers 21:5-6 *The people spoke against God and Moses: "Why have you brought us from Egypt to die in the wilderness, because there is no bread, no water, and our very spirits detest the despicable food? 6 So ADONAI sent poisonous*

serpents among the people, and they bit the people and many of the people of Israel died.

Lesson ten is: Don't be impatient with how long it takes God to lead you to your Promised Land. Now **lesson 11:**

> I Corinthians 10:12 *Therefore, let anyone who thinks he is standing up be careful not to fall!*
>
> Numbers 16:1-3, 13-14, 32-33 *Now Korah, son of Izhar son of Kohath son of Levi, and sons of Reuben—Dathan and Abiram, sons of Eliab, and On son of Peleth— 2 rose up against Moses and took 250 men from Bnei-Yisrael, men of renown who had been appointed to the council. 3 They assembled against Moses and Aaron. They said to them, "You've gone too far! All the community is holy—all of them—and A<small>DONAI</small> is with them! Then why do you exalt yourselves above the assembly of A<small>DONAI</small>?" 4 When Moses heard this, he fell on his face. ... 13 "Isn't it enough that you brought us from a land flowing with milk and honey, only to kill us in the wilderness? And now you would lord it over us? 14 What's more, you haven't brought us into a land flowing with milk and honey, nor given us an inheritance of fields and vineyards. ... 32 The earth opened its mouth and swallowed them, along with all their households, all of Korah's people and all their possessions. 33 They went down alive into Sheol, they and everything that was theirs. The earth closed over them and they were gone from among the community.*

Eleven is Don't grumble against the leaders God has appointed. That was the grumbling which ended up with the earth opening up and swallowing those who grumbled.

So, what will be the result of not learning the lessons of the Israelites in the desert? It actually will be the same as what the people of Israel experienced, which is stated in Numbers 14:

> Numbers 14:32-33 *But your bodies will drop in this wilderness. 33 Your children will be herdsmen in the wilderness for 40 years. They will suffer because of your unfaithfulness until your corpses are consumed in the wilderness.*

So what's the lesson? **Twelve** is a lesson I think most people have heard about. **If we don't learn the lessons, we'll have to go around the mountain again.** That was

1. LIFE IN THE SUKKAH

actually the source of the grumbling. It was when they had gone around the mountain a few times and come back. Can you imagine that? You come back to the same place you've been. I don't know how long it took them to get around the mountain. It was a big mountain. But there are the footprints you made the last time you were there. So you set up camp there again and get ready to go around the mountain again—for 40 years!—until you've learned these lessons. Have you had to go around the mountain two or three times?

This was also after they had been told what their punishment was for being afraid of the giants in the Promised Land: they will not get to go in. So we can understand their despondency.

So Paul exhorts us to learn these lessons of history and to heed these warnings. We all know that we learn from experience, right? That's called learning the hard way. That's how our ancestors learned in the desert. But I believe, and I hope you see this, that it's God's desire that we would not have to learn the hard way, that we would learn from His Word, that we'd be able to study His Word to learn these lessons, so we don't have to go through those difficult experiences of going around the mountain again and again.

Here's the key to learn and apply all the lessons that God wants to teach us: we must humble ourselves and be willing to obey, and be willing to change. That's really what the lessons are all about—changing us from glory to glory, meaning changing us from what we are to being more and more in the image of Messiah from day to day. That requires us to humble ourselves and allow the Lord to change us.

The converse of lesson 12 is that if they had trusted the Lord, they would have been in the desert only two years instead of forty years! If they had obeyed God's direction to take the Promised Land and had trusted Him to go with them, they wouldn't have had to learn lesson 12. Here are some Scriptures to show that God had planned just a two-year journey for them.

> Numbers 10:11-12 **On the twentieth day of the second month of the second year,** the cloud lifted up from above the Tabernacle of the Testimony. 12 Then Bnei-Yisrael set

*out on their travels in the Sinai wilderness. The cloud came to rest in the wilderness of Paran. 13 **So they set out the first time** by the mouth of Adonai by Moses's hand. ... 33 So they advanced from the mountain of Adonai, a trip of **three days**....*

The place where they then camped is where they craved meat and God sent quail and some died from a plague. So at least a couple of days have passed. The place was named Kibroth-hattaavah, which means *graves of lust or craving or greediness.*

Numbers 11:34-35 *...that place was called Kibroth-hattaavah, because they buried the people who were craving. 35 From Kibroth-hattaavah the people journeyed to Hazeroth and stayed in Hazeroth.*

Here in Hazeroth is where Aaron and Miriam complained against Moses, and Miriam got leperosy. Aaron pleaded, and God healed her, but they had to wait seven days before moving on.

Numbers 12:15-16 *So Miriam was restricted to outside the camp **for seven days**. The people did not move on until Miriam was brought back. 16 Afterward, the people left **Hazeroth** and encamped in the Wilderness of **Paran**.*

Numbers 13:1-3, 26 *Adonai spoke to Moses saying, 2 "Send some men ... to investigate the land of Canaan.... Each ... a prince of the tribe of his fathers, a man from each tribe." 3 So according to the word of Adonai, Moses sent them **from the wilderness of Paran**. ... 26 They traveled and returned to Moses, Aaron and the entire community of Bnei-Yisrael **at Kadesh in the wilderness of Paran**.*

 So if you do the math, they started out from Sinai on the 20th day of the second month, traveled 3 days, ate quail and a plague came so maybe 3-5 more days. So we are at the 28th day or so of the second month that has only 29 days. Then we have the 7 days to wait for Miriam, so we are on the 6th or so of the third month, which has 30 days. Then there's the 40 days for the spies to spy out the Promised Land. That covers the 24 days to the end of the third month. So now they are on the 16th day or so of the fourth month which has only 29 days. Jewish tradition adds 22 more days somewhere scattered in there, and say the spies returned on Tisha b'Av, the ninth of Av, the fifth month.

But for sure, they are still in the second year when God wanted them to go in and take the Promised Land. Caleb and Joshua encouraged the people to obey, but they refused:

> Numbers 14:8-9 *If ADONAI is pleased with us, He will lead us into that land and will give it to us—a land flowing with milk and honey. 9 Only don't rebel against ADONAI, and don't be afraid of the people of the land. They will be food for us. The protection over them is gone. ADONAI is with us! Do not fear them." 10 But the whole assembly talked about violently stoning them.*

So you see that if they had not shrunk back in fear because of the giants, but instead had trusted the Lord and obeyed Him, their journey would've only been two years. So **the bonus lesson is: If you don't trust the Lord, your two-year trial and testing time can turn into forty years!**

So building a sukkah and doing as much as possible in it for seven days can help us to remember that extremely important lesson. It can help us to become more humble and to remember to reverence the Lord and to trust Him for everything, to not fear what He is telling us to do no matter how hard or scary it looks, but to obey Him. Then we will reach our personal promised land of changing from glory to glory into the image of Messiah in the shorter time God has planned.

If you haven't started observing this Moad yet, I invite you to try it and see how humble you feel after seven full days and how much you learn about trusting the Lord and depending on Him. If our congregants don't have a place to build a sukkah, if they live in an apartment complex, for example, we invite them to build one on our synagogue's property.

Mini Tabernacle / Sukkah

As I thought about this humbling, I realized that we as children born into the Kingdom of God have already been humbled. Living in a sukkah every year is a good reminder of that humbling.

We are each a temporary, portable sukkah for Yeshua living in us, for the Holy Spirit filling us and dwelling inside us. Right? Our bodies are flimsy, mobile, and temporary, right? And we have invited Yeshua in to be Lord of our lives, and have been filled with the Ruakh HaKodesh, following His leading. Rabbi Sha'ul (Apostle Paul) wrote about it. He uses the word, *Temple*, but let's think about it as the Tabernacle in the wilderness, as each of us being a mini tabernacle or sukkah for the Ruakh.

I Corinthians 6:19 *Or don't you know that your body is a temple for the Ruach HaKodesh who lives inside you, whom you received from God? The fact is, you don't belong to yourselves;*

So how does this connect with becoming humbled when we live in a sukkah? Well, how did we become His sukkah? How did we become part of the Kingdom of God? We had to humble ourselves. I had to humble myself. How about you? Did you have to humble yourself? You had to come to that place to admit your need for His atoning sacrifice in your life, to admit your need for His salvation, for His Blood to cover and wash away your sins, for Him to take away your iniquity. That was the humbling experience.

So, as we think of ourselves as a mini tabernacle of the Ruakh, let's take a little time to review what all went into building the Tabernacle in the wilderness. Here is a list.

So, there was the outer curtain surrounding the **courtyard**.

There was the structure around it with poles holding up the curtains of the courtyard, with a base for each pole and a horizontal crossbar holding the poles together.

There was only one gate to enter. (Yeshua is our gate.)

There was the **altar of burnt-offering** made of **bronze,** and all the **utensils for the altar.**

There were basins for carrying the blood of the sacrifices for sprinkling for atonement.

There were poles for carrying the altar.

There was a thick covering over the **Holy of Holies** and the **Holy Place** inside the outer court. The covering had four layers to it: **fine linen, goat hair, ram skin, and badger skins.**

1. LIFE IN THE SUKKAH

Then there were pegs and hooks and loops to hold all these together and loops and the poles that hold it up

Then there was the Holy Place entrance curtain.

Inside the Holy Place, there was the table where the **showbread** (the Bread of the Presence) was put out before the Lord.

There was the **menorah**.

The **altar of incense**.

All these things were carried with poles and there were rings for the poles.

There was a curtain between the Holy Place and the Holy of Holies behind it.

Then there was inside the Holy of Holies: the **Ark of the Covenant** which had the **cherubim** on top of it and again the **poles to carry it**.

Inside that Ark of the Covenant was **Aaron's rod** that budded, a **jar of manna,** and the **tablets of the Ten Commandments**.

Then they had to make the **priestly garments**, the robes and the **ephod**, and the **breast plate for his chest**.

There were **stones in the breast piece**.

There's also a **turban or headdress with a precious stone on it**.

And there was the anointing oil to anoint all these things and to anoint the kohanim (priests).

So there were all these things—let's call them—components of the Tabernacle. You can read about all this in Exodus chapter 28.

So they brought all those components for building the Tabernacle. The reason I listed them all is I want you to get a feel for how much there was: poles, rings, curtains, furniture, the menorah, the table, and the basins, etc. Can you get the picture that there was a lot of stuff that went into building this Tabernacle?

Exodus 39:33-35 *Then they brought the Tabernacle to Moses, along with the tent and all of its furnishings, its clasps, its boards, its crossbars, its pillars, and its bases; 34 along*

> with the covering of ram skins dyed red, and the covering of sealskins, the veil of the curtain; 35 as well as the Ark of the Testimony with its poles, and the atonement cover;

The rest of chapter 39 lists all of these items that they brought, and Moses was also given very important detailed instructions to make anointing oil, then what all to anoint with it.

> Exodus 40:9-16 *"Take the anointing oil and anoint the Tabernacle, and everything within it, and consecrate it, along with all of its furnishings, and it will be holy. 10 Also you are to anoint the altar of burnt offering with all of its utensils and consecrate the altar. The altar will be most holy. 11 Then you are to anoint the basin along with its base and sanctify it. 12 "Bring Aaron and his sons to the entrance of the Tent of Meeting, and ... anoint them, ... so that they too may minister to Me as kohanim. ... 16 Moses did so, just as A<small>DONAI</small> had commanded him.*

In the rest of this chapter, verses 18-33, Moses set up the Tabernacle, placed all the furnishings in it, set up the burnt offering altar, the laver, and the enclosure. And again in reading this, I was just so amazed with how God gave Moses such detailed instructions for making the Tabernacle and how He provided all the materials and the craftsmen to do the work. After everything was finished, look what happened!

> Exodus 40:34 *Then the cloud covered the Tent of Meeting, and the glory of A<small>DONAI</small> filled the Tabernacle.*

Think of all that as somewhat how we were prepared and formed to be able to become a tabernacle or sukkah for the Holy Spirit. We became a new creation, a new temporary, portable dwelling for Yeshua to be inside us. A lot went into making us cleansed and anointed and ready, so His glory can fill us!

So there was an initial humbling that allowed us to be a sukkah for Yeshua. But what about as we walk day to day, seeking to obey Him, seeking to follow Him. I don't know about you, but that's been a humbling experience for me, too. It's learning to depend on Him daily and not on our own abilities, learning to turn to Him when we're stuck, learning to follow Him, learning to spend time with Him to get the strength that we need for each day.

So here's what I saw in this. We, as disciples of Yeshua, should be a people who have already been humbled. We should be people who are open to how the Lord would want to teach us and change us. And we are! That's why most of us are believers. That's why you're reading this book and why I wrote it. That's why we read and study His Word. It's not just because it has some beautiful phrases in it. It's because we want that Word to work in us and to transform us.

So, I believe we can learn from all these things in history. We've just studied the forty years' lessons in the desert and we're going to pray right now that we can apply them.

Let's Pray

Father, we thank You for the lessons of the wilderness. We humble ourselves right now to learn them. We confess, Lord, that we need Your help to live the way You want us to live, and to change the way You want us to change because You are the agent of change in our lives. So we thank You for being our Sukkah, for showing us how living in You is a humbling experience. We just want to lift these lessons before You.

[I know that each of us has struggled a little bit with some of these lessons.]

I pray, Father, that You would just begin to work these lessons in each of us. Teach us that You will provide, that as we seek to follow You, we don't need to worry or fear because You will be our provision. You will meet all of our needs.

Teach us, Lord, to be reverent, to fear You, to be in a state of wanting greatly to obey You, O God. Teach us to be thankful for all that You've done and all that we have.

Teach us, Lord, that You will protect us from dangers and from the enemy. When we are on Your mission, going where You want us to go, You will protect us.

Teach us, Lord, that our ability to gain wealth is a gift from You, and that we are to use what we gain to establish Your Covenant and build Your Kingdom.

Teach us, O Lord, how pride leads to idolatry, which will lead to our destruction. Keep us from that pride.

Teach us, Lord, that You will make a way of escape from our enemies, and You will destroy our enemies. Teach us to fight the enemy in the power of Your hand, Lord, that You would be with us when we have to fight.

Father, for each of us struggling with some kind of illness, teach us the truth of this promise, that You will provide health and healing for us. You are the Lord who heals us. Teach us, Lord, to appreciate that You gave us Shabbat, one day a week to rest for our physical, emotional, and spiritual health.

Guard us from sexual immorality, O God. in this world that is flashing it in our faces all the time.

Give us patience with the walk that You have brought us on and You've called us to, O God, to walk that path and wait on You.

Keep us from grumbling against those whom You've appointed to lead us.

Make it very real in us, Lord, that if we don't learn these lessons, we're going to keep on going around the mountain until we learn them or our time comes to an end.

So we thank You, today, Father. We thank You for all that You're doing in our lives, and we bless You and praise You, in Yeshua's Name. Amen.

CHAPTER 2
Sukkot Fellowship

Now, if you think about it, building a sukkah really is a strange thing for God to command us to do. It's not like His commands to make offerings or go from here to there or build a Temple. He says to build a temporary, portable dwelling and live in it for seven days at the end of the harvest season. I mean, we're used to it, but that's a weird thing to do.

> Lev. 23:42-43 *So ...when you have gathered in the fruits of the land, you are to keep the Feast of Adonai for seven days. ... 42 You are to live in sukkot for seven days. All the native-born in Israel are to live in sukkot,*

Now notice again that it says only the *native-born* Israelis **in Israel** are commanded to live in the sukkot. In the diaspora, we're very thankful that God is merciful to us in allowing us to build a sukkah and just visit it, and not require us to stay out in it the whole time or to sleep in it. Thank You, Lord.

So one year as I was thanking God for His mercy in this, as the rain was coming down and the wind was blowing in the sukkah, when I was trying to stay out there for a little while, I started thinking about what Sukkot is like in Jerusalem today and what it was like in ancient times. Here's the account of the Jewish exiles, returned from Babylon, building their sukkot in Bible times:

> Nehemiah 8:15-17 ... *"Go out to the hill country and bring olive branches and wild olive branches, myrtle branches, palm branches and branches of other leafy trees to make sukkot, just as it is written." 16 So the people went out and*

> brought branches, and made sukkot for themselves, each on their own roof, in their courtyards, in the courtyards of the House of God, in the plaza before the Water Gate and in the plaza of the Ephraim Gate. 17 The entire assembly who had returned from the captivity made sukkot and dwelt in the sukkot. Since the days of Joshua the son of Nun until that day Bnei-Yisrael had not done so—and the joy was very great.

People in Israel actually live in their sukkot for the seven days as those exiles did because that is the command, and we see that they used branches to build their sukkot, which is still the tradition today for the roof.

On a typical, narrow, crowded street today in Jerusalem, people build their sukkot out front in their courtyards or on their roof tops. In some neighborhoods, the streets are blocked off from traffic the whole week, and the people build their sukkot right out on the street.

This kind of makes you think of what small towns used to call "sidewalk days" when they closed the main streets for a few days, and the store owners brought all their products out onto the streets into the open air for display for special sales. People really enjoyed browsing around between the tables and racks without having to worry about traffic. Children enjoyed the merry-go-round and other special rides set up for them. This was before shopping malls were built. Those were fun days, a little bit like Sukkot.

In apartment complexes in Israel during Sukkot week, people build their sukkot on the balconies. They are really small because the balconies are small. In some apartment buildings, people build their sukkot on the roof. There are so many sukkot up there, they have to mark off little squares, one for each family to build their small sukkah in. So all the people in the apartment building spend the week together.

The sukkot in Jerusalem are of all sorts and sizes. Some elaborate ones are mansion-type sukkot on the streets. They look pretty big compared to others. The insides of people's sukkot are nicely decorated with a table and chairs for eating.

Some even have windows. They are always decorated very beautifully.

Then there's a new innovation, sukkah on a bike, called a pedi-sukkah! It actually is portable! They are from Chabad, which is an orthodox Jewish organization that's very outreach oriented. They pedal around Jerusalem with a little sukkah on the back of their bicycle. They stop and people come in the sukkah and wave the branches in the sukkah. So those who don't have a sukkah at home can fulfill the commandment to wave the branches in a pedi-sukkah. I think it is a really cute idea.

For our congregation, everyone sets up their own sukkah at home, but we also always build a large sukkah in our congregation's yard. Some years we rent a huge tent and have Sukkot dinners out there. For the final one on the last night, we invite community people who don't know anything about Sukkot. The first time we did it in 2001, more than 300 people total came, so it was at least 100 guests. It was one of our most well attended outreaches we had ever had up to that point.

We really like the idea of having a portable sukkah, so we created our own for inside a van that we have used several times. It is a wonderful way to reach out to the community to teach them about Sukkot and bless them.

Remember that Sukkot is a pilgrimage Moad.

Deut. 16:16 *Three times a year all your males are to appear before ADONAI your God in the place He chooses—at the Feast of Matzot, the Feast of Shavuot, and the Feast of Sukkot. No one should appear before ADONAI empty-handed—*

So, first of all, *"the place He chooses"* is Jerusalem. So, everybody had to come to Jerusalem. Many people from outside Jerusalem would come to Jerusalem and claim a spot, and say, "I'm going to build my sukkah here." Or they would rent a space to build a sukkah. They did this to be in compliance with that commandment, but look at verse 14.

Deut. 16:14 *So you will rejoice in your feast—you, your son and daughter, slave and maid, Levite and outsider, orphan and widow within your gates.*

So not only were the men commanded to come, but the families were commanded to come. It even says, *outsider*. That means if there was someone who was not Jewish in your town, they were invited to come along. Maybe you were to help pay for them. It also mentions widows and orphans. You were to help support them by bringing them along, paying for their travel and whatever they needed. So you can see, this would get to be quite a crowd.

> Deut. 16:15 *Seven days you will feast to Adonai your God in the place He chooses, because Adonai your God will bless you in all your produce and in all the work of your hand, and you will be completely filled with joy.*

Not only were all these people supposed to come to Jerusalem, but it was to last for seven days and be a time of great joy, Z'man simkhatenu, "the time of our rejoicing."

So, in Biblical times, every family in Israel came to Jerusalem for Sukkot, built a sukkah, lived in it for seven days, feasting and rejoicing, along with their servants, if they had them, along with inviting foreigners who were part of their community at home, and along with the widows and orphans. We're talking about several million people! They all came to Jerusalem to feast and rejoice for seven days!

Actually, it's also similar to two other Appointed Times. Families had to come to Jerusalem for Passover, and it says to keep the Feast of Matzot, the Festival of Unleavened Bread for seven days. So they came to Jerusalem a whole week for Passover. They didn't stay in sukkot then, so they must have rented places to stay. For Shavuot, people were to come to Jerusalem, but it was for only one day. It also included feasting.

So as I was looking at this, I realized that we don't grasp how big a deal this was. I want you to try to get a picture of this in your mind. Envision a giant camp meeting. Now they didn't have canvas or nylon tents, but they built their sukkot all around Jerusalem and lived in them for seven days.

Just think about it. This was a major interruption of life, a major temporary life style change. I was thinking about why God commanded this coming to Jerusalem three times a year,

2. SUKKOT FELLOWSHIP

bringing your family, feasting for a day or a week, building sukkot, living in them for a week. Then it finally hit me. Our God is really big on bringing His people together for fellowship, really big! He commanded us to do this so we would have close fellowship!

Not only at Moadim, but He set it up that we get together every week for fellowship. In Lev. 23, there is a very foundational verse for this:

> Lev. 23:3a *Work may be done for six days, but the seventh day is a Shabbat of solemn rest, ...*

You're probably familiar with that part, but notice what it says in the next phrase:

> Lev. 23:3b *... a holy convocation. You are to do no work—it is a Shabbat to ADONAI in all your dwellings.*

A holy convocation means we're supposed to get together on Shabbat. So not only three times a year on the Moadim, but **weekly,** God's people are commanded to have a worship gathering! Actually, this verse is the reason we have a Shabbat service. It's a holy convocation. Right? It's also the reason churches meet weekly. And it's the reason Islam meets weekly. All of it came out of this command to come together once a week.

While they were in captivity in Babylon, the Jewish people began gathering in Synagogues on Shabbat. Since the Temple was far away and had actually been burnt down, they began to have local worship places where they would study the Torah. When they returned to the Land, in their towns and sections of their cities, they gathered on Shabbat in synagogues and studied the Torah. Of course, those gatherings always included fellowship, talking with each other, maybe having a meal, etc. So, that was a local fellowship with your neighbors every Shabbat. But three times a year, you got to gather with people from all across the Land, people from the other side of Israel, for example, people from Galilee and Beer Sheva—people from the mountains and the desert gathering together to celebrate Sukkot, getting to know each other.

By Yeshua's time, there were thousands, maybe millions of Jewish people living in other countries in the cities of the

Roman Empire, and they would come to Jerusalem for Sukkot and live there for seven days also. So you got to fellowship with people from Macedonia and Greece and all these other countries. It's just amazing.

Sukkot was, I believe, the most effective of the Moadim in encouraging fellowship. Why? Because everybody had to live in a sukkah for seven days. Why would that encourage fellowship? Have you ever gone to a camp meeting where everyone is camping out? You're like wandering around the campground, meeting people all the time. People are trading sugar and coffee because they ran out. They're helping each other start fires. Community happens! That's why camping has been such a valuable thing.

So this was like a giant camp meeting. The whole city of Jerusalem, millions of people, gathering together, sharing the space. Where did they get water? They had to go draw water from somewhere, so they all got together for that. They needed to go get firewood for lighting fires. Where did they throw their garbage and what did they do for toilets? I have no idea. Where did the kids play? They must have had playgrounds or places for the kids somewhere. Imagine all the noise from everything!

So this gave me a whole different picture of what Sukkot was like. How often did God want us to do this? Once every year forever! But how often did He also command us to have a holy convocation, plus how many days would we be celebrating Moadim together?

Well, I'm an ex-engineer, so I like to deal with numbers. So I counted all these days that foster fellowship. There are 52 Shabbatot (plural of Shabbat) in a year, right? There are six days of Passover plus one Shabbat. There's one day of Shavuot, seven days of Sukkot, actually eight, but there are two Shabbatot in there, the first day and the eighth day. Then we have Purim, which got added in later for feasting, and Hanukkah, which also got added. So I figured out that there are 56 Shabbatot, but there are a total of 75 out of 365 days, which is about 21% or one-fifth of our days when God expects

2. SUKKOT FELLOWSHIP

us to be in fellowship! Isn't that amazing?! That is amazing! I think we miss it. Everybody is glad that we have the five day instead of 6 or 7 day work week. We all get to go to our homes, and we often do things alone. But this was commanded that everyone had to get together. Do you catch this? It's really wonderful.

So let's talk a little bit about what fellowship is. How is it different from just hanging out for group activities?

Well, in Hebrew, the word for *fellowship* is *khaverah*. That's why we call our fellowship groups, khaverah groups. In Greek, the word is *koininia*. That's why our friends in East Rochester call their church Koininia Fellowship. It's actually redundant, a repetition of the same word. If you look up the definition of koininia, it's *spiritual fellowship*, *fellowship in the Spirit*. So, true fellowship is a work of the Holy Spirit. You can be together with other Believers and it not be in fellowship. Fellowship is when the Holy Spirit is amongst you.

Matthew 18:20 *For wherever two or three are assembled in my name, I am there with them.*

So fellowship between people happens when we are assembled in His Name. When it does happen, Yeshua is there with us, in the midst of us.

So what does this mean, assembled in His Name? Well, if somebody was assembled in your name, what would you think it would mean? I think, when we are assembled in Yeshua's Name it means, He is the focus. He is the subject of the meeting. When we are gathered in Yeshua's Name, we are gathered to seek His will and to do His will.

Let's talk about some things that are fellowship. Certainly, a worship service is fellowship. A Bible study is fellowship. A prayer meeting is fellowship. When we go out on the street together, trying to reach people with the Gospel, that's fellowship with each other. These are all times of fellowship, but fellowship is not limited to these organized events. Fellowship can happen whenever two or more are gathered, and they are seeking God or serving Him together in some way.

So if two of you are just praying together, that's fellowship. You're doing it in His Name. Our congregation's times of consecrated prayer are quiet times. People are not chatting with each other. Sometimes we used to say, "No talking. If you have to talk, leave." But we are there praying together. It's fellowship.

Also getting together with people, sharing your stories, telling about how you came to the Lord, telling about your life experiences about how God showed you how to walk with Him; or seeking or giving Godly counsel is fellowship. Getting to know one another is fellowship, sharing insights, networking—that's a buzz-word these days—networking for the Kingdom, getting to know people and what they do, so you can connect with them and do things together, that's fellowship. A shared lunch, a ride that you give someone, a walk, a phone conversation, a time of helping someone out can all be fellowship. Working on something together for the Kingdom of God can be fellowship. And I'm afraid to say this, but even interacting on Facebook and an email discussion can be fellowship. But the most important thing about fellowship is that it's interactive. In a worship service, during the sermon, it is more like a lecture because we're not interacting, but afterwards it will be fellowship. It's really the discussion back and forth that distinguishes fellowship.

So why is fellowship so important to God that He gives us all the Moadim and Shabbatot, a fifth of our time, that we're supposed to be participating in it?

> I John 1:3 *What we have seen and heard, we are proclaiming to you; so that you too may have fellowship with us. Our fellowship is with the Father and with his Son, Yeshua the Messiah.*

So the way I understand this is that the thing that *"we are proclaiming to you"* is the Gospel. It's speaking the Word, and we're proclaiming it to you for a reason. Why? For fellowship! Right? *"So that you can have fellowship with us."* And when we're having fellowship together, we're having fellowship with the Father and the Son. One of the main reasons God created each of us is to have fellowship with Him. He also created us as social beings. We are not like some total loner animals that mate and then separate. The mother has the babies and the father never sees them. We are social beings, like many other

2. SUKKOT FELLOWSHIP

species that live in flocks and herds, even fish live in schools. We are social beings. We need each other. The Gospel was proclaimed to us so we could have fellowship with other Believers.

Hebrews 10:24-25 And let us keep paying attention to one another, in order to spur each other on to love and good deeds, 25 not neglecting our own congregational meetings, as some have made a practice of doing, but, rather, encouraging each other. And let us do this all the more as you see the Day approaching.

The Day is the end. So as we get closer to the end, the author is saying that we need to fellowship more because we need the strengthening. Why? I made a little list here:

We inspire each other to love and to do good deeds.
We disciple each other through fellowship, so we are discipled.
We need the gifts others have, both supernatural and natural.
We learn what those gifts are through fellowship.
We need the love and acceptance we receive from each other.
We can accomplish so much more when we're together, than when we try to do something alone.
We get creative. I've been in fellowship when someone has an idea, "Let's try this. Let's do that." And we have a new vision or new strategy.
We enjoy each other. I enjoy being with people. It's amazing the sense of humor that people have—the funny things they've been through, the funny things they say.
We need to pray for each other.

All that is why we have fellowship. Then this last reason. Yeshua said this, speaking about us loving one another:

John 13:35 (TLV) "By this all will know that you are My disciples, if you have love for one another."

So one of the most powerful ways to demonstrate that we are witnesses for the Lord is to show our love for each other. Now that best happens when we are helping each other, but it also happens when people observe how we treat each other, when they observe that we don't get down on each other, and we don't criticize each other, but we love each other, we forgive each other, we hug each other. When people observe that, they see that we love each other, and that's a witness for the Lord.

So I am always very passionate about this because fellowship has been a vitally important part of my life and walk with the Lord. Before I gave my heart to the Lord, I had the desire always, maybe you have had this, to be part of some group where people loved each other and worked toward something good, some kind of a good goal. So I joined several different groups to be a part of them. I was on sport's teams. I joined a fraternity. I was a member of neighborhood associations where we lived. I got involved in political parties. All of these involvements turned out to be disappointments to me. No matter how lofty the group's goals were, human nature always rose up. Egos would come out of hiding, and ambition would raise its ugly head. Someone would try to gain power by intimidation or lying. Jealousy and envy, anger and bitterness would rise up, and the lofty goals would go out the door. Have you had that experience in worldly organizations?

Well, in 1977, six months before I gave my heart to the Lord, Dianne came to trust in the Lord through participating in a fellowship group, a home fellowship Bible study in our neighborhood. You might have heard this story. People in that group prayed for me for six months. That prayer miraculously removed my opposition to reading the Bible because I was not at all interested in reading the Bible, and one day I just decided to read it. After I decided that, I talked about it, saying, "Somehow those people's prayers gave me a spiritual lobotomy. They cut out that portion of my brain that was resistant to reading the Word." Within a few weeks, and after some traumatic events, but without attending any service anywhere or anybody witnessing to me, I gave my heart to the Lord. And I found what I was searching for, a relationship with God. It was awesome!

Then for the first time, I decided to attend one of those home groups with Diane. As soon as I got there and the people started interacting with each other, and we started to

2. SUKKOT FELLOWSHIP

have a little Bible study and a little prayer time, I knew I had found something else I had been looking for. When I found the Lord—I was looking for Him—but I also found what I had been looking for previously in a group—a family, a community, a mishpokhah where there was a lofty goal and people were truly able to love each other and work together. Why? Because their lofty goal was not simply accomplishing this or that, but was to seek God and learn from Him and follow Him. Because of that, the Spirit of God in that group gave them victory over all those egos, jealousies, ambitions, and all that other baggage that had disappointed me in other groups. They were able to interact in a Godly way.

I remember thinking, "This is amazing. This is what I've longed for all my life." I didn't grow up in a Godly family. Maybe you grew up in a Godly family and you had that around the dinner table, or you had that in a youth group or something, but I had none of that. And it was like, "Oh, this is absolutely amazing." That group didn't have complete victory over the flesh, but I've got to say, it was like day and night compared to working at Xerox or being part of the neighborhood association. It was like day and night how people behaved toward each other. So for me, that was part of the life-changing experience.

And the Spirit of God showed me that fellowship was so important that as a really new believer, maybe I was a few weeks old in the Lord, I immediately started to seek out other believers at work and arranged to meet with them, like once a week. They didn't ask for it. I said, "Can we get together once a week and have lunch together?" It was clear to me that that was important. And that's how I got discipled—at work with other believers there. Then that turned into a lunch hour Bible study where I participated and eventually began to lead. So it just was always part of my walk to have these fellowship times.

Then when I became an elder in our Messianic congregation, and later as the rabbi, I always made fellowship a high priority, encouraging people to participate in one of our khaverah groups, and to try to start more. When people have a gifting from God to teach and lead, I tell them to go start a group.

I have personally led the Messianic Judaism class twenty-five years now (since 1998)—the same class, but different people rotating through it. I always call it a group, not a class because we structure it as a fellowship. It's a discussion group. It's not a lecture. There's time to worship. There's time to share. There's time to pray. And that's why it takes so long to complete the class! People complain about that, but I'm like, "I don't care. This is really valuable."

But you know what the most valuable thing about it is? I get to know people! I get to know the new people in our congregation over the course of the year or so that it takes to get through that class, and the people get to know each other. I can't tell you how many friendships have formed out of that group. It's amazing.

In our congregation, we do our leadership meetings once a month, and we do fellowship things there, too. It's interactive. We do interactive Bible study. We pray. We worship. We pray for each other. I've led four other groups over the years. For every one, I felt led to not make it a lecture. Even if it's a video, we watch the video, then we discuss it because it is so important to do the fellowship thing.

Godly, Spirit-led fellowship is so important. As I said, this can happen in other ways besides in organized groups. When two people get together, that can be Godly, Spirit-filled fellowship. And you know what? After our services, it happens in our **oneg** (עֹנֶג.*oh-neg*) room. Lots and lots of fellowship, one on one, three, four, sitting around at tables. Fellowship is vitally important. That's why we do **oneg**. In Hebrew, it actually means *"delight."* It's used in Isaiah 58:13 *call Shabbat a delight*. In Judaism, it has come to mean the time for finger food and fellowship after the Shabbat meeting.

So the Spirit wants me to point out that sometimes we miss those unstructured fellowship opportunities because we're too busy. We're focused on our plans. We don't think this is really God's thing for us. But I believe God wants to give us the ability to discern when a fellowship opportunity arises and realize that it could be a very important life-changing experience for that

2. SUKKOT FELLOWSHIP

other person or for you. So we need to learn that when God brings a situation where there's an opportunity for fellowship, we need to put aside that agenda we have for the day, and enter into it with all our heart.

Recently, I had another opportunity for fellowship when three or four people who were relatively new to the congregation asked to make an appointment with me to sit down and talk. It was such a blessing to get to know them, to hear their stories, to see how the Lord touched them and what they've been through. It was inspirational. Things like that really bless me.

Before I end this chapter, I just want to say that there are many enemies of Godly fellowship that we must stand against. We must keep our fellowship Godly, uplifting, and healthy. Carnal behavior is almost always rooted either in pride, trying to show that you're better than everybody else because you really think you are, or what we call false pride, which is trying to prove yourself because you really don't think you're very good at all. Out of that comes competition, contention, jealousy, gossip, rejection, emotionalism, and people who push for control. As a leader, allowing fleshly behavior to go on without confronting it is wrong. It should be confronted. We can allow it to go on when we're one on one with somebody just to show them love, but when it happens in a group, whoever is leading that group should say, "I'm sorry. We need to change the subject now." or "I'm sorry. We need to not deal in that now. We can deal with it later in private. It's not acceptable here because it's affecting all the other people."

That's what I hope we do as group leaders. We need to be able to know what things are from the enemy, trying to destroy fellowship and recognize them. And if we find it in ourselves because that's certainly possible, we need to repent and stand against it.

So I'm going to continue to promote fellowship. When the fall Moadim end, there is no Moad from the end of Sukkot and Simchat Torah to Hanukkah. It is like ten weeks before Hanukkah. So what can we do? Well, in our congregation, we go back to having kiddish in our oneg room every first and third Shabbat of the month. Again, it's not a time that you can really eat lunch because it is really light stuff, just bagels and cream cheese, but it's a time where we can have fellowship.

I want to end here by just encouraging you, if you are not involved in a khaverah or small group, please get involved. In our congregation, we have several small groups. Even our worship team meets as a small group to encourage each other and pray for each other. We have an Español (Spanish) group and a T'shuvah group. Then once a month our women's group and men's group meet. And for our new people we always have our ongoing Tuesday evening Messianic Judaism class group. So, I just want to encourage your participation in some sort of small group that meets to study the Bible, worship, and pray together every week because it's important.

Has fellowship been a blessing to you? Let's thank Him.

Let's pray.

Father, I just thank You for knowing us so well that You understand that we need fellowship with You and with each other. I thank You for the blessing fellowship has been to me. Thank You, Lord, for that blessing.

I pray, Lord, You would teach us to keep our times of fellowship led by Your Spirit and focused on Messiah. Deal with the traits that destroy fellowship, Lord. If any of those things that get in the way of fellowship have been revealed in us, we repent of them. We want nothing to do with them! We repent of competition and rejection and emotionalism, judging people, all those kinds of things. We repent and ask for Your forgiveness. Help us to stay away from them.

I pray You would bless our times of fellowship in our groups. I pray You would bless spontaneous, unstructured times.

And I pray, Father, that You would just give all who read this the ability to recognize fellowship opportunities. When we run into somebody and are just standing there talking to them, help us to realize that it could be a valuable fellowship opportunity, that we don't need to rush off because we've got to go do something, but we can participate in fellowship with them with all of our heart. Help us to do that more.

Finally, Lord, give us all an appreciation for the value of fellowship like You did for me. Cause us to be seekers after it, to seek it out, and to appreciate it and to participate in it, to be open when we're in fellowship with other believers and to be able to experience all the blessings of it. In Yeshua's Name. Thank You, Lord. Amein .

CHAPTER 3
SPENDING TIME IN YOUR SUKKAH

So we've learned that the result of people obeying the Sukkot commandments, of everyone coming to Yerushalayim (Jerusalem) to build sukkot and rejoice together developed into a giant camp meeting in Yerushalayim every year with great rejoicing for seven days, rejoicing over the Yom Kippur atonement, their harvest, and the presence of God in the Temple.

So besides knowing our need for fellowship, why else did God direct this? Well, He knows that people need to get away from their routines. People can begin to think their routine is the only reality. We all periodically need a vacation to rejuvenate and refresh us, draw us closer to the Lord, and renew our worship. Spiritual retreats and conferences are fruitful for this. But our getaways have to have the right atmosphere to revive us spiritually.

Retreats are best when they are in beautiful locations. The setting is important. For me nature's beauty draws me to the Lord. It's nice to visit cities, museums, historical sights. But it's seeing the Glory of the Lord in the woods, mountains, rivers, and seas, feeling so close to His presence that refreshes me.

Think how spiritually uplifting it must have been to go up to Yerushalayim, camping in a Sukkah for a week, being near the presence of the Lord in the magnificently, beautiful

Temple, praying in it, singing and dancing to the music of the Levites, making offerings, and listening to the Torah teachers. I was in Jerusalem several times, and it was always spiritually renewing even without the Temple being there.

Jewish people in the Diaspora have this Sukkot get-away in a small way by building a sukkah in their back yards. That is a small approximation to getting away, having a sukkah right outside your door, but let's take a moment to picture yourself in a sukkah. If you are reading this during Sukkot, you can actually be sitting in your sukkah and experience the real thing!

So, now we're out in our sukkah, in that different environment. What does the Lord want to show us through our being here? Well, first of all, let's enjoy the beauty of His creation. We can look up to the sky and see the clouds. We can see the trees in our yard, hear the wind blowing, listen to the birds singing, feel the breeze, and watch the falling leaves. As I prayed about what we are supposed to learn, the Spirit showed me that the purpose of being here is to revive our worship; to reconnect with Him in a fresh way. In Genesis 11 men tried to connect with God in their own way:

Genesis 11:4 And they said, "Come, let us build ourselves a city, and a tower whose top is in the heavens.

This made the Lord very angry because we can only connect with God through what He builds, like being out in His awesome creation, or through what He commands us to build like the Tabernacle or Temple, and like a sukkah.

Leviticus 23:42 You are to live in sukkot for seven days. All the native-born in Israel are to live in sukkot,

It is so fitting that He directs us to build sukkot—temporary dwellings—to restore life to our worship. Remember that sukkot are purposefully flimsy, humble structures to help us remember when He was in our midst in the wilderness, to remind us to be thankful for how He provided in the desert:

Food – manna   Water – from the rock
Shade – pillar of cloud   Light & warmth – pillar of fire
Direction – the pillar moved
Clothing & sandals – didn't wear out

    Medical treatment – not needed, no sickness
    Cure for snakebites – snake on the pole

    As you are worshiping in this temporary dwelling place, I want you to ponder again that we actually dwell in a sukkah all year. The Bible teaches that God is a Spirit, and because we are made in His image, we are spirit beings. Your spirit is the real you, the immortal you, able to connect with God's Spirit. As spirit-beings we have souls—personalities, emotions, and wills—and we dwell in physical bodies. But, these bodies are temporary dwelling places, and portable for following God.

    Someday we'll have immortal bodies that are not temporary. Our bodies are wondrous structures but, like sukkot, they really are quite flimsy. We can exercise our bodies to make them strong, but they are still not very strong compared to other creatures or machines. Injury and sickness can quickly destroy our flimsy bodies.

    3500 years ago when our ancestors wandered for forty years in the desert, the Lord's manifest presence appeared above His temporary sukkah—the Tabernacle—in the desert in the form of the pillar of fire by night and the cloud by day. His presence was also in the Temple in Jerusalem in the Holy of Holies in the same form.

    2000 years ago He came to earth in a different visible manifestation. Here's a verse about it that you might not have connected to Sukkot. It's a familiar verse. You can probably quote it from memory. Right?

> John 1:14 (**NKJV**) *And the Word became flesh and dwelt among us, and we beheld His glory....*

    Now, look up that word *"dwelt"* in your *Strong's Concordance,* and you'll see that it's the Greek word, *skenu* which means *to tent* or *encamp,* in other words *to dwell temporarily!* It's the Greek way of saying *to live in a sukkah!* Yeshua came and dwelt in a sukkah of human flesh. It was a temporary dwelling place. It was not very strong. After 33 years, His flimsy sukkah of human flesh was destroyed by evil men. He went back to heaven, but before He went, He made an amazing promise, that He was going to send the Ruakh HaKodesh, which He called our Comforting Counselor:

3. SPENDING TIME IN YOUR SUKKAH

John 14:15-17 *"If you love me, you will keep my commands; 16 and I will ask the Father, and he will give you another comforting Counselor like me, the Spirit of Truth, to be with you forever. 17 The world cannot receive him, because it neither sees nor knows him. You know him, because he is staying with you and will be united with you."*

This Comforting Counselor is for those who love Yeshua and keep His commands. He will be in us! How is it possible for the Holy Spirit of the Holy God to dwell in a sinful man? It is only possible because of the work done by His Son.

1 Peter 1:22 (NIV) *Now that you have purified yourselves by obeying the truth, ...*

Yeshua made the way for us to purify our hearts by making atonement through His Blood for all who receive Him. Today He is present not as a pillar of fire or cloud over the Sukkah in the desert, not over the Mercy Seat in the Temple, but in us. There is a place inside each follower of Yeshua, in your heart, in your spirit where the Ruakh HaKodesh dwells.

But it's bigger than that because speaking to God, Yeshua also says this about His followers.

John 17:23 (TLV) *I in them....*

Yeshua Himself is saying He is in us. In what form? He and the Ruakh HaKodesh are one. He is in us in the form of His Spirit. Paul refers to this as a great "mystery."

Colossians 1:26-27 (TLV) *[T]he mystery that was hidden for ages and generations, but now has been revealed to His kedoshim* [holy ones]. *27 God chose to make known to them this glorious mystery regarding the Gentiles—which is Messiah in you, the hope of glory!*

This is the essence of the Kingdom of God, Mashiakh (Messiah) in us. But notice what else Yeshua says:

John 17:23 (TLV) *I in them, and You in Me....*

The Father is in Yeshua, and Yeshua is in us. So, the Father Himself is in us. How can this be? Remember, God is echad, one. We describe Him as Father, Son, and Ruakh, but they are all one. They are all fully the one God. So, the Father, the Messiah and the Ruakh HaKodesh are all in us! There is a Holy of Holies inside our tabernacles, our sukkot of human flesh.

The Bible calls it our heart, our innermost being, our belly; a *cavity,* figuratively the heart where the Ruakh HaKodesh dwells and therefore where Yeshua and the Father also dwell! The Ruakh wants you to grasp how significant this gift is. I did a search on *"Spirit"* through the Tanakh. Twelve times it says the Spirit was on people using the Hebrew word, *alav,* which means *clothed, enwrapped.* This happened to Moses, the seventy Elders, Gideon, Samson, David, Elisha, and Zachariah. Four times it says the Spirit was in people using the Hebrew prefix *b',* which means *in,* and can also mean *entered.* Those four people are: Joseph, Joshua, Ezekiel, and Daniel. God Himself said His Spirit was *in* Joshua (Num. 27:18). Two times it says the "Spirit is in them" spoken by non-Hebrew speakers: King Nebuchadnezzar and a queen about Daniel (Dan. 4:8; 5:11).

Ezekiel seems to have a revelation for a time in the future (to him) when there will be a new way the Ruakh HaKodesh will interact with people:

> Ezekiel 11:19-20 *Then I will give them one heart, and I will put a new spirit within them, and take the stony heart out of their flesh, and give them a heart of flesh, 20 that they may walk in My statutes and keep My judgments and do them; and they shall be My people, and I will be their God.*

The Hebrew word for *"within them"* used there is בְּקִרְבָּם *b'kerbehkhem.* There are four other predictions in Ezekiel that use the term *"Spirit in"* God's people. How important is this understanding that since Yeshua sent the Ruakh HaKodesh, He is not just on us but in us?

It's very important because the Ruakh HaKodesh had been moving on the earth for a long time already, coming upon God's people. Yeshua meant He was going to send the Ruakh HaKodesh in a new way, to live in, rather than be upon, His followers.

> Matthew 11:11 *Yes! I tell you that among those born of women there has not arisen anyone greater than Yochanan the Immerser! Yet the one who is least in the Kingdom of Heaven is greater than he!*

How are we greater? Because we're immersed in the Ruakh. He in us and we in Him. In Acts, it is amazing how strong the emphasis is on this Ruakh immersion. It's recorded five times!

Acts 2 in Jerusalem on Shavuot (Pentecost).
Acts 8 in Samaria - Peter & John were sent to pray for them.
Acts 9 Sha'ul (Paul) when Ananias was sent to pray for him.
Acts 10 Gentiles at Cornelius' house.
Acts 19 in Ephesus when Paul found believers there.
[You can read much more about this in my *Shavuot* book.]

Today on follow-up cards after an altar call, we ask people if they've prayed to receive Yeshua. But in Acts the emphasis seems to be on being filled with the Ruakh HaKodesh. Why? It is wonderful for people to come to trust in Yeshua, but usually the only evidence that something happened is what the person says. But in Acts, something much more notable and observable was recorded, not when a person did something, but when God did something, placed His Ruakh inside a person.

What was observable? In four out of the five instances, it was observable because they spoke in tongues or prophesied. In the fifth instance, Sha'ul went from being blind to seeing. Today the Lord wants to raise your level of appreciation for His Ruakh HaKodesh in you.

Our Tabernacle within us

What advantage is it to have the Ruakh HaKodesh inside us instead of upon us? Well, for one thing, we don't have to go somewhere like the Wailing Wall, a shrine, a mega-church's altar, or a concert to spend time with Him. We can be with Him simply by going inside ourselves to that place in our hearts where the Ruakh HaKodesh who is Yeshua lives. It's a tabernacle, a sukkah, a Holy of Holies inside us. It's the place where we experience God's glory. His glory fills us as it filled the Tabernacle in the wilderness, which was, at that time, the temporary, portable dwelling place for God's presence.

Exodus 40:34 *Then the cloud covered the Tent of Meeting, and the glory of ADONAI filled the Tabernacle.*

What can this Tabernacle teach each of us about how to worship in our own sukkah? Let's learn about that. We will start outside and work our way in. (See the list on pp. 32-33.)

The first thing to understand is there was an enclosure around the Tabernacle, called the Courtyard, surrounded by a barrier made of fabric on a wood frame 5 cubits (7.5 feet) tall, too high to see over. Second, there's only one gate covered with a curtain. There's only one Way in. What does this mean for us? It shows the division between two realms, God's Kingdom and the kingdom of darkness. Yeshua is the Way in:

> Colossians 1:13 *He has rescued us from the domain of darkness and transferred us into the Kingdom of his dear Son.*

What does that barrier teach us? It shows that not everyone is allowed in. We must guard our inner tabernacles against ha-satan's forces that want to destroy it and us. And remember that I Cor. 6:19 says your body is the tabernacle of the Holy Spirit. So we need to realize that when we put things into our body that defile it, we're defiling our tabernacle. Ponder that a minute....

The next thing that we see is the altar of burnt-offering where the unblemished flesh of animal sacrifices was burned up. A sacrifice had to be made to atone for, cover over, take away people's sins. If a kohane (priest) tried to come further into God's presence, without confessing his sins, repenting, and making an atoning sacrifice, he would be consumed.

> Exodus 33:3 (NKJV) *"... I will not go up in your midst, lest I consume you on the way, for you are a stiff-necked people."*

Imagine all the smoke going up from all those offerings. In Hebrew, the word for *spirit* is *ruakh,* which also means *breath* or *wind.* Smoke is a kind of breath or wind that has an aroma. The Bible always talks about sacrifices being a pleasing aroma to the Lord. Why? Because sacrifices cleansed from sin, and were worship, and allowed the kohanim and Levites to come closer into His presence.

However, ordinary people were not able to go any further. A greater, more precious sacrifice, Yeshua's sacrifice, had to be made for every person to be able to come closer to God.

> 1 Peter 1:18, 19 *You should be aware that the ransom paid to free you from the worthless way of life ...19 ... was the costly bloody sacrificial death of the Messiah, as of a lamb without defect or spot.*

Yeshua's sacrifice was more precious because He is the only begotten Son of God. He was God Himself come as a sinless man. God's plan was that Yeshua's sacrifice would be credited to cover all the sins of all who repent and receive it.

> II Corinthians 5:21 *God made this sinless man be a sin offering on our behalf, so that in union with him we might fully share in God's righteousness.*

When you receive Yeshua's sacrificial sin offering, you receive a new identity. Peter says this awesome thing:

> I Peter 2:9a *But you are a chosen people, the King's cohanim, a holy nation, a people for God to possess!*

Other translations say *a royal priesthood.*

> I Peter 2:9b *Why? In order for you to declare the praises of the One who called you out of darkness into his wonderful light.*

After you receive Yeshua's sacrifice, He ordains you a kohane, a priest or priestess, so you can come closer to God. As kohanim today, we must continually place our flesh on the altar.

> Colossians 3:5 *Therefore, put to death the earthly parts of your nature—sexual immorality, impurity, lust, evil desires and greed (which is a form of idolatry);*

You must place your flesh, your old nature, your iniquity on that altar of burnt-offering to sacrifice it, to put it to death and burn it all up.

So the altar was where sacrifices were made for the people's sin and for guilt offerings for forgiveness. But that altar was also there for something else. It was also for fellowship and peace offerings as worship, which included burning part of it and eating the rest in fellowship. The kohanim were to burn up all those offerings made by the people. So we can minister to others to help them learn to place their flesh upon that altar but also to give sacrifices of praise and thanksgiving as worship.

Now there's one more step before entering into the Tabernacle. The next item in the Courtyard was the laver, a big basin. The kohanim had to wash with water before entering the Tabernacle. Washing was to remove physical dirt. What is the prophetic meaning of the laver? Believers in Yeshua, royal kohanim, need to be immersed in water *t'vilah*, baptism as a prophetic act of turning away from sin and turning to God.

II Corinthians 5:17 *Therefore, if anyone is united with the Messiah, he is a new creation - the old has passed; look, what has come is fresh and new!*

Baptism is acting out the death of your old carnal nature, your old self in the water and your resurrection as a new creation. Once you have received Yeshua's sacrifice and been immersed in water, you are a kohane and can draw closer to God by entering the Tabernacle.

So you've made the sacrifices and you've washed. Now you can go through the second curtain into the Holy Place. In Moses' Tabernacle, there were four thick layers covering the Holy Place, so there was no sunlight or moonlight in there. The only light came from the seven-branch Menorah. So what does this tell us? When you go into your Holy Place, what's the light that you have in there? The Light of the World! Yeshua is our only Light, expelling darkness and revealing Truth. Through the Ruakh, He guides us into all Truth. So, drawing back this curtain reveals the Light of Truth.

In the Holy Place, there was also the *shulkan*, the table with the Bread of the Presence on it. Only the kohanim were allowed to eat these loaves of bread. This symbolizes in my mind, eating with God which is having fellowship with Him. So your Holy Place is where you can eat the Bread of Fellowship with the Lord, teaching that the Tabernacle is a place of relationship. This is so important. It's not just a place of rules, do this and don't do that, and rituals. It's a place of relationship.

Also in the Holy Place, before the curtain leading into the Holy of Holies, there's the **altar of incense** made of pure gold. On this altar, sweet smelling incense was burned. Again because the Hebrew word *ruakh* means both *spirit* and *breath*, this incense symbolizes the presence of the Ruakh Hakodesh, the Holy Spirit, teaching that your tabernacle is a place to breathe in the Spirit and be filled with the Spirit. The Bible also talks about the incense being the prayers of the saints:

3. SPENDING TIME IN YOUR SUKKAH

Psalm 141:2a *May my prayer be set before You like incense.*

Revelation 8:4 *on the gold altar in front of the throne. The smoke of the incense went up with the prayers of God's people from the hand of the angel before God.*

Revelation 5:8b (TLV) *...each holding a harp and golden bowls full of incense—which are the prayers of the kedoshim [saints].*

When the Kohane HaGadol (High Priest) came into the Holy Place, he wore the breast piece with the twelve stones over his heart. Do you know what is written on those stones? The names of the twelve tribes, one on each stone. So whenever he went in, he bore their names close to his heart. Yeshua is our Kohane HaGadol and He is in our individual tabernacles, and He has your name written on His heart. So, you know that He is noticing you and interceding for you. And this is where He leads you to pray and intercede for those He puts on your heart.

So you're filled with the Spirit. You've had fellowship with God. You've got the Light of Truth. Now you go through the third curtain, called the parokhet. It leads directly into the Holy of Holies where the manifest presence of God appeared over the Ark of the Covenant. It is where God, who gives us Eternal Life, dwells.

This is one of the most powerful things I find in the New Covenant. I taught about this in my *Yom Kippur* book. Notice what this verse says about Yeshua:

Hebrews 10:20 *He inaugurated it for us as a new and living way through the parokhet, by means of his flesh.*

What happened to this curtain when Yeshua died on the Cross? This curtain in the Temple was ripped in two from top to bottom, symbolizing that we can now go in there. Yeshua made a living way through the curtain by sacrificing His flesh, so we can enter. Even today you can come boldly into the presence of God. Understand that this was where only the Kohane HaGadol could come and only once per year on Yom Kippur to make atonement for the entire nation of Israel. So here's another miracle that's so amazing. You can go into the

Holy of Holies in your tabernacle how often? Every day! You can be in there all the time, any time you want.

This is another gate to enter to go deeper with God. How do we enter this gate into this holiest chamber?

> Psalm 100:4 *Enter His gates with thanksgiving and His courts with praise! Praise Him, bless His Name.*

So to go into your Most Holy Place, you have to start with a thankful heart. In other words, you can't go in there moaning in bitterness or anger. You have to be thankful for all that God has done and has given you, and you have to praise Him.

In the Holy of Holies, there's the Ark of the Covenant. In Hebrew, it's also called the *Aron Kodesh*, the Holy Ark. Inside were the Tablets with the Ten Words (Commandments) on them, Aaron's rod that budded when there was a controversy about who should be the Kohane HaGadol, and a jar of Manna, the supernatural food that God gave the Israelites in the wilderness.

On top of the Ark is the covering, which in Hebrew is called the *Kaporet*, which is from the same root word as what I wear on my head, a kippa, which means *covering*. It's called the Kaporet because it represents a covering over sin. In English it's also called the Mercy Seat. On the covering, there are the keruveem (pronounced *kehr-oo-veem*), the two creatures carved in gold. There is an awesome, prophetic significance to these keruveem.

> Genesis 3:24 *And He expelled the man; and at the east of the Garden of Eden He had cheruvim dwell along, with the whirling sword of flame to guard the way to the Tree of Life*

Keruveem guarded access to the Tree of Life, which would give those who ate its fruit eternal life. Keruveem being on top of the Ark signifies that the Ark is the source of eternal life. So when the torn parokhet curtain between the Holy Place and the Most Holy Place is parted, it reveals the keruveem guarding the source of eternal life, but they are not wielding swords of flame. Instead their wings are extended to welcome those who come near. So the way is open to the **Eternal** Tree of Life.

So these things are in your Holy of Holies. Let's do a little imagining now. Just close your eyes, and imagine you're in your Holy of Holies inside you. It might seem a little weird, but the Holy of Holies really is inside you, in your spirit. So there's the Ark of the Covenant, and what do the things inside represent and teach you? Well, the jar of Manna is God's provision for your life. Aaron's rod that budded confirms that you are one of His kohanim. The Tablets represent the Word, the Torah. And over the Tablets is the covering, the Mercy Seat and the keruveem. They can also represent the angelic presence in your life. Angels are working in our lives all the time. We don't see them, but they are there.

The Mercy Seat, the Kaporet, is God's throne. That's where He's seated—above the Tablets in the Ark. The fact that the Mercy Seat is over the Tablets of the Law is full of powerful meaning. It symbolizes that mercy is above judgment. Yeshua said this, which James echoed:

> Matthew 12:7 *If you knew what 'I want compassion [mercy] rather than animal-sacrifice' meant, you would not condemn the innocent....*
>
> James 2:13b (TLV) ... *Mercy triumphs over judgment.*

So, there are three entrances we must go through to get to the presence of God at the Mercy Seat. The first is the only **Way** to enter the Kingdom of God. The second reveals the Light of **Truth**. The third leads to the Kaporet, the throne of God, the source of Eternal **Life**.

> John 14:6 *Yeshua said, "I AM the Way—and the Truth and the Life; no one comes to the Father except through me.*

So Yeshua, our sacrificial Lamb, who is the Way, the Truth and the Life leads us to the Kaporet where we meet with Almighty God, HaShem Himself. It's where He met with Moses.

> Exodus 25:22 *"I will meet with you there. I will speak with you from above the atonement cover—from between the two cheruvim that are on the Ark of the Testimony...."*
>
> Hebrews 4:16 *Therefore, let us confidently approach the throne from which God gives grace, so that we may receive mercy and find grace in our time of need.*

So what do you do in your inner sukkah when you come into your Holy of Holies? Well, I think the primary thing is it's the place to listen and hear the voice of the Lord, and receive His direction and maybe His correction. It's the time to be connected to experience His Love and His Glory! Yeshua said if you're not connected to the Vine, you can't bear any fruit.

But let's not forget. It is also a time of interceding and praying for those whom the Spirit puts on your heart. You're right there in the presence of God. It would be selfish to come into His presence and listen to Him and all that and not bring forth the things that as a kohane, you are to pray for. The Holy Spirit wants to challenge you, when you go, to intercede.

This revelation changes our attitude towards our brothers and sisters in Messiah. How can we hate, judge, or take advantage of a brother or sister in whom God dwells in this way? Instead our hearts filled with His mercy and compassion should be overflowing with love for them and feel compelled to pray and intercede for them and minister to meet their needs.

So, are you spending enough time in your sukkah? We can enter the Holy of Holies in our sukkah, where the Ruakh is, any time we want to enter. He will meet with us there. He has opened the way through the veil. We can only go through it because of Yeshua's sacrifice for our sin. We must come with His Blood. We must get alone with the Lord, worshiping Him, to enter, which can happen even in the midst of a crowd.

Things like music and teachings can help us get there, but we must purpose to get there. We must shut off all the competing voices—voices of pride, fear, self-exaltation, depression, vanity, and control. Inside we can experience His presence.

One of the greatest benefits of being a rabbi is that almost every week I must go to that place to receive a Shabbat message. I know I can't come seeking just that because what's in there is not a bunch of knowledge or an inspiring thought. What's in there is personality—Yeshua Himself, the Father Himself! When I come, I have to relate to Him first. I have to take my mind off my need for a sermon. I need to greet Him, worship Him, listen to Him, love Him, know Him.

Then what happens in there is the source of life for me. It can be the source of life for you too.

Interestingly, Yeshua spoke of this when He went to the Temple on Sukkot.

> John 7:37-39 *Now on the last day of the festival, Hoshana Rabbah, Yeshua stood and cried out, "If anyone is thirsty, let him keep coming to me and drinking! 38 Whoever puts his trust in me, as the Scripture says, rivers of living water will flow from his inmost being!" 39 (Now he said this about the Spirit, whom those who trusted in him were to receive later—the Spirit had not yet been given, because Yeshua had not yet been glorified.)*

In the Holy place inside you, there is the source of Mayim Khayim—Living Water. He is that source. He wants you to go in and drink. When you drink your fill, you will overflow.

We can bring His Ruakh HaKodesh out to people. His Ruakh within us will be like multiple rivers of Living Water flowing out to others.

Yeshua also promised we would hear His voice.

> John 10:27 *My sheep hear my voice, I recognize them, they follow me,*

We hear His voice in that place in our hearts, not outside. It's like in our thoughts. Hearing Him is so vital to keeping close to Him. It's a huge part of having an ongoing, living relationship with Him.

Let's end by talking about sukkah maintenance. How do we keep the river flowing into our sukkot? We will dig much deeper into this in later chapters in Section 3, but let's just touch on it here.

> Ephesians 5:18 *Don't get drunk with wine, because it makes you lose control. Instead, keep on being filled with the Spirit—*

Stern correctly translates it: *keep on being filled*. We must be refilled, like our gas tanks. Paul goes on to tell us how:

> Ephesians 5:19 *sing psalms, hymns and spiritual songs to each other; sing to the Lord and make music in your heart to him;*

This is worship.

SECTION 1 THE SUKKAH

Ephesians 5:20 *always give thanks for everything to God the Father in the name of our Lord Yeshua the Messiah.*

This is a thankful heart.

Ephesians 2:22 *in whom you also are being built together for a dwelling place of God in the Spirit.*

When we come together, there is a greater measure of the Ruakh HaKodesh present. That's why we experience a stirring—in all our spirits. It is measures of His Spirit come together to make a fuller measure. And it doesn't work without unity. The smaller measures cannot flow together if they are blocked by discord between us.

Your sukkah is not a sturdy place, so keep it protected and maintained. Don't let it be buffeted by strange doctrines, or cares, or pleasures. Don't let just anyone in. We had a fire in our sukkah one year because we let a person traveling through sleep in it. He lit a fire in the morning and almost burned it down.

Who might you let in that would be a problem? Not only other people, but also other gods, the god of achievement, vanity, pleasure, lust, control, anger. Those are gods of this world. Don't let them in. Keep your sukkah for Yeshua only.

So, yes, be careful who you invite into your inner sukkah, but it is important to welcome guests into your physical one in your yard. There is a tradition that has developed around this idea of having fellowship in your sukkah. It is the tradition called **ushpizin, honored guests**. It is the Sukkot tradition of welcoming the patriarchs into your sukkah. As I said in the introduction to this book, every night one of the patriarchs (Abraham, Isaac, Jacob, etc.) is honored and there is a place set for them at the table, like we do for Elijah at our Passover Seder. During Sukkot, we welcome Abraham one day, Isaac the next day, Jacob the next, etc.—in our minds. They are our unseen honored guests.

As we noted before, these honored guests were all wanderers, which is another spiritual lesson. We are wanderers, pilgrims on this earth, so we need to be hospitable to other wanderers who come our way. This is Sukkot hospitality, bringing the wanderers into our sukkah. It also embodies the hope and desire that guests will come to your sukkah and excitement when someone does come. You can learn all about that traditional hope in the movie *Ushpizin*.[2] To have strangers or long lost friends or non-observing Jews show up during Sukkot brings great delight. They are quickly and eagerly invited to come in and eat in the sukkah and even to sleep there.

Did you know that the patriarch usphizin were in the New Covenant? You probably never saw this Bible passage this way before:

> Matthew 17:1-2 *Six days later, Yeshua took Kefa, Ya`akov and his brother Yochanan and led them up a high mountain privately. 2 As they watched, he began to change form—his face shone like the sun, and his clothing became as white as light.*

So what was happening? First of all, the manifest presence of God was appearing. Right? Yeshua who before looked like a man was suddenly looking like something beyond a man.

> Matthew 17:3-6 *Then they looked and saw Moshe* [Moses] *and Eliyahu* [Elijah] *speaking with him.*

Wow, that's awesome. Those are two of the patriarchs there with Him! And look at what Peter tries to do.

> Matthew 17:4 *Kefa said to Yeshua, "It's good that we're here, Lord. I'll put up three "skianus"*

That's actually the word *sukkot* there. It's the same Greek word that Yochanan used in John 1:14! "I'll put up three skianus—three sukkot—for you!" Other English translations say *three tabernacles* or *tents*.

> Matthew 17:4b *I'll put up three "skianus" shelters if you want—one for you, one for Moshe and one for Eliyahu."*

So what was happening here? Peter was slipping into doing what he had been doing all his life, "Here are the patriarchs! What an honor! Yeshua is with the patriarchs!" This raised Yeshua's esteem in Peter's mind. He now saw Yeshua as being as great as Moshe and Elijah! So he wanted to say,

---

2 *Ushpizin*, a film written by Shuli Rand, directed and produced by Gidi Dar, about Sukkot in the Ultra Orthodox community. It starred Rand, and his wife, Michal, who had never acted before. Israeli film, Gilgamesh Productions, 2004.

"I'll make a sukkah for each of you!" Do you see that? So there is Sukkot on the Mount of Transfiguration. But, of course, God was about to reveal more. This is awesome because it gets back to that Sukkot theme of the manifest presence of God.

Matthew 17:5 *While he was still speaking, a bright cloud...* There's a Sukkot theme, right?

Matthew 17:5b *...enveloped them; and a voice from the cloud said, "This is my Son, whom I love, with whom I am well pleased. Listen to him!"*

Obviously a rebuke. So what was God saying to them about Yeshua? He was saying, "He's not an ushpizin. He's not one of the patriarchs. You've got your sights too low, folks. He is much more than that. He is My Son! Don't go making little tabernacles for Him. He is much greater than that!"

Matthew 17:6 *When the talmidim heard this, they were so frightened that they fell face down on the ground.*

Let's bow in prayer.

Thank You, Lord, for Sukkot and all its lessons. We bow in worship and honor and adoration to You. We thank You for making a way for the Ruakh HaKodesh to dwell in each of us. We pray, Father, give each reader of this book a revelation of living in the sukkah of their flesh. Give each person a revelation of Your presence in their sukkah.

We pray that any who don't have Your Spirit would be filled in a mighty, powerful way, and may we keep on being filled.

May we walk in the knowledge all through our days that You are in our sukkah and will be with us to the end of the age. Help us to be strong and courageous. Help us to trust You and obey You no matter how insurmountable Your orders seem. Help us to trust that if You tell us to do something, You will be with us and will do miraculous things through us. Help us not to shrink back in fear. Help us not to rebel against You or the leaders You have set over us.

Help us to hear Your voice inside us and to be comforted and strengthened and encouraged by Your voice. May we all experience the power of coming together in unity. Not

3. SPENDING TIME IN YOUR SUKKAH

only is each individual who trusts in Yeshua a Tabernacle for Your Ruakh individually but also all of us are corporately a Tabernacle of worship. Help us to stay in love and kindness and unity of Your Spirit to be a mighty Tabernacle/Temple for You! In Yeshua's Name, we pray. Amein.

Section 2

THE LULAV

Father in Heaven, we pray that You open our hearts and our minds and our ears to be able to receive from You what You have for us concerning the Lulav, the branches and the fruit that You commanded for Sukkot. In Yeshua's Mighty Name. Amein.

CHAPTER 4
TREES IN ISRAEL

For these next three chapters, I was led by the Spirit to focus on something in the Sukkot commandments that you don't find in many teachings. The Lord told us to do two unique things on Sukkot. They're both kind of strange or different from what we do for the other Moadim. One, which we just studied, is to live in a sukkah, the other is about the branches.

> Leviticus 23:40 *On the first day you are to take choice fruit of trees, branches of palm trees, boughs of leafy trees, and willows of the brook, and rejoice before ADONAI your God for seven days.*

That verse is the origin of what is called the Lulav, the three different kinds of branches together with the one fruit: a palm branch, a willow branch, a leafy branch, and a lemon-like citrus fruit. I sometimes use an orange because, according to the command, it's just got to be a citrus fruit. But traditionally it is a very special fruit, called an etrog, which is very expensive, but an orange is also Scriptural. For the leafy tree branches, I usually get some from our local trees like a maple or birch. But in Israel and in Jewish traditions, the "leafy tree" is also a very specific tree. We will get into that in Chapter 6.

Every year for our Sukkot meetings, I make sure to have all around the sanctuary the branches and citrus fruits commanded, along with all sorts of branches of local species like maple, oak, and birch for the unspecified leafy branches to make sure that everybody can put together a Lulav to wave.

4. TREES IN ISRAEL

Yes, it makes a mess. I always apologize in advance for the clean up that will be needed afterwards. One year I even brought some Rose of Sharon branches since it is mentioned in other places in Scripture.

Today, trees are very important in Israel. We have an abundance of trees where I live, but that is not the case in Israel. There must have been a lot more trees there before, otherwise why would God give a commandment to collect tree branches for this Moad? The Lulav is supposed to have three branches—from trees, of course, and the fruit comes from a tree. So there must have been enough trees over the centuries for thousands or maybe millions of men to each have a Lulav every year. But something happened to trees in Israel after Rome exiled the Jews from the Land because when the pioneers began to return to the Land in the late 1800s, it was desolate. Here's what Mark Twain had to say about the condition of the Land when he visited it in 1867:

> Chapter 46[3] ... Here were evidences of cultivation — a rare sight in this country — an acre or two of rich soil studded with last season's dead corn-stalks of the thickness of your thumb and very wide apart. But in such a land it was a thrilling spectacle. Close to it was a stream, and on its banks a great herd of curious-looking Syrian goats and sheep were gratefully eating gravel. I do not state this as a petrified fact — I only suppose they were eating gravel, because there did not appear to be any thing else for them to eat. The shepherds that tended them were the very pictures of Joseph and his brethren....
> ....
> We could not stop to rest two or three hours out from our camp, of course, albeit the brook was beside us. So we went on an hour longer. We saw water, then, but nowhere in all the waste around was there a foot of shade, and we were scorching to death. "Like unto the shadow of a great rock in a weary land." Nothing in the Bible is more beautiful than that, and surely there is no place we have wandered to that is able to give it such touching expression as this blistering, naked, treeless land.

---

3 "The Innocents Abroad," Jewish Virtual Library, https://www.jewishvirtuallibrary.org/the-innocents-abroad#47

Here you do not stop just when you please, but when you can. We found water, but no shade. We traveled on and found a tree at last, but no water.

....

Chapter 47 We traversed some miles of desolate country whose soil is rich enough, but is given over wholly to weeds — a silent, mournful expanse, wherein we saw only three persons — Arabs ... shepherds they were....

....

Gray lizards, those heirs of ruin, of sepulchres and desolation, glided in and out among the rocks or lay still and sunned themselves. Where prosperity has reigned, and fallen; where glory has flamed, and gone out; where beauty has dwelt, and passed away; where gladness was, and sorrow is; where the pomp of life has been, and silence and death brood in its high places, there this reptile makes his home, and mocks at human vanity. His coat is the color of ashes: and ashes are the symbol of hopes that have perished, of aspirations that came to nought, of loves that are buried. If he could speak, he would say, Build temples: I will lord it in their ruins; build palaces: I will inhabit them;

... A desolation is here that not even imagination can grace with the pomp of life and action....We never saw a human being on the whole route....There was hardly a tree or a shrub anywhere. Even the olive and the cactus, those fast friends of the worthless soil, had almost deserted the country."

"Israel in Bible Prophecy," [4] p. 4

Concerning the Valley of Jezreel (or the Valley of Armageddon, as Christians call it), Twain observed, "A desolation is here that not even imagination can grace with the pomp of life and action." He described the central highlands of Samaria by stating, "There was hardly a tree or a shrub anywhere. Even the olive and the cactus, those fast friends of a worthless soil, had almost deserted the country." Continuing with his description of Samaria, he wrote: "No landscape exists that is more tiresome to the eye than that which bounds the approaches to Jerusalem." Twain's summary description of the land was a dismal one: ". . .

---

4 "Israel in Bible Prophecy," lamblion.com, http://lamblion.com/xfiles/publications/books/Israel-in-Bible-Prophecy_Chapter4.pdf

it truly is monotonous and uninviting . . . It is a hopeless, dreary, heart-broken land."

The pioneers soon began a tree planting campaign to try to reforest the Land. So there has been over a hundred-fifty years of reforestation going on in Israel, and it's no longer desolate. There's still lots of arid land there in some areas, but there are also many forests there now, which have actually changed the climate. There's more moisture that's retained in the Land. I mean, after all, Israel is right on the Mediterranean Sea, and the breeze comes across, so why should it be dry? The sky should be dumping rain there all the time, but nothing was catching the moisture because it was just all desert. Now there are enough trees to catch and retain moisture.

When you think about how much effort has gone into planting trees, you can understand, if you read the news from Israel, why there is so much of an uproar when there's a forest fire. It's because this has taken them a hundred-fifty years to do this reforesting. This is why it is such a horrible problem when Gaza was sending incendiary balloons and kites into Israel that started fires.

So having enough trees for everyone to have a Lulav at Sukkot is a blessing that came with lots of effort. What is the Lulav supposed to remind us to do? To be **thankful for the harvest**—for the grain, for the vegetables, for the fruit, etc., and we can also be thankful for trees. So let's do that right now. Hold your Lulav up, stand up, and let's give thanks for the harvest.

Let's pray.
Thank You, Lord, for the harvest. Thank You for our delicious food. Thank You for the rain that brings the harvest. Thank You that You make things for us that taste so good. Thank You for fruit! That is just Your grace that You make it so pleasurable for us to eat. We thank You that You gave us taste buds that would love something that is so good for us. Thank You, Lord, that You made us this way, to give us joy.

SECTION 2 THE LULAV

And thank You, Lord, for trees. Thank You that Israelis have been able to reforest their Land. Thank You for the beautiful trees across the world. Their beauty and majesty are a great pleasure to behold. We are blessed by their shade and by how they refresh and moisturize the air. And the colors the leafy trees turn in autumn in my area around the time of Sukkot are such a delight to behold. Children love playing in the piles of fallen leaves. So we thank You for creating trees, Lord.

We wave our branches to You, Lord, as we thank you, Lord. Thank You! In Yeshua's Name! Amein.

CHAPTER 5
THE MYSTERY OF THE ETZ TAMAR (PALM TREE)

Here again are the only instructions in the whole Bible for making the Lulav and what to do with it:

Leviticus 23:40 *On the first day you are to take choice fruit of trees, branches of palm trees, boughs of leafy trees, and willows of the brook, and rejoice before ADONAI your God for seven days.*

So, we're to lift the Lulav up and—notice what the verse says—*"rejoice before the Lord for seven days."* That's a lot of rejoicing, don't you think? This is really amazing that our God is a God that commands us to rejoice. It is not something we made up. He commands us to rejoice! To me it's a sign of God's love, of how deeply He loves us! And He loves to see His people happy! Joyful!

We're to rejoice by waving the branches and the fruit. So let's just take Him at His Word and do it. If you are reading this book during Sukkot, and you have your Lulav, let's just take a moment and not just wave it, but let's rejoice and be thankful while we wave it. And I mean really rejoice. When we do this in our congregation on Sukkot, our people really know how to be joyful!! I tell them, "You guys got it!!" It really lifts my spirit! So rejoice now with all your heart!!

Thank You, Lord! We give You thanks, Father. We wave the branches before You. We stir up our spirits to rejoice in You. We thank You, Father, for Your Ruakh. Thank You for Your provision for us. Thank You for all the things that You've done. Thank You for reconciliation, Father. Thank You, Lord. We praise You. Hallelujah!!

> Leviticus 23:41 *You are to celebrate it as a festival to Adonai for seven days in the year. It is a statute forever throughout your generations—you are to celebrate it in the seventh month.*

This is one of the Appointed Times of the Lord that was not affected as badly when the Temple was destroyed. And the command is to keep it forever wherever you are.

In the next chapter, we are going to dig into each of the branches and the etrog to see what the deep meanings are for them. But first in this chapter, we need to focus on the big question that comes up about the palm branch.

The Hebrew term for palm tree is: etz tamar. This big question has caused a great mystery, and is one crucial point used by Orthodox Jewish leaders to discredit the Church and Messianics. When people who have participated in the church see us waving palm branches on Sukkot, they usually think of the palm branches they wave on Palm Sunday to remember when Yeshua entered Yerushalayim (Jerusalem) riding on the colt of a donkey, often called the Triumphal Entry.

> Matthew 21:8 *And a very great multitude spread their clothes on the road; others cut down branches from the trees and spread them on the road.*

Here, instead of waving them, they are putting the branches on the road for the donkey to walk on. Yochanan (John) tells us a little more in his account:

> John 12:13 *They took palm branches and went out to meet him, shouting, Hosanna!!! "Blessed is he who comes in the name of Adonai, the King of Israel!"*

Yochanan specifically mentions palm branches, and it sounds like they were also waving them. Now, we are getting to the big question about this event. We find the question in these verses:

5. THE MYSTERY OF THE ETZ TAMAR

John 12:1-2, 12-13 *Six days before Pesach, Yeshua came to Beit-Anyah, where El'azar lived, the man Yeshua had raised from the dead; 2 so they gave a dinner there in his honor. ... 12 The next day, the large crowd that had come for the festival heard that Yeshua was on his way into Yerushalayim. 13 They took palm branches and went out to meet him....*

Yeshua's entry into Yerushalayim was just five days before Pesakh (Passover), but palm branches are commanded to be waved during Sukkot, not during Pesakh. So that's the mystery of the etz tamar (palm branch): why palm branches at this time? Unless we understand this mystery, we won't understand a critical turning point in Yeshua's life.

Palm branches are the first of three connections between Sukkot and Yeshua's Triumphal Entry into Yerushalayim. If we read on in either account, we see **the second and third connections** with Sukkot. The **second** is that they shout, **Hosanna**; and the **third** is that they call Him **king**:

Matthew 21:9 (NKJV) *Then the multitudes who went before and those who followed cried out, saying: "**Hosanna** to the Son of David! 'Blessed is He who comes in the name of the Lord!' **Hosanna** in the highest!"*

John 12:13 (NIV) *They took palm branches and went out to meet him, shouting, "Hosanna!" "Blessed is he who comes in the name of the Lord!" "Blessed is the **king of Israel**!"*

Blessed is He who comes in the Name of the Lord. In Hebrew, it is: *Barukh haba b'shem Adonai.* It is a Hebrew way of greeting. In Yochanan (John) verse 13, they are calling Yeshua, *King of Israel* and crying *Hosanna*. The NIV footnote says Hosanna is a Hebrew expression that became an expression of praise (in Christian tradition). What is that Hebrew expression? What were they really saying?

Well, *Hosanna* is an English transliteration of the Greek *Osanna*, which is a transliteration of the Hebrew, *Hoshiana* הוֹשִׁיעָה נָא which is a compound word consisting of two words combined. The first word is *Hoshia* or *Hoshiah*. The root word is *yasha* which means *salvation, deliverance*. Yeshua's

Name comes from the same root word. The second word in the compound word, *Hoshia-na,* is *Na,* which means *I beseech you, now,* or *Please, now!* So they were actually saying, "Please save now!" or "Please *yasha* us now!" Here are those verses:

> John 12:13 (TLV) *So they took palm branches and went out to meet Him, shouting, "'Hoshia-na! Baruch ha-ba b'shem ADONAI! Blessed is He who comes in the name of the Lord!' The King of Israel!"*

> Matthew 21:9 (TLV) *The crowds going before Him and those following kept shouting, saying, "Hoshia-na to Ben-David! Baruch ha-ba b'shem ADONAI! Blessed is He who comes in the name of the Lord! Hoshia-na in the highest!"*

Matthew records them saying, *"Please save now, Son of David!"* That is a title of Mashiakh (Messiah). John writes that they said, *"Please save now, ... King of Israel!"* Why do all the Gospels note that they cried out these particular things? Well, it's because these words are the traditional prayer recited on Sukkot. As I mentioned earlier, Sukkot became a time of prayer for rain for the coming year because in Israel's dry climate, rain was needed for national salvation. This prayer became the focus of every day's worship during Sukkot. (We will go into much more detail about this in chapters 8 and 9.)

Every day they brought water up from the Pool of Siloam and recited this prayer as people circled the altar in the Water Libation ceremony. On the last day, during the great celebration at night, they circled the altar seven times while they shouted this prayer. What prayer? In Sukkot liturgy from Temple times and also today, we recite Psalm 118. The prayer is in this verse:

> Psalm 118:25-26 (CJB) *Please, ADONAI! Save us!* [Hoshia-na!] *Please, ADONAI! Rescue us! 26 Blessed is he who comes in the name of ADONAI.*

This is exactly what the people were shouting as Yeshua entered Yerushalayim, as they greeted Him with palm branches. So the Triumphal Entry passage is very connected with Sukkot. Non Messianic Jewish critics of the Brit Hadashah say the palm branches and the Hosanna prayer here show that

5. THE MYSTERY OF THE ETZ TAMAR

the Gospel authors were ignorant of the Torah and Jewish tradition. They say the Gospel writers are all confused about the holidays of Pesakh and Sukkot, that they have them all mixed up. These critics say this proves their written accounts are not really authentic.

But were Matthew, Mark, and John confused or are there even more solid connections? Let me tell you that they were not confused. I will show you the connections. Sukkot is a memorial of our ancestor's wandering in the desert. During those forty years, God was in their midst as the pillar of cloud and fire.

> Exodus 40:38 (NKJV) *For the cloud of the LORD was above the tabernacle by day, and fire was over it by night, in the sight of all the house of Israel, throughout all their journeys.*

As the Israelites lived in sukkot (temporary dwellings), in the desert, God's manifest presence was among them above the Tabernacle. Sukkot is a time to remember the presence of God in their midst, and not only His presence but His direct ruling over them, His direction and guidance, and His judgment.

Were Matthew, Mark, and John making up a story and confusing the Moadim? No, they were not confused at all. The people were welcoming Yeshua with a **three-fold** Sukkot welcome:

First, they understood that He was the Messiah.

Second, they were welcoming Yeshua as God Himself coming to dwell amongst them the way the pillar of fire and cloud dwelt among their ancestors.

Third, they were welcoming Him as the coming King!

Pesakh is about a sacrificed lamb, whose blood on the doorposts protected them from death. It represents Yeshua's first coming and His sacrificial Blood on the doorposts of our heart, protecting us from eternal death. Sukkot is about God coming as the King, coming to rule the earth. It represents Yeshua's second coming as the King of kings! The people understood that Yeshua was that King above all kings! And they believed that the time was near! It tells us that in this verse:

84 SECTION 2 THE LULAV

> Luke 19:11 ...*Yeshua went on to tell a parable, because he was near Yerushalayim, and the people supposed that the Kingdom of God was about to appear at any moment.*
>
> Luke 19:11 (TLV) ...*He was near Jerusalem and they supposed that the kingdom of God was about to appear at once.*

How important was it that they realized this? Look at the Pharisees' reaction in Luke's record of this event:

> Luke 19:39 *Some of the P'rushim* [Pharisees] *in the crowd said to him, "Rabbi! Reprimand your talmidim!"*

Why were they so upset? It was because the crowds were proclaiming Yeshua to be God come as a man as the Messiah as the King of kings!

> Luke 19:40 *But he answered them, "I tell you that if they keep quiet, the stones will shout!"*

Why were these words so important that the stones would cry out? It's because this was a pivotal moment in Yeshua's life here on earth. He had demonstrated His power to be the ruling King. He had just raised Lazarus from the dead, and many people were believing on Him as the King because of it and were leaving the Temple leaders to follow Yeshua. It says so here:

> John 12:10-13 *The head cohanim then decided to do away with El'azar too, 11 since it was because of him that large numbers of the Judeans were leaving their leaders and putting their trust in Yeshua. 12 The next day, the large crowd that had come for the festival heard that Yeshua was on his way into Yerushalayim. 13 They took palm branches and went out to meet him,*

So the crowd was honoring Him as the coming King. However, Yeshua knew that He first had to be the Pesakh, sacrificed lamb. Immediately after His Triumphal Entry on the colt of a donkey into Yerushalayim, Yeshua says this:

> John 12:23, 27-29 *Yeshua gave them this answer: "The time has come for the Son of Man to be glorified. ... "Now I am in turmoil. What can I say — 'Father, save me from this hour'? No, it was for this very reason that I have come to this hour. I will say this: 28 'Father, glorify your name!'" At this a bat-kol came out of heaven, "I have glorified it before,*

5. THE MYSTERY OF THE ETZ TAMAR

and I will glorify it again!" 29 The crowd standing there and hearing it said that it had thundered; others said, "An angel spoke to him."

This was a revelation to the people about Yeshua's true nature. This was the turning point that sent Him to the Cross. It was the signal that He had accomplished His work of power to show His Kingship. The time had come for His sacrifice to show His suffering servanthood.

That's the mystery. For the people, using the etz tamar branches on a different Moad was purposeful and very honoring to Yeshua Messiah as the King of kings. He first had to became the suffering servant, our Savior to redeem us and conquer the enemy by His shed Blood. He will soon return as the King of Heaven in His power and authority over all! That will be His final Triumphal Entry into Yerushalayim!

Let's pray.

Yeshua, we thank You for coming as the suffering servant to conquer all evil and to rescue us from the enemy and redeem us from our sins. We are so grateful. We praise You! We honor You. We glorify You! We give you all our praise.

We give you our whole lives, all our energy; all our plans; all our ambitions; and all our ideas and creativity. We want to live only for You, only to fulfill our destiny that You planned for us in Your Kingdom. You are our all in all. You are the King above all kings, the Ruler of the whole universe. You love us more than we can fathom. You suffered all to have us near You. We come to You, Lord. We want to be filled with Your Ruakh and to obey Your Ruakh in everything we do. Bless you, Yeshua!! Praise You. We rejoice in You and in all You have done!! Hallelujah!!! Amein!

CHAPTER 6

The Mystery of the Etrog and Lulav

So now in this chapter, we will study each item in the whole Lulav. Let's look at this verse again, which, as I said, is the only verse in all of Scripture that commands us about the branches and fruit, and what to do with them.

> Leviticus 23:40 *On the first day you are to take choice fruit of trees, branches of palm trees, boughs of leafy trees, and willows of the brook, and rejoice before ADONAI your God for seven days.*

One year the Spirit began to talk to me about digging into what these particular branches mean. Why did God choose those certain branches and that fruit? The only details He gives us about them is He tells us what they are, and the only thing He says about why He wants us to wave them is to rejoice with them. Well, I guess it doesn't specifically say to wave them. We are assuming that to rejoice with them means to wave them as we rejoice.

In a way, it's enough for me that God, who knows all things, commands us to rejoice with these things. Therefore, I've come to the conclusion that somehow it must gladden His heart when we actually do it. Certainly it's also good for us to do it because all the things that He tells us to do are good for us. Amen? Amen!

So the Spirit of the Lord led me to focus on another kind of mystery—it's always been a mystery to me anyway—about what the significance is of these four distinct objects that we are told to wave before the Lord in thanksgiving. I'm calling them "distinct objects" because you really can't just call them branches, right? The etrog is a lemon-like fruit. So is it a branch? No, it's a fruit. So traditionally in Judaism they're called the four species, but that's a little strange, too, because there are three branches from trees and then you've got the one fruit. So what is all this about?

As I studied this, the solution to the mystery came forth—a hidden message actually. When I started to see this happening, I remembered my former assistant, Rabbi Ben's message about the sounds that we make with the shofar on Rosh Hashanah, where he took the calls and put them together and it actually said something. It was a sentence. So what I found here is that there's a message, if you will, in the things that we are supposed to wave. But I will save that for the end, just to keep you on the edge of your seat.

As we look at the purpose—as to why God chose each of these objects—I also want to say something here just as kind of a general instruction for Bible study. I have found over the years that when you see things in the Word of God where it says do this and this, it is so inspiring to dig in and say, "What exactly did He mean by that? What's the symbolism? Why?" It's so much more profitable and life-giving to do that rather than just accepting it blandly, saying, "Oh, He just chose that." Because I have found that nothing in the Word is chosen just to choose it. Nothing is random. Nothing is just by chance.

Everything in the Word has a purpose. Everything in it means something. As we dig in, we find the deep meanings and significance. That has always been a very fruitful method of Bible study for me.

So as I prayed about this, the Spirit of God showed me that each of the objects that we wave represents a Godly character trait that the Spirit of God wants to instill in us. If we've seen that trait grow over the past year, we can give thanks for that trait. That's one thing the waving is about, to give thanks. But it is also a reminder to pray for these things. So now let's dig in and see what meaning is hidden in each commanded item of the Lulav.

Willow עַרְבֵי־נָחַל Arbe Nakhal

The last kind of branch mentioned in the commandment is a **willow** branch, but we are going to talk about it first. I have my reasons. Don't worry. *Willow* in Hebrew is *"arbe nakhal."* *"Arbe"* (pronounced *arbeh*) is *"willow"* and *"nakhal"* is *"brook."* So it's saying to bring willows of the brook. If you know anything about willows, you know they grow beside streams of water because they need a lot of water. When you see a stream, you will often find willows growing along its shores, at least in a climate such as where I'm from.

So grab your willow branch. Look at it. Enjoy its beauty. I've found that the leaves don't last very long. They kind of curl up soon after you cut them. Now just hold it and kind of wave it around as you read on.

So, what's the willow all about? Well, immediately the Spirit sent me to Psalm 1, which is about what grows by the streams of living water. First of all, it tells us that we need to reject the wisdom and counsels and activities of this world.

> Psalm 1:1-2 *Happy is the one who has not walked in the advice of the wicked, nor stood in the way of sinners, nor sat in the seat of scoffers. 2 But his delight is in the* Torah *of* ADONAI, *and on His* Torah *he meditates day and night.*

So we must delight in the Word of God and meditate on it. If you're not familiar with what the word *"meditate"* means in Hebrew, it actually means, *"to roll it around in your mind."* In other words: *Go over it. Think about it. Consider it. Ponder it.*

If it's a parable or a story, visualize it in your mind. Go over the scenes. Ponder each part. We are to do that with the Word of God. In some teachings by Dr. Caroline Leaf, she explains that neuro scientists now understand that things go from our short-term memory to our long-term memory when we meditate on them. So if we just see something, it's in our short-term memory and doesn't stick around very long. But if we think about it, and then we come back to it and think about it again, pretty soon it gets into our long-term memory and stays. The beautiful thing about our long-term memory is that scientists understand now that the neurons in our brain actually become configured chemically and electrically to hold our memories. So in a sense, when something goes from short-term memory to long-term memory, it becomes part of your body. I hope you can grasp that. It becomes part of your flesh in the sense that it is really part of your brain.

So here in Psalm 1, it says we're supposed to meditate on the Word of God. In other words, we're supposed to read it, but then we're supposed to think about it and read back over it and memorize it maybe. And when we do that, it goes in and actually becomes part of us. See how beautiful that is? That's the value of meditating on the Word. (We will learn a lot more about meditating on God's Word in chapters 28, 29, and 30.)

So, if you do those things—stay away from the scoffers and meditate on God's Word, etc., what will happen?

> Psalm 1:3a (ASV) *And he shall be like a tree planted by the streams of water,*

What kind of tree is that? A willow!

> Psalm 1:3b (CJB) *they bear their fruit in season, their leaves never wither, everything they do succeeds.*

Wow, that's a pretty wonderful promise for those who are like the arbe nakhal, the willows of the brook. We know that by staying in the Word, we stay connected to the Vine, which is Yeshua. So that's how we continue to flourish! To succeed in everything we do, we need to be meditating on the Word, which will make us be like a willow tree by the brook! We will be planted by Yeshua's river of Living Water!

Then there's the other side of the promise, which we should read because it's there, but it's not so pleasant.

> Psalm 1:4 *The wicked are not so. For they are like chaff that the wind blows away.*

> Psalm 1:6 (CJB) *... the way of the wicked is doomed.*

So the warning here is not just that it will dry up and not be so fruitful, but it's pretty bleak for those who don't stay by the river of Living Water, who don't continue to meditate on the Word.

So lift up your willow branch and wave it, as we pray.

Let's pray.

Lord, help me stay near to You, the source of Living Water. Help me reject the counsel of the wicked, not stand in the way of sinners, nor sit in the seat of scoffers, but instead to delight in Your Word and meditate on it day and night.

[Now, this is supposed to be an annual thing so think back over this last year. If you have been sustained by the streams of Living Water, by Yeshua's Living Water during this year— if you've grown; if you've borne fruit instead of withering; if you've been successful at something, this is a time to give thanks for the *arbe nakhal*, the willow of the brook. Okay? So let's give thanks.]

Lord, thank You for Your Living Water. Thank You that You have sustained me by it. Without Your Living Water, I would be withered; I would be nothing. I would have no success. So I thank You for everything in my life that has flourished instead of withering. I give all the credit to You. Thank You, Lord. In Yeshua's Name. Amein.

Palm Branches כַּפֹּת תְּמָרִים Capote Tamarim

Okay, the second thing we are to wave is the **palm branch**. In the Scripture in Hebrew, it is *capote tamarim*. It actually is a very interesting phrase. *Tamarim* means *palm trees*, plural. *Tamar* is *palm tree*, singular. *Capote* is really interesting as to the language. *Capote* is the plural of כַּף *caf*, which actually means *hand, palm, palm of the hand*, etc. (יָד *yad* also means *hand*, but *caf* is generally referring to an *open hand* or *palm*.) So why do they call them palm of the hand palm trees or palm, palm trees? Well, you can see that the palm frond of some palm trees actually look like a hand, like the palm of a hand. (To me, most of them don't, but I guess to others they do.) So that's why they're called palm trees. So *capote tamarim* is literally the *hands of palm trees*. So you have a palm tree and the branches growing out of it are the hands. So hold up your palm *hand* as you read.

So why did the Spirit tell us to give thanks with palm branches? I was led to **three reasons**. **First** of all, you are probably aware that palm trees are known for their ability to survive storms, including hurricanes. That's because of their extreme flexibility. The trunks can bend horizontally and not break. You've probably seen pictures of them bending in the powerful wind. That flexibility is something that the Spirit of God wants each of us to have so that we can survive the storms and trials of life.

The **second** thing is that their ability to bend also applies to something else. This is apropos especially to Jewish people because the Lord has told us that we have part of our body that's very stiff—our necks. So bending our necks is being like the palm branch. The trees that don't bend in the wind or in a hurricane, what happens to them? They break! We need to be able to bend our necks. Capote can also mean bow. In other words, we need to be willing to humble ourselves, and bow in submission to God's discipleship—and His correction—with contrite hearts.

Third, palm branches were waved at the coronation of kings. That's why in John 12:13, as we noted, people waved palm branches when Yeshua entered Jerusalem. It wasn't Sukkot! It was in the spring near Passover. They knew it was off season, but they did it to acknowledge Yeshua as the King of kings. That's why.

So wave your palm branches as we pray.

Let's pray.

Lord, help me to be flexible to withstand the storms that come my way and to humble myself before You. We repent of stubbornness, of having a stiff neck. We humble ourselves before You. We submit to You as King of Kings and Lord of Lords, Ruler of all the universe. We wave these branches in honor of You. Amein.

[Once again, if you think back over this last year and you've learned to be more flexible because of the storms that came your way this year, or you've had some instruction or correction from the Lord, and you humbled yourself to receive it, then you can give thanks.]

Lord, thank You for making me more flexible this last year. Continue to help me be not stiff-necked, but flexible, humble, contrite, submitting to Your discipline and Your correction. And thank You for revealing Yourself to us as the King of kings. In Yeshua's Name. Amein!

Thick Tree עֲנַף עֵץ־עָבֹת Anaf Etz Avot

Okay, the third one is *anaf etz avot*. This is also kind of interesting. *Anaf* means *bough* or *branch*. *Etz* is *tree*. You probably recognized that. But the word *avot* is really interesting. This is not the *avot* that means *fathers*. That *avot* is spelled differently in Hebrew: אָבוֹת This *avot* עָבֹת means *dense foliage*. It can also mean *thick*.

Different translations have different ways of expressing this: *"boughs of leafy trees" "boughs of thick trees" "boughs of intertwined trees."* So you sort of get the picture that these are trees in a forest, and when you look through it, all their branches are intertwined. But what jumped out to me about this was that it is *"thick boughs."* In other words, strong boughs. What I thought of is boughs that are thick enough to build with. You know, a branch of a tree that would be thick enough that you could make a 2 x 4 out of it, or larger, a 4 x 4 or a 4 x 8 or something like that.

So when I started to think about what I should get, I thought of evergreens because really most of our construction is done with pine, which is an evergreen. And a pine tree has dense foliage. How many pine needles does one branch have? Thousands! Imagine if they were leaves. It would be so dense. So sometimes I bring a bunch of evergreen branches to our synagogue to represent the "thick boughs."

That strength of the thick boughs is the strength that the Spirit of God gives us—strength to endure hardship, strength to overcome ha-satan, strength to crucify our flesh—to control our tempers, our appetites, control our tongues. Also think of this: strength to be used to build the Kingdom! That's what came to me for this.

So when your strength increases, God is able to use you in greater ways for His Kingdom, right? The stronger you become in the Lord, the more He will use you. This verse came to me:

> Revelations 3:12a *I will make him who wins the victory a pillar in the Temple of my God, and he will never leave it.*

So what better picture of a strong piece of wood than a pillar? Right? So how can you be a pillar in His Temple? He's not speaking of the Temple in Jerusalem made of wood and stone because we know in another verse in Ephesians, He speaks about what His Temple is that we're to be pillars in.

> Ephesians 2:21 (TLV) *In Him the whole building, being fitted together, is growing into a holy temple for the Lord.*

So each of our individual bodies, the Scripture says, are Temples of the Holy Spirit, but we as a congregation are also a Temple for God, and the entire body of Messiah is a Temple for God. We are a local Temple for the Lord. Being a pillar in God's Temple, what immediately came to mind was that it doesn't mean a pillar standing alone, a building needs more than one pillar. It means being in His Temple, being part of one of His congregations, along with and connected to other pillars, so that we're holding up the house because if you just have a bunch of pillars standing around and they're not secured to the floor and the ceiling, which connects them to each other, you're not going to hold up the house, right? The house needs connected, weight bearing pillars.

One way to get connected and strengthened is to be a part of a small group. That's what small groups are all about. They're about strengthening our walk with the Lord, connecting us together for accountability, for discipleship, and for strength. So we are not pillars standing alone, but are connected together, holding up the spiritual dwelling place of the Lord.

There's a beautiful picture from nature about this. I don't know if you've ever seen it before, but redwood trees can grow to something like 300-400 feet tall. When I look at a redwood tree, the first thing I think of is, for a tree to grow that tall, it must have really deep roots, right? And the concept of deep roots is a great concept spiritually. We're supposed to have roots down to the solid rock.

But when the biologists looked at the root system of the redwood tree, you know what they found? Very shallow roots! Yet they're standing up so tall. So how do they do it? Well, they grow in groves. The roots of the redwood, rather than being deep, spread out and intertwine with the roots of other redwood trees. Isn't that amazing? That's why they're the tallest of trees, taller than any other trees, even taller than the sequoias. Those are broad, but not as tall as redwoods. The reason that redwoods can be the tallest tree is because they link arms, if you will, with other trees.

So you see how that fits in with us being part of the body of Messiah and supporting each other to make us pillars in His House.

So pick up your thick tree branch.

Let's pray about this.

Lord, help me be a thick bough, strong in spirit, and overcoming my flesh. Help me to use that strength to build Your Kingdom. Make me a pillar, Lord, in Your Temple. Connect me to the other pillars so that I can stand. In Yeshua's Name. Amein.

[So now, I'm going to ask that same question about the past year. Has the Lord strengthened you this past year in some way? Has He connected you to others to make you stand stronger in some way? If so, let's wave the branch some more and give thanks.]

Lord, thank You for making me a thicker bough this year, for increasing my strength, and connecting me to other pillars to be stronger in Your Temple. Amein.

Fruit of the Citrus Tree פְּרִי עֵץ הָדָר Pri Etz Hadar

Okay. Now we come to the citrus fruit. The Hebrew is pronounced *pree etz ha-dar*. *Pri* (pree) means *fruit*. *Etz* by itself, as we've learned means *tree*. Together with *hadar*, *etz hadar*, it means *citrus*. The plural, *citrus fruits* is *perot (peh-rote) etz hadar*.

According to this commandment, it is to be a citrus fruit. Remember, this is the only verse in the whole Bible explaining the Lulav. The tradition is a very special lemon-like citrus fruit, called an etrog, which is very expensive. If you've watched the movie, "Ushpizin," you know that already. But any citrus fruit would be Scriptural. One year when I taught on the Lulav in my congregation, I brought mandarin oranges. By the time we got to the fruit in my teaching, we didn't have enough to go around because some of the kids were eating them. So we ended up with some people just having orange sections to hold up. Everyone was laughing about that.

> Leviticus 23:39a *So on the fifteenth day of the seventh month, when you have gathered in the fruits of the land, you are to keep the Feast of ADONAI for seven days.*

> Deuteronomy 16:13 *You are to keep the Feast of Sukkot for seven days, after gathering in the produce from your threshing floor and winepress.*

So from these two verses, we can see that Sukkot is about the harvest. Sukkot comes at the end of the final harvest—in our cold climate. In Israel, the fruit harvest has come in, including the grapes, but the olive harvest doesn't even start until after Sukkot.

What's the significance of waving this pri etz hadar, this citrus fruit? Well, first of all the focus is on being thankful for the harvest. In America, we should be filled with gratitude to live in a land of overflowing abundance. We know people in many parts of the world are in great need. This is particularly meaningful to us at Congregation Shema Yisrael in Rochester, New York because we have been active participants in the distribution of overflow. Over the twenty one years that we gave food away through our Sharing Our Bread program, we supplied about two million meals. (That's like McDonald's counting the millions of burgers they've served.) All of this was provided from overflow of the harvest God gives our nation!

Yes, since covid, there are supply chain problems causing shortages, but we still have an abundance compared to other places, especially places where there is war, like Ukraine, and persecution, like Nigeria. So, we have great reasons to be thankful for the bountiful harvest.

But, God wants us to see that each of us is reaping another harvest, a spiritual harvest. We can be even more thankful for that harvest of spiritual fruit. So what is our fruit according to the Bible? Well, I did a study on this and found that there are references in the Bible to fruit in five places, five different times. The first type of fruit we find in Galatians 5. It is probably the one that occurred to you as soon as I mentioned it.

> Galatians 5:22-23 *But the fruit of the Spirit is love, joy, peace, patience, kindness, goodness, faithfulness, 23 humility, self control. Nothing in the Torah stands against such things.*

So the **first** variety of choice fruit is internal and in Hebrew it is *pri haRuakh, the fruit of the Spirit.* Look carefully at that list. Would you agree with me that it's simply describing God's character? Yes? So it's a list of God's character traits, and the Spirit of God grows that in us. It's internal. Yes, it's very visible sometimes, but it comes from inside us.

By the time I became a new believer, I had worked in the business world for a long time. I worked for Xerox in the high tech, hard core, corporate world, and most of the managers, the vice presidents, and the department heads that I had met were intimidating. They were tough. They were harsh and hard and in your face. That was how they led, mostly by intimidation. When I started to meet some leaders in the Kingdom of God, I was so surprised and shocked as I saw the fruit of the Spirit in them. They were kind and caring and joyful! They had gentleness, humility, and love! That's exactly how it should be because that fruit should be in those who are maturing in the Lord. They should have that visible, Godly character.

So, as the Holy Spirit conforms us to be more and more like Yeshua, that fruit comes forth in our lives. But it is important to understand that fruit takes a long time to grow. It's the slowest growing of anything that we grow in our gardens and fields. Fruit doesn't grow quickly. So don't be too hard on yourself, expecting your character to be instantly Messiah-like.

The **second** variety of fruit is the fruit of righteousness grown by the Holy Spirit. It's found in this verse in Hebrews, which is speaking about God's discipline.

> Hebrews 12:11 *Now, all discipline, while it is happening, does indeed seem painful, not enjoyable; but for those who have been trained by it, it later produces its peaceful fruit, which is righteousness.*

Righteousness, as I hope you know, means "right standing with God," but it also means the ability to live in victory over sin. And another thing it can mean is taking a stand on Godly issues, being a righteous person, meaning, "I'm going to take a stand when I see injustice." "I'm going to take a stand when society champions immorality." "I'm going to take a stand and be compassionate where there needs to be compassion." So that's the second kind of fruit.

Here's the third kind of fruit:

> Hebrews 13:15 *Therefore by Him let us continually offer the sacrifice of praise to God, that is, the fruit of our lips, giving thanks to His name.*

So the **third** kind is the fruit of praising God, but there's a little bit of a condition there. I wonder if you noticed it. Did you notice the word "... *continually*" there? So this is **not** just someone who comes and praises the Lord once a week because they're in a worship service. This is someone who praises God continually. That means giving Him praise in all their speech when they're talking with believers, when they're talking with unbelievers, and just giving Him praise and thanks in their thoughts and in praise all day. The Holy Spirit grows this fruit of thanksgiving in us. So that's the third kind of fruit.

The **fourth** kind of fruit is very precious. It is the fruit of our offspring, which the Holy Spirit grows through us. Our physical children whom we raise in Godly families, and our spiritual children whom we lead to the Lord or disciple or both. This fruit comes forth when we obey the Great Commission.

> Matthew 28:19-20 *Therefore, go and make people from all nations into* talmidim [disciples], *immersing them into the reality of the Father, the Son and the Ruach HaKodesh, 20 and teaching them to obey everything that I have commanded you.*

This fruit is the biggest of all spiritual fruit. It's the watermelon of them all. Okay? It's a prize watermelon. So this fruit is those that we help bring into the Kingdom or that we disciple. If you've led someone to the Lord this past year, you need to rejoice because you bore fruit, watermelon-size fruit. Or if you discipled someone this year, that's also like a watermelon fruit.

Now we have one more fruit and then we will get to the mystery I promised you. The **fifth variety** of fruit is our good works. So what are our good works? Helping the needy, helping friends, organizing others to help, teaching the Word, giving, etc.

> Matthew 5:16 *In the same way, let your light shine before people, so that they may see the good things you do and praise your Father in heaven.*

So it's not just doing those good things, but it's also giving glory to God, letting people know that you're doing this good deed because of God's Love and His Spirit in you. Otherwise you get the glory instead of God. So I'm going to describe some of this fifth kind of fruit, and I believe you probably have, at some time in this past year, borne this fruit because every deed that we do that is led by the Holy Spirit is this kind of fruit.

Every prayer that we pray for ourselves even, if we pray for ourselves to follow the Lord, that's this kind of fruit. Every prayer that we pray for others for healing, for help with their problems, for spiritual growth, or just to bless them, that's this fruit.

Every time we humble ourselves, exercise self control, go the extra mile, that's this kind of fruit. Every time we turn the other cheek, every time we give out of a generous heart or act unselfishly, that's this kind of fruit. Every time we do anything in service for the Lord, that's this fruit of good works. When we help out our congregation, such as, cut the grass or fix the plumbing or paint or serve in Shabbat School or lead in singing or take some responsibility for some Kingdom thing, all those things are fruit.

So the Spirit grows fruit in our lives, five varieties. Two of them are internal: the fruit of the Spirit and the fruit of righteousness. Three of them are external, praising God, discipling or leading people to the Lord, and our good deeds. How do we make sure we have a harvest of this fruit? This verse tells us:

> John 15:5 " ...Those who stay united with me, and I with them, are the ones who bear much fruit; because apart from me you can't do a thing.

> John 15:5 (TLV) "... The one who abides in Me, and I in him, bears much fruit; for apart from Me, you can do nothing."

So the secret to fruit bearing is to stay united with Yeshua and abiding in Him. He chose us for this purpose of bearing fruit for His Kingdom.

> John 15:16 *You did not choose me, I chose you; and I have commissioned you to go and bear fruit, fruit that will last;*

So, by staying connected to Yeshua, we will bear fruit that will last into eternity. Being united with Him and abiding in Him means spending quality time with Him, spending time in His word, reading, studying, in worship, prayer, listening, and in doing what He directs us to do. God is glorified when we bear spiritual fruit.

> John 15:8 *This is how my Father is glorified—in your bearing much fruit; this is how you will prove to be my talmidim.*

After becoming disciples of Yeshua, our primary purpose on earth is to bear fruit, much fruit for the Kingdom of God.

So, I trust the Spirit has borne some fruit in you this year. God is delighted that you bear fruit. So this is another reason to be rejoicing on Sukkot. .

So let's wave this fruit and pray.

Lord, grow more fruit in me. Grow my character and my righteousness. Lord, grow more fruit through me. May I become a greater praiser of You. May I lead many to You. May I disciple many. And may I do deeds that are fruitful that demonstrate Your Glory. I just thank You, Lord, for the fruit that you've grown in me.

Let's say it. Thank You, Lord, for the fruit that You've grown in me. Thank You, Lord. Thank You, Lord.

Okay, now, for the mystery. If you take the four objects, and put them in the order we just went through. Okay? We did the willow, the palm, the thick branches, and the fruit. They form a message, which is a promise of God that has certain conditions to it.

So here's the promise. If you will be like a willow planted by Living Water for nourishment, and if you will be like a palm tree flexible to survive the storms and humble to be disciplined, and if you will be like the thick branches applying your strength to build the Kingdom of God and stay connected to Him, then you will bear much fruit, the fruit of the Spirit, the fruit of righteousness, the fruit of praise, the fruit of disciples, and the fruit of good deeds.

How about that? Is that a message? Alright let's read it again. Let's make it more personal this time.

"If I will be like a willow planted by Living Water for nourishment, and if I will be like a palm tree flexible to survive the storms and humble to be disciplined, and if I will be like the thick branches applying my strength to build the Kingdom of God and stay connected to You, then I will bear much fruit."

Let's say it, "Then I will bear much fruit, pri haRuakh, the fruit of the Spirit, the fruit of righteousness, the fruit of praise, the fruit of disciples, and the fruit of good deeds or good works. Amein."

So now, if you are reading this during Sukkot, I suggest you go into your sukkah and wave your whole Lulav and give praise and honor to Yeshua, the King of kings. If it is not Sukkot, how about going into your inner sukkah to worship Him.

Hallelujah!!! Lord, we praise You! We love You! We honor You and glorify You! May Your Name be magnified in all the earth!!

[Go ahead and keep on praising Him in your own words....]

CHAPTER 7
WE ARE LULAVS!

We are going to dig deeper into this theme of fruit now in this next passage of Scripture. You probably never saw it as a Sukkot passage before, but it is so connected to Sukkot.

> John 15:1-2, 5 *I am the real vine, and my Father is the gardener. 2 Every branch which is part of me but fails to bear fruit, he cuts off; and every branch that does bear fruit, he prunes, so that it may bear more fruit. ... 5 I am the vine and you are the branches.*

Now, He's talking about a grape vine here, and who's He saying the branches are? Us! Okay, so **we are branches!! We are the Lulav!** Did you ever think of yourself that way before? When you are waving the Lulav, you are symbolizing us! Believers! **The Lulav is made of branches, and we are branches on the vine.**

Now, He's also teaching something else very interesting here. He says that every branch in Him that fails to bear fruit, He cuts off. I'm assuming you are not cut off. So if you are not cut off, then we can infer from these verses that you are bearing fruit! Isn't that great? You are bearing some fruit, otherwise you would be cut off. But if you are bearing fruit, He prunes you.

Let me explain a little about **growing fruit**. When you have a branch that is going to bear fruit, you may have buds for maybe 20 or 30 pieces of fruit on that branch. If you let them all grow, you would get tiny, little fruit. So instead what you do is you clip off a bunch of them. With the skill of a vine grower or a gardener, they know how much fruit a branch can support well. So you clip off a bunch of them and the ones that are left, they grow big and delicious. That's what **pruning** is all about. And pruning in our lives is something that the Spirit is always doing to us, cutting away that which is not productive, that which is not going to support bearing good fruit.

> John 15:3 *Right now, because of the word which I have spoken to you, you are pruned.*

Yeshua's Word, the Word of God, prunes us.

> Ephesians 5:25-26 (TLV) *Husbands, love your wives just as Messiah also loved His community and gave Himself up for her 26 to make her holy, having cleansed her by immersion in the word.* (NKJV: *26 that He might sanctify and cleanse her with the washing of water by the word....*)

So the Word, reading the Word, receiving the Word, meditating on the Word is the thing that prunes us and cleanses us. Only, of course, if we let it sink in, and we do it, and it changes us, not if we just hear it and ignore it or hear it so we can tell someone else about it. We must receive it for ourselves.

> John 15:4 *Stay united with me, as I will with you—for just as the branch can't put forth fruit by itself apart from the vine, so you can't bear fruit apart from me. 5 I am the vine and you are the branches.*

We are Lulavs!

> John 15:5b *Those who stay united with me, and I with them, are the ones who bear much fruit; because apart from me you can't do a thing.*

Now that's a harsh reality.

> John 15:6-7 *Unless a person remains united with me, he is thrown away like a branch and dries up. Such branches are gathered and thrown into the fire, where they are burned up. 7 If you remain united with me, and my words with you, then ask whatever you want, and it will happen for you.*

Now let me explain. This doesn't mean that as long as you are reading the Word you can go ask for a Cadillac or a great big boat, and it's got to happen for you because it says so. It's not that at all. What it means is that if you put God's Word into you enough and you're connected with Him enough, your desires will become His desires. And what you will find is that as you pray, you will be praying His will for your life, and it will happen because it is His will.

> John 15:8 *This is how my Father is glorified — in your bearing much fruit; this is how you will prove to be my talmidim.*

So we are the branches. We are to bear a harvest of fruit, the five kinds of fruit, and here's the amazing thing. That brings glory to God! As we do good works, as we bring people into the Kingdom, as our character develops, that brings glory to God. That is an amazing responsibility. We can glorify God!!

> John 15:9 *Just as my Father has loved me, I too have loved you; so stay in my love.*

He loves you! As much as the Father loves the Son, the Son loves you. That's why He wants us to stay connected with Him. He loves us!

> John 15:10 *If you keep my commands, you will stay in my love—just as I have kept my Father's commands and stay in his love.*

So, what's the key to staying connected and in His Love? Obedience, yes, absolutely. It's the key. And understand that it has to be obedience that is led by the Spirit of God because there is an obedience that comes out of legalism which is from a wrong spirit. It is the Living Spirit of God that we need to be following.

> John 15:11 *I have said this to you so that my joy may be in you, and your joy be complete.*

Remember that Sukkot is the **time of our rejoicing**. "Z'man simkhatenu" is what it is called, "the time of our rejoicing." The joy of Yeshua is what is promised here if we stay connected. His joy is nothing like the world's joy. The joy of Yeshua is deep and lasting. It is totally different from the joy of this world. Do you know His joy? Before I came to the Lord, I had good times at certain times, and I was happy that certain things happened to me, but it wasn't that joy. It was weak and fleeting. His joy is overflowing and is only found in Him.

7. WE ARE LULAVS

John 15:12 *This is my command: that you keep on loving each other just as I have loved you.*

Whoa. That's a big challenge. Remember we just learned how He loves us. Do you get the progression here? God loves Yeshua with an infinite, incredible Love. We can be sure of that. Then He says He loves us that way, right? Then He tells us that we've got to love everybody else that way. Just a little challenging!

John 15:13 *No one has greater love than a person who lays down his life for his friends.*

Now, He's not saying here that we need to look for ways to be martyrs and sacrifice our lives for other people, although that may happen. What He is saying is that we are to lay down our wants and desires and live a life submitted to Him in love. That's laying down our lives, being committed to Him and following Him.

Here's a really neat part of this.

John 15:14 *You are my friends...*

We, His branches, are His friends!

John 15:14 *...if you do what I command you.*

The friendship is based on obedience.

John 15:15 *I no longer call you slaves, because a slave doesn't know what his master is about; but I have called you friends, because everything I have heard from my Father I have made known to you.*

So here we have an incredible promise of the revelation of God's plans. I believe that's the plan for us. In other words, we are supposed to know what God has planned for us. This is one of my favorite verses:

John 5:19 *Therefore, Yeshua said this to them: "Yes, indeed! I tell you that the Son cannot do anything on his own, but only what he sees the Father doing; whatever the Father does, the Son does too.*

So as Yeshua walked this earth, what I get is that He got up in the morning and He asked the Father, "What are You going to do today?" And the Father would say, "I want You to go here and pray for this person, go there and heal that person." And that's how we're supposed to live. We're supposed to know what God's plan is for us today. And that's the promise there, the promise of that knowledge because we're friends. He tells us His plans for us.

> John 15:16a *You did not choose me, I chose you; and I have commissioned you to go and bear fruit...*

So it is not even up to us. We've been chosen to bear fruit. You have been chosen to bear fruit. It is by His choosing. We've been commissioned and ordained to bear fruit. Then He describes what kind of fruit we will bear.

> John 15:16b-17 *...fruit that will last; so that whatever you ask from the Father in my name he may give you. 17 This is what I command you: keep loving each other!*

What is **fruit that will last?** Well, when you do something good for someone and it has an effect on their eternal life, that is lasting fruit. When you help bring someone into the Kingdom, that's lasting fruit! They're going to live forever! When fruit of the Spirit character traits become developed in you, that's lasting fruit. Those characteristics are not going to go away when you go to Heaven. If God's kind of love develops in your life, you don't lose that. It's going to be there forever. So that is lasting fruit.

So how do we do this? How do we connect with the vine? Well, you know this. I'm just going to remind you, and I'm going to give you one more insight in how to do this. Read, memorize, meditate on, study what? **The Word!!** That's the first way. And receive teaching on it. Teaching is important. I teach a couple times every week, but I like to listen to other people teaching because it is an awesome thing when someone digs into the Word and brings out what the Spirit of God is saying to them about it. We all need that. So there's **learning and prayer**—spending time in prayer—being with God in His presence, praying. **Fellowship**, being with other believers who will encourage you, inspire you, and correct you. All of those things are part of being connected.

Finally, there's **worship**. I want to show you something that the Lord showed me awhile back. I was asking the Lord what it is when we get before Him, "How is it that Your Spirit comes into us and fills us and we become empowered by Your Spirit? What's the mechanism? What do we have to do in order to receive that?" And this is the picture that God showed me. It's a picture of myself on the left and God on the right with a line down the middle. It is me in my normal activities. God is on the other side, and He's got all kinds of things for me. He has His Spirit, His Love, the sap of His vine, Living Water, the oil of His Spirit, the Bread of Life, the True Manna. I know and you most likely know, too, that during times of intense worship more of that is flowing to you than at other times. Right? That's why we like to worship. But God showed me that there is like a wall between us. There is a door in the wall, but it's got a one-way hinge on it. It only opens one way. God wants His Spirit to come over to me, and I want Him to come and permeate me, but the Spirit can't get through the wall and the door doesn't open towards me because He doesn't force His way in. Can you visualize that?

Then God showed me what happens when we begin to worship. So we have the same picture with the wall and the one way door between me and all that God has for me. But now I begin to worship and adore and exalt God and express gratitude toward Him and my love for Him and my desire to listen—all the things we do during worship when we are praising God and thanking Him and magnifying Him. Well, the door gets pushed open by that. It opens toward God. Then the Spirit rushes in through that opening.

What is critical to understand here is that if you're worshiping God and you're just saying, "God, fill me, fill me, fill me." I don't think it works. It's when you get your mind off of yourself and focus on Him, when you begin to praise and worship Him and begin to acknowledge who He is and what He is like and offer yourself to Him, that the door gets pushed open. To me, that's the connection. That's when the sap flows. That's when the power of the Lord comes through.

Let's pray.

Thank You, Father, that You brought us salvation and made us to be branches, lulavs connected to You, with rivers of Living Water flowing out from within us. Help us to stay connected to You, the True Vine, and to bear much fruit!!

[Now, if you are willing, pray this hard prayer with me.]

Father, prune me so I can bear more fruit. Prune away the things that are not from you that hinder my fruit, things that keep me so busy that I took on myself that You had not assigned to me. Prune away all my fleshly things like anger, frustration, unforgiveness, pride, etc.

Help me to grasp how much You Love me. Help me to know Your Love deep down in my hearts. Let it be the thing that sustains me. And help me to love others the way You Love me.

Thank You for the promise of showing us what Your will is. Thank You for choosing us to be part of Your Kingdom. Help us to connect to other believers and to learn from each other as we study Your Word together.

We worship You, Yeshua. We honor You. We glorify You, our Savior, our Lord, the King of the Universe, the One whose Name is above all names, who has conquered the enemy and holds all the power in Heaven and on earth. We praise You. We adore You. You are all we need. You are our help in times of trouble! You are our shelter in the storm. You are the One who comes to us in our sukkah and communes with us. You want to be with us always. Help us not to drift away. We ask You that the fullness of Your Glory would come!! Come soon, Adonai Yeshua Mashiakh! In Your Name we pray. Amein!

Section 3

THE GREAT DAY

and

MORE MYSTERIES

CHAPTER 8
HOSHANA RABBAH

This chapter is about the Last Day, the Great Day, also called Hoshana Rabbah. Let me explain what that means. The words mean the *great salvation*. *Hoshana* means *salvation*. *Rabbah* means *great*. It was the day in the times of the Temple when the prayer of "Please Save!" was prayed. And it has been carried right down to today to the modern synagogues where that same prayer is prayed on this day.

We get our English word *Hosanna* from *Hoshana*. But remember that *Hoshana* doesn't mean Praise the Lord like we have grown up mistakenly thinking. *Hoshana* means in Hebrew "Please save!" I want to give you a sense of what was happening in the Temple in Bible times every year on the seventh day. They thanked the Lord for the harvest. Then they prayed for rain—for water for the next harvest. Then they spiritualized that to be praying for salvation in the Spirit. Here's the prayer for spiritual water:

ושאבתם מים בששון	Ushaftem mayim b'sassone
ממעייני הישועה	mimainei haYeshuah
ושאבתם מים בששון	Ushaftem mayim b'sassone
ממעייני הישועה	mimainei haYeshuah
הי הי הי הי	Hey, hey, hey, hey
מים מים מים מים	Mayim Mayim Mayim Mayim
הי מים בששון	Hey, mayim b'sassone
מים מים מים מים	Mayim Mayim Mayim Mayim
הי מים בששון	Hey, mayim b'sassone

8. HOSHANA RABBAH

Here are some links so you can hear it and watch some dancing to it:

Older people dancing to it:
https://www.youtube.com/watch?v=IL7aAiqw8Us
Young people dancing to it (with instructions):
https://www.youtube.com/watch?v=YYEk0qalvsU
Really good, fast dancing, music only, no voices:
https://www.youtube.com/watch?v=X15ODiDDev8

Do you know what it means? They are singing in Hebrew, this verse in Isaiah:

Isaiah 12:3 *With joy you will draw water from the wells of salvation.*

In Hebrew: *Ushaftem – and you shall draw, mayim – water, b'sassone – with joy, mi mai nei* (pronounced: "me my nay") – *from the wells of, ha-Yeshuah – (the) Salvation.*

Salvation is *Yeshuah* pronounced the same and (except for the added last letter) spelled the same as YESHUA! So every time they sang that, they were calling on His Name! "From the well of Yeshuah. *Mi mai nei ha-YESHUAH!* That is His Name! They were calling His Name while praying for salvation! Even still today, they are calling on His Name every Sukkot on this Great Day!! Just think about that for a minute!

So that's the prayer for the water of salvation. Now, let's look at the Hoshana prayer, first in English and then in Hebrew. Read it aloud, and when you get to the word, *Hoshia-na* (pronounced Ho-shee-AH NAH), you need to shout it!

Please save us for Your sake, our God. Hoshia-na!
Please save us for Your sake, our Creator. Hoshia-na!
Please save us for Your sake, our Redeemer. Hoshia-na!
Please save us for Your sake, our Attender. Hoshia-na!

Hoshana l'mankha Elohenu, Hoshia-na!
Hoshana l'mankha Borenu, Hoshia-na!
Hoshana l'mankha Go'elenu, Hoshia-na!
Hoshana l'mankha Doshenu, Hoshia-na!

I want you to get this picture very clear. They had been singing, "mee mai nei ha YESHUAH" "the water of salvation," and then they were saying, "Please save! Please save!" This was choruses being sung by thousands and thousands of people and then all of them crying out this way. It was a time of great joy like in the Isaiah song. The Talmud (Sukkot 51a:16[5]) says, "One who did not see the Celebration of the Place of the Drawing of the Water never saw celebration in his days."

These prayers were a calling out for the salvation which only the Messiah can bring. So the coming of Messiah became associated with the prayers for rain.

Now let's look at what happened. It is so awesome!

> John 7:37a *Now on the last day of the festival, Hoshana Rabbah....*

Other translations call it the "great day."

> John 7:2,37 (NKJV) *Now the Jews' Feast of Tabernacles was at hand. 3 ... 37 On* **the last day, that great day** *of the feast,*

Yeshua did something so astoundingly amazing on that Great Day of Hoshana Rabbah! Let's read on:

> John 7:37b-38 *...Yeshua stood and cried out, "If anyone is thirsty, let him keep coming to me and drinking! 38 Whoever puts his trust in me, as the Scripture says, rivers of living water will flow from his inmost being!"*

In the midst of them crying for water, in the midst of them crying for salvation and saying His Name, Yeshua was saying, "Here I am! I'm answering your prayer. You're crying for salvation. Here I am!! Come to Me and drink!"

What awesome, incredible power in what He said there! And if you don't understand Jewish tradition, you don't even get this. You wouldn't have any idea of what was going on around Him at this time when He said this!

Now look at the theme here, the theme of the manifest presence of God. He didn't say, "If anyone is thirsty, let him come to God and drink." What did He say? "Let him come to ME and drink." What chutzpah! He was saying, "I am the presence of God. This is celebrating the presence of God. I'm here! I'm here! I'm bringing you salvation. Come to Me and drink!"

---

5 Seferia.org, https://www.sefaria.org/Sukkah.51a.16?lang=bi&with=all&lang2=en

Then there is the dependence on God theme. Your translation may say, "Come to Me and drink." David Stern's *Complete Jewish Bible* translation I believe has the right tense of the verb, which is, "Keep coming to Me and drinking." That's dependence on Him. You don't just come once and drink. You keep coming and drinking. Keep coming to Him. (We will talk about this much more in the next chapter.)

Let's pray.

Yeshua, we thank You that Jewish people all over the world during Sukkot cry out to You every year for Your Living Water and for Salvation, for You to save them!! But our hearts are broken because they don't even realize that it is You they are crying out to.

We thank You, that when You were on earth as a man that You interrupted their crying out and revealed Yourself as the One they were calling out to. We pray that through the Ruakh HaKodesh You will again interrupt this celebration all over the world and reveal Yourself that way again to Your Jewish people. Open their eyes and hearts to realize that You are the One who is the answer to these prayers; that You are their Messiah; that You are the One who is their Salvation; that You are the source of Living Water and the well of salvation.

We pray, Lord, for more and more Jewish people every year to come to this realization, whether observant or not, whether they are Orthodox or secular. Open their eyes to see, and their ears to hear, and open their hearts to understand and receive You, we pray. In Your Powerful, Holy Name, Yeshua, we pray. Amein.

CHAPTER 9
THE WATER DRAWING CEREMONY

Now let's go into even more detail about the Hoshana Rabbah, the Great Day, which some say is the eighth day, but the Orthodox Jewish people, including the Chabad, say it is the seventh day. Here's the commandment again:

> Leviticus 23:34-42 ADONAI *spoke to Moses saying: 34 "Speak to Bnei-Yisrael, and say, On the fifteenth day of this seventh month is the Feast of Sukkot, for seven days to* ADONAI. *35 On the first day there is to be a holy convocation—you are to do no laborious work. 36 For seven days you are to bring an offering by fire to* ADONAI. *The eighth day will be a holy convocation to you, and you are to bring an offering by fire to* ADONAI. *It is a solemn assembly—you should do no laborious work. ... 39 ... The first day is to be a Shabbat rest, and the eighth day will also be a Shabbat rest. ... 40 On the first day you are to take ... branches ... and* **rejoice** *before* ADONAI *your God for* **seven days**. *... 42 You are to* **live in sukkot** *for* **seven days**.

Why has this seventh day been named the Great Day? Well, as you can see in verses 40 and 42, it is the last day to wave the Lulav and the last day to live in the Sukkah, so that might be one reason why. But the main reason might be because it is the culmination of the tradition that had already developed by the time of Yeshua called the **Water Drawing Ceremony**. As we saw, this day was already called the Great Day by Yeshua's time. Let's look again at what Yeshua said when He made that powerfully shocking, bold interruption:

9. WATER DRAWING CEREMONY

> John 7:37b-38 (NKJV) ... *"If anyone thirsts, let him come to Me and drink. 38 He who believes in Me, as the Scripture has said, out of his heart will flow rivers of living water."*

What do the rivers of Living Water represent? The Ruakh HaKadosh, the Holy Spirit:

> John 7:39 (TLV) *Now He said this about the Ruach, whom those who trusted in Him were going to receive; for the Ruach was not yet given, since Yeshua was not yet glorified.*

Why did He choose to make this analogy between water, Himself, and the Ruakh on the Great Day, the seventh day of Sukkot? We saw the connection to the prayer for spiritual water and salvation in the last chapter. But there's so much more! There's even a bigger reason. The answer can only be found in the traditions recorded in the Talmud where the **Water Drawing Ceremony** is described.

Throughout the seven days, a kohane (priest) carried water in a gold pitcher from the Pool of Shiloach (Siloam), up the hill to the Temple. Then it was poured into a basin at the foot of the altar by the Kohane Hagadol. The whole thing every day was a big celebration. A whole crowd would follow the Kohane down to the pool and then back up in a ceremonial processional. For six days the priest led the processional once around the huge altar before the water was poured out.

On Hoshana Rabbah, the seventh day, the priest led the procession around the altar seven times. This is still done around the bima without the water, in synagogues today. On the seventh day, the water was poured out on the altar.

The processional each day was accompanied by kohanim blowing shofars, L'vi'im (Levites) singing sacred songs, and people waving their Lulavs and dancing. The sacred songs included chanting the Hallel (Psalms 113–118) culminating with these verses:

> Psalm 118:25–27 *Hoshia-na! Please, ADONAI, save now! We beseech You, ADONAI, prosper us! 26 Baruch haba b'Shem ADONAI—Blessed is He who comes in the Name of ADONAI. We bless you from the House of ADONAI. 27 ADONAI is God, and He has given us light. Join the festival with*

branches, up to the horns of the altar. 28 You are my God, and I will praise You; You are my God, I will exalt You. 29 Oh, give thanks to the Lord, for He is good! For His mercy endures forever.

The Hoshana prayer/song, "Save now!" "Hoshia-na!" led to the day being called Hoshana Rabbah, the Great Hosanna. Again, remember, *Hoshana* means *Please save.* The rabbis associated this Water Drawing Ceremony with the verse in Isaiah which led to the traditional song we looked at in the last chapter:

Isaiah 12:3 *"With joy shall you draw water from the wells of salvation."*

This ceremony became a crying out for more than physical water. It became a cry for an outpouring of the Ruakh HaKodesh on the people of Israel. Here's a quote from the *Encyclopedia Judaica,*[6] volume 14, page 365:

"A connection between the possession of the Ruach ha-Kodesh and ecstasy, or religious joy, is found in the ceremony of water drawing, Simchat Beit-HaSho'evah [literally: joy of house of water-drawing], on the festival of Sukkot. The Mishnah said that he who had never seen this ceremony, which was accompanied by dancing, singing and music, had never seen true joy (Sukkot 5:1,4). Yet this was also considered a ceremony in which the participants, as it were, drew inspiration from the Holy Spirit, which can only be possessed by those whose hearts are full of religious joy (Jerusalem Talmud, Sukkot 5:1, 55a)."

Messianic redemption was associated with the prayers for rain, when the Ruakh would be poured out like water.

Another source to help us understand what went on in the Temple on Sukkot is the Siddur (prayer book) we have today. The Sukkot prayers in the traditional Siddur today is for more than just rain. Israel is calling out for the salvation that only the Messiah can bring. Still in modern Jewish tradition, each day one of seven prayers requesting salvation is recited. On the seventh day, all seven are recited. This verse is also one they recite in the prayers:

---

[6] A 22-volume English-language encyclopedia of the Jewish people and of Judaism, published in Jerusalem by Keter Publishing House, and in New York City by the Macmillan Company, 1971-1992.

9. WATER DRAWING CEREMONY

Ezekiel 34:26 *I will make them and the places around My hill a blessing. I will cause the rain to come down in its season. There will be showers of blessing.*

As I've studied the traditional prayers for this day in the Siddur and the Brit Hadashah account of what Yeshua did on this day, I am convinced, maybe you are also, that the Water Drawing ceremony and the prayers for salvation in the Siddur were already the custom during Yeshua's time on earth. Some think tradition and customs are invalid or even bad because they are just things made up by man. Sometimes they are. Yeshua even said about those kind that they *"make the Word of God of no effect."* But, here we have some traditions that Yeshua Himself observed. In fact, as we saw, He used the existing traditions to "make the Word of God have a **greater** effect." So, if Yeshua observed this tradition, it gives us a clue of what we should do on this day.

Now, let's try to grasp further the impact of what He said on that day. After the prayers for rain, salvation, and pouring out of the Holy Spirit associated with the coming of the Messiah, after carrying the water around the altar seven times and pouring it out, at that very moment on that Great Day of Sukkot, Hoshana Rabbah, Yeshua had something to say to the crowd of people In the midst of this water pouring, shofar blasting, palm branch waving, dancing, psalm chanting and singing with ecstatic joy on the part of people seeking salvation, Yeshua cried out in the Temple court those amazing, powerful words. Let's meditate on them again and let more of their power flow in.

> **John 7:37** *"If anyone is thirsty, let him keep coming to me and drinking! Whoever trusts in me, as the Tanakh says, rivers of living water will flow from his inmost being!"*

Yeshua was declaring, "I am the answer to your prayers for salvation and for the water of the Ruakh. I bring rain, the showers of blessing. I am the water of salvation. I am the One who can satisfy your thirst for God.

Again I say, "What chutzpah!!!" He was saying not that He will **show** us the source of Living Water, but that He **IS** the **source** of Living Water. He was saying, I am the Messiah. I am the One who saves. If you want to be in God's presence like our forefathers in the desert who dwelt in Sukkot, come into My presence. I am the manifest presence of God Himself come among men tabernacling with them.

So now do you see the other reason why Yeshua chose to say this on Hoshana Rabbah? It was because of the whole Water Drawing Ceremony, and yes, also because He was responding to the people's prayers for water, salvation, the Ruakh, and the Messiah.

So, who did He make His offer to? Anyone who is thirsty, Jew or Gentile, rich or poor, young or old, knowledgeable or ignorant. How was this statement received?

> John 7:40 *On hearing his words, some people in the crowd said, "Surely this man is 'the prophet';" 41 others said, "This is the Messiah." But others said, "How can the Messiah come from the Galil? 42 Doesn't the Tanakh say that the Messiah is from the seed of David and comes from Beit-Lechem, the village where David lived?" 43 So the people were divided because of him.*

The controversy continues in verses 44-52. Now, many Bible scholars today believe the next few verses, telling the story of the woman caught in adultery (7:53-8:11) is an insert. It is a real, true event, but that it was inserted later. If we assume it was, then the next thing Yeshua said on that Great Day was this:

> John 8:12 *Yeshua spoke to them again: "I am the light of the world; whoever follows me will never walk in darkness but will have the light which gives life."*

Do you see a connection between this statement and the Water Drawing Ceremony? We also see this connection in the passage of Psalm 118:27 quoted above, *"ADONAI is God, and He has given us light."* But Yeshua's statement provoked an agitated reaction recorded in all of John 8. Here are some of the leaders' angry reactions:

> John 8: 13,25,53,57-59 *So the P'rushim said to him, "Now you're testifying on your own behalf; your testimony is not valid." ... 25 At this, they said to him, "You? Who are you?"*

9. WATER DRAWING CEREMONY

> *... 53 Avraham avinu died; you aren't greater than he, are you? And the prophets also died. Who do you think you are?" ... 57 "Why, you're not yet fifty years old," the Judeans replied, "and you have seen Avraham?" 58 Yeshua said to them, "Yes, indeed! Before Avraham came into being, I AM!" 59 At this, they picked up stones to throw at him; but Yeshua was hidden and left the Temple grounds.*

The religious, Jewish leaders of the day, did not like what Yeshua was saying on this Great Day. They were so enraged, they wanted to kill Him! That's the enemy ha-satan at work.

So, if Yeshua observed the Simchat Beit-HaSho'evah, (Water Drawing Ceremony) and the Hoshana Rabbah, the Great Prayer for Salvation, how should we observe this tradition today? We don't have an altar we can pour the water out on, but you will see later what we can do symbolically.

RIVERS OF LIVING WATER!

In the natural, Sukkot is a Harvest Festival, so it's a good time to give thanks for the water that enabled the harvest, and to pray for rain for next year's harvest. In the spiritual, we can pray for revival, for salvation for our loved ones and for the Jewish community. And we can keep coming to Him and drinking. Let's dig deeper into that verse.

> *John 7: 37 ... "If anyone is thirsty, let him keep coming to me and drinking! 38 Whoever puts his trust in me, as the Scripture says, rivers of living water will flow from his inmost being!"*

What additional promise, beyond having your spiritual thirst satisfied, does Yeshua make here to those who trust in Him? He promises you will be filled with so much of the Ruakh HaKodesh that it will be like rivers flowing out of you to others. Notice He didn't say "a river." He said "rivers"—plural! Multiple rivers of God's Love will flow to other people. He didn't say a "well" which you have to dip down into to bring the water up from. He didn't say an eyedropper, or a straw, which are like a trickle. He didn't say a cup or bucket. He didn't even say a hose or hydrant, which are men's creations. He didn't even say a stream or creek or river. He said rivers, plural, not just one river, but many rivers. Not only will you be able to drink of the water of salvation, but there will be so much of it that it will be like rivers flowing out of you to others.

Why rivers? Well, like we learned in my *Shavuot* book, rivers have awesome power, so this describes the power of God's Spirit. Rivers are harnessed for electricity. Rivers can change landscapes. A river moves you if you get out into it.

So, if we're supposed to have *"rivers of living water flow from our inmost beings,"* how do we keep them flowing? We can't block them up, we have to let them flow out. How do we let the rivers out? Through outreach, good works, love, prayer, and praise. We have to get rid of our trickle mentalities. God is not about trickles:

> 1 Corinthians 2:9 *But, as the Tanakh says, "No eye has seen, no ear has heard and no one's heart has imagined all the things God has prepared for those who love him."*

What else is needed to keep the rivers flowing out? We have to let them flow in. How do we let them in? Through worship, studying the Word, teaching, having fellowship and through prayer. When people come together and let their streams flow together, the flow becomes an even mightier river like Ezekiel saw in a vision in chapter 47. At the first measurement of a thousand cubits, it was only ankle deep. At another measurement of a thousand, it was knee deep, then waist deep. Then it was too deep to walk in.

We are praying for rivers of revival that change lives, cities, regions, and people groups. What does it mean to let our streams flow together? It requires unity of vision and purpose. It requires submitting one to another, and it requires commitment and sacrifice for the goal.

These rivers of Living Water represent the flow of the Ruakh HaKodesh in our lives. Why would a person want to have the Ruakh HaKodesh active in their life and be led by the Spirit? This passage tells us why:

> Romans 8:6-8, 13-15 *Having one's mind controlled by the old nature is death, but having one's mind controlled by the Spirit*

is life and shalom. 7 For the mind controlled by the old nature is hostile to God, because it does not submit itself to God's Torah—indeed, it cannot. 8 Thus, those who identify with their old nature cannot please God. ... 13 For if you live according to your old nature, you will certainly die; but if, by the Spirit, you keep putting to death the practices of the body, you will live. 14 All who are led by God's Spirit are God's sons. 15 For you did not receive a spirit of slavery to bring you back again into fear; on the contrary, you received the Spirit, who makes us sons and by whose power we cry out, "Abba!" (that is, "Dear Father!").

Why else do we want the Ruakh HaKodesh active in our lives?

Acts 1:8 *But you will receive power when the Ruach HaKodesh comes upon you; you will be my witnesses both in Yerushalayim and in all Y'hudah and Shomron, indeed to the ends of the earth!"*

We cannot be witnesses for Yeshua unless we are filled with His Ruakh. We cannot be filled with His Ruakh unless we want to be witnesses for Yeshua. Once we ask and receive the Ruakh HaKodesh, we have a responsibility. We are commanded to live by the Spirit or "walk in the Spirit."

Galatians 5:16 *So I say, live by the Spirit, (walk in the Spirit) and you will not gratify the desires of the sinful nature.*

Your sinful nature is your old nature, your nature before you knew Messiah, your flesh. It's still around. It doesn't go away. It has its own desires. Only by walking or living by the Spirit can we rise above the desires of our sinful nature.

Galatians 5:17 *For the sinful nature desires what is contrary to the Spirit, and the Spirit what is contrary to the sinful nature. They are in conflict with each other, so that you do not do what you want.*

Old sinful natures' desires are opposed to what the Spirit wants for us. Those desires are the things that get us into trouble, open the door for satan, and mess up our lives. Walking in the Spirit leads to fruitfulness, peace, and an end to striving.

How do we walk in the Spirit? It's like floating in a river. We need to stay within its banks. We dry up when we try to walk away from the river. We need to flow in the river's direction, and not try to go upstream, trying to do things in the flesh that are against the flow of the Spirit.

Rivers can flow nice and slow and smoothly, or into a lake where there is barely any movement, or they can flow very fast over rapids. Likewise, the Ruakh HaKodesh can lead us into smoothly flowing easy times. He can also lead us safely through turbulent times. He can guide us into and through times when nothing seems to be happening. In dry climates, such as in Israel, rivers can even disappear in the summer and yet still be flowing underground. We can't tell what the river of the Ruakh is doing by its surface appearance.

Here's what is most important. We call God's Spirit the Ruakh HaKodesh. *Kodesh* means *holy*. The Spirit of God is holy. The Ruakh HaKodesh will not lead us to do anything unholy.

I am frequently amazed at how people equate the strength of their feelings with the Ruakh HaKodesh. God gave us feelings for a purpose, but we are not to be guided by our feelings. Just because you feel strongly about something, does not mean that it is the leading of the Ruakh HaKodesh.

Feelings can be unholy. Jealousy, envy, hatred, greed, lust, rejection, and pride are all feelings that are unholy and lead to trouble and sin. Even good feelings are not necessarily from the Ruakh HaKodesh. Love is a good feeling, but love for another person's spouse is wrong and breaks Torah commandments.

Diligence is a good feeling. It helps us accomplish tasks that need to be done. But it can be motivated by pride or envy, which are of the flesh and against the Ruakh HaKodesh. What does the Spirit lead us to do?

> Galatians 5:22-23 *But the fruit of the Spirit is love, joy, peace, patience, kindness, goodness, faithfulness, 23 humility, self control.*

How do we tell the difference between the old nature and the Spirit? By looking for those fruits of the Spirit.

> Hebrews 4:12 *See, the Word of God is alive! It is at work and is sharper than any double-edged sword—it cuts right*

9. WATER DRAWING CEREMONY

through to where soul meets spirit and joints meet marrow, and it is quick to judge the inner reflections and attitudes of the heart.

Our feelings are part of our soul. The Word, the Bible needs to be in our heart for the Spirit to work. The Ruakh HaKodesh will not contradict the Word. The Spirit will not violate God's written Word concerning morals. So without a knowledge of what the Word says, how would you know if a leading was violating the Word? If we don't know the Word very well, it will be difficult to follow the leading of the Ruakh HaKodesh because we will have trouble discerning whether it is the Ruakh leading us or our own flesh or a false spirit trying to lead us astray.

Let's look at the story of **another incident** in the life of Yeshua that deals with "Living Water." In John 4 Yeshua asked a **Samaritan woman at a well** for a drink. Samaritan women did not expect Jewish men to talk to them. She answered, "Why are you asking for a drink from me, a woman?"

> John 4:10, 14 *Yeshua answered her, "If you knew God's gift, that is, who it is saying to you, 'Give me a drink of water,' then you would have asked him; and he would have given you living water."…14 …whoever drinks the water I will give him will never be thirsty again! On the contrary, the water I give him will become a well of water inside him, welling up into eternal life!"*

Different versions translate that Greek word, *pegey,* as *spring, fount, well.* **Because this conversation happened at Jacob's Well, I believe the KJV translation is correct — a well.** A well today has pipes and motors to make the water run out, but to get water from a well in those days, you had to let down a bucket and draw it up. At Jacob's Well, Yeshua was describing salvation, which is also described here:

> Isaiah 12:3 *Then you will joyfully draw water from the wells of salvation.*

Salvation is a well from which we can draw Living Water, which will satisfy our thirst for God forever. He gives us eternal life, a home in heaven in God's presence. When you trust in

Yeshua for salvation, He will put a well in your heart, and you will never be spiritually thirsty again. You can always let your bucket down and take a drink of the Living Water, and your spiritual thirst will be satisfied.

How does a person keep coming to Him and drinking? He has to start by coming for the first time. It starts with personally receiving the atoning sacrifice He made for my sin, making Him Lord, and obeying Him. But the drawing of water must continue, and getting water out of a well takes effort. It takes spending time connected to Him, reading His Word, praying, worshiping, studying, fellowshipping, and obeying. Now back to the Temple on Sukkot to look again at the Living Water He promised there:

> John 7:38-39 *Whoever puts his trust in me, as the Scripture says, rivers of living water will flow from his inmost being!" 39 (Now he said this about the Spirit, whom those who trusted in him were to receive later—the Spirit had not yet been given, because Yeshua had not yet been glorified.)*

Here the Ruakh is described as Living Water. On Hoshana Rabbah, Yeshua told us we can have this Living Water, but in a very different way. He didn't say "a well, which you have to dip down into to bring water up from," but rivers. So at salvation, we receive the Ruakh, but then when we are immersed in the Ruakh and are filled to overflowing, we experience the rivers of Living Water ever flowing out of us. Salvation and being filled with the Spirit are two separate experiences that can both occur when we receive Yeshua's atonement. Or being filled can happen at a separate later time.

So, we can see that Yeshua took part in this traditional Water Drawing Ceremony on Sukkot. How awesome if we could take part today! We could try to simulate it, but we don't have the altar to pour the water out upon. However, according to the Brit Hadashah, we do have a temple:

> 1 Corinthians 6:19 *Or don't you know that your body is a temple for the Ruach HaKodesh who lives inside you, whom you received from God?*

So we can pour the water out on the altar of our bodies. Today's Moroccan Jews pour water on each other on Sukkot.

I'm not suggesting that we douse each other. In our congregation, we have done a ceremony with cups of water. I filled enough cups with water for each person to have one. Then we did a ceremony with them that I will walk you through in a minute.

The water represents the Ruakh. On Rosh Hashanah, we begin a time of introspection and repentance. On Yom Kippur, we repent and ask to be cleansed. Sukkot became a time for asking and receiving the Ruakh HaKodesh. Shavuot's (Pentecost's) main focus is on the Ruakh and the Word. Sukkot is also focused on the Ruakh and the Word, very much so. Of course, every day is a day we can focus on any or all of these things. We need to repent of any sins we've been made aware of and be cleansed every day. We need to be continually in the Word and to keep coming to Yeshua to keep on being filled with the Ruakh every day. But the Moadim help us to sharpen our focus on each of these vital, spiritually important things.

Simulating the Water Drawing Ceremony

Now you can take a glass of water and an empty bowl and go outside into your sukkah to participate in some prophetic acts to celebrate the Living Water. If you have others with you, have them each take a glass full of water with them to the sukkah. You need only one bowl for the group. If no one is with you, it would help with the visualization and symbolism if you bring a couple other glasses of water to represent other people joining you.

Maybe sing the Mayim song on the way out to the sukkah or sing it when you get there. Here are the words again:

Ushaftem mayim b'sassone
mimainei ha'Yeshua .
Ushaftem mayim b'sassone
mimainei ha'Yeshua
    Hey, hey, hey, hey

Mayim - Mayim - Mayim - Mayim
Hey, mayim b'sassone
Mayim - Mayim - Mayim - Mayim
Hey, mayim b'sassone

First spend a few moments giving thanks for the water we have received this year without which our land would be destitute. ... Then pray for rain for the coming year. ...

Now pray the traditional Hoshana prayer for Sukkot as you wave the branches:

Please save us for Your sake, our God. Hoshia-na!
Please save us for Your sake, our Creator. Hoshia-na!
Please save us for Your sake, our Redeemer. Hoshia-na!
Please save us for Your sake, our Attender. Hoshia-na!

Hoshana l'mankha Elohenu, Hoshia-na!
Hoshana l'mankha Borenu, Hoshia-na!
Hoshana l'mankha Go'elenu, Hoshia-na!
Hoshana l'mankha Doshenu, Hoshia-na!

Please save Israel, Lord, we pray!

Now, we are going to do three prophetic acts. First, take your glass and drink some of the water as a picture of pouring the water on the altar in the temple of our bodies. Then pray for more infilling of the Ruakh HaKodesh and for being filled continuously with that Living Water. Go ahead and pray in your own words. ...

Next drink some more living water from your glass, and pray that the Spirit will become the spring welling up within you.

Then pour some water out on the ground and pray the Spirit in you will become those rivers of Living Water flowing out of you to others. Pray it will flow out from your innermost being in love and prayer to fellow believers. And pray it will also flow out in compassion and intercession for the lost, both Jewish and Gentile.

Now have everyone pour the rest of their water from their glass into the bowl and then spill it out all at once. Look at how powerful the flow is when all our rivers flow together.

Pray it would become mightier rivers of Living Water resulting from all our rivers flowing together, flowing out into your community in love to family, friends, strangers, and the whole world.

Now sing some songs about Yeshua's Living Water.

CHAPTER 10
THE MYSTERY OF SH'MINI ATZERET— THE EIGHTH DAY ASSEMBLY

The name of this day comes from this verse in the Torah: Numbers 29:35 (NKJV) *On the eighth day you shall have a **sacred assembly**. You shall do no customary work.*

B'yom ha'sh'mini atzeret... בְּיוֹם הַשְּׁמִינִי עֲצֶרֶת is how that verse (Num. 29:35) starts out. As we said, some say this eighth day is the Hoshana Rabbah, the Great Day, but the Orthodox Jews do not. They consider it a separate Moad, and have a different traditional celebration gathering with different prayers for this Eighth Day. Let's look at what is specifically commanded by God for the eighth day:

> Leviticus 23:34 "*Speak to Bnei-Yisrael, and say, On the fifteenth day of this seventh month is the Feast of Sukkot, for seven days to ADONAI. 35 On the first day there is to be a holy convocation—you are to do no laborious work. 36 For seven days you are to bring an offering by fire to ADONAI. The **eighth day** will be a **holy convocation** to you, and you are to bring an offering by fire to ADONAI. It is a **solemn assembly**—you should do no laborious work. ... 39 ... The first day is to be a Shabbat rest, and the **eighth day** will also be a **Shabbat rest**. ... 40 On the first day you are to take ... branches ... and **rejoice** before ADONAI your God for **seven days**. ... 42 You are to **live in sukkot** for **seven days**.*

God says Sukkot lasts seven days, but then He tells us what to do on the eighth day. It's another mystery that we will try to solve in this chapter. Notice that living in the sukkah is only for seven days, and celebrating with the Lulav is also only for seven days. So we aren't commanded to do either of those things on the eighth day. (However, the Orthodox still eat in their sukkot on this eighth day.) So that sets the eighth day apart from the seven.

Another thing that sets it apart is that the pattern of the Sukkot sacrifices (Num. 29:12-38) is broken for the eighth day. For seven days the number of bulls decreases by one each day, but on the eighth day it decreases by six, from seven to only one. The number of rams and lambs is suddenly cut in half on the eighth day. So that makes the eighth day look different from the seven also. (We will look into the mystery of those sacrifices in the next chapter.)

So what are we to do on the eighth day? There is no Temple so we can't bring that offering by fire of a bull, rams, lambs and a goat to Adonai as He commands. Yet God commanded us to keep this day as a Moad **forever**, and He knew that the Temple would be destroyed a couple of thousand years [in 70 CE (AD)] after He commanded this.

So, God must have an agenda for us to do in this post-Temple age for Sh'mini Atzeret, this Eighth Day of Sukkot as He does for all the other Appointed Times. Well, it says we are to keep it as a Shabbat day and to have a holy convocation. Then it says we're supposed to have a solemn assembly. What is the difference between a holy convocation and a solemn assembly, and how can we do both on the same day?

The Hebrew word for *holy convocation* is מִקְרָא קֹדֶשׁ, miqra qodesh (mikra kodesh). This is used for every Moad in commanding us to have a holy gathering.

The Hebrew word for *solemn assembly* is עֲצֶרֶת atzeret. This is used twice in the commandments for this eighth day and once for Passover's seventh day. It is also used twice in describing when the people were actually celebrating this eighth day, then two other times when God is saying how

10. MYSTERY OF THE EIGHTH DAY

displeased He is that they have mixed it with sin, and twice yet again when God says to call a fast because the days are evil.

Here's the list of when this word is used. Notice that the very first time it is used in Scripture is for this eighth day:

> Leviticus 23:36 ...*The **eighth day** will be a **holy convocation** to you, and you are to bring an offering by fire to ADONAI. It is a **solemn assembly**—you should do no laborious work.*

> Numbers 29:36 (NKJV) *On the eighth day you shall have a **sacred assembly**.*

> Deut. 16:8 *For six days you are to eat matzot* [unleavened bread]. *On the seventh day there is to be a **solemn gathering** for ADONAI your God—on it you are to do no work.*

> II Chron. 7:9 *And in the eighth day they made a **solemn assembly**: ...*

> Nehemiah 8:18 *And they kept the feast seven days; and on the eighth day was a **solemn assembly**....*

> Isaiah 1:13 ... *—I cannot endure it—iniquity with **solemn assembly**.*

> Joel 1:14 *Sanctify ye a fast, call a **solemn assembly**....*

> Joel 2:15 *Blow the trumpet in Zion, sanctify a fast, call a **solemn assembly**....*

> Amos 5:21 *"I hate, I despise your festivals! I take no delight in your **sacred assemblies**.*

The only other times this term is used are in II Kings 10:20 for a gathering to worship a false god, and Jeremiah 9:2 for an evil gathering.

Now here's where it gets interesting. The root word for עֲצֶרֶת *atzeret* is *atzar* עָצַר. It is used 15 times to mean *"shut up,"* as in Sarah's womb being *shut up* and all the wombs in King Abimelech's household being *shut up* while he kept Sarah; a few times God uses it as punishment for Israel's sins that He will *shut up* the heavens to keep it from raining. It is used 7 times as *stayed* as when Aaron stopped the plagued by standing between the dead and the living with the censor full of incense in Numbers 16, and Phinehas stopped the plague caused by idolatry and sexual sin in Numbers 25. David's sacrifice in II Samuel 24 stopped a plague. In modern Hebrew it still holds this meaning of *stop* and *stay*.

> [It reminds me of the Hebrew word for praise, יָדָה *yadah*, which is used 53 times as *praise*, 32 times as *give thanks*, and a few times as a few other words, one time as *cast* and then one time in Zechariah as *cast out*.
>
> > Zechariah 1:21 *(KJV)* ...but these are come to fray them, to **cast out** the horns of the Gentiles, which lifted up their horn over the land of Judah to scatter it.]

The Orthodox take this meaning of *stop* or *stay* to mean that the Lord is asking us to pause after Sukkot and spend one more day with Him. They see it as a kind of guarding and closing of Sukkot, which is nice and meaningful.

But it looks to me like this special kind of solemn assembly can also be a time of powerful spiritual warfare to stop the enemy! And the word *yadah* meaning *praise*, but being used also to mean *casting out* the enemy shows that our praise can be a spiritual weapon in that spiritual warfare against ha-satan and his hordes. So perhaps it is a holy convocation for yadah worship and serious, Spirit-guided, powerful, conquering, victorious spiritual warfare, a gathering like this final one:

> Revelations 19:11-14 *Next I saw heaven opened, and there before me was a white horse. Sitting on it was the one called Faithful and True, and it is in righteousness that he passes judgment and goes to battle. 12 His eyes were like a fiery flame, and on his head were many royal crowns. And he had a name written which no one knew but himself. 13 He was wearing a robe that had been soaked in blood, and the name by which he is called is, "THE WORD OF GOD." 14 The armies of heaven, clothed in fine linen, white and pure, were following him on white horses.*

The armies of Heaven following Yeshua, clothed in pure, white linen, riding on white horses is us! To be ready to follow Him into that final battle, we need to follow Him in spiritual warfare now. Perhaps God designed Sh'mini Atzeret for post Temple times to be a forerunner to that final battle to defeat ha-satan's kingdom before the thousand year Millennial reign.

10. MYSTERY OF THE EIGHTH DAY

And one final note. The number eight in Hebrew represents *new beginnings*. And Sukkot represents the Millennial reign when Yeshua will come to "tabernacle" with us on this earth and reign for a thousand years after defeating ha-satan and locking him up in the bottomless pit (Rev. 19-20). That will for sure be a wonderful new beginning! After the thousand year reign, ha-satan will be loosed and defeated again and will be thrown into the Lake of Fire forever. Then there will be another awesome new beginning:

> Rev. 21:1-5 (TLV) *Then I saw a new heaven and a new earth; ... 2 I also saw the holy city—the New Jerusalem—coming down out of heaven from God, prepared as a bride adorned for her husband. 3 I also heard a loud voice from the throne, saying, "Behold, the dwelling of God is among men, and He shall tabernacle among them. ...God Himself shall be among them and be their God. 4 He shall wipe away every tear from their eyes, and death shall be no more. Nor shall there be mourning or crying or pain any longer, for the former things have passed away." 5 And the One seated upon the throne said, "Behold, I am making all things new!" ....*

Let's pray.

Hallelujah!! Praise the Lord!! Father, we thank You for this extra day that You have designed for us to continue our time with You after living in the Sukkah and waving our Lulavs for a whole week. And we thank You for the special kind of solemn assembly that You gave us for this day for praise and spiritual warfare. Help us to use all the spiritual weapons You have made available, for us to be victorious over the enemy. Help us to listen carefully to Your Ruakh to fight the spiritual battles you want us to fight on this special day. Help us to be in unity in this spiritual warfare, so that our power will be multiplied and will have greater power and effect and accomplish the conquests You have planned.

We praise You, Father. We thank You. We glorify You. We shall conquer the enemy in every battle You call us to fight on this Eighth Day Moad and every other day of our lives. In Yeshua's mighty, all-powerful Name. Amein.

CHAPTER 11
THE MYSTERY OF THE SUKKOT SACRIFICES

God commands a very interesting, very out of the ordinary set of Temple sacrifices for Sukkot. He commands quite a large number of animals to be sacrificed each day. What is really fascinating and mysterious is that the number of bulls commanded to be sacrificed is a descending number, one less each day, starting with thirteen bulls the first day:

> Numbers 29:12-35 *"On the fifteenth day of the seventh month you are to have a sacred assembly. You are not to do any of your work, and you are to celebrate the Feast to ADONAI for seven days. 13 You are to offer a burnt offering by fire to ADONAI as a pleasing aroma: thirteen young bulls from the herd, two rams, and fourteen year-old male lambs without defect, 16 plus one male goat as a sin offering, besides the regular burnt offering with its grain and drink offering. ... 17 "On the second day, you are to offer twelve young bulls from the herd, two rams, and fourteen year-old male lambs without flaw, 20 "On the third day, offer eleven bulls, ... 23 "On the fourth day, ten bulls, ... 26 "On the fifth day, nine bulls, ... 29 "On the sixth day, eight bulls, ... 32 "On the seventh day, seven bulls, ... 35 "On the eighth day ... one bull, one ram, and seven male lambs....*

The chart (on the next page) shows the animal numbers commanded each day and the totals for each animal for all eight days. Notice that the total number of bulls is 70 for the seven days and 71 if you add the one for the eighth day.

11. MYSTERY OF THE SUKKOT SACRIFICES

Sukkot sacrifices

Day 1	13 bulls	2 rams	14 lambs	1 goat
Day 2	12 bulls	2 rams	14 lambs	1 goat
Day 3	11 bulls	2 rams	14 lambs	1 goat
Day 4	10 bulls	2 rams	14 lambs	1 goat
Day 5	9 bulls	2 rams	14 lambs	1 goat
Day 6	8 bulls	2 rams	14 lambs	1 goat
Day 7	7 bulls	2 rams	14 lambs	1 goat
Day 8	1 bull	1 ram	7 lambs	1 goat
Total:	71 bulls	15 rams	105 lambs	8 goats

[King Solomon offered 22,000 oxen (2 Chron 7:5)]

So the question is why? Why so many animals? Why the descending number of bulls? Why seventy bulls for the seven days? Why suddenly only one on the eighth day? We will look at possible answers to these questions in this chapter.

These sacrifices cannot be done anymore since Yeshua's sacrifice fulfilled all animal sacrifices and the Temple was destroyed. However, God, of course, knew there would be nearly 2000 years of not doing the sacrifices, yet we are commanded to celebrate the moad *forever throughout your generations* (Lev. 23:31). So surely there is still significant meaning and in the sacrifices for us today. What is that meaning? It's a mystery. I asked the Lord to reveal this mystery, and He led me to this article by a physics professor at Bar-Ilan University in Tel Aviv: [7]

> But why are the offerings made in decreasing order...? This question is answered only in later sources (*Midrash Aggadah* [Buber], Numbers 28): [8]
>
>> The total comes to seventy, which is for the nations of the world, of which there are seventy, so that the Lord shall deliver us from their hands and they disappear from the world; hence the number steadily decreases.
>
> A similar interpretation is found in *Pesikta Zutreta* ([*Lekah Tov*],[9] Numbers, *Parashat Phinehas*, p. 137a):

---

[7] Prof. Ido Kantor, "The Rationale of the Sukkot Sacrifices" Bar-Ilan University, Parashat Hashavua Study Center, Parashat Phinehas. Tel Aviv, Israel, July 16, 2011, studylib.net/doc/7822047/the-rationale-of-the-sukkot-sacrifices
[8] Midrash Aggadah is an anonymous midrashic commentary on the Torah, first published by Solomon Buber in 1894 based on a rare manuscript that he discovered in Aleppo (from Sefaria.org). sefaria.org/Midrash_Aggadah?tab=contents.
[9] Tobiah ben Eliezer, a Talmudist and poet of the 11th century, author of Lekach Tov or Pesikta Zutarta, a midrashic commentary on the Pentateuch and the Five Megillot (from en.wikipedia.org). en.wikipedia.org/wiki/Tobiah_ben_Eliezer

> Seventy bullocks were sacrificed on the festival, for the seventy nations of the world. One bullock and one ram on Atzeret, for Israel being the one nation in the land. Just as the bullocks decreased in number as the festival progressed, thus the Canaanites are diminished, but Israel is not diminished.
>
> The decreasing number of bulls symbolizes the drop in the number and status of the nations of the world who oppose Israel.
>
> Thus we see that in the course of the seven days of the festival, **seventy** bulls are to be sacrificed, as against the **seventy** nations of the world, and it is significant that the number steadily diminishes.

That's prophetic! I like it. Sukkot is a prophetic Moad, looking toward the Millennial Reign, as you know. So it makes sense that the Sukkot sacrifices would also be prophetic. So, while sitting in the sukkah, we can be reminded to pray that this prophesy be fulfilled that Israel will soon have no more enemies.

Here's another meaning, a personal meaning that God may have also intended. Notice that these sacrifices are to be "burnt offerings," in Hebrew: עלה קרב *qerev olah*. *Qerev* means *offering* or *sacrifice*, but it also means **to draw near.** *Olah* means **to go up, to ascend.** A burnt offering is a very special worship offering. It is not done for the forgiveness of sin. It is to be done out of a heart of worship to Adonai. It is different from the shelem, peace or fellowship offering that you eat part of in fellowship with your family and the kohane. For the burnt/olah offering, the animal is to be completely consumed in the fire. So that is a lot of animals being totally burned during Sukkot! What can this possibly mean for today?

One thing is God asks us to give ourselves as a sacrifice and when we do, it should be an ascending offering that draws us near to Him. We should give our all to be completely consumed in Him and in the work of His Kingdom.

> Romans 12:1 *I exhort you, therefore, brothers, in view of God's mercies, to offer yourselves as a sacrifice, living and set apart for God. This will please him; it is the logical "Temple worship" for you.*

11. MYSTERY OF THE SUKKOT SACRIFICES

As we give up ourselves on the altar every day in worship, we are also placing our flesh, our old nature, there to be burned up. Our expectation might be that each day there should be less and less flesh left to be burned. Perhaps that is one significance of the decreasing numbers of the bulls.

Now let's look at the sheep. The two rams and fourteen lambs is the same number that is commanded to be sacrificed on Rosh Hashanah / Yom Teruah / the Day of Sounding the Shofar / the Feast of Trumpets.

> Numbers 29:1-2 *"On the first day of the seventh month you are to have a sacred assembly. ... 2 You are to prepare a burnt offering as a pleasing aroma to* ADONAI*: one young bull from the herd,* **one ram, and seven male lambs** *a year old, without flaw, ... 5 as well as one male goat as a sin offering... 6 Also offer the burnt offering for the month* [New Moon] *with its grain offering, the regular burnt offering....*

Here's the commandment for the New Moon offering:

> Numbers 28:11 *"On the first of the month you are to present to* ADONAI *a burnt offering of two young bulls,* **one ram, and seven flawless male lambs** *a year old, ... 15 Also, one male goat as a sin offering to* ADONAI *beside the regular burnt offering.*

So the total for Yom Teruah would be the same number of rams and lambs as the number for each day for Sukkot. And notice that for Yom Teruah and for each day of Sukkot, they are to also offer the regular daily offering, which is one lamb in the morning and one in the evening, like our daily offering of praise to the Lord every morning and evening.

So the lamb sacrifices for each day of Sukkot are the same as for Rosh Hashanah, the Feast of Trumpets! That's the Day we are looking for and expecting to hear the sound of the great Shofar when Yeshua will come in the clouds with a shout and with great glory!! Sukkot prophetically speaks of the Millennial reign when Yeshua will reign from Jerusalem over the earth. So every day will be as joyful as the day of His coming! Maybe that is what the numbers of the rams and lambs is supposed to signify for us.

Back to the number seventy. Terah was 70 when he fathered Abraham (Gen. 11:26). Seventy souls from Jacob moved to Egypt when Joseph was ruler over the food during the famine (Ex. 1:5). Seventy elders along with Moses and Aaron ate with God on Mt. Sinai (Ex. 24:1,9).

This seems to signify the beginning of very important things. Abraham is the first person of the Covenant that became the Jewish people! From Jacob's family came the first heads of the twelve tribes of Israel. Moses and Aaron and the seventy elders were the first leaders of the Sinai Covenant!

Sukkot signifies the beginning of the Millennial reign of Yeshua! And the New Covenant of the Cross of Yeshua was the beginning of the most important Covenant of all time, which leads to the Millennial reign! All who enter the New Covenant become leaders, kings and priests, in Yeshua's royal Kingdom. So there's the theme of new beginnings again.

Another significance of the number 70 in the Bible is the Israelites were in captivity in Babylon seventy years. Being in captivity taught the Israelites to truly stay away from idolatry and to spend their lives studying and observing Torah. Because of that, they became a nation living according to the Covenant and thus were ready for the birth of the Messiah!

So may all of our trials and troubles also teach us to study and obey God's Word, so we are ready for what He has planned for us, and ready for the Messiah's return when He comes to Tabernacle on earth to rule and reign!!

Thinking of sacrificing bulls brings this verse to mind:

> Psalm 69:31-32 *I will praise God's Name with a song, and magnify Him with praise. 32 It will please ADONAI better than an ox or a bull with horns and hoofs.*

A burnt offering of a bull was the biggest and best, most worshipful sacrifice you could make to God in Temple times. Yet this verse says praising Him pleases Him even more than sacrificing an ox or bull to Him. So these Sukkot sacrifices of all these bulls can remind us that when we keep on praising Him with songs and magnifying Him with shouts of joyful praise every day, we are pleasing Him more than these sacrifices that He commanded.

11. MYSTERY OF THE SUKKOT SACRIFICES

Let's pray.

Father, we thank You for this mystery of the sacrifices You commanded for Sukkot. Help us to understand more and more what it means for us today.

We thank You, Father, that Sukkot does signify Your perfect Millennial reign which will be the beginning of awesome great things! Help us to allow You to prepare us for that and for every other "beginning" You have for us. Help us to allow You to remove all baggage from us as we keep laying ourselves on Your altar so we will be free and ready.

We thank You that you have all timing set according to Your plan. We rest in knowing that all is in Your control. We bless You. We love You. We trust You. We praise You. We will continue to worship and praise You all our days. May it please You more than any sacrifice we could've made to You in Temple days. In Yeshua's Name we pray. Amein.

Section 4

Z'MAN SIMKHATENU

THE TIME OF OUR REJOICING

CHAPTER 12

THIS IS THE TIME OF OUR REJOICING [Z'MAN SIMKHATENU]

Lev. 23:40 ... *and rejoice before A*DONAI *your God for seven days.*

Notice again that the verse says to "rejoice before the Lord for **seven days**." That's a lot of rejoicing, don't you think? Isn't it amazing?! God commands us to rejoice! He loves to see His people happy and joyful!

As we learned, we are to rejoice by waving the branches and the fruit. So let's just take another moment like we did before. Wave your Lulav and rejoice and shout out thankfulness and praise with all your heart.

Thank You, Lord! We rejoice in You, Father! ....

As we noted earlier, this time is called z'man simkhatenu, which in Hebrew means, *the time of our rejoicing*. *Z'man* is *time*, *tenu* is *our*, *simkha* is *rejoicing*.

So I was meditating a little bit on that English word, "rejoice." You know, we just throw around words in English. And I realized that it's made up of two parts *re-* and *-joice*. Right? *Re-* often means *to repeat, return, turn back; restore*—*make it back the way it was*. So *re-joice* means *repeat your joy*! So I realized that what this is about is remembering the things that made you joyful and repeating the joy. *Rejoice! Bring back the joy!* Think of the Psalm where David says this:

Psalm 51:14a *Restore to me the joy of Your salvation. ...*

So that's what this is about, reliving the joy that we experienced when God did great things in our lives. Has God done great things in your life? Yes? So every once in awhile, you should go back and relive that joy! Rejoice in that. This is really a wonderful commandment of God. It really shows His Love for us. He wants us to remember the great times and rejoice in them.

But why? Why would He command this to especially be done once per year? I thought about that, and I realized it's because of all the tsuris, all the troubles of this world. They gang up on us. They overwhelm us, and after awhile, we forget the great things the Lord has done, and we just get weighed down. Do you get burdened by all the things of the world? We get discouraged by them, and we need to break through that.

So what's the way to break through it? Remember the great things God has done for you, and re-joice, be re- joyful!

This is why, I believe, that we in the United States actually established a day to do this in the end of November, Thanksgiving Day, because that's really the purpose of Thanksgiving Day, to give thanks for what you have, and rejoice in those things.

So what are we to be rejoicing and thankful for together as the Body of Messiah? I know you have something individually, probably many things. We will rejoice about a few of those. Then in the rest of the chapter I am going to focus on things our congregation can rejoice about.

Individual harvest and fruits to rejoice about

There are tons of things we could all rejoice about as individuals. But I will focus on just four of them to rejoice in right here. They are kind of a review from the Lulav section. See if you remember.

So the **first** one is to rejoice and be thankful for the harvest. It's why we wave the branches. You know, we take for granted the abundant provision we have in my country. If you travel much, you've seen that It really is not as abundant in many places in the world, with overflowing shelves in the stores. In our congregation, we get leftovers from the local grocery chain, Wegman's, and we give them away. It's an incredible abundance. Instead of taking it for granted, we need to keep being thankful and praying for the continuation of that abundance, especially since covid and the Ukraine war.

When we think of this rejoicing for the harvest, we can get a little bit spiritual about that because there's a physical harvest, the fruit and the abundance we have, but there's also a spiritual harvest that we can rejoice in.

What's that? Answered prayers! Have you had a prayer answered this year? Healings! Have you had a healing this year? Yes? Praise the Lord! How about breakthroughs and salvations? Do you know anyone you love that got saved this year? Okay! That's a fruit! Did you grow or mature spiritually? That's a fruit.

Did you take a stand for what is right some time in your life? That's a fruit of maturity. Then, of course, the fruits of the Spirit, love, joy, peace, patience, kindness, goodness, faithfulness, gentleness, and self-control. Do you feel like some of that grew in you this year? Let's hope it grew in us, right?

Finally, the fruit of good relationships or of reconciliations after they've gone sour. Did you have a reconciliation this year? Awesome! Those are some of the spiritual fruits that we've all experienced that we can rejoice about.

Rejoicing for our congregations

Second, if you are part of a congregation, you can rejoice in being a part of it, and rejoice in what God has done for and through that congregation over the years. Write some of the things out on a paper and spend some time rejoicing in them.

I want to rejoice about our congregation. I think it will bless you too as part of the global Body of Messiah. Rabbi Sha'ul said to rejoice with those who rejoice. So I hope you can rejoice with me here. (But feel free to skip this part.)

12. THE TIME OF OUR REJOICING

The year 2022 was our thirty-eighth anniversary. Two more years will be our fortieth anniversary as a congregation! So I just want to celebrate by sharing some of our historical highlights, the things God has done for and through us, to give Him the glory. We remember those things with joy and are thankful for the almost 40 years of Him doing this. Also, for the 38 years of being part of the revival of the Jewish people, the Messianic Movement.

So, I'm going to start out with two of our people, Randy Katz and Ann Malak, who were the faithful ones before Congregation Shema Israel existed. Before us, in the 1970s, there was a Messianic congregation in Rochester called Beth Elohim. They actually owned a building and had a leader. Randy is the designated historian for Beth Elohim. At some point that group folded, and a small prayer group from them started meeting at Bethel church. They were praying for someone to come and revive the Messianic Movement in Rochester.

Around the same time in 1983, a group of us, some of whom have gone on to be with the Lord and others who have moved away, were part of a group that Chosen People Ministries was leading here in Rochester. We were reaching out to Jewish people. Then the Lord did an amazing thing. In 1984, just 38 years ago, a young Jewish man just out of college came to Rochester with the call to start a Messianic congregation, young Jonathan Bernis.

If you know what Jonathan has gone on to do, it is absolutely amazing that God sent him to this little city, to this little prayer group because he has proven to be mightily used by God in awesome ways. We will talk about some of those ways a little bit later. It was just an amazing thing that I rejoice about still that God answered the prayers of those two little groups and sent Jonathan Bernis here to start Congregation Shema Yisrael.

The next thing to rejoice in is that Pastor Ron Domina gave us access to Bethel church to meet there for four years without any cost. We met in the youth chapel, which is now part of the coffee shop, the place where people sit around and drink their coffee. That was the grace of God! Most pastors at that time were not favorably inclined toward the Messianic Movement. Pastor Ron somehow heard God speak to him, and he opened up that building for us.

My family and I started attending in 1985. The reason we got connected was that our son, Jason, turned 13, and we wanted him to have a bar mitzvah. So we went and got connected with Rabbi Jonathan and had a bar mitzvah.

In 1988, we purchased the building on North Winton Rd in the Irondequoit section of Rochester replete with wonderful cracks in the walls. But this is reason for amazing rejoicing. We were only 40 people, yet somehow we were able to raise the money to buy that building. It was absolutely a miracle that such a small group was able to do that.

Then it took some other miracles to renovate the place. The main room was a kitchen. We tore everything out, tore out the walls and turned it into a sanctuary. There were lots more renovations, upstairs, etc.

What was amazing about that is God sent to our congregation people who were experts at this kind of work, two in particular. I call them our Bezalel and Oholiab from Exodus 31 where God raised up two craftsmen for Moses to build the Tabernacle. These two gentlemen came in, and they had all the tools and all the knowledge, and they just did it. It was absolutely the grace of God. Absolutely!

Then just within two years, a world-shaking event happened that affected us mightily. That was in 1989 when the iron curtain came down. I believe it came down because the Soviet Union was not allowing Jewish people out to move to Israel. This was part of God's plan. So that wall had to come down, and it did!

So in 1990, the Spirit of God guided Jonathan Bernis to pay a visit to Moscow. The reason he wanted to do that was because in the Messianic Movement in our community outreaches, we experienced that most Jewish people in the West were very closed to the Good News. They've been taught against it. We experienced lots of prejudice for all kinds of reasons. But nobody knew what the Jewish people's attitude in the former Soviet Union would be toward the Gospel.

So Jonathan took a group of people, and they took Bibles and tracts in Russian and went to Moscow. They didn't know a soul. They opened up their suitcases on the streets of Moscow and said, "Anybody want a Russian Bible?" Well, they didn't actually say those words because they couldn't speak Russian. They just held them up and offered to give them away, and they were mobbed! Absolutely mobbed! You see, the Soviet Union had not allowed any spiritual literature in for seventy years, and the people were curious. What's this all about? What is spiritual life all about? Then, while they were being mobbed by these people wanting Bibles, they started asking through an interpreter they met, "Are any of you Jewish?" About half the people said, "Yea, I'm Jewish." "I'm Jewish."

From that Jonathan began to understand that the Jewish people in their seventy years of captivity in the former Soviet Union had been totally isolated from any Jewish or Christian teachings, so they had not been taught to be against the Gospel. They hadn't been taught to be closed to it. They were open and curious.

So, God led Jonathan to organize an outreach in the city of St. Petersburg for October of 1993. He called it the Festival of Jewish Music and Dance. Then a miracle happened. Somehow people found out what Jonathan was planning to do, and the finances came in. A hundred people, about twenty from our congregation, including me, went with him to put on this festival.

We held it in a 3000 seat auditorium and it was pretty much filled up the first night. That was another amazing thing of God! We had no idea whether people would actually come!

After the music on the first night, I still remember and still get chills from what happened next. Jonathan got up and gave a short Gospel presentation and invited people to come down and receive the Lord, and more than half of the almost 3000 people there came forward and prayed to receive the Lord. We gave them little cards to find out their background, and as we analyzed the cards, we found out that half of those people were Jewish. So that night, I would say close to 750 Jewish people at once prayed to receive the Lord!

This was unprecedented. Nothing like this had happened, as far as we knew, since the days of the Book of Acts. We were so privileged to be part of it. So there's another reason for rejoicing. Yes, go ahead and applaud!!

Then it got even better! Jonathan continued to organize these outreaches in other cities of the former Soviet Union, in Moscow, Kiev, Odessa, Minsk, and the hand of God continued to move, supplying the resources, the money, the people to go with him, favor with the Russian authorities, which was one of the biggest miracles—to let us do these things. And it resulted in tens of thousands of Jewish people coming to the Lord over the next ten years. Again, unprecedented since the Book of Acts. So we can rejoice in that! I rejoice that I was able to be a part of that first festival, and then was able to support Jonathan for the other times that he went.

Now, even though we were rejoicing greatly about all this, our congregation at home was really struggling because Jonathan was our leader, but he was gone overseas all the time. It was getting harder and harder to function not having him around, so we were praying for a new leader.

In the meantime, Jonathan was friends with David Levine, a Jewish man who had found the Lord and had become the assistant pastor at a church right near our congregation. He had felt no call to his own people, and Jonathan had been trying to convince him for years that he should start reaching the Jewish people.

Soon after Jonathan's first outreach festival, David Levine and his wife Sandy decided to visit Israel. When they were in Israel, the Lord began to speak to them about reaching his own people. Then they were instructed by the Lord to start attending services at our congregation. So they began to attend our Shabbat meetings on Friday evenings and Saturday mornings while David continued as assistant pastor on Sundays at that church.

12. THE TIME OF OUR REJOICING

Then during one of our meetings, David had a vision! In the vision, he was in outer space, looking back at the planet earth. Between him and planet earth was the figure of a man, whom he took to be God. God was saying, "Favor on Zion." And the question was posed to David, "Do you want to be part of this?" And it was left up to David what to do. What he did was absolutely amazing. Without any kind of offer from us, he quit his job as a pastor of that church, telling them, "We're just going to start attending over at Shema Yisrael." I was one of the elders at the time, and we were praying about what to do about the fact that Jonathan wasn't around anymore. We needed to hire someone, and all of a sudden, David showed up. We found out his qualifications and it was like, "Well, what do you think? Might this be the Lord?" And it was!

So David came on as our assistant pastor. At the time, we were called pastors, not rabbis. Again, the amazing provision of God.

At that time, Jonathan started an organization called Hear Oh Israel Ministries. He eventually moved to St. Petersburg to start a congregation. A few years later, he returned to the US and took over the television ministry, Jewish Voice broadcast, in Phoenix, which he still runs today. It's now called Jewish Voice Ministries International. They do online programs and mission outreaches all over the world.

What happened then? It was again the grace of God. You can see the hand of God in this. As Jonathan was going to each of these cities and bringing these outreaches, it became obvious, especially to those of us who were on the eldership team, that someone needed to take the responsibility to see that congregations were planted in each of those cities. We couldn't just leave those people without spiritual leaders.

So David participated in one of the festivals, and he was assigned to do follow-up. That drew him in to that role of doing the planting. Over the next ten years, through Jonathan's continuing evangelism and David's planting, around fifty Messianic congregations were started in the former Soviet Union! Fifty! Many of them are still flourishing! Some in Ukraine are still meeting in spite of the invasion, giving hope to the community, and are seeing many new people come to faith.

That leads us to the provision of God that affected me the most. It soon became too much for David to lead our congregation and also do this planting of congregations around the former Soviet Union. So he and I and the other elders prayed about this in September of 1995. Then the Lord spoke to me, and I started as Assistant Rabbi in March of 1996.

And I've got to say, you know, 90-95 percent of the rabbis in the Messianic Movement started their congregations by a little meeting in their home with their own family and a couple of friends. They were pioneers and planters. They were working a job while trying to start a congregation, which was a hard road. For me, I quit a very good job with Xerox, but I stepped into a congregation that was already flourishing, that had a building, and leadership, and a salary! It was an amazing, amazing thing to be able to do that and not have to go through that hard stage. I just praise God and rejoice when I think about that.

Then out of our congregation in Rochester, a congregation was planted in Syracuse by Mark and Daniah Greenberg in 1997. (The same Daniah Greenberg who organized the publication of the Tree of Life Bible!) That congregation had amazing favor. They were able to buy a building right on the Syracuse University campus, which is a very Jewish campus. They still have that building, and Jacob Rogers and his wife Teresa are leading that congregation now.

In 2000, we started something here called Sharing Our Bread. It was to reach the Russian Jewish immigrants that were living here in Rochester. At the peak of that ministry, we were helping 38 holocaust survivors by giving them groceries every week. Through that and other outreaches to them, many of them received the Lord. I love thinking back to the amazing provision when we started that. We didn't have any food to give away. We didn't have any place to give it away. We didn't even have any people to do the giving away! And we didn't know who to give it to! So we just began to pray and, within a month, we had Wegman's grocery store chain giving us food. We had a place to give the food away, and we had 80 families show up the first time we offered the food! We also had drivers with vans for getting the food and for picking up the people who needed rides. It was so amazing! We invited them each week to a short worship service before we handed out the food. Most of them came regularly to that service, and after a few years, became believers. After, a decade or so, most of them died or went into nursing homes, and so we closed the program.

Here's another amazing thing for me to rejoice about. I still shake my head when I think about this one. Right away, I started fellowshipping with some of the pastors in this city in a group called Greater Rochester Association of Evangelicals (GRAE). I did that for a few years and got to know the other pastors in the city, and it was great. Then all of a sudden in 2001, they asked me to be president! Now you know, that's a great honor, but me being in the Messianic Movement is why I'm so amazed at what God did. Remember that when we first started the Messianic Movement, it wasn't that positively received by many pastors at all because they thought we were going back "under the law." But all of a sudden, this association of like 120-130 pastors decided that a Messianic rabbi should be their president!! I just shake my head!

So for four years, I was able to be the president of that. It was actually quite humorous because I had to go and represent that organization at many functions. And they would announce that they were being supported by this organization and that one, and they would introduce the leader of each organization. Every time they would come to GRAE, "...and Greater Rochester Association of Evangelicals, with Rabbi Jim Appel representing them." It was just really humorous. But it raised awareness so much of the Messianic Movement and of our existence in the community. So I rejoice in that.

There are other things to rejoice in. Our young people heading overseas. We've had two international trips, one to

Ukraine and one to Budapest. Others in the congregation served in amazing roles as God called. We planted Beit Emanuel in Naples with Jim and Anna Copening, and Tenei Adonai in Eugene, Oregon with David and Keri VanSlyke. Then we had some folks that served a few years overseas, some in Ukraine and one in Haiti. So it was just awesome that we were able to participate in sending all these folks.

[The current war in Ukraine is such a huge tragedy. I'm particularly affected when I hear the names of the cities being attacked by Russia. Jonathan Bernis organized Festivals of Jewish Music evangelistic outreaches in most of those cities, and I still remember their names. We pray fervently for Ukraine's victory and an end to this war.]

Then we had many great people fulfill their calling by coming on as staff in our congregation. I rejoice that we could be part of enabling them to fulfill the call of God on their lives.

Then we rejoice in the renovation of our old building in 2014. We put up a big thermometer to try to raise the funds because we thought it would take like six months or so, but it all came in just two weeks! And the Lord provided the people to do the work. We thought all that was awesome.

Then the favor for our future came in! That absolutely amazing move of God that Edgewood Free Methodist Church offered us their building, saying, "We want you to have this building because it is in the middle of the Jewish community, right near the Jewish Community Center, so we believe a Messianic congregation should have this building. We're going to do everything we can to make it possible for you to have it!!" Whew! And we've been in that building since the fall of 2020. You can read all about that in my *Counting the Omer* and *Shavuot* books.

So I rejoice in all those things! Now take your list, maybe add to it, and rejoice about all the things in your congregation!

12. THE TIME OF OUR REJOICING

Rejoicing in Yeshua's birth

Okay, so that's two things to rejoice in: our physical and spiritual harvest and what God has done in and through our congregations. That's a lot so far, right? But I've got a couple more things to rejoice in.

The **third** thing to rejoice in is that, as I and many others believe, our **Messiah Yeshua** was born on the first day of Sukkot! If you are curious, I'd like to show you, so you can show your friends, where we get this from in the Scriptures. It is hard, but not *too* hard to follow.

First let me give you the background as to why December 25 was chosen. In the fourth century, the church made a decision to remove all Jewish practices. So Hanukkah could no longer be celebrated. Hanukkah is the 25th day of the month of the winter solstice on the Hebrew calendar, and they chose the 25th day of the month of the winter solstice on the Gregorian calendar to be the day the Savior was born. It's too much of a coincidence for it to not be related. I believe, December 25 was also chosen as a concession to the pagans who celebrated the winter solstice around that time of year.

But we can date Yeshua's birth directly from the Scriptures. It's not for sure, but here's how you do it. First of all, we take a look at Yochanan the Immerser's (John the Baptist's) father, Zechariah.

> Luke 1:5 *In the days of Herod, King of Judah, there was a kohen [priest] named Zechariah from the priestly division of* **Abijah**. *Elizabeth, his wife, was from the daughters of Aaron.*

Remember that **Abijah** division. Can we find anything more about these divisions of the kohanim (priests)? Yes we can!

> I Chron. 24:3, 5-7, 10 (NKJV) *Then David with Zadok of the sons of Eleazar [priests], and Ahimelech of the sons of Ithamar [Levites], divided them according to the schedule of their service. ... 5 Thus they were divided by lot, ... 6 And the scribe, ... one of the Levites, wrote them down before the king... 7 Now the first lot fell to Jehoiarib, the second to Jedaiah, ... 10 the seventh to Hakkoz,* **the eighth to Abijah**,

So there we have that same name of a division, and David dividing them for what?

I Chron. 24:19 (NKJV) *This was the schedule of their service for coming into the house of the Lord according to their ordinance by the hand of Aaron their father, as the Lord God of Israel had commanded him.*

So what we are seeing here is that David organized a schedule for the kohanim for when they were to come to Jerusalem from wherever they lived throughout Israel and serve in the Temple. If you count them, you find there are 24 divisions.

Now this next step is where we cannot say this is for sure, but it definitely looks this way. Keep in mind that back in that day, travel was done mostly by walking. These kohanim had to walk from all parts of Israel to Jerusalem to serve in the Temple. So if we assume they served for two weeks because to serve for one week and then go right back home again would've been too much travel and twice as often. So that would cover 48 weeks of the year. 24 x 2 weeks. Right?

But we know that a year has 52 weeks. So in the Scripture, there are three pilgrimage Moadim. All of the kohanim had to be there for those Moadim, which are Passover, Shavuot (Feast of Weeks) and this one, Sukkot. So that would make 48 plus 3. What does that make? 51. But Sukkot is actually eight days. It takes up two Shabbats. So that would be the 52 weeks of the year.

They all had to follow this schedule. So if we put this into rotation for the 52 weeks, Zechariah was in the eighth division. So the cycle, we assume, would have begun in the first of the month of the Biblical year on the Jewish lunar calendar, which is Nissan, the month that Passover is in.

So the eighth division, if they served for two weeks, would have served in the 15th and 16th week. Do you follow that? Okay? But in those first 16 weeks, both Passover and Shavuot fall. So instead of the 15th and the 16th, it would have been the 17th and 18th weeks. Follow me so far? Okay. I know this is math, but hang in there.

So Zechariah would have been in the Temple during the 17th and 18th weeks of the year. Got that? So he would've gone home in the 19th week of the year, which, if you do the

12. THE TIME OF OUR REJOICING

math, is in the fifth month of the year. You can do that math in your head, right?

> Luke 1:24 *Following this, Elisheva [Elizabeth] his wife conceived, and she remained five months in seclusion....*

Now here again, we have to make another assumption, which is that she got pregnant in that first month when her husband Zechariah got home. God had promised them a miracle. So if we make that assumption, what we have is the dating of when Yochanan the Immerser was conceived. Do you see how we've gotten here? He was conceived in the fifth month of the year on the Biblical Jewish calendar.

Then we have another clue.

> Luke 1:26 (TLV) *Now in the sixth month the angel Gabriel was sent by God to a city of Galilee named Nazareth,*

That's in the sixth month of Elizabeth's pregnancy, not the sixth month of the year. So we go from the fifth month of the year when she conceived to six months later. Okay? I know it's getting a little hard to follow. So five plus six is eleven, so we are in the eleventh month, but really it would be the tenth month because the fifth month when she conceived would technically be considered her first month of pregnancy. So the angel would've visited Miriam (Mary) and she would've conceived in the tenth month of the year on the Jewish calendar. Do you follow me so far? Okay?

Now you move ahead nine months around the year, and because a year is twelve months, 10 plus 9 is 19, but you subtract 12, so you come out with what month? The seventh month of the year! Now all of the great events in Messiah's life happened on Appointed Times. Right? He was crucified on Passover. He arose from the dead on Firstfruits, and He sent the Holy Spirit on Shavuot (Pentecost). So in the seventh month, are there any Appointed Times of the Lord? There's three! Rosh Hashanah, Yom Kippur, and Sukkot.

So now, the next question is: are any of those somehow connected to the Messiah being born? Immediately we think of Sukkot because we understand that Sukkot is about reminding us of God dwelling amongst us temporarily in the wilderness! Does that speak of the Messiah coming? Yes! What was Yeshua's sukkah? His body! His body was His temporary dwelling place here on earth. In fact, as I pointed out on page 54, I believe that John alludes to this in the actual Greek. We saw it when we looked up the words in this next verse.

> John 1:14 (TLV) *And the Word became flesh and tabernacled among us.*

For the phrase, *"tabernacled among us,"* some translations say *"dwelt"* or *"lived" among us*, but *"tabernacled"* is the best translation. Remember, in Greek it's *"skenu,"* which means *"to dwell temporarily"* Again, that would be the Greek way of saying *"Sukkot"!* So He tabernacled among us.

So this is my conclusion, and you can agree with me or not, but my conclusion is that Yeshua was born on the first day of Sukkot, which is in the seventh month. It would've been the 15th day of the month. So Happy Birthday, Lord! The Hebrew way to say that is *Yom Huledet Samayakh!*

Now I'm not trying to convince people to stop celebrating Christmas. I know it's important to lots of families, mine included, because of the light it has been telling the whole world that the Savior was born. But Sukkot is the date I believe the Bible says. And many people have begun to adopt this.

So what was the Holy Spirit trying to teach us by arranging for Messiah to be born on Sukkot? Well, obviously, God was coming to dwell where? In the midst of His people. Right? Yeshua's body was a sukkah. And that is something awesome to rejoice about!!

We rejoice that our Messiah grew up amongst us. It wasn't like He came down to this planet as a full grown being somehow. But He came as a baby. He went through all the stages and struggles of childhood: of being born, of being a small child, of being a teenager even, and a young adult. He experienced all the tsuris, as we call it in Yiddish, all the troubles, all the difficulties, and the exhaustion at times. Then as He became a man, we read that He experienced opposition, frustrations, envy of Him, betrayal, false accusations, and finally, He experienced being murdered. And He overcame all of that to fulfill His destiny to be the Messiah, the Savior of the whole world.

So can you rejoice with me that He was born? Thank You, Yeshua, for coming to earth as a babe to know life as a human, to understand us on that deep level. We are grateful!

Rejoicing in Messiah's atonement

Now for the **final thing to rejoice about**. We've touched on three things: abundance, our congregations, and the Lord's birth. The **fourth** is Messiah's atonement. First we need to understand the way God set up these holidays, to have these three fall holidays in sequence so close to each other. It's really kind of interesting that God scheduled three holidays within two weeks. It makes life kind of crazy this time of year. But the Lord did that for a purpose. The purpose is all about atonement. Rosh Hashanah is a day of rejoicing, but also begins the Ten days of Awe for repentance. Yom Kippur is the day for atonement and forgiveness, and then Sukkot is the time of **giving thanks for that forgiveness** that happened on Yom Kippur.

So we Messianic believers **give thanks**, not just for what happened on Yom Kippur, but **for what the Messiah did through His atonement**. I'm just going to highlight a few things about the atonement of the Messiah. We need to remember what He did and to rejoice about it.

First of all, the book of Hebrews tells us that **His atonement is greater** than the atonement made by the animal sacrifices.

> Hebrews 10:1-2 *For the Torah has in it a shadow of the good things to come, but not the actual manifestation of the originals. Therefore, it can never, by means of the same sacrifices repeated endlessly year after year, bring to the goal those who approach the Holy Place to offer them. 2 Otherwise, wouldn't the offering of those sacrifices have ceased? For if the people performing the service had been cleansed once and for all, they would no longer have sins on their conscience.*

So, let's dig in to this. First of all, who are those who "approach the Holy Place"? Well, we know that's the Kohane HaGadol, High Priest. But he did it for all Israel. He was making atonement for all of the people of Israel. In verse 1, it talks about a goal, that those sacrifices didn't bring the people to the goal. So what's the goal? Well, we don't have to guess because it's answered in verse 2: *"For they would no longer have sins on their conscience."* That's the goal, to have a clean conscience. That's the greater thing Messiah's sacrifice does that the animal sacrifices could not do. It brings people to the place where they have **cleansed consciences**. This verse also speaks of this:

> Hebrews 9:14 *[T]hen how much more the blood of the Messiah, who, through the eternal Spirit, offered himself to God as a sacrifice without blemish, will purify our conscience from works that lead to death, so that we can serve the living God!*

So when we confess our sins to God and ask His forgiveness and ask Him by the power of Yeshua's atoning sacrifice to take away our sin, His sacrifice doesn't just get us forgiven. It is important to understand this. **He sets us free from shame and guilt**, from what we carry around with us when we have done things that we know were wrong.

Shame and guilt is an awful burden to carry around. It is part of what Yeshua paid for when He made His atoning sacrifice. What other things did He pay for? Forgiveness, healing, deliverance, freedom from the curse, shalom, eternal Life, and the gift of receiving the Holy Spirit and so much more! Cleansing our conscience is part of this. Now, I've done a lot of counseling, and I've seen that there are many believers who suffer from guilt and shame because they have not received this. They don't realize that guilt can be taken away by Yeshua.

So that's **the first thing** I believe we can rejoice about in Yeshua's atonement. **He cleanses our conscience.** No matter what we've done, if we confess it to Him, **He cleanses us from all unrighteousness, and removes it, and we have a clean conscience**. Can you rejoice in that? Amen!! Thank You, Yeshua!

12. THE TIME OF OUR REJOICING

Another thing that Yeshua gained for us through His atoning sacrifice that we can rejoice in is what we studied in chapter 9, that all those who trust in Him will have rivers of Living Water flow out of them from being filled with His Holy Spirit. And remember that the Holy Spirit in us is **God Himself in us**! That's how He dwells in us, by His Spirit! Yeshua says that He is in the Father and the Father is in Him and we are in Him and He is in us. That's how it is, through His Holy Spirit. So Sukkot is also a day to remember and be thankful and rejoice that not only did He say that the Holy Spirit would flow out of us, but **He and the Father would be in us**.

Here's another thing Yeshua's sacrifice won for us:

Ephesians 2:10 *For we are of God's making, created in union with the Messiah Yeshua for a life of good actions already prepared by God for us to do.*

Why is this a source of rejoicing? **This is purpose**. Life without a purpose is meaningless. It's hopeless. What this is saying is that God created you for a purpose, not just to come and trust in the Lord, but to move on to fulfill the plan that God has for you in this life. I know many believers suffer from hopelessness and depression and a sense of not being of value because they haven't fully received this promise that each person has a purpose in God's Kingdom. There's something specific for you to do.

And then here's another one. Yeshua says this to His disciples:

Luke 10:19 *Remember, I have given you authority; so you can trample down snakes and scorpions, indeed, all the Enemy's forces; and you will remain completely unharmed.*

Luke 10:19 (TLV) *Behold, I have given you authority ...over all the power of the enemy; nothing will harm you.*

Now I know most of you are not worried about trampling down snakes and scorpions. We lived in California for awhile and that was a big worry there actually. But how about the enemy's forces? Do you have any opposition from the enemy? Yea! All of us have that. This says Yeshua has given us authority over all the enemy's forces. Can you rejoice in that?

Yes! Hallelujah!! Thank You, Lord, for **giving us authority over the enemy**!

Then finally, we're going to end with this one:

Mark 16:17-18 *And these signs will accompany those who do trust: in my name they will drive out demons, speak with new tongues, 18 not be injured if they handle snakes or drink poison, and heal the sick by laying hands on them."*

God gave each of the followers of Yeshua **healing power in your hands and in your prayers.** It's part of the atonement. It's part of what He paid for.

So what are the four things we can rejoice about when we're reminded of His atonement? That He cleanses our consciences; that He gave us purpose, and authority over all the power of the enemy, and healing power in our hands and prayers. We haven't even mentioned so many other things. It's a long list that could go on and on:

- He made a way for us to know Him personally.
- He gave us eternal Life.
- He gave us a forever family that we're going to be with forever in Heaven.
- Our names are written in the Book of Life and not blotted out.
- He's given us the Spirit of Truth so we can tell the Truth from lies. So awesome!!
- He's making us ambassadors for the Kingdom, a very high office for breaking bondages and speaking freedom.
- We are healed by His stripes.
- We're seated with Him in Heavenly places!
- He brings us abundant life.
- He gives us His Shalom.
- We could go on and on forever! Praise His Name.

Okay, get your Lulav and rejoice over all those things!

Let's pray.

[Can you agree with me that you'd like to have a thankful heart?]

Father, give us thankful hearts. We sing a song that says, "A thankful heart prepares a place for You, O Lord." That is so true. So, Father, we just obey Your easy commandment to rejoice today. We rejoice in You, Lord. We're going to rejoice and give thanks for the whole seven days. We thank You, Father, for You being a God who commands us to rejoice. We rejoice in all that You are and that You do. We thank You for the harvest. We thank You for Your provision for our physical needs, for the provisions which are so abundant in this country. We thank You for the spiritual harvest. We rejoice in salvations, healings, discipleship, and the fruits of the Spirit, and relationships, and reconciliations. We thank You for what You've done for and through our congregations, and we thank You that it's going to go on.

I personally thank You, Father, for the favor we've seen from pastors for Shema Yisrael Congregation. Thank You for our new building. Thank You for sending Jonathan Bernis to us. Thank You for the revival we participated in in Russia. Thank You for us being able to feed the Holocaust survivors for almost ten years! I thank You for all these things and many more.

And Father, we thank You for coming to earth as a human. Thank You that you didn't just come as a grown man, but as an infant, born on Sukkot, living among us, suffering and struggling as human beings do. So we thank You, Yeshua.

And thank You for Your atoning sacrifice, for bringing us all the things that we listed here: forgiveness, cleansed consciences, purpose, the Truth, power over the enemy, healings, all these things and so much more. Thank You so much, Lord. Thank You, Lord. Thank You that our names are written in the Book of Life, Father. Thank You! In Yeshua's Name. Amein.

Wave your branches and rejoice!

CHAPTER 13
BORN A KING AND PRIEST

Let's look again at that familiar New Covenant verse that you now know is very much connected to Sukkot:

John 1:14 (NKJV) *And the Word became flesh and dwelt among us, and we beheld His glory, the glory as of the only begotten of the Father, full of grace and truth.*

John 1:14a (TLV) *And the Word became flesh and tabernacled among us. ...*

John 1:14b (CJB) *...and we saw his Sh'khinah, the Sh'khinah of the Father's only Son, full of grace and truth.*

So again, Yochanan (John) is saying that God came as a human and temporarily lived among His people. That is what the Tabernacle was all about. It was the place where God temporarily dwelt amongst His people.

In the last chapter, I revealed through Scripture that Yeshua was born in the seventh month. Surely you remember by now the three Moadim in the seventh month: 1. Yom Teruah (Rosh Hashanah, Feast of Trumpets), 2. Yom Kippur (Atonement), and 3. Sukkot (Tabernacles). And when we think about it, Sukkot speaks of God dwelling with us temporarily in the cloud and in the fire, and when Yeshua was born, what was that? God dwelling amongst us temporarily! Right? So again, that's why I believe He was born on the first day of Sukkot and on the Eighth Day what would have happened? He would have had His Brit Milah—His circumcision—and that would have been on an Appointed Time, too! Isn't that amazing?!

So I believe the Bible tells us that this is when Yeshua was born. However, there is nothing wrong with celebrating His birth on another day, since the Scripture doesn't make it totally explicitly clear.

Now for this chapter I was led to dig into some of the details about the birth of Yeshua, about His ancestry and His DNA. We know Yeshua had to have descended from the tribe of Judah. Right? He's the Lion of the tribe of Judah. We know that from several prophecies in the Old Testament. Jacob actually prophesied it all the way back in Genesis.

> Genesis 49:10 *The scepter will not pass from Judah, nor the ruler's staff from between his feet, until he to whom it belongs will come. To him will be the obedience of the peoples.*

Scepter is the symbol of the King's power. It would not depart from the Tribe of Judah. Some translations say, "until Shiloh comes." But it could also be translated as it is here by the Tree of Life Version, "until he to whom it belongs will come."

Then Psalm 89 says some very specific things. This is the Lord speaking. David is recording what the Lord is saying:

> Psalm 89:35-38 *"I will not violate My covenant, nor alter what My lips have uttered. 36 Once for all I have sworn by My holiness—surely I will not lie to David— 37 his descendants will endure forever, and his throne as the sun before Me, 38 and as the moon, established forever, and a trustworthy witness in the sky." Selah*

So here the Lord is saying specifically that the Messiah and all the kings who sit on the throne will come from David's line, and will be on the throne forever. Forever! So how was Yeshua descended from David? Well, most people think it was through Joseph. It says Yosef (Joseph) was from the tribe of Judah, right? But Yeshua was not Yosef's blood son. You understand that, right? Whose son was He? God's Son because Miryam (Mary) was a virgin. So the only DNA that Yeshua had that was human DNA was whose? Miryam's! Yosef was his adopted father, which meant that Yeshua could be his heir. He could leave property to him, but if Yosef were the king, Yeshua would not have been able to be the king following him because an adopted son did not inherit the kingdom. They inherited things, but they couldn't be royalty in the kingdom.

So how is it that Yeshua was from the line of the tribe of Judah? Well, Miryam was also from the line of King David, and she was His real mother, not His adopted mother. So He fulfilled the requirement to be Israel's eternal King through His mother Miryam.

Now another very interesting thing comes out about this. In my *Yom Kippur* book, I showed how Yeshua fulfilled the scapegoat sacrifice. And I mentioned that He not only fulfilled it by His own body being the sacrifice, right? But what else did He fulfill? He fulfilled being the Kohane HaGadol (the High Priest) who offered the sacrifice in Heaven. Remember that?

> Hebrews 9:11-12 *But when the Messiah appeared as cohen gadol* [the high priest] *of the good things that are happening already, then, through the greater and more perfect Tent which is not man-made (that is, it is not of this created world), 12 he entered the Holiest Place once and for all. And he entered not by means of the blood of goats and calves, but by means of his own blood, thus setting people free forever.*

It's hard to grasp this scene with your mind. Yeshua is in the throne room of God, before the throne of God offering His own Blood. I always struggle with what that was like. Was it dripping from His wounds? Or had He caught it in a basin or something? How did He do this? We don't know, but somehow He offered His own Blood. So in offering His Blood, He was fulfilling the role, not of the scapegoat, but of who? The Kohane who offered the blood. And because it was His body He was also offering, He fulfilled the role of both the scapegoat and the sacrificed goat.

So the Kohane HaGadol had to have descended from who? Aaron. And since Yosef and Miryam were both descendants of King David of Judah, how could Yeshua be a descendant of Aaron? How could He fulfill Aaron's descendant being the one who is supposed to be the Kohane HaGadol? Well the mystery to that goes back to a verse in Luke that we looked at in chapter 12:

13. BORN A KING AND PRIEST

Luke 1:5 *In the days of Herod, King of Y'hudah, there was a cohen named Z'kharyah who belonged to the Aviyah division. His wife was a descendant of Aharon, and her name was Elisheva.*

Now, not only was Zechariah a descendant of Aaron because he was a priest, but his wife was a descendant of Aaron also. Notice that she was not just a Levite, she was a descendant of Aaron. So why is that statement important? Well, after Gabriel told Miryam that she would bear a child by the Holy Spirit, this is what he said.

Luke 1:36 *You have a relative, Elisheva [Elizabeth], who is an old woman; and everyone says she is barren. But she has conceived a son and is six months pregnant!*

So Miryam, from the tribe of Judah, had a relative Elisheva who was from which tribe? From the family of Aaron from the tribe of Levi. And if you look up the Greek word there for relative, it's a close, blood relative, not just a distant relative. She was a cousin, and she was from the family of Aaron. So Miryam was a descendant from King David from the Lion of Judah, but she was also descended from who? Aaron.

So how is this possible? Well, it's pretty simple. She had a mother and she had a father, right? Her father was from the line of King David. That's why she was called from the tribe of Judah, but her mother must have been from the line of Aaron or else she wouldn't be a cousin of Elisheva, and she must have been a close relative because look at the situation. She showed up supposedly a virgin pregnant and Elisheva welcomed her into their home. Miryam lived with her for about three months, so there must have been a pretty close connection there. It wasn't like they were third, fourth, or fifth cousins. They must have been quite close.

So Miryam, being Yeshua's real mother, brought human DNA to Yeshua from both families, the family of King David and the family of the Kohane HaGadol Aaron. His DNA from King David was through Miryam's father, and his DNA from Aaron was through Miryam's mother. So Yeshua fulfilled the requirement that He be descended from one of the kohane.

So He fulfilled the prophecies we just read from Genesis and Psalms about sitting on the throne of Israel eternally. Listen to what He Himself said.

John 18:36 *My kingdom is not of this world.*

So where is His Kingdom? It's in Heaven. And how long will His Kingdom last? It's eternal! It is the Kingdom of God. It is the Kingdom of Israel. This is the throne of Israel. So He's seated on that eternal throne over the house of Israel forever. So Yeshua fulfilled this promise.

Nobody else could have fulfilled this promise because Israel's throne in the world disappeared when Israel was conquered by Rome and other nations. There was no king anymore. If Yeshua hadn't fulfilled this promise, it would have been broken.

So I think maybe what happened was that Miryam's parents must have intermarried between the two tribes for all of these Messianic prophecies to come together in Miryam, and then to come together in Yeshua. She received from the Holy Spirit the seed of God the Father when she conceived. So God's Son could be born as the divine child and as a human being. The Son of God and also, as He often called Himself, the son of man. He was both.

So Yeshua's lineage is from the two families of his mother, of King David and of the Kohane HaGadol Aaron. In the natural He fulfilled all the Messianic prophecies concerning the Messiah, regarding Him coming from both David and Aaron.

Now to what's really kind of a side note in this from somebody else's study. I found this to be amazing. If we look back at the history of the start of the Aaronic priesthood when Aaron was first ordained, it was interestingly formed from the same two tribes. From Levi, yes, and also from Judah. Why? Because Aaron married someone outside the tribe.

Exodus 6:23 (NKJV) *Aaron took to himself Elisheba* [another way to spell Elisheva], *daughter of Amminadab, sister of Nahshon, as wife; and she bore him Nadab, Abihu, Eleazar, and Ithamar.*

13. BORN A KING AND PRIEST

Now most people would just say, "Oh, okay. So she's got a name." But if we go into the Book of Numbers, it's listing the people who are going to help Moses with the first census count of the people. Look at what it says:

> Numbers 1:4 -7 *One man from each tribe, each head of his father's household, is to assist you. ... 5 These then are the names of the men who will assist you: ... 7 From Judah, Nahshon son of Amminadab.*

That's the same name! And then it says this:

> Numbers 1:16 *These were those selected from the community, princes of their ancestral tribes. They were heads of the thousands of Israel.*

So Nahshon the son of Amminadab was basically the head of the tribe of Judah. Aaron married Elisheva, the daughter of Amminadab, Nahshon's sister. So Aaron's wife Elisheva was the sister of the leader of the tribe of Judah, Nahshon. So if you haven't seen it yet, in the foundation of the Aaronic priesthood, both tribes were involved because who were the ones that were born of the union between Aaron and Elisheva? It was Nadab, Abihu, Eleazar, and Ithamar, the four sons who became the kohanim. So what was in their DNA? The DNA of Levi and Judah!

But you know what else is astounding in this? Look at this. In the foundation of the priesthood that was given to Aaron, two women were involved. The first was Elisheva, and who was the other woman that was instrumental in the founding of that priesthood? Aaron's sister Miryam! Two names, Elisheva and Miryam. Do you see that? What were the names of the two women instrumental in the founding or the beginning of Yeshua's priesthood? Miryam and Elisheva. I don't know the deeper meaning of that, but I find it to be beyond coincidental. It is amazing!

So how does this apply to all of us? How does it apply to you? Well, first of all, this should strengthen your faith that Yeshua fulfilled the prophetic requirement as the Son of Man. He was a descendant from the Kohane HaGadol as well as from the king. Secondly, and this, to me, should increase your appreciation of God's amazingly intricate plan, how He has arranged these things to be fulfilled and revealed in His Word. It's amazing to see this. And thirdly, Peter writes this to all of you who are chosen.

> I Peter 2:9 (TLV) *But you are a chosen people, a royal priesthood, a holy nation, a people for God's own possession, so that you may proclaim the praises of the One who called you out of darkness into His marvelous light.*

So all of us who trust in the Messiah Yeshua, including you, what are we? We are a chosen people, chosen by God, chosen to be what? A royal priesthood! Do you see that? A royal priesthood, called and ordained to be kohanim in His Kingdom, a royal priesthood, descendants of the king. We are royalty who are also kohanim. Do you see the connection between you and Yeshua? He came from the kings and the kohanim, and spiritually those who have received Him become royal priests. Who do you descend from spiritually? The King and the Kohane HaGadol (High Priest). This is what Peter is telling us. You are part of a royal priesthood.

> John 1:12 *But to as many as did receive him, to those who put their trust in his person and power, he gave the right to become children of God, 13 not because of bloodline, physical impulse or human intention, but because of God.*

You have been adopted into God's family. So you and I are adopted children, but we're children of the King! See that? We're also children of the Kohane HaGadol. Yeshua is our Great High Priest. Yeshua and God are one, so we are children of the King and the Kohane HaGadol. So our spiritual DNA is just like His is. We are descendants from the King and the Kohane HaGadol. That includes you!

And, you know, we don't use this word much, but we are priests and priestesses of Yeshua. Whenever you talk about priestesses people talk about it like it's a cult. But it just means a female priest, right? You are children of the Great High Priest because Yeshua is the Great High Priest, and He is one with God. So you are His child. You got that? Okay.

So how should this affect you? It should have a huge effect! Knowing you are royalty should be a tremendous help to you.

13. BORN A KING AND PRIEST

If you struggle with low self-esteem, you are a royalty!
If you struggle with rejection and feeling like you're not accepted? Know that you're part of the royal family!
If you struggle with depression, you're royalty!
If you lack the feeling that you belong? You are royalty!
How about not feeling like you are loved? You are royalty! You are a child of the King who Loves you!
How about envying somebody else's position or somebody else's circumstances. You are royalty.
How about being bitter for the circumstances you're in? You are royalty.

You found out you are royalty because of all that you've gone through and you turned to the Lord. So this knowledge should affect you and give you great gratitude. And I want you to just receive these words from the Spirit. I speak them prophetically.

Now you, and yes, I'm talking about you, you are a child of the King. You are part of the royal family. Receive that. Are you receiving it? Speak it out.

I am a part of the royal family.

I am accepted. I rejoice in that acceptance. I belong!

I belong to the royal family. I am beloved by the King Himself as His child. Others should be envious and jealous of me. I shouldn't be envying them; they should be envying me! No matter how hard my situation is, rather than be bitter about it, I can rejoice.

You are chosen to be part of Messiah's royal family. And you know what else? This family will last how long? Forever!

And you know what else? You have a home in the castle! I think that is what Yeshua is saying, "I'm going to prepare a place for you." What is the King's home? It's a castle! You have a home in the castle in Heaven forever!

Now on the other side, if you decide, as royalty, to imitate the descendants of most earthly kings, that's not such a good idea. That can make you begin to act entitled, prideful, conceited, spoiled, and above the law. But you're not children of an earthly king. You're children of the Eternal King of Israel!

And this is what He is like.

> Philippians 2:5-8 *Let your attitude toward one another be governed by your being in union with the Messiah Yeshua: 6 Though he was in the form of God, he did not regard equality with God something to be possessed by force. 7 On the contrary, he emptied himself, in that he took the form of a slave by becoming like human beings are. And when he appeared as a human being, 8 he humbled himself still more by becoming obedient even to death—death on a stake as a criminal!*

So we are to imitate King Yeshua, and what does it say? Let's look at some of those words. You must empty and humble yourself and be obedient. Empty yourself. As sinful humans, we need to get rid of all ungodly attitudes and fears. Humble yourself. Have a realistic understanding of who you are as God sees you. Also have faith that God can enable you to do whatever He calls you to do. Be obedient to God even when His direction goes against your desires. Walk in the authority of the children of the King. Operate in the authority over the King's enemies.

Now this is very important. Children of royalty must accept the responsibility of their birth. They need to be model servants to the King. The King is their Father. Their behavior needs to bring honor to Him.

So you are not just royalty, but also of the royal priesthood. This should also be a tremendous help to you. You are to imitate our Great Kohane HaGadol Yeshua. You're called to fear and serve God by worshiping Him and being His representative before people. You are His hands and His feet and His lips and His voice. You are to come into His presence to hear His voice and know His heart. You are to speak words to other people, demonstrating God's love to other people because that's the way He demonstrates it. It's through you.

You are to be intercessors. That's a big part of what a priest does. He is someone who goes to God for other people and prays for them, being faithful to that. You are to offer yourself as a living sacrifice as Yeshua did. We are talking spiritually offering yourself, but many have had to do this physically also.

13. BORN A KING AND PRIEST

Your Great Kohane HaGadol says, *"Well done good and faithful servant enter into the joy of your master."*

Now finally, this understanding should drastically affect your relationships with other people. At your Shabbat meetings, the people sitting near you, on your right and your left, in front of you and behind you are also royalty. All your believing neighbors, friends, and relatives are royalty, too. Do you appreciate that?

So, as a child of your royal Father, you should treat your believing brothers and sisters as what? Royalty! As God's children, He loves them just the way they are. The person sitting near you is also a priest or a priestess. You need to respect his or her calling. He or she may be in the early stages of kohane training, but he's still a kohane. God sees his potential. This verse is such a challenge, but I think it applies here:

> Philippians 2:3-4 *Do nothing out of rivalry or vanity; but, in humility, regard each other as better than yourselves — 4 look out for each other's interests and not just for your own.*

You're royalty but he's royalty and she's royalty too! Regard each other as better than yourselves.

Let's pray.

Father, we thank You for Sukkot and all its amazing, deep meanings. We thank You that You came and "skenu-ed" amongst us, coming as a man to save us. Thank You for being the king who humbled Himself and was obedient to death. Thank You for being the Great Kohane HaGadol who sacrificed His own life. We ask, Lord, that you would show us how to walk as royal kohanim of Your Kingdom. We pray You will strengthen us in our authority over the enemies of Your Kingdom.

And Father, we ask You to empty us of all ungodly attitudes. You emptied Yourself. The Word says so. Now as royal kohanim, we command these things to leave:

- rejection
- low self-esteem
- jealousy, envy
- inability to believe that we're loved
- bitterness

We command them to leave. We empty ourselves of these ungodly things. Help us to resist them. Help us to resist their return, oh Lord. We humble ourselves, Father, before You. Help us to be obedient to You, to be model servants of our King. We ask You to fill us to the overflowing with Your Ruakh, just like You spoke on Sukkot that rivers of Living Water would flow out of our innermost beings. Fill us to overflowing, Father.

[Just raise up your hands and say, "Fill me, Lord, fill me to the overflowing. On Sukkot fill me, O Lord, fill me."]

Renew our minds, Father, to think the way You think. Anoint our priestly worship of You. Anoint our prayer, Father. Enable us to see our brothers and sisters as royalty. Enable us to esteem them greater than ourselves, Father, to hold them up. Anoint our speaking of Your Word, Father, and our demonstration of Your Love as we reach out. Help us to regard others as better than ourselves. In Yeshua's awesome Name. Amein.

CHAPTER 14
CONNECTED BY LIGHT

In this chapter, I want to talk about the connections between two Biblical holidays, between this holiday, Sukkot, and the next holiday coming up, Hanukkah. The Hanukkah celebration is not commanded in the Torah. The event being remembered is not recorded in the Bible, but there is a record of Yeshua being in the Temple when it was being celebrated (John 10:22-23 on the next page), so I'm going to still call it a Biblical holiday.

The symbol of Hanukkah is the nine branched Hanukkiah. It is not the seven branch Menorah that was inside the Holy Place in the Temple. That one was not out in the courtyard for everyone to see, like the Hanukkiah is. On the Hanukkiah, we light the candles, one each day for the eight days in remembrance of the miracle of the oil lasting eight days.

Hanukkah is very near the winter solstice, the darkest day and night of the year. The theme of Hanukkah is light. It is actually known as the Festival of Lights. It is on the 25th day of the tenth Hebrew month named Kislev, which is 10 weeks after Sukkot.

The Talmud describes the festivities on the evening of **first day of Sukkot**. It says that "very tall candelabras were erected in the Court of the Women" (*Carter's Illustrated Encyclopedia of the Holy Temple in Jerusalem*, pp.192-193). Each candelabrum had four bowls, which held 7.5 gallons of oil. [These were bowls of burning oil like the Olympic flame.]

171

The Talmud says, "The light was so brilliant that it seemed more like day than night. The lights could be seen from every house in Yerushalayim."

So, both Hanukkah and Sukkot are Festival of Lights. Lighting up the Temple courts would not seem so significant today because in our culture, having bright lights at night is normal. But, in Biblical times, most of the year people only saw candles and torches at night. The seven branched Menorah was lit every night and morning, but it was inside the Temple. No one saw it. Only the kohanim who trimmed it and lit it each morning and night got to see it.

On Sukkot the candelabras were lit for eight days, and on Hanukkah the nine branched Hanukkiahs were lit for eight days. Coincidence? I don't think so. I find it very interesting.

These two times of great light were considered awesome. And these were two seasons of light separated by only nine weeks between the last day of Sukkot and the first day of Hanukkah. So this whole time came to be known as the season of lights. This "season of lights" started on Sukkot ten weeks before Hanukkah and lasted through Hanukkah. Realizing this prompted me to look at this season with a new understanding.

What did Yeshua do and talk about during this season of lights? We know Yeshua participated in Sukkot, especially the last day in John 7 as we looked at in depth in chapter 9. We also know He participated in Hanukkah recorded in John 10.

> John 10:22-23 *Then came Chanukkah in Yerushalayim. It was winter, 23 and Yeshua was walking around inside the Temple area, in Shlomo's Colonnade.*

Between John 7 and 10 we have chapters 8 and 9. Is there a connection between this "season of lights" in Yerushalayim and what Yeshua said during that season?

> John 8:12 …*"I am the light of the world; whoever follows me will never walk in darkness but will have the light which gives life."*

> John 9:5 *"While I am in the world, I am the light of the world."*

Now that we understand that there was more to the season of lights than Hanukkah, that it stretched from Sukkot to

Hanukkah, we can see that Yeshua was building on the season of lights that was happening around Him to communicate who He was. Prior to understanding there was this season, I used to wonder why Yeshua's proclamation of being Light of the World happened before Hanukkah rather than on Hanukkah.

So then I was led to do a search for other connections to the lights during this season, especially in events surrounding His birth, which I believe was on Sukkot.

Here's the first other connection with light that I found. Yeshua's birth was also a very lit up day. As we pointed out, the Talmud says great lights were lit in the Temple court on the first day of Sukkot. So, the Light of the World was born on the day that the great four-bowled candelabrum were lit in the Temple courtyard.

The second connection was another light on the first day of Sukkot, the night of His birth. But, this light was not in the Temple courts. It was outside Yerushalayim.

> Luke 2:8-9 *In the countryside nearby were some shepherds spending the night in the fields, guarding their flocks, 9 when an angel of ADONAI [the LORD] appeared to them, and the Sh'khinah [glory] of ADONAI shone around them. They were terrified;*

Yeshua's birth was announced to the shepherds with the appearance of another great light, so bright it terrified them. It was the light of the Glory of the Lord, Sh'khinah, announcing His birth!

The third light connection continues with the events of Yeshua's first few weeks.

> Luke 2:21 *On the eighth day, when it was time for his b'rit-milah [circumcision], he was given the name Yeshua, which is what the angel had called him before his conception.*

If Yeshua was born on the first day of Sukkot, His circumcision would have been on the Eighth Day of Sukkot.

> Luke 2:22-23 *When the time came for their purification according to the Torah of Moshe, they took him up to Yerushalayim to present him to ADONAI 23 (as it is written in the Torah of ADONAI, "Every firstborn male is to be consecrated to ADONAI")*

This did not happen on the Eighth Day. This was Pidyon HaBen פדיון הבן – the consecration of the firstborn. It happened later. Every firstborn son's parents had to pay a ransom for him, according to Numbers 18:15-16. We learn the date when His Pidyon HaBen happened from the next verse in Luke.

> Luke 2:24 *and also to offer a sacrifice of a pair of doves or two young pigeons, as required by the Torah of A<small>DONAI</small>.*

This sacrifice was to fulfill Miryam's purification after childbirth. So, they combined the Pidyon HaBen with Miryam's purification, which refers to a mother's ritual purification after childbirth.

> Leviticus 12:4 *She must wait during the blood of purification for 33 days. She is not to touch any holy thing, nor come into the Sanctuary, until the days of her purifying are completed.*

So we can date this ceremony at the Temple—Pidyon HaBen and the purification ceremony of Miryam—to the 33rd day of Yeshua's life. So it would've been in the middle of Chesvan, the eighth month, about halfway between Sukkot and Hanukkah. And, since it was during the season of lights, it's not surprising that we find the theme of light arising once again. When Yeshua's parents brought Him to the Temple for these ceremonies, a man named Shim'on (Simeon) received the revelation that He was Messiah.

> Luke 2:28-31 *Shim`on took him in his arms, made a b'rakhah* [blessing] *to God, and said, 29 "Now, A<small>DONAI</small>, according to your word, your servant is at peace as you let him go; 30 for I have seen with my own eyes your yeshu`ah* [salvation], *31 which you prepared in the presence of all peoples –*

Pay attention! Here's the third light connection:

> Luke 2:32 *a light that will bring revelation to the Goyim* [nations] *and glory to your people Isra'el."*

Shim'on is paraphrasing Isaiah 49:6, prophesying that a light would come, and it would not just be for Israel but for Gentiles too.

> Isaiah 49:6 *So He says, "It is too trifling a thing that You should be My servant to raise up the tribes of Jacob and restore the preserved ones of Israel. So I will give You as a light for the nations, that You should be My salvation to the end of the earth."*

14. CONNECTED BY LIGHT

Here's the fourth connection. Another light appeared in the heavens at this season. Some men known as the Magi had followed that special light to see King Messiah. You might think I have them out of chronological order because of nativity scenes you have seen with the Magi there. But we can see from the Bible that the Magi were not present at Yeshua's birth:

> Matthew 2:1-2 *After Yeshua was born in Beit-Lechem [Bethlehem] in the land of Y'hudah during the time when Herod was king, Magi from the east came to Yerushalayim 2 and asked, "Where is the newborn King of the Jews? For we saw his star in the east and have come to worship him."*

This star is the fourth light connected to Yeshua's birth. Herod consulted with Bible scholars and learned the Messiah was to be born in Beit-Lechem (House of Bread).

> Matthew 2:7 *Herod summoned the Magi to meet with him privately and asked them exactly when the star had appeared.*

The Magi found Yeshua, still in Bethlehem, worshipped Him and gave Him gifts. Then warned in a dream not to return to Yerushalayim, they left secretly.

> Matthew 2:16 *Meanwhile, when Herod realized that the Magi had tricked him, he was furious and gave orders to kill all the boys in and around Beit-Lechem who were two years old or less, calculating from the time the Magi had told him.*

So, we know they had told Herod the star appeared two years earlier. So, the Magi didn't visit Yeshua on the day He was born. It was two years later that they showed up, either two years from His conception or from His birth. So Yeshua's family must have stayed in Bethlehem after His birth. Why did Herod murder all baby boys under 2 years old in and around Bethlehem? It's because he was afraid this baby would grow up and usurp his throne.

This mass murder was very much in line with Herod's character. History records that he also murdered all the men in his own family whom he also feared would usurp his throne.

So, the star the Magi followed is the fourth light connected with Yeshua's birth, and He called Himself the Light of World during the Season of lights, while the nation was celebrating the Festival of Lights. But, what did He mean when He said I am the Light of the World? Light is associated with Truth in the Bible—Yeshua also said I am the Truth, and He said His Word, the Bible is Truth. Another prophesy of light in Isaiah speaks of Mashiakh (Messiah) being a Light:

> Isaiah 9:1 (2) *The people walking in darkness will see a great light. Upon those dwelling in the land of the shadow of death, light will shine.*

Who are these people living in darkness? The Israelis, who had the Bible and the Temple, were obeying God's laws, and celebrating the Jewish holidays. Isaiah says these Jewish people were in the dark because they were living in the shadow of death. Does this mean in danger of being attacked and killed by an army? No. They were in the shadow of spiritual darkness, destined for spiritual death.

What is spiritual death? Separation from God and all the goodness and Love He created in this life and the next life when those separated from God in this life will remain separated from Him for eternity in the place the Bible calls hell. What then is spiritual life? It's the opposite. Spiritual life is being connected with God, knowing God, being in fellowship with God, serving God, experiencing all the goodness and Love He created in this life and in the next life. Those who are connected with God in this life will remain connected with Him for eternity in the place the Bible calls Heaven.

What's it like to be in spiritual darkness in this life? It's the inability to see the spiritual side of life, the spirit world, the inability to understand the spiritual laws of the universe and how they affect our lives.

We say a person who is physically blind is "in the dark" because they can't see this physical world. A person in spiritual darkness is spiritually blind. They are unable to see the Truth about life. Why can't they see the Truth? Because our enemy, ha-satan, uses deception to keep us from the Truth.

> II Corinthians 4:4 *They do not come to trust because the god of the 'olam hazeh* [this world] *has blinded their minds,*

in order to prevent them from seeing the light shining from the Good News about the glory of the Messiah, who is the image of God.

Only the Truth can enable us to see through the deception. No one wants to be deceived but many are. Many people understand the physical laws of the universe, like the law of gravity—if you jump off a high building you will go down. You will hit the ground hard enough to kill yourself. Engineers and scientists use physical laws all the time for our benefit. If you claim you don't believe in the law of gravity and try to defy it by jumping off a roof, you will still go down and hit the ground.

Spiritual laws are as unchangeable and unyielding as physical laws. Whether you believe in them or not, they will still hold and will affect your life. They are still true. Yet most people don't understand or apply them to their own lives.

Galatians 6:7-8 *Don't delude yourselves: no one makes a fool of God! A person reaps what he sows. 8 Those who keep sowing in the field of their old nature, in order to meet its demands, will eventually reap ruin; but those who keep sowing in the field of the Spirit will reap from the Spirit everlasting life.*

When you sow or plant seeds in the field of your old nature—sin and disobedience, you will reap ruin, darkness, separation from God, and spiritual death. When you sow in the field of the Spirit—obeying God, you will reap everlasting life, light, life connected with God and with His blessings, anointing, provision, and joy. This is a law of our universe—even if you don't believe it, it holds true. Your life will be governed by it, and you will reap what you sow. Here's another spiritual law:

Proverbs 3:5-6 *Trust in ADONAI with all your heart, lean not on your own understanding. 6 In all your ways acknowledge Him, and He will make your paths straight.*

When you trust God with all your heart, over your own wisdom, and you acknowledge His wisdom and authority in your life, He will make your paths straight, lead you, and level the path before you. If you don't, He will not lead you and your ways will be difficult. This is a law of our universe. Even if you don't believe it, it still holds. Your life will still be governed by it.

Psalms 119:105 *Your word is a lamp to my feet and a light to my path.*

God has given us His Word, the Bible, as a Light, the true Light, so we can understand these spiritual laws, the true laws. Yet Isaiah says even the Israelites who had God's Word were in darkness because they weren't able to understand and apply the spiritual laws. Their minds were still blinded by ha-satan's deceptions.

I walked in spiritual darkness for 31 years. I would attempt something that looked like a good thing to do, and it would turn out to be a mess. I followed some worldly philosophy that sounded good and it wasn't. I tried some new drugs that were supposed to make me happy, but they didn't. I had studied some exotic religious paths to peace and they didn't bring peace. I had gotten involved in a scheme to make money and it failed. I said the wrong thing and messed up a friendship.

But the Israelites Isaiah was referring to were not in darkness forever. He predicted that a great light would come. Yeshua, the Light of the World, is that great light that has dawned. When you repent and put your trust in Him, He turns on the lights. He opens your spiritual eyes and you're able to see and understand the Bible and learn the Truth about the spiritual nature and the laws of the universe. You can see that if you obey His laws you will experience the blessings of God.

I began seeking spiritually around the age of 21, but I didn't have Yeshua's Light. I searched through psychedelic drugs, New Age, Hinduism, and yoga. I was searching without Yeshua's Light because of ha-satan's deception.

As a Jew, I thought of Yeshua as the leader of the religion that had persecuted my people, so, I didn't want His light, but I kept getting burned, growing bad fruit, and reaping destruction. It seemed like I'd been stumbling in the dark all my life.

Ten years later, at the age of 31, because people were praying for me, I decided to put my trust in Yeshua and committed myself to following Him. It was like a light turned on, and I could see the Truth—the Truth about the importance of the spiritual laws of God and that Truth was in the Bible. It

14. CONNECTED BY LIGHT

was like a blindfold came off my eyes and I understood the spiritual side of life! The Truth was obvious—things had gone bad because I wasn't obeying Him, and I began to experience God's blessings, and found a purpose for my life.

But, when you don't trust in Him, don't obey His teaching, and don't seek to know Him, you will continue to stumble in spiritual darkness and deception. If you feel like you've been stumbling through life in the dark, the Holy Spirit is inviting you today to put your trust in Yeshua. If you do, He will open your spiritual eyes and you'll see the spirit world. But, it's not just a one time turning on of His Light. When you put your trust in Him, He turns the Light on, opens your eyes, but, only in the areas of your life which you yield to His guidance.

If you trust Him for finances, His Light will shine on your finances. What will you see when He shines His Light on your finances? Tithing, give and it shall be given, honesty, responsibility, self control.

If you don't trust Him in relationships His Light won't shine on your relationships. What will you see when He shines His Light on your relationships? Faithfulness and patience, who you should be close with and who not, who you are angry with, and who you have to forgive.

If you trust Him for health, His Light will shine on your physical condition. What will you see when He shines His Light on health? Spiritual roots, moderation, exercise, diet, motivation, etc.

If you don't trust Him for your relationship with Him, He won't shine His Light on your worship. What will you see when He shines His light on your worship? What's keeping you from really connecting with Him? Idols, fear? What's keeping you from doing it frequently? Busyness, priorities?

If you trust Him for your future, your career and ministry, He will shine His Light on those things, and what will you see? If you have any stubbornness, false expectations, fears, greed, or ego, it will all be exposed.

How valuable is this Light? How valuable is the ability to see into the spirit world and to understand Truth? The Ruakh spoke to me through an experience about the value of physical light or sight. I had two critical problems with my eyes a few years ago. I had the sudden appearance of thousands of specks, floaters in my right eye. The optometrist said it could lead to retinal damage if not treated immediately. How fast did I get in to have it checked? Faster than lightning!

It was material that had broken off and was floating around in my eye. Praise the Lord, there was no damage. Over time the specks were absorbed and disappeared.

Then a month later it happened in my left eye. This time I was really concerned. I got in to the retinal specialist immediately and he found a small tear in my retina. I needed laser treatment to keep it from growing. I was so thankful for the procedure because it saved my sight. How much would I have been willing to pay for that procedure? A lot! Why? Because it made me realize how precious sight and light is.

After the laser repair, I came back in to be checked. I thought this would keep happening and could keep needing repair. The doctor said it is a very common occurrence for this part of the eye to break off. Once it does, there's nothing more to break off, so it won't happen again. His statement brought great relief and gratitude for his expertise. That knowledge was like light to me. The light of knowledge is very valuable.

If the light of physical sight and the light of knowledge are so valuable, how much more precious is spiritual sight and Light? Gaining more spiritual Light, more understanding of God's ways and the spirit world is my lifelong, ongoing quest. I want greater understanding of how those spiritual laws work, how they affect my life and the lives of my loved ones. I need Yeshua's Light to continue to be a lamp to my feet and a light to my path. There's lots more for me to learn, how about you? Are you hungry to have more Light?

> Luke 11:9-10 *"Moreover, I myself say to you: keep asking, and it will be given to you; keep seeking, and you will find; keep knocking, and the door will be opened to you. 10 For everyone who goes on asking receives; and he who goes*

on seeking finds; and to him who continues knocking, the door will be opened.

God will honor your desire for more Light. If you feel like you've been stumbling through life in the dark, the Ruakh HaKodesh is inviting you today to put your trust in Yeshua in every area of your life. If you do, He will open your spiritual eyes and you'll see the spirit world.

Let's pray.

Thank You, Father, for Sukkot starting the Season of Lights even as our days shorten. Thank You for being the Light of the World. Thank You for being the Truth, for giving us Your Word which is Truth. We don't want to walk in spiritual darkness any more, nor in the shadow of death. We put our trust in You, Yeshua, in Your atoning sacrifice with all our heart. We acknowledge You in all our ways and trust You will direct our paths.

Shine your Light on us. Help us to understand the spiritual laws of the universe and apply them to our lives. Be a lamp for our feet and a light for our paths. We want to continually have more Light in our lives so we will keep on asking, seeking, and knocking.

Show us areas where Your light has not penetrated—finances, relationships, health, future, relationship with You, etc. Shine Your Light on those areas, we pray, and we will repent and surrender to You. In Yeshua's Name, we pray. Amein.

Section 5

PROPHETIC

CHAPTER 15

Sukkot Themes in Prophecies About the Future

So now, let's take a look at how Sukkot is connected through prophesy to the future. One of the traditional readings on Sukkot is Zechariah 14. Zechariah wrote his prophesies about 2,600 years ago, and several of them, along with some of Isaiah's reveal how Yeshua will fulfill Sukkot in the future. We will be going back and forth between Zechariah 12-14 and Isaiah 4. I think you will be surprised at all the Sukkot themes in these passages. Here Isaiah is speaking of a day still yet in the future:

> Isaiah 4:5 *[T]hen ADONAI will create over the whole area of Mount Zion and over her convocations [*מִקְרָא *miqra (not* עֲצֶרֶת *atzeret)], a cloud by day, and smoke and shining of a flaming fire by night. For over all, glory will be a canopy.*
>
> Isaiah 4:5 (NKJV) *...the LORD will create above every dwelling place of Mount Zion, and above her assemblies, a cloud and smoke by day and the shining of a flaming fire by night. ...*
>
> Isaiah 4:5b (CJB) *...for the Glory will be over everything like a hupah.*

This is the Sukkot theme. Do you see it? Sukkot is for reminding us of when the Israelites lived in sukkot in the wilderness, right? And there's that manifest presence again of God being among them in the form of the pillar of cloud and of fire. Notice that it's not just the Temple, but it says in the NKJV, over all the dwelling places and their assemblies. In other words, all the houses will be houses of worship. Making your home a place of worship is a good thing for us to do. (That word for assemblies is the normal word מִקְרָא *miqra*, used many times. It's not the special one, עֲצֶרֶת *atzeret*, used for the Eighth Day.)

And notice that the *canopy* or *covering* is actually the Hebrew word *khupah* that the CJB translates correctly but transliterates incorrectly.. This connects the future fulfilling of Sukkot by Yeshua with the *wedding feast of the Lamb* in Revelations:

> Revelations 19:7-9 *"Let us rejoice and be glad! Let us give him the glory! For the time has come for the wedding of the Lamb, and his Bride has prepared herself —8 fine linen, bright and clean has been given her to wear." ("Fine linen" means the righteous deeds of God's people.) 9 The angel said to me, "Write: 'How blessed are those who have been invited to the wedding feast of the Lamb!'" Then he added, "These are God's very words."*

So this wedding will be during this future fulfilling of Sukkot! The very next verse in Isaiah confirms it:

> Isaiah 4:6 *Then there will be a sukkah for shade by day from the heat, and for refuge and for shelter from storm and from rain.*

The word "*sukkah*" there is *"tabernacle"* in your English Bibles, but it is actually the Hebrew word *"sukkah."* There will be a Sukkah over Jerusalem. Can you imagine how big that Sukkah will be? This Sukkah over Jerusalem is definitely not flimsy because besides providing for shade and refuge, it provides shelter from the storm! This is God's Sukkah. It is strong and safe. And there's that theme of dependence on God, this time for protection from the storm and the rain and the scorching sun.

Now let's go backwards to verse 3 to look at some other connections with Sukkot there.

> Isaiah 4:3 *So it will come to pass that whoever is left in Zion and whoever remains in Jerusalem will be called holy—everyone who is recorded among the living in Jerusalem.*

Now you have to understand what is happening. The prophet is connecting with the book of Zechariah here. Zechariah lived after Isaiah, but somehow in the Spirit, these two books are connected. The ones who are left in Zion are the ones who are the survivors of the great battle in Jerusalem that is described in Zechariah chapters 12-14. I encourage you to read that and really get to know it because it is a very relevant passage for today. It is the passage that has the part about Jerusalem becoming a cup of trembling that will make all the nations around it stumble and that all the nations will come and besiege Jerusalem, and then there will be war. We will look into all that in the next chapter.

So these are the survivors of that battle of Jerusalem and it says that they will be called holy—everyone who is recorded among the living. And then the next verse:

> Isaiah 4:4 *After ADONAI has washed away the filth of the Daughters of Zion and has purged the blood of Jerusalem from her midst by the spirit of judgment and by the spirit of burning,*

Now here we see another one of those themes that we saw in the Tabernacle in the desert, that it was a place for cleansing. It was a place for making atonement. And there's going to be a cleansing of Israel, making them righteous, enabling the manifest presence of God to be there. Then in Zechariah 12, there is an amazing passage. It speaks about all Israel that survives recognizing Him whom they have pierced, and mourning for Him as one mourns for an only son. Then right after that section, it comes to this verse:

> Zechariah 13:1 (NKJV) *In that day a fountain shall be opened for the house of David and for the inhabitants of Jerusalem, for sin and for uncleanness.*

Do you see how that is connected to Isaiah 4? That's the cleansing fountain doing the "washing away" that Isaiah is speaking about in chapter 4. And that's going to happen

15. SUKKOT THEMES IN PROPHECY

through the Jewish people recognizing Yeshua as the Messiah as it says in Zechariah 12.

What is the liquid going to be in that cleansing fountain? Yes, it is the Blood of the Messiah! That's the cleansing agent in that fountain. It is Yeshua's Blood that will enable the presence of God to dwell in all of Yerushalayim (Jerusalem). Let's read verse 5 again because this comes after that cleansing.

> Isaiah 4:5-6 *Then ADONAI will create over the whole area of Mount Zion and over her convocations, a cloud by day, and smoke and shining of a flaming fire by night. For over all, glory will be a canopy* [covering or khupah]. *6 Then there will be a sukkah for shade by day from the heat, and for refuge and for shelter from storm and from rain.*

Now another interesting connection I found that I never understood before is that God has to remove one covering before He brings another covering. Did you know that there is already a covering over Yerushalayim, actually over all the nations? Let's look at Isaiah 25. I believe this is going to happen just before He puts the covering or canopy on of Isaiah 4.

> Isaiah 25:7a *On this mountain...*

That same mountain, Mount Zion.

> Isaiah 25:7 *On this mountain He will swallow up the shroud that enfolds all peoples, the veil spread over all nations.*

Not just Israel, but all the nations. Then in the next verse he explains what that covering is! Listen to this. It is amazing.

> Isaiah 25:8 *He will swallow up death forever. My Lord ADONAI will wipe away tears from every face. He will remove His people's reproach from all the earth. For ADONAI has spoken.*

Do you see what that is? There's a veil over the whole earth now, the veil of death that came in from the Garden of Eden with the sin of Adam and Eve. This verse is speaking about that time when death will be defeated as it says in I Corinthians 15 and in the Book of Revelation 20. And here it is in Isaiah—way back in Isaiah. He will remove that veil, and *"He will swallow up death forever,"* and then He will put His covering, His khupah over them that is spoken of in Isaiah 4.

So that's some of the future connections concerning the sukkah. Now let's look at the connections with the branches and the fruit.

> Isaiah 4:2 *In that day the Branch of A<small>DONAI</small> will be beautiful and glorious, and the fruit of the land excellent and appealing for Israel's survivors.*

So right there we see that there is someone called the "Branch of ADONAI" who will be "beautiful and glorious." The Hebrew word for *branch* there is *samakh* which means *a branch or a sprout*. Of course, this is a Sukkot theme—the branches and the fruit. Who is that Branch of ADONAI? Yes, it is the Messiah Himself. So the Messiah Himself is the Lulav! It is speaking again in this verse of the manifest presence of God that we are talking about here—the main theme—the manifest presence of God in Messiah being there in Yerushalayim in that future day.

All that we have read so far has been about Israel experiencing Sukkot. Now let's look at calling in all the nations. This happens after the battle. After the Lord has come and defeated the nations that surrounded Yerushalayim, then Yeshua stands on the Mount of Olives. It splits open and Living Water goes out to the east and the west. It is an incredible future event. That is all from Zechariah 12 and 13 and the beginning of 14.

> Zech. 14:16a (CJB) *Finally, everyone remaining from all the nations that came to attack Yerushalayim....*

Before it was just those who were left in Yerushalayim, remember? This is all who are left from the nations who came against Yerushalayim.

> Zech. 14:16b (CJB) *...will go up every year to worship the king, ADONAI-Tzva'ot, and to keep the festival of Sukkot.*

Remember, Sukkot is a harvest Festival of gathering and bringing in the fruit, and this verse is talking about the ingathering of all the nations. But Sukkot is also called the Feast of Ingathering in the Bible:

> Exodus 23:16b *...as well as the Feast of the Ingathering at the end of the year, when you gather your crops from the field.*

15. SUKKOT THEMES IN PROPHECY

Exodus 34:22 *You are to observe the Feast of Shavuot, ...as well as the Feast of Ingathering at the turn of the year.*

All through the Gospels when Yeshua speaks about the angels going out and the people being gathered in, He refers to it as a harvest. Right? The angels are going to go out and reap the harvest. And that is exactly what the imagery is here. There's going to be an ingathering of all the peoples at the end of the age at the time of the return of Yeshua.

Then Gentiles will also keep Sukkot. These verses are why Sukkot is known as the holiday for the Gentiles. We have seen a partial fulfillment of this prediction in our lifetime. Thousands of non-Jews come to Jerusalem each year from all nations to celebrate Sukkot in expectation of this prediction. The pandemic interrupted that, of course. But after this future ingathering, everyone will be required to go to Jerusalem to celebrate Sukkot:

Zech. 14:17 (CJB) *If any of the families of the earth does not go up to Yerushalayim to worship the king, ADONAI-Tzva'ot, no rain will fall on them.*

Right there you see the connection with the prayers for rain on Sukkot. There will be *"no rain"* on those who don't go up to celebrate Sukkot. The nations will worship the Lord on Sukkot in Yerushalayim! I believe that this will be the beginning of what is called the Millennial Kingdom. It will be a thousand year reign when Messiah will be actually physically present in Jerusalem. I mean you will be able to get on an El-Al plane and go there and see Him (*smile*). He will rule the earth with a rod of iron for a thousand years. Ha-satan will be bound and it will be a time of shalom (peace). That will begin on Sukkot with all the nations coming up and celebrating the Feast of Tabernacles.

Since Yeshua's coming is so close, we had a city-wide celebration of Sukkot once (right before covid) because most people don't know how to celebrate this Moad. We wanted to let people know about it, so they will know what they are doing when they go up to Yerushalayim. We don't want them to come and wonder what they are supposed to do. Hopefully, we can do this again soon.

Let's move further down in the chapter to see another one of these themes.

> Zechariah 14:20 (CJB) *When that day comes, this will be written on the bells worn by the horses: "Consecrated to ADONAI"; and the cooking pots in the house of ADONAI will be* [as holy] *as the sprinkling bowls before the altar. 21 Yes, every cooking pot in Yerushalayim and Y'hudah will be consecrated to ADONAI-Tzva'ot. Everyone who offers sacrifices will come, take them and use them to stew the meat. When that day comes, there will no longer be merchants in the house of ADONAI-Tzva'ot.*

I never understood this until I saw the connection with the Tabernacle in the desert being the place where atonement was made, and the people were made holy so the presence of God could dwell amongst them. That is what this is talking about. Even the pots and even the bells on the horses will be holy to ADONAI, so that His presence can be there. So we see that theme of cleansing again.

Notice something else here. Sacrifices will be made. So that is saying that the Temple will be rebuilt. There is a Jewish organization, the Third Temple Institute, that is working right now on being prepared to rebuild that Temple in Yerushalayim.

There is one more passage about the future that I don't know if you have ever connected to Sukkot, but once you see it, you will be amazed at this incredible connection. This is the vision that Yochanan (John) had.

> Revelation 22:1 *Next the angel showed me the river of the water of life, sparkling like crystal, flowing from the throne of God and of the Lamb.*

Remember I mentioned that in Zechariah 14:4, it says Yeshua is going to come and set His feet on the Mount of Olives, and the mountain is going to split and Living water is going to flow to the east and to the west? That is what this is referring to. The "Water of Life" is coming from the "throne of God." Do you see that?

15. SUKKOT THEMES IN PROPHECY

Revelation 22:2 *Between the main street and the river was the Tree of Life producing twelve kinds of fruit, a different kind every month; and the leaves of the tree were for healing the nations—*

This is an amazing Tree. Every month it produces a different kind of fruit. So here we see that same theme of fruit, of a tree and branches, and the nations. Sukkot is the Moad that really connects with the nations because they are the ones that are going to come up and worship at this time.

Sukkot is also a time to think about our future glorious time with Yeshua when He comes to rule and reign.

Let's pray.

Thank You, Father, for all these Sukkot connections. We long to see Your strong Sukkah over Jerusalem, and to be under Your Khupah for the wedding feast of the Lamb. Our hearts will be so full! Our joy will be overflowing!! We look forward longingly to that day!

Thank You, Lord, for the promise of salvation of the people of Israel. We long to see that! Thank You for the promise of the removal of the shroud of death from over all this world, and that all nations will come up to Jerusalem to worship You. We long to see that awesome, amazing day too.

Thank You for the promise of the Water of Life coming forth from the Temple in Jerusalem, and for the promise of the healing power of the leaves of the trees along that River. We look forward so much to seeing all that happen. How marvelous it will be! What glory!

Thank You for strengthening our faith through the amazing connections of all these prophecies. In Yeshua's Name. Amein.

CHAPTER 16
THE BATTLE AND THOUSAND YEAR REIGN

We give thanks for the spiritual fruit harvest on Sukkot. Part of the fruit of the Spirit is faith which comes by hearing God's Word. The prophecies of Zechariah have been instrumental in my life in increasing my faith. So let's look at the future battle in Jerusalem that Zechariah predicted that I mentioned in the last chapter.

> Zechariah 14:3-4 (CJB) *Then ADONAI will go out and fight against those nations, fighting as on a day of battle. 4 On that day his feet will stand on the Mount of Olives, which lies to the east of Yerushalayim; and the Mount of Olives will be split in half from east to west, to make a huge valley. Half of the mountain will move toward the north, and half of it toward the south.*

These two verses predict the physical return of the Messiah. He Himself will fight against the attacking nations. His physical feet will stand on the Mount of Olives. This prediction ties in with a prediction in the Brit Hadashah about His return.

> Acts 1:9-12 *After saying this, he was taken up before their eyes; and a cloud hid him from their sight. 10 As they were staring into the sky after him, suddenly they saw two men dressed in white standing next to them. 11 The men said, "You Galileans! Why are you standing, staring into space? This Yeshua, who has been taken away from you into heaven, will come back to you in just the same way as you saw him go into heaven." 12 Then they returned the Shabbat-walk distance from the Mount of Olives to Yerushalayim.*

16. BATTLE & THOUSAND YEAR REIGN

Yeshua ascended into heaven from the Mount of Olives. Two men (angels) in white told His followers that He will come back in the *"same way as you saw Him go into heaven."* Six hundred years before the disciples heard this from the angels, Zechariah said it!

Now let me tell you about amazingly prophetic things that have been done in that area in Jerusalem by people who don't believe in Yeshua. There is a huge Jewish cemetery on the western slope of the Mount of Olives facing Jerusalem. Even though most Jewish people don't believe Yeshua is the Messiah, many Orthodox Jews believe Zechariah's prediction that the Messiah will appear there first, so they have purchased grave sites there on the Mount of Olives so they can be among the first to be resurrected.

When Jerusalem was under Muslim control, the Eastern gate of the city that faces the Mount of Olives was bricked over by the Muslims to prevent the Messiah from entering as predicted by Zechariah! In addition, the Muslims have put a cemetery just outside that bricked-over gate because they know Jewish people won't step on a grave because the Torah says it would contaminate them and would make them unable to enter the Temple without first going through a long ceremonial cleansing. So by putting the cemetery there, the Muslims are attempting to prevent the Messiah from entering the city and the Temple through that gate!

Let's look at some of the other amazing predictions in Zechariah 14. Here's one I mentioned in the last chapter:

> Zechariah 14:8 (CJB) *On that day, fresh water will flow out from Yerushalayim, half toward the eastern sea and half toward the western sea, both summer and winter.*

This river is also described by the prophet Ezekiel and by John in Revelation 22. In Ezekiel 47, its water brings life to the Dead Sea in the East.

> Zechariah 14:9 (CJB) *Then ADONAI will be king over the whole world. On that day ADONAI will be the only one, and his name will be the only name.*

This simple statement predicts the Messiah ruling the whole earth, reigning as King. John speaks of this:

> Revelation 20:4 *Then I saw thrones, and those seated on them received authority to judge. And I saw the souls of those who had been beheaded for testifying about Yeshua and proclaiming the Word of God, also those who had not worshipped the beast or its image and had not received the mark on their foreheads and on their hands. They came to life and ruled with the Messiah for a thousand years.*

We call this the Millennial Kingdom. This is how Yeshua will fulfill Sukkot. The temporary period of a thousand years when He will reign (and dwell) on the earth will begin on Sukkot, the Moad of temporary dwellings. Where will His throne be located? The White House? The Kremlin? Buckingham Palace? The Knesset? No! He will reign in the Holy of Holies in a rebuilt Temple, on the Temple Mount. Some of Yeshua's followers will help Him rule in that Kingdom. According to Rev. 2:27 and Psalm 2:9, He will rule with a *"rod of iron."* There will be perfect peace, justice, wisdom, and no ha-satan to disrupt. I will love being there, helping Him during those days.

Before that reign, this horrible thing will happen:

> Zechariah 14:12 (CJB) *ADONAI will strike all the peoples who made war against Yerushalayim with a plague in which their flesh rots away while they are standing on their feet, their eyes rot away in their sockets, and their tongues rot away in their mouths.*

This is what the incredible heat of the atomic bomb actually did to the people of Hiroshima and Nagasaki. So it looks like Zechariah was predicting that some kind of atomic weapon will be used against those attacking Jerusalem, something that could not have happened until 1945. How did Zechariah know about the effects of a nuclear attack? He didn't, of course. So it had to be God speaking through Zechariah. This is one passage that caused the spiritual fruit of faith to grow in me. Let's go back to chapter 12 to look again at another faith growing passage.

> Zechariah 12:10 (CJB) *"[A]nd I will pour out on the house of David and on those living in Yerushalayim a spirit of grace and prayer; and they will look to me, whom they pierced." They will mourn for him as one mourns for an only son; they will be in bitterness on his behalf like the bitterness for a firstborn son.*

16. BATTLE & THOUSAND YEAR REIGN

This is a special passage that has also caused the fruit of faith to grow in me. Most Jewish people living in Israel and around the world don't believe Yeshua is the Messiah, but because this Spirit of grace will be poured out upon them, they will recognize the One whom they pierced, Yeshua, God's firstborn Son. Those who had refused before that to believe He is the Messiah will mourn because most Jewish people have rejected Him for centuries. Now this verse again:

> Zechariah 13:1 *In that day a spring will be opened to the house of David and to the inhabitants of Jerusalem to cleanse them from sin and impurity.*

This *spring* (*fountain* in other translations) will cleanse people from sin. Again what cleanses people from sin? Yeshua's Blood! So this is the spring of Messiah's Blood that cleanses us from sin. There's an old hymn about this, written by William Cowper in 1771. Here are the first two of the five verses:

> There is a fountain filled with blood
>   Drawn from Immanuel's veins;
> And sinners, plunged beneath that flood,
>   Lose all their guilty stains.
>
> The dying thief rejoiced to see
>   That fountain in his day;
> And there may I, though vile as he,
>   Wash all my sins away.

So far we know what time of year this siege of Jerusalem will occur. When? Right before Sukkot. We even know what weapons will be used in the battle. Nuclear. But what about what year it will occur? That leads us to another Zachariah passage that has also grown fruit of faith in me.

> Zechariah12:2 (CJB) *"I will make Yerushalayim a cup that will stagger the surrounding people. Even Y'hudah (Judea) will be caught up in the siege against Yerushalayim.*

What kind of a drink causes people to stagger? Strong alcoholic drink. People who drink from it will stagger like drunkards. Who are the people surrounding Jerusalem today? Palestinians. This prediction is being fulfilled today. From 1917 to 1948 Great Britain ruled all of Israel and Jordan. In May of 1948 a UN resolution created two states, one Jewish, one Arab. The Jordan River—east of Jerusalem—was to be the border. Israel accepted the resolution; the Arabs did not. The Jordanian Arab army attacked and occupied the Old City of Jerusalem and the Temple Mount. The Old City contained a Jewish neighborhood. Jews living there had to flee. For nineteen years, Jerusalem was divided. Jordan controlled the Old City; and Israel the new.

Then in 1967, four Arab nations attacked Israel, but were driven back by the Israeli army, the IDF. This miraculous victory brought the Old City of Jerusalem back under Israeli control again and was annexed.

Since the Oslo Accords in the 1990s, Israel has been willing to give the Palestinians almost all the land they want for their own state, except Jerusalem. But, the Palestinians won't accept that. They keep insisting on having Jerusalem as their capital. Whenever the negotiations focus on the future borders of Jerusalem, they break down. Jerusalem has become a cup that causes the surrounding people to behave foolishly, as if they are drunk. The Palestinians' refusal to accept almost all the land they want without Jerusalem is the fulfillment of this prophesy of foolish behavior.

Judea is the territory surrounding Israel—also caught up in this dispute. The Palestinians are demanding to be given places where Israelis have already settled. Israelis continue to build in areas they believe will be theirs. These verses sound like they came from today's news.

> Zechariah12:3 (CJB) *When that day comes, I will make Yerushalayim a heavy stone for all the peoples. All who try to lift it will hurt themselves,...*

Other translations say, *all who try to move it will hurt themselves*. How can you move a city? Certainly not by physically picking it up, but by changing its borders or by changing who it belongs to. All who try to change its borders will injure themselves, like when someone tries to lift something too heavy for them and injures their back or it causes a hernia.

16. BATTLE & THOUSAND YEAR REIGN

This is a warning to the U.S. and other nations that if they pressure Israel to give up Jerusalem to the Palestinians, they will injure themselves.

> Zechariah 12:3 (CJB) ... *and all the earth's nations will be massed against her.*

This hasn't happened completely yet, but it is close. A large majority of the UN nations are Muslim or Communist. Since 1980, they have used the UN as a means of attacking Israel. Only the U.S. and its western allies stand with Israel.

Zechariah says someday all the nations will actually attack Israel. We can see how close this day is by the rate the attacks have intensified, and by how many nations turn against Israel: Arab spring – Egypt; Flotilla incident – Turkey.

Why are these nations turning? It's the David and Goliath effect. From 1948 to 1972 the media saw Israel as little David fighting the giant Arab Goliath. Since the Palestinian intifada began in the 1980s, the Palestinians are seen as David and Israel is seen as evil Goliath.

The Palestinians have visited heads of states and nations on the UN Security Council, nations from all over the world, to convince them to vote for Palestinian statehood.

These Scriptures show the supernatural inspiration of the Bible. Amazingly, Zechariah is actually predicting today's current events. This is only possible if it is inspired by God who is outside of time. God put these predictions in the Bible as proof He inspired it. These predictions and their being worked out in current events have greatly increased my faith in the validity of the Bible.

But, you may be thinking, "They may increase your faith, Rabbi Jim, but, they don't increase my faith. They just increase my fear." Why do they increase my faith? Because I have chosen to obey what Yeshua said when discussing the future and His return with His disciples.

> Luke 21:28 (NKJV) *Now when these things begin to happen, look up and lift up your heads, because your redemption draws near.*

What does "*look up and lift up your heads*" mean? It means to be expectant that Yeshua's return is coming soon.

Psalm 27:5 *For in the day of trouble He will hide me in His sukkah, conceal me in the shelter of His tent, and set me high upon a rock.*

Trust Him! He will be with you through the turbulent times! He will hide us in His Sukkah!

Let's pray.

Thank You, Father, for putting proof of predicting the future into the Bible, so our faith in it will be strengthened. Help any who doubt to put their trust in Your Word through these passages as they see them coming to pass. Help us to trust that other things You say in the Bible are the Truth and to be obedient to those Words and live by them.

We pray, Father, for Godly leadership for the Palestinians who would be able to be obedient to Your will. We pray for the soon fulfilling of that prophecy, that the Spirit of grace will be poured out on Israel, so Israelis will come to believe in Yeshua, their Messiah. We thank You that many are. We pray for more and more until the nation as a whole recognizes and receives.

And, Father, we pray that the United States will not be one of those nations trying to move Jerusalem, or one of the nations attacking Jerusalem. We pray the U.S. will always stand as a support to Israel. Protect our nation from false leaders who would go against You or would do anything against Israel. We pray for revival across our whole nation that all would turn to You from the least to the greatest. We pray this for the whole world. Please bring repentance and revival, we pray, Father.

We pray, Father, for faith for everyone reading this book to look up and lift up their heads to trust that You will be with us as we go through turbulent times. You will hide us in Your strong Sukkah for our protection. We thank You for that, Father. In Yeshua's Name we pray. Amein.

CHAPTER 17
Before and After the Millennial Reign

We will now look, in this chapter, at the rest of the story of what led up to the Battle of Jerusalem and what will happen after the thousand year reign, after the Millennial Kingdom, and how the whole story fits together into God's plan over the centuries. As you read this chapter, keep in mind that Yeshua said, *When you see these things begin to take place*—What did He say we're supposed to do? *Lift up your heads because your redemption is drawing near.*

So just to recap a bit. We showed the amazing, divine inspiration of the Word of God in three prophecies about Israel and Jerusalem that the prophet Zechariah made some 2600 years ago. A couple of them have been fulfilled and one of them is yet to be fulfilled.

The first one was that Jerusalem will be like a cup of strong alcoholic drink that causes the surrounding people to act foolishly. Second, Zechariah predicted that all who try to change or move Jerusalem's borders would injure themselves. Then finally, he predicted that more and more nations would turn against Israel, and we're seeing this even today as Egypt and Turkey, and some of our own government people have turned against Israel from being allies in the past.

It is just amazing that we can see these predictions coming to pass in our day. It should be proof to you that the Word of

God, the Bible, was inspired by God who is outside of time, and it should strengthen your faith.

We also read Zechariah's predictions of some great conflicts between the forces of our enemy ha-satan and God's people. He tells about a siege of Jerusalem that is coming. And then there's Yeshua's return to destroy Israel's enemies.

That conflict between ha-satan and God's people has it's roots all the way back in the beginning in Genesis. Do you know that at the end of Sukkot, the Parashah reading comes to the end of the Torah scroll? Then we have to roll it up from the end back to the beginning. So I want to start this chapter in that first Parashah that comes after the scroll is rolled back up, Genesis chapters 1 - 6. It contains the first incident in this conflict between ha-satan and human beings. It's the wonderful account of creation and then the terrible account of the fall of man caused by ha-satan's deception. So just after the fall, speaking to the serpent, we read what God said.

> Genesis 3:15 *I will put animosity between you and the woman—between your seed and her seed. He will crush your head, and you will crush his heel.*

Some translations say *enmity* instead of *animosity*. The Hebrew word is אֵיבָה *eyva,* which means *hatred, contention,* and *conflict*. This is the first prediction in the Bible. God predicts this conflict between ha-satan and Eve's offspring. And who is the serpent's seed? Well, that would be the spirits allied with ha-satan, evil spirits. Who is the woman's seed? That would be us! That would be human beings. And, of course, we've had enmity and animosity, we've been in conflict in this great battle for about 6000 years now.

But there's something interesting about this prophecy. The Bible usually uses the term *seed* for the descendants of men. If you think about it, the term is used in the seed of Abraham, the seed of Israel, the seed of Jacob, but here it refers to the seed of a woman. So in this prophecy, I believe we also see that it points to the Messiah because Yeshua was the only person who was the seed of a woman but not the seed of a natural man. And ha-satan bruising the heel of Eve's seed, Yeshua, we can say is Him being nailed to the Cross by his feet, or as many think, through the heel. And Messiah bruising ha-satan's head refers to a head blow, a fatal blow, which Yeshua did by defeating him on the Cross. He will finish the blow when He returns to reign on the earth.

So there's been this animosity between the two, this constant conflict between ha-satan and the descendants of Adam and Eve. This conflict began with ha-satan deceiving Eve in the garden. I'm sure you're familiar with the story of her deception. The conflict went on for another 1600 years to what, I think you will agree with me, is the low point of human existence:

> Genesis 6:6 *So ADONAI regretted that He made humankind on the earth, and His heart was deeply pained.*

It pained and grieved God's heart. I don't think we could've gotten any lower than that. Just think about this. God was basically saying, "I can't work with these people anymore. There's nothing I can do to turn them around. They've all gone so far down that slippery slope of iniquity that there's nothing I can do to stop them. I can't fix them!"

His only recourse was to wipe out all of the evil. We all know what happened. He only allowed one family to survive. So how did this decline happen in those 1600 years? Well, ha-satan used the same tactics he used on Eve. Deception. The reason we are all here today as descendants of Noah is because that one man refused to listen to ha-satan's lies.

So that was a low point. As I thought on this, I wondered why we who have lived after the flood haven't become as corrupt as the people who lived before the flood. It's been something like 5000 years. Yes, we're pretty bad, but not so bad that God has had to wipe us out completely. I began to see that soon after the flood, God began putting His Spirit on certain people, and began sending His Word.

He established His covenant with one family, the descendants of Abraham. He grew one branch of that family into a nation of several million people. He led them out of slavery. He established His Covenant, in writing, with this new nation, Israel. He gave us His Laws and promises, and the promise of our own Land. Then He led us into our promised Land where we could live according to His Laws. He did all this to strengthen the human race in our battle against the enemy.

Then Moses predicted that someday God would send someone like him.

> Deuteronomy 18:15 A‍DONAI *your God will raise up for you a prophet like me from your midst—from your brothers. To him you must listen.*

This is the One who defeated ha-satan, Messiah Yeshua, Himself. When Yeshua came, He strengthened us astronomically more by providing atonement. This enabled us each to have a relationship with God Himself.

And the biggest difference, I believe, is He enabled His Spirit to live within us. And through His Spirit living in us, He gave us spiritual weapons, the only kind that are truly effective against ha-satan. He gave us His Word, His Blood, the Truth, His righteousness, our salvation, the Good News of the Gospel, the guidance and power of His Spirit, a measure of faith for each of us, the power of praise, the power of His Name, and the power of prayer. And the Bible says we have His mind, the mind of Messiah. All these things are mighty weapons against the enemy.

Because of Yeshua, there's been a change in this conflict. Sometimes I think we forget that this is really what's going on. Today, we, God's people, are on the offensive. Do you believe that? Some people think we are on the defensive. But look what Yeshua said!

> Matthew 16:18 (KJV) ...*upon this rock I will build my church;* and **the gates of hell shall not prevail against it**.

Gates are defensive. We are on the offensive, tearing down the gates of hell around individuals and setting them free! Many have been set free because people have engaged in this warfare and have used these weapons and prayed for them! That's how I was set free. The gates came down around me and I was able to enter the Kingdom of God.

There's been a change. We are the aggressors and the conquerers. (For more on how to operate as aggressors over the enemy, ha-satan and his hordes, see my *Counting the Omer* book, "Red Sea to Mt. Sinai" section, Week 6, page 167.)

There's another turning point coming in this conflict. The time is coming when Yeshua will put ha-satan in a pit in chains for a thousand years. And so there will be shalom. That's called the Millennial reign of Messiah. But before that time there will be great tribulation described by John in Revelations: famine, earthquakes, and wars, great judgments on humanity for our disobedience. But now let's take a look at John's vision beyond that of what comes after the thousand year reign.

> Revelation 20:7-9 *When the thousand years are over, the Adversary will be set free from his prison 8 and will go out to deceive the nations in the four quarters of the earth, Gog and Magog, to gather them for the battle. Their number is countless as the sand on the seashore; 9 and they came up over the breadth of the Land and surrounded the camp of God's people and the city he loves.*

So here we read about a final rebellion against God. Notice the *"city that He loves"* term. This really struck me. What city would that be? Yes, Jerusalem, of course. So this will happen in the land of Israel because that's where Jerusalem is. I don't know why God releases the enemy for another period of time. Do You? But for some reason He does. However, we can take hope in the rest of verse 9:

> Revelation 20:9b *But fire came down from heaven and consumed them.*

So this time the forces of darkness will be defeated forever.

> Revelation 20:10 *The Adversary who had deceived them was hurled into the lake of fire and sulfur, where the beast and the false prophet were; and they will be tormented day and night forever and ever.*

This is the final destiny of ha-satan and his hordes, when Yeshua will finish crushing his head, that fatal blow, and he will be punished forever.

Revelation 20:11 *Next I saw a great white throne and the One sitting on it. Earth and heaven fled from his presence, and no place was found for them.*

If you've ever heard that term used, "the great white throne," this is the verse that it comes from.

Revelation 20:12 *And I saw the dead, both great and small, standing in front of the throne. Books were opened; and another book was opened, the Book of Life; and the dead were judged from what was written in the books, according to what they had done.*

This is the time when all the dead will be resurrected to face the judgment of God. An earlier verse talks about the seas even giving up their dead. Notice it said that there are books, plural. This is where we get the understanding that God has a book on every person. On you and me, there's a book. He has a book on me that records all that I have done, all that I have said, and even, I believe, all that I have thought. He's got that in a hard drive somewhere up there. And some day it's going to be opened.

It makes me think of the movie, "Bruce Almighty." God takes him up there and shows him this file cabinet, and God opens the file on him, and the drawer goes out like a hundred feet. It was a great scene.

Did you know that Moses mentions the Book of Life? Look here:

Exodus 32:31-33 *Then Moses returned to Adonai and said, "Alas, these people have sinned greatly, and made gods of gold! 32 Yet now, please forgive their sin. But if not, please blot me out of Your book that You have written." 33 Adonai said to Moses, "Whoever has sinned against Me, I will blot out of My book."*

Do you see that? From this we can ascertain that our names are all written in the Book of Life when we are born, and we stay there until we've sinned against God beyond measure! This was before Yeshua's sacrifice when there were many sins that could not be atoned for by animal sacrifices. Idolatry was one of those sins. So if your name is not found in the Book of Life at the end of the age, it means it was blotted out when your last chance for repentance before you died was over.

17. BEFORE AND AFTER THE MILLENNIUM

Revelation 20:15 *Anyone whose name was not found written in the Book of Life was hurled into the lake of fire.*

As we saw in verse 10 on page 203, this punishment doesn't end. This is a hard thing. There's a lot of Bible teachers who don't say this these days. But it says in verse 10 that the torment in this *lake of fire* goes on *day and night forever and ever.* And it says here in verse 15 that anyone whose name is not written in the Book of Life will be cast into that lake of fire.

Revelation 21:1 *Then I saw a new heaven and a new earth, for the old heaven and the old earth had passed away, and the sea was no longer there.*

This goes beyond my imagination. I don't know if this is a new planet or a new universe. And how about the new heaven? Is that a new heaven around the earth or the place where God is in Heaven? I don't know. Then John sees some more interesting things.

Revelation 21:2 *Also I saw the holy city, New Yerushalayim, coming down out of heaven from God, prepared like a bride beautifully dressed for her husband.*

Artists portray this as a cube because of the measurements given. It comes down out of Heaven. Some people think it's like a pyramid shape. We don't know. I hope to find out some day.

Revelation 21:3 *I heard a loud voice from the throne say, "See! God's Sh'khinah [Glory] is with mankind, and he will live with them. They will be his people, and he himself, God-with-them, will be their God.*

So at this time, in this new city on the new earth, God's presence will be very real. Then here's what I think is the best news out of all this:

Revelation 21:4 *He will wipe away every tear from their eyes. There will no longer be any death; and there will no longer be any mourning, crying or pain; because the old order has passed away.*

That's the ultimate good news! No more death. No more pain. No more sorrow. This is my great hope for the future, a world much better than this one. These predictions increase my faith. And as I said, I've chosen to obey this that Yeshua said:

Luke 21:28 (NKJV) *Now when these things begin to happen, look up and lift up your heads, because your redemption draws near."*

So I hope you are in a place where you can look up. We can hold our heads up because our redemption is drawing near. So now let's dig into what this actually means to look up and lift our heads? First of all, it means that as followers of Yeshua, we should be eagerly expectant that His return is coming soon. Be confident that you are one of His chosen, and that He will bring you through all of these judgments and frightening events that we see here, that He will stand by you at that great white throne judgment and when your name comes up, and they are about to open your book, Yeshua will say, "This one is mine. I paid his/her penalty." And the One who sits on the throne will look at your name still in the Book of Life, not erased, will close your book and say, "Case dismissed." That's what we should lift up our heads expecting. This should increase our faith.

But, you may again be thinking, "That may increase your faith, Rabbi Jim, but, it doesn't increase my faith. It just increases my fear." You might be wondering, "What will happen to me when I stand at that great white throne and my book is opened?" Well, if you are not one of His chosen, there is every reason for you to be afraid.

You need assurance that you are one of His chosen ones, that He will intervene for you at the judgment seat and will bring you safely through the wars of the tribulation. There's only one way to have that assurance. I want to share that with you in case you have even a little bit of doubt.

Here's how you can have that assurance. First of all, recognize that you have fallen short of God's standards and have broken his Laws, in action, in words, and in thoughts, and take responsibility for that breaking of His Laws and don't blame it on other people. Take responsibility for what the Bible calls your own sins. And then repent, which means more than just to say you're sorry. It certainly means to say you're sorry, but you've got to turn away from that, and then realize that you can't pay the penalty for the things that you've done against

God. The price is way too high. There's no way anyone can pay the penalty. You must receive Yeshua's sacrifice to pay for your sin and receive God's undeserved forgiveness for you. Then commit yourself to following the leading of God's Holy Spirit to help you obey Him in the future and to help you receive His assurance that you are His child. Then you can know Him, and He'll lead you and guide you and protect you and live in you, even through the frightening events that are predicted here.

So that's the first step to lifting up your head. You can't lift up your head and be expectant and wanting the Lord's return unless you've done that. And we're going to pray later together if there's anything in you that says, "You know. I'm not ready to endure."

But more than that, once you've done that, you have His soon return to look forward to. I've been amazed, that in the book of Matthew, Yeshua thought that our need to know how to live with the knowledge of His soon return was so important that He gave five messages about this right in a row! It's one thing to repeat what you said because you want to make sure somebody gets it, but can you imagine repeating it five times, and each time giving it in a different way, like in a parable so they get it? If you want to check this out, go to the end of Matthew 24 where there are two and the beginning of Matthew 25 where there are three. So it just runs right through—five times—that He teaches on this subject. We will look at two of them here. The first one is just after Yeshua has made a lot of predictions which would have scared His disciples. We're going to try to glean what He means about how we are to live in these times.

> Matthew 24:42-44 *So stay alert, because you don't know on what day your Lord will come. 43 But you do know this: had the owner of the house known when the thief was coming, he would have stayed awake and not allowed his house to be broken into. 44 Therefore you too must always be ready, for the Son of Man will come when you are not expecting him.*

So here's His first instruction. Stay alert! Live as if Yeshua could return at any moment. He could come a minute from now because when He comes, He will come like a thief in the night. He will return when you're not expecting Him. I have to admit that I don't always manage to obey this. Do you? But I try, and I have found that trying to obey this has had a profound effect on my life on several different levels, and I want to share those with you to see if you can get something out of it.

When I keep that in my mind, that the Lord is coming back, it really helps to keep me from thinking, saying, or doing things that I would not want Him to find me doing when He returns. Do you know what I mean? Things that I would be ashamed of that I think, "I don't want to be doing that when He comes." I don't know what that would be for you, but there are a few things like that for me. You know, it's silly to think that way, because we just learned that God has a book where He records everything we do. Right? So it doesn't matter if He didn't come back when we were doing it, it's still recorded there. It doesn't matter that He's not standing right in front of me to see me do what I'm not supposed to be doing, it's still in the book, right? But it still helps me to think that way.

Secondly, staying alert, expecting His coming at any time, prevents me from getting caught up too much in the cares and pleasures of this world. And when I'm really struggling with something, I think,"You know, these things will pass. The Lord's going to come back and everything's going to change." It helps me make time to be with Him now. It helps me to consider spiritual things instead of just the things of this life, of this world. I need to make time to do the work of His Kingdom and not worry about other things.

Thirdly, to me, staying alert means remembering that I am a spirit man living in this body. My body is my sukkah! It's a temporary dwelling place. It means staying alert to the fact that there's spiritual warfare going on around my sukkah and in my mind and around me and the people around me all the time. We need to stay alert to the spiritual nature of our lives. It's like what the shofar is to awaken us up to, that there is a

17. BEFORE AND AFTER THE MILLENNIUM

spiritual side to our lives. It's staying alert to what God is doing in me and in the people around me.

The fourth thing it means is living according to the knowledge that my time for accomplishing anything in my life is limited, not just because I'm in my 70s, but your time, even if you are only in your 20s is limited, too. You have a finite time. And it's not just limited by how old we are. If you're 20 years old, you might say, "Well, I've got a lot more time than you do, Rabbi Jim!" But you might not! The Lord might return before I die, and then we have the same amount of time left. Right?

I remember a quote from Herman Cain who ran for president in 2012. He decided to run after he had stage IV cancer when you're supposed to be dead in a couple months, and he was miraculously healed. This is what he said when asked if that had any effect on his decision to run for president. He said, "It made me painfully aware of how precious life is, and we know not the day when it could be gone. I had been blessed to achieve my American dreams and then some. I know the reason I am totally cancer free is because God wanted me to do something different than stay in cruise control the rest of my life." And that's the point here. He had accomplished great things. He was the CEO of a couple corporations and obviously had a lot of money. He was in his 60s. He could've just sat back without any goals except to enjoy life. But God said, "Turn off the cruise control." He ended up dropping out of the race, but became very active in helping the conservatives. (Sadly, he died in 2020 from the virus.)

I believe part of staying alert is realizing that we have a calling. God has a plan, a goal for us to accomplish.

The second parable also refers to a house. The first one was about a house that got broken into. This one refers to someone who is a servant in the house, and he's left in charge when his master goes away.

> Matthew 24:45-47 *Who is the faithful and sensible servant whose master puts him in charge of the household staff, to give them their food at the proper time? 46 It will go well with that servant if he is found doing his job when his master*

comes. 47 Yes, I tell you that he will put him in charge of all he owns.

So in this parable, God is the master of His house, and we, His followers, are His servants. So what He's saying here is that our goal should be more than just not being spiritually asleep. Our goal should be to be found serving Him, doing our job for Him when He returns. This would be like working for a boss that is usually out of sight, but he frequently appears without any warning. Have you worked on a job like that? I have. Actually, most people really dislike that. You may not be happy with it, but it does make you more diligent. "I can't slough off because who knows, I might be checking social media on my phone and there he comes!" So that's how alert we are to be.

This parable is about a servant put in charge of the house, so really this is about leaders. It's about anyone with responsibility over other people whether at home or at your job or in your congregation. In our congregation, we have small group leaders who are considered under-shepherds, and then we have people in charge of functions like worship, outreach, finances, etc. So the parable promises that if we faithfully care for our fellow servants or for the ministry God has given us for as long as it takes until He returns, we will be greatly rewarded.

But then the warning is actually very unpleasant.

Matthew 24:48-51 But if that servant is wicked and says to himself, 'My master is taking his time'; 49 and he starts beating up his fellow servants and spends his time eating and drinking with drunkards; 50 then his master will come on a day the servant does not expect, at a time he doesn't know; 51 and he will cut him in two and put him with the hypocrites, where people will wail and grind their teeth!

Not a pleasant picture. So if we're not faithful until He returns, if we take advantage of our position, the punishment will be much greater than that in the first parable where the person just lost the reward because he didn't stay alert.

If we think of history, this was the downfall of many of Israel's kings. That's exactly what David did. "Oh, I can take that woman because I'm the king." This is a timely warning, considering all the leaders in Messiah's Body who have fallen in recent times, causing a real mess. Usually they fall because they take the money, or a relationship, or the glory for themselves.

So you might be thinking, "Whew! I don't have to worry about that because God hasn't assigned me to be in charge of anything! And I'm going to keep away from that because this is dangerous!" Right? "I'm not a ministry leader, so I don't have to worry about this." Well, we all have responsibility for something or someone. Certainly your children and your spouse. But even if you don't have children or a spouse, God has given us all the responsibility to be praying for others, and to be a witness and an example to those around us, our extended family, our neighborhoods, our schools, our workplaces. In a sense, we are His representative, His ambassador there. This is part of it. When He comes back He wants to find that you have been praying for your neighborhood, for your school, for your coworkers, and you have been witnessing to them and sharing with them.

So if we are diligent in taking care of the responsibilities that God has given us as if Yeshua were to come back today and evaluate our work today, that's what He is saying to us about how we are to live in these days. It's a heavy charge.

There are three more parables about this, the ten bridesmaids, the talents, and the sheep and the goats that you can read and learn more about how to be ready for Yeshua's return.

Let's pray.

Lord, we thank You for the predictions of the amazing and frightening things that are coming.

[If you are not completely sure that you are a citizen of the Kingdom of God, that you are His child, that He will bring you safely through all these events and the judgment, I'd like you to pray this prayer right now.]

Father, I recognize that I've fallen short of Your standards. I've broken your Laws written in Your Book in my actions, words, and thoughts. I take responsibility for disobeying You, for sinning. I repent of this. I turn away from disobedience, and I confess my sins to You. I realize, Lord, that I can't possibly pay the penalty for my sin. The price is way to high. I ask you to forgive me. I receive Yeshua's atoning sacrifice to pay for my sin. I receive Your undeserved forgiveness, and I thank You, Lord, for Your great grace and mercy. I ask You to fill me with Your Ruakh and dwell within me. I commit myself to following the leading of Your Spirit, and obeying You. Help me obey You in the future. And I ask, Lord, that I would receive assurance that I am Your child, that I have been born from above, that there's a place reserved for me with You in Your Heaven, that my name is written in Your Book of Life and will not be blotted out, and that You will guide me and protect me from all these coming frightening events. In Yeshua's Name. Amein.

[Now for us believers. If you just prayed that prayer, you are now also a believer!]

Father, give us hope for that future world that is better than this one, a world without death, without pain, without sorrow, and without tears. Lord, we want to see that world. Help us, Lord, to live each day as if you are returning today. Keep us from doing, saying, or thinking anything You would not want to find us doing when You return, oh Lord. Make that be an image in our brain whenever we are tempted, "Well, why don't you do this. Nobody will see it." Make that image of You standing right in front of us to pop into our brain to help us stand strong and firm; or an image of a page in a book and of someone writing on it where it's being recorded, or of someone typing on a laptop, or even more for today of someone holding up their phone, recording it!

Father, keep us from getting caught up in the cares and pleasures of this world. Help us to keep our eyes on You. Keep us awake and alert spiritually, so we can see what's happening. Help us to see, Lord, the battle that we're facing, the enemy who is a spirit, who is not flesh and blood. Help us to see that we need to battle in the spirit, Oh Lord, with the spiritual weapons that You have given us. Help us to realize that our battle is not against people, that people are not our enemy. It's the enemy working through them against us.

Father, help us to live as if our time is short because we don't know when our time is up. We don't know when You are coming.

Finally, Lord, help us to fulfill the responsibilities that You've given us, caring for Your people, for the work of Your Kingdom, interceding for people, being ambassadors and intercessors in the places where You have placed us.

We thank You, Lord, for Your soon coming return. We pray that would just stick with us, that You are coming soon and to walk with our heads lifted up.

[Lift up your head right now.]

Lord, we lift our heads to You!!!

[Wave your Lulav, lift up your head, and shout!]

My redemption is drawing near!! Thank You, Lord!!! Thank You!!! In Yeshua's Name. Amein.

CHAPTER 18
A Special History Tour of Israel

I want to share about the time my daughter Elizabeth and I recently spent in Israel. Let me just start out by explaining the reason for this tour. We went with a group called **The Jerusalem Institute of Justice** which is a ministry that our congregation has been supporting for many years. They are attorneys who advocate for Messianic Jews that are trying to make aliyah, trying to immigrate to Israel. They also advocate for other righteous causes in Israel like pro-life and stopping prostitution, etc. So they sent an offer for pastors and leaders to go on this tour. I had been on two other tours of Israel, but this was very different. We did visit Biblical sites, which are always awesome connectors to the things we read about in the Bible, like the Garden Tomb, the hill of Calvary, Gethsemane, the Mount of Beatitudes, the Sea of Galilee, Capernaum, all those. I highly recommend seeing them in the flesh. But we were privileged to see some other special sites.

We visited what I'll call restoration sites that memorialize what has happened in the restoration of Israel and of Jerusalem to the Jewish people. So the Biblical sites are wonderful because they strengthen our faith and the reality of God's written Word, but the restoration sites strengthened my faith even more because they memorialize events that fulfill God's plan, events that were carried out by people who didn't necessarily even believe in God's plan. They fulfilled those events by overcoming tremendous opposition, and they fulfilled them not two or three thousand years ago but in our own lifetime. The fulfillment of these events was recorded by the media. The people involved are still alive. They can be interviewed.

This is really kind of the main point of what we're going to talk about in this chapter, which is that if we were here 150 years ago, none of these restoration of Israel events would have happened yet. The only things they had back then to hang their faith on that God fulfills His promises, besides His promises fulfilled personally to them, would've been those that are recorded in the Bible. Those fulfillments are wonderful and amazing and very faith building, but isn't it awesome to also have current events proving God's faithfulness to keep His Word? 150 years ago they didn't have political things happening around them in the world fulfilling His promises like we do today.

Now I don't mean to be diminishing God's Bible promises. We love the promises that God fulfilled in the Bible. They build our faith very much. For instance, David was promised he would be the King of Israel, but the accounts of his life's struggles to arrive at that promise is what makes it real. It's something that we can all relate to, and it's all recorded in the books of 1st and 2nd Samuel. Those details give us faith in God and His promises and help us trust in His Word.

So God's promise that Israel would be restored has been fulfilled! But most of us know only the surface details of what it took to bring that promise to fulfillment and what opposition had to be overcome. We can study and learn the history of it. Israelis do that through their schools in every grade, but most of us don't even know where to start.

I want to say that if you love Israel, and are working, praying, and giving for the salvation of the Jewish people and the restoration of Israel, like people in my congregation, then the Ruakh wants to inspire you today by showing you that people who had that same motivation and calling were instrumental in making the restoration of Israel come to pass. They were integral parts of God's plan, and He wants you to see that you are an integral part of God's plan, too, and that you can trust that His promises that you are working to fulfill will come to pass.

So let's start with where this wonderful idea that the Jewish people should regain their ancient homeland came from. By the year 1800, the Jewish people had been persecuted in Christian Europe for many hundreds of years, but for the last 300 years it had been the worst. For 300 years the Inquisition had been going on throughout Europe, and the Muslims ruled over the Jewish homeland of Israel. The church was steeped in Replacement Theology, believing that God was done with the Jewish people, and that the church had replaced them as God's chosen people. They believed the Jews had killed Jesus, so were forever cursed by God, and the Catholic church was to be God's agent in bringing about this curse. (Read and learn lots more about Replacement Theology and antinomianism and the effect it has had on the church and Jewish people in my *Shavuot* book in Section 4, titled, "TORAH.")

But God's Word promised there would be a restoration. So I'd just like to read one of the many Scriptures promising Israel's restoration. What's always amazing to me about this promise is that it's not given by one of the latter prophets like Isaiah or Jeremiah, it's Moses, 3500 years ago! And listen to how specific he is about the fact that the Jewish people are going to be scattered everywhere, and then they are eventually going to be restored.

> Deuteronomy 30:1-5 *Now when all these things come upon you—the blessing and the curse that I have set before you—and you take them to heart in all the nations where A‍DONAI your God has banished you, 2 and you return to A‍DONAI your God and listen to His voice according to all that I am commanding you today—you and your children—with all your heart and with all your soul, 3 then A‍DONAI your God will bring you back from captivity and have compassion on you, and He will return and gather you from all the peoples where A‍DONAI your God has scattered you. 4 Even if your*

outcasts are at the ends of the heavens, from there ADONAI your God will gather you, and from there He will bring you. 5 ADONAI your God will bring you into the land that your fathers possessed, and you will possess it; and He will do you good and multiply you more than your fathers.

Amazing detail! Specific promises of God. If you want to look them up, Ezekiel, Jeremiah, and Isaiah have very similar promises of this restoration. Now you might not be aware of this. The European Jewish people had read these promises, but they were discouraged from believing them by their own leaders, our own Jewish leaders, who thought it would bring on further persecution to believe them. The attitude of most Jewish leaders during this period was, "Let's keep a low profile. Don't make any waves because we've been persecuted so badly, we don't even want to be seen. We're just going to keep out of sight." So there was no belief, no movement toward restoration to the Israel homeland.

Now here's what's so amazing. Christian Zionists saw the falsity of Replacement Theology. Even though they were being taught anti-Semitism, even though it was all around them, they saw through all that. They saw the promise of Israel's restoration as God's plan. Christian Zionists saw it first.

So one of the things that was so powerful for me and my daughter, when we were in Jerusalem, is they took us to a **museum called the Friends of Zion**. It was **created by Mike Evans** and **dedicated to Christian Zionists**. It reveals the amazing power of God's Word to bring the truth. It was Gentile Christian Zionists who were heroes in that. They inspired the idea of the return. Let's learn about a few of them.

First of all, George Bush of the **1800s**. He is actually an ancestor of both of our presidents Bush. He was a professor of Hebrew at New York University, and in **1844,** he **published a book** titled *The Valley of Vision Or The Dry Bones of Israel Revived?* In it, he denounced, "The thralldom and oppression which has so long ground them [the Jews] to the dust." **He called for elevating the Jews**, "to a rank of honorable repute among the nations of the earth by allowing the restoring of the

Jews to the Land of Israel." His writings were read by millions of people. This was **before the Civil War!!** This was before radio or TV or the internet! So the 1844 George Bush was the first Gentile Christian Zionist hero.

The next one is **William Eugene Blackstone. In 1890,** Blackstone organized The **Conference On The Past Present And Future Of Israel.** He advocated strongly for the resettlement of the Jewish people in Palestine. He lobbied U.S. presidents for the restoration of the Jews. He created a **petition signed by 413** prominent Americans, and this is how it read, "Why shall not the powers which gave Bulgaria to the Bulgarians and Serbia to the Serbians now give Palestine back to the Jews? These provinces were rested from the Muslim Turks and given to their natural owners. Does not Palestine rightfully belong to the Jews?" He also obtained endorsements of the Presbyterian Church and most of the mainstream American Protestant movement, and these endorsements were presented to President Wilson, which **caused President Wilson to strongly support the Balfour Declaration**, where Britain decided to give land to the Jewish people, which we're going to learn about in just a minute.

Then we have another interesting gentleman, **Jean-Henry Dunant.** This man is just incredible. He is the man who founded the **International Red Cross in 1864.** He is also the man who put forth the ideas of the **Geneva War Convention**, the rules of warfare that say things like, innocent people should not be killed, that there should be military hospitals, that they shouldn't shoot at the ambulances, etc. The first Geneva Convention was held in 1863, when 12 nations signed a treaty drawn up from this man's idea. He was the **first winner of the Nobel Peace Prize in 1901.** His advocacy for Israel stemmed from his staunch Christian Protestant belief in the Bible.

The next Gentile Christian Zionist is someone you might recognize: **Casper Ten Boom** and, of course, somebody else you might know, his daughter, **Corrie Ten Boom.** You probably know that Corrie and her family saved about 800 Jews from the Nazis by hiding them in their house while waiting for them to be secretly transported to freedom. They did this until they were caught and were sent to the death camps where Casper and Corrie's sister Betsy died.

But what you may not be aware of is that they held a weekly prayer meeting in their house for the restoration of Israel and the peace of Jerusalem. It was started, now get this, by Cory's grandparents in 1844 and was continued by her parents and their siblings for a hundred years! They met every week for a hundred years, praying for the restoration of Israel and the peace of Jerusalem until they were captured by the Nazis in 1944. That's what stopped the prayer meeting.

Only God knows the importance of that prayer meeting in the fulfillment of His plan for Israel. It makes me think about those bowls in Heaven with the prayers of the saints finally tipping over when they get full. Who knows whether this prayer meeting was the critical thing that tipped the prayer-for-Israel bowl.

What's so amazing about these things is that all of this was done in the face of widespread, virulent, anti-Semitism. These Christian Zionists were moved by God's Word to stand in the midst of opposition for the restoration of Israel. Then these Christian Zionists with their writings, their speeches, and their personal one-on-one interactions influenced **Jewish** leaders to become Zionists.

So what about these **Jewish Zionists**? When and how did that movement arise? Well, as I touched on earlier, for many centuries, there were no Jewish Zionists because Jews were forced to live in ghettos in Europe and Russia, and they just wanted to hang in the background. They were also not able to interact with non-Jews. The ghettos were run by religious Jewish leaders who kept the people from participating in the culture around them, again out of fear of more persecution. "We're just going to stay in our little town and care for our people and not make any waves." Every once in a while they were attacked, but they thought, "If we go out there, if we get into society, it's going to be even worse."

So what enabled **Jewish Zionists** to break from this ghetto culture? Well, it goes way back to the late 1700s when the United States was established with freedom of religion as the law. If you remember your American history, this was first implemented in Rhode Island by **Roger Williams**. The influence of this idea began to spread, especially to the oppressed French people.

As a result, years later the French Revolution adopted religious freedom as one of its pillars, one of its foundations, and in the early 1800s a very unexpected hero arose. Yes, the man, **Napoleon Bonapart**. As you might be aware, he built a personal, enormous empire. He took most of Europe and Russia, and he ruled over that Empire for about ten years. But what you're probably not aware of is that as he built that personal empire, he incorporated religious freedom everywhere that he conquered. It was a foundational freedom in all the lands he conquered.

So that was when the Jews were freed from the ghettos, and it led to the Zionist ideas taking hold amongst Jewish leaders. The most important Jewish Zionist at that time was **Theodor Herzl**. In Jewish History, this period is called the Enlightenment. (Other great Jewish intellectuals from that period that you might have read about are Karl Marx, Sigmund Freud, and Carl Jung.) Herzl published a book in 1896 called *Der Judenstaat* in German, which means *The Jewish State*. The book argued that the Jewish people should leave Europe for Palestine, their historic homeland, and that only through a Jewish state could they 1. Avoid anti-Semitism, 2. Express their culture freely, and 3. Practice their religion without hindrance.

Here's where we see what a struggle it was to bring this about. You'd think this vision would have been applauded and welcomed in the Jewish community, right? But rather than get behind Herzl's vision, the established Jewish leaders opposed and vilified him. They considered his ideas as a threat to their goal, which was assimilation. They wanted the Jewish people to assimilate. They said things like, "Now that we're out of the ghettos, you should always just assimilate. Don't hold on to your traditions. Don't hold on to your ways of worship. Just become like everybody else. Then we'll finally be able to avoid all of the persecution that we have had." They saw Herzl as rebelling against God. But in spite of this great opposition, Herzl's ideas spread rapidly throughout the Jewish world and attracted international attention. Soon the Zionist's vision began to bring about real actions, and here's where our tour comes in. The tour took us to the sites that were memorials of some of those actions and showed us the struggles involved in carrying them out.

Our tour

So the first Zionist place we went was called **The First Aliyah Museum**. *Aliyah* means *to go up* or *to emigrate to Israel*. The first aliyah was between 1882 and 1904 and was actually financed, interestingly, by the wealthy **Rothschild** family who bought land in the Palestine area and paid for Jewish people to move there. It was motivated by the terrible persecution the Jewish people were suffering, especially in Russia. It was also motivated by the desire for freedom, for land, and to live by the Bible. 35,000 people came, but many of them died due to sickness. Malaria was rampant there. Many that survived failed financially, but a few succeeded. So this was a museum that showed the struggles of these early pioneers.

Then in the early 1900s, God began to move on the international stage. During World War I, England was under a German naval blockade and was running out of gunpowder. And one important ingredient needed to make gunpowder was not available in Great Britain. It had to be imported from Europe, but there was a blockade. **Chaim Weitzman**, a **Jewish chemist** in England, invented a way to make gunpowder without that ingredient, using ingredients available on the island of Great Britain. Thus he saved England from certain defeat in World War I.

After the war in 1917, a declaration by another **Christian Zionist, Lord Balfour**, was written out of gratitude to Weitzman for England's survival. This declaration declared that England was going to set aside a homeland for the Jewish people.

The other thing that happened during this war was that Turkey, which ruled over the current land of Israel, at that time called Palestine, had sided with Germany in World War I against England, France, and the U.S., and was defeated. So the Turkish empire was divided between the allies. Britain took the land they were given and set aside one portion for Arabic people, which is now Jordan. Then what Britain did with the rest began the amazing fulfilling of God's promise of Israel's restoration. What did they do? They set aside the rest for the Jewish people to come and settle, which is now Israel.

But again, there was tremendous opposition to this fulfilling of God's plan. Britain came under tremendous pressure from the Arabs to prevent Jewish emigration to their Land. Why was the pressure so tremendous? Oil. The Arabs controlled the oil. So the Brits had to succumb to the pressure, and they severely limited Jewish immigration into this land that they had set aside for the Jewish people.

That terrible thing went on from 1917 until 1933, but from 1933 to 1939 it was worse because the Nazis came to power in Germany in 1933, and Jewish people were trying to escape. None of the nations of the world would receive them. Not even the United States! Even Israel was not allowed to take them because Britain was still caving to the Arab pressure upon them. So this was a terrible catastrophe. Many of the people were sent back into the hands of the Nazis.

However, heroic smuggling organizations developed to bring Jewish people illegally to Israel in fulfillment of God's promises. When people were caught escaping the Nazis and being smuggled to Israel, the Brits put them into detainment camps. We visited one of them called the **Atlit Immigration Camp** in Israel. The captured escaping Jewish people came in railway cattle cars. The rooms in the camp looked strikingly similar to Nazi concentration camps. The buildings were surrounded by barbed wire. Men and women were separated and put through showers. Can you imagine what the Holocaust survivors were thinking when they were told, "You have to go through these showers"?! There were huge furnace-looking

18. A SPECIAL HISTORY TOUR

monstrosities to purify the clothing from bugs, lice, and things like that. It would have been so traumatic for the people escaping the Nazi camps to come to these places looking too eerily similar. They were in the land of Israel but were going into camps just as if they were in Poland or Germany. Just imagine what a trauma that was!

But the smuggled-in immigrants were cared for in those camps by the Brits who held them there until 1948 when Israel became a nation. I want to recommend that you read about some of these attempts at immigration to Israel. One book I read is *The Story Of The Ship Called The Exodus*. I also recommend watching movies and documentaries about it, too.

So this was a very difficult 30-year period when Britain controlled Palestine and kept the Jewish people out. During that difficult time, Jewish leaders somehow knew they would eventually have to fight either the British or the Arabs for the Land. So in the 1930s before the war, they developed many **secret ammunition factories**.

We visited one called the **Ayalon Institute** and saw the machinery that made bullets in the underground factory. Now what's amazing about this is, it is thirty feet underground! It's in a concrete bunker with a concrete roof over it that's like ten feet thick. It was located, this was also amazing, one-tenth of a mile from a British depot train station where the British unloaded supplies. That's where they set up this factory. When you walked into it on the upper level, on the ground level, it was a communal farm. There were orchards and crops around it. There was a bakery and a school. There were bedrooms and a laundry. But underground was this concrete bunker. We saw the actual bunker as it's now set up with some statues of people. It was about 20x15 feet in size. It was just an amazing subterfuge and deception.

They imported old bullet-making machines, and brought them into the bunker. While people were working on the farm on the surface, other people came into the bunker and worked like twelve hours a day, every day. The farm workers didn't know that there was a bullet factory underneath them. There was a laundry machine, a great big commercial washing machine that was on like little railroad tracks, and when the time came, they pushed the laundry machine out of the way and it revealed this staircase. That's how the people came down. So the people working in the factory had breakfast with the rest of the people who worked on the farm, and then a few minutes later they all disappeared and went down there and made bullets for the rest of the day. Then they came out and had dinner with everybody. The supplies were brought in at night, and the bullets were taken out by the same truck that brought the supplies in. When the War of Independence started in 1948, Israel had ammunition! It is absolutely amazing! I had no idea that this was there. Such amazing prophetic foresight. This was not the only one. There were many factories like this.

So on November 29, 1947, the newly formed United Nations voted to create the State of Israel. That was a fulfillment of a very specific prophecy given by Isaiah.

> Isaiah 66:8 *Who has heard such a thing? Who has seen such things? Can a land be born in one day? Can a nation be brought forth at once? For as soon as Zion was in labor, she gave birth to her children.*

So about six months later, the nation of Israel was established on May 14, 1948, the day that the British control ended. To commemorate that, we visited the **Independence Hall where the Declaration of Independence was read**. Inside, a lot of the seats are the original seats that were there when the Declaration was read.

Immediately after the Declaration was read, war broke out between Israel and the five Arab nations around them. There actually had been civil war going on since the UN declaration. The British had been trying to keep it down. The neighboring Arab states were opposed to the vote of creating the Jewish state and declared they would intervene to prevent its implementation. So as soon as the declaration was read, the armies of Egypt, Jordan, Iraq, Lebanon, and Syria attacked Israeli troops inside the area that they had been given. That is called the **1948 Arab-Israeli war**.

Now what I didn't know about this was that things were so dangerous that the signers of this document took great risk of their lives just to sign it. In fact, they said that they did not give out the invitations to this event until the morning of the day of the event because they were afraid the Arabs would come and attack or that the British would come in and say you can't do this. The people were notified in the morning and they showed up at 4:00 in the afternoon and the declaration was read.

The war went on for about a year and in July 24, 1949, there was an armistice agreement. By that time, amazingly, Israel had retained its independence and had increased its land area by almost 50% compared to the 1947 UN Partition Plan. Sadly, 6,373 people sacrificed their lives in that war.

Now, many Bible scholars thought that the establishment of the State of Israel was not part of God's plan for the end times. The main reason was that most of the people who established the state were secular or socialists. They were not at all believers in the Bible. Even Orthodox Jewish scholars doubted that this was a fulfillment of prophecy because their eschatology dictated that only the Messiah could restore the State of Israel.

However, it was the undeniable miracles of Israel's survival of the War of Independence that made people realize that this is the hand of God. It was undeniable. There are many books and documentaries about that war, and I recommend them to you.

Now let's go on to the next two Wars. 19 years later in 1967, Israel was again attacked by five Arab neighbors, and again Israel triumphed in what's called the **Six-Day War**. It is another miraculous victory against the overwhelming Arab forces. In that war, Jerusalem was restored to the Jewish people. We saw powerful exhibits on this miraculous victory.

Then six years later, in 1973, Israel was attacked on the Day of Yom Kippur, the Day of Atonement by five Arab armies while most Israelis were in synagogues. It's called the **Yom Kippur War**. They almost lost this war. It really is astoundingly miraculous. Israeli tanks on the Golan Heights in the north were enormously outnumbered by the Syrians. The air force was not able to help because the Syrians had anti-aircraft guns in place. Amazingly, a dozen Israeli tanks held off a force of two hundred Syrian tanks that were attacking.

We were there on that battlefield in our tour, and we saw a film with reports from the tank drivers. They were saying they were sure all was lost, but they said, "We're just going to take a stand!" They drove their tanks up to a ridge where they could be seen by the Syrians, a dozen of them against hundreds of Syrian tanks, and the Syrians said, "Well, I guess we can't win," and turned around and left. Some Syrians have reported seeing angels. God made them see and hear things that made them flee. It was miracles of Biblical proportions. Just amazing!

So after Israel survived these three wars and over the next 46 years, something else happened which you might be familiar with. Israel as a land was completely desolate. It was desert and swamp, but during the next 46 years an agricultural miracle happened. Now today, date palms and orchards of all kinds are all over the place. This is a fulfillment of a prophecy in Isaiah

> Isaiah 27:6 *In days to come Jacob will take root, Israel will blossom and bud and fill the face of the world with fruit.*

So we saw orchards covering what had been desert. So with that plus the three miraculous war victories, it's to the point now that really all true Bible believers are convinced that this is God's plan. There's no way Israel could have survived these wars except by the hand of God.

We were scheduled to visit Sderot on the Gaza border, but we had to cancel because rockets were being fired out of Gaza. Instead we visited the northern border with Lebanon where Hezbollah rules just across the border. We were guided by a security chief for one of the kibbutz there, named Eitan. He brought us right up to the border to the soldiers and placements, and we prayed for two of the Israeli soldiers. They were around 19 and 20 years old, and we laid hands on them and prayed for them as they were guarding that post. Then they told us to look up the hills. They pointed out that there were a couple of cars up there with people with binoculars, watching us. Hezbollah was watching what we were doing!

So the last thing I want to talk about is a Biblical site that is in the midst of the struggle to fulfill God's plan, and that's the Temple Mount.

The Temple Mount is administered by Jordan and the Muslims there, but it's policed by Israeli police who will arrest you if you look like you're praying or reading on the Temple Mount. This is because this would change what they call the "status quo." Whenever the "status quo" has changed, the Muslims riot, so the police try to prevent the "status quo" from being changed.

So we had to be careful not to read anything or let our lips move. Two American congressmen were arrested on the Temple Mount in February of 2018 because they lifted up an olive branch as a symbol of peace. So I did a panorama picture there of the Temple Mount. What impressed me about it was, it is an immense platform, flat area. No one knows where the exact location of the Temple was, and, of course, archaeologists are not allowed to investigate because the Muslims don't want any evidence to be found that there really was a Jewish Temple there. So that is forbidden.

So, again, we can see how it has been a struggle, and how it will be a struggle for the Temple to be rebuilt on that site. I hope you're getting the picture here that every step is a struggle. God has a plan. He says what's going to happen. He promises it's going to happen, but it doesn't just happen like that. There's a struggle and people are involved in that struggle at every step.

Yet one of the things that we saw was the amazing vibrancy and energy of modern Israel. We had a great tour of the Knesset. We also got to visit an organic communal farm. It was a wonderful, informative, educational, and eye-opening tour of Israel.

My walk, your walk with the Lord is directly dependent on how much you trust His Word, that He'll fulfill His promises. Right? The promises that we all cling to are the promises of salvation, of healing, of provision, of peace, of fruitfulness, of wisdom, of protection, of His presence, of His guidance.... I could probably go on for another five paragraphs naming the promises that we all cling to. But here's what I saw in this. For many centuries, the only examples of God fulfilling His promises were from the Biblical texts that recorded things that happened thousands of years ago. Noah's family surviving the flood; Sarah having a baby at 90 years old; Joseph rescuing the people from the famine in Egypt; Moses leading Israel out of Egypt; the Egyptian army being destroyed; Joshua conquering the Promised Land; Yeshua healing the blind, the deaf, the lame, the sick, and raising the dead; Yeshua arising from the dead; the Apostles healing the sick, turning the world upside down, all wonderful, amazing accounts of God doing great miracles and fulfilling His promises, but all very ancient.

But we who are alive today and for the last 50 years, have personally observed in the news, God doing miracles in fulfillment of His promises. The promises of the restoration of Israel; the people returning to the land; the land becoming fertile and fruitful; even the language being restored; overcoming fierce enemies; and overcoming betrayals by supposed friends. You may have heard this. When the Queen of England asked the archbishop for proof of God's existence, his answer was, "That's simple, your Majesty. Israel. Israel is the proof of God's existence." Yeshua said this of those who walk with Him:

> Matthew 13:17 *Yes indeed! I tell you that many a prophet and many a tzaddik* [righteous man] *longed to see the things you are seeing but did not see them, and to hear the things you are hearing but did not hear them.*

Now, of course, Yeshua was speaking of them seeing Him, right? But I believe we can apply this to ourselves today. Many prophets and righteous people longed to see what you have seen, but never saw it; to hear what you have heard but did not hear it. Well, you have seen what they longed to see: God's promises in the Bible dramatically fulfilled in your days through the restoration of Israel and eventually the salvation of the Jewish people. So may your faith be strengthened by what you've just seen for yourself and what you've read here.

If you want to go to Israel, the purpose of this tour for us was that we as leaders would come back and then bring other people on a tour like this. Well, we planned one other tour, but then covid got in the way.

Let's pray.
[Can you say thank You with me to God for His Word and His promises?]

Father, we realize that our faith is based on the evidence of You fulfilling Your promises. We thank You for all the promises, all the fulfillments recorded in the Bible. They are awesome, but we also thank You that we are alive today to see and hear Your promises being fulfilled on our radios, TVs, computers, tablets, and phones, and in our newspapers.

Father, help us to appreciate what a blessing it is to be alive to see and hear these things that so many up until 70-80 years ago longed to see but never saw. So I pray, Father, for each of us that our faith would be strengthened through what we saw here, and that we would take the time to go and look into and study some of these things and understand the amazing ways in which You have fulfilled Your promises.

So we pray, Father, for the peace of Jerusalem, as you command us. We pray for the restoration of the Temple Mount. We pray for the fulfillment of the rebuilding of the Temple. Some people think that's a bad thing. I believe it's going to be Your office when You come back and reign for a thousand years. It's going to be Your throne room. So, Father, we pray for that fulfillment.

We pray, Father, for the acceptance of Messianic Jews in the Land of Israel that those of us who have been trying to make aliya and have been thwarted at every step by the bureaucracy there, that there would be a breakthrough, that the Jerusalem Institute of Justice can help bring that about.

We pray for Prime Minister Netanyahu who is now in great danger of a scandal that could take him down. We pray for the truth to come out in that, Father. We pray for these next elections to result in a clear majority for his party. We pray for wisdom for Israel's leaders to follow Your guidance.

And finally, Lord, the thing that I so much want to see is You've made a promise that all Israel will be saved. We don't understand how that could be fulfilled, but we don't understand how all this could have happened either. I mean, it's beyond imagination how what we've seen could have happened. So, Lord, we want to see all Israel saved. We want to see it with these earthly eyes, not looking down from Heaven. We pray that in our lifetime, we would see all Israel saved! In Yeshua's Name. Amein.

CHAPTER 19
JERUSALEM JUBILEE

In 2018, before covid, my assistant Pastor Tom and I went to the Annual Conference of Messianic Rabbis in Orlando. Whenever I go to these conferences, the high point is always Rabbi Jonathan Cahn's message. He's usually the final speaker. Are you a fan of Jonathan Cahn? Okay. I've read through his books and I've heard him speak probably a couple of dozen times. What he is gifted with is he can see Biblical patterns happening in our lives in modern times in history. So if you haven't read *The Harbinger*, it takes the events around 9/11 and shows how they followed the pattern in Isaiah 9:10, the pattern of apostasy of the nation divided. Then it deals with the bricks versus the cut stones and the sycamore trees versus the cedar trees. If you don't have any clue what that's all about, you've got to read the book because it's amazing.

The Harbinger was published in 2011. Then in 2017, he came out with two more books, *The Secrets,* which is a devotional, and then the book *The Paradigm*. Have you read *The Paradigm?* If you haven't, let me just encourage you to read it. What he did in *The Paradigm* is again this thing with patterns. He found the pattern for leaders of the United States over the past 30 years, and he lined it up with what happened in ancient Israel during the time of Ahab, Jezebel, Jehu, and Jonadah. He identifies each of our leaders with one of those people. It is mind-boggling the detail to which they line up in terms of the timings and things like that.

The thing that it did for me (and I'm sure it's similar for you if you read it) is it enabled me to understand former President Trump's personality. I'm sure if you haven't read the book, you were as befuddled and amazed and sometimes offended at how Trump functioned. But if you read *The Paradigm*, you will completely understand why he was like that, and why he had to be like that. So that's my infomercial for Jonathan.

What I'm going to share here is what Jonathan shared at the rabbi's conference. (I shared this with my congregation, but I told them, "I'm not going to share the way he did because over the years I've learned if I try to do that it flops. I just can't do it." They laughed.) So what it was though was a revelation about an event that year that revealed a pattern concerning the Jubilee years. Rabbi Jonathan shared this at the Rabbi's conference in 2018, then he published basically the same revelation in his next book a year later in 2019. That book is titled *The Oracle* and is 280 pages long. I highly recommend you get that book also. It will greatly strengthen your faith and understanding of the world. *The Oracle* is all about the Jubilee (*Yovel* in Hebrew).

So let me first start out by talking about the Temple and the Temple Mount. Then I will get into the Jubilees. Here's what God had to say about it to King Solomon:

> I Kings 9:3 A<small>DONAI</small> said to him: "I have heard your prayer and your petition that you made before Me. I have consecrated this House, which you have built, to put My Name there forever, and My eyes and My heart will be there every day.

So the Temple and the Temple Mount upon which the Temple was built is not just a nice place to worship God. God consecrated that place. The meaning of the word, *consecrated*, is *to set it apart for Him*. The thing that really grabbed me, is that He said He put His Name there on that Temple and on that mountain. What I see is this. If you come to most people's house, they've got their name on the mailbox. (Well, at least it used to be that way.) What does that signify? It signifies who lives in that house. So God is saying, "I put My Name on the Temple on the mountain." It belongs to Him. It belongs to God.

19. JERUSALEM JUBILEE

He said in that verse that it would be there how long? Forever! His eyes and heart will be there forever.

If you want to look at some other places about this, look at Leviticus 17:8-9 where He says that no sacrifices can be made anywhere else in Israel or in the world. In Deuteronomy 16:16, He commanded that all the men of Israel had to come to that Temple Mount to worship three times a year. Now this, of course, is in the city called Yerushalayim (Jerusalem).

Jerusalem became Israel's capital when King David conquered it about a thousand years before Yeshua. In the year 70 CE (AD), the Temple was destroyed and the priesthood ceased functioning. Then in the year 135 CE, the Jewish people were exiled from Jerusalem by the Romans and forbidden to set foot on that mountain for a hundred years. The Romans brought plows and plowed the Temple Mount. So there was no structure left on it at all, and Rome ruled over Jerusalem and all Israel. Then over the centuries, many other Gentile nation rulers conquered it and ruled over the Temple Mount in Jerusalem: the Muslims, the Crusaders, the Ottomans, the Egyptians, and the British all ruled over Jerusalem after Rome did. As you know, in 1948 Israel fought the war of independence and became a nation. Part of Jerusalem was conquered in that war. For the next 19 years, Jerusalem was a divided city. Part of it was Israel and the other part of the city was Jordan. The border between the nations ran right through the middle of the city. The Temple Mount where the Temple had stood was in the Jordan part. The city was called the Old City.

In 1949 one year after Israel became a nation, they made Jerusalem their capital and moved the government from Tel Aviv to Jerusalem. Then 18 years later during the Six-Day War in 1967, all of Jerusalem, including the Temple Mount, was restored to Israel. So we again see this restoration happening.

For Jonathan and for myself whenever you see restoration, it makes us think of Leviticus chapter 25 where it gives the instructions for the year of Jubilee

Leviticus 25:10 *You are to make the fiftieth year holy, and proclaim liberty throughout the land to all its inhabitants. It is to be a Jubilee to you, when each of you is to return to his own property and each of you is to return to his family.*

So I want to focus on that phrase *"return to his own property."* When the Land of Israel was first conquered by Joshua, it was divided amongst the Israelites. So if an owner became impoverished—fell into financial straits and had to sell his land, he was actually only renting it out for the number of years that there were until the next Jubilee. So if the Jubilee was 40 years off, he would rent it out for a pretty good price. But if the Jubilee was only two years off, he would rent it out at a very low price because in the year of Jubilee the land had to come back to the ancestral owner.

The word in Hebrew for *Jubilee* is *Yovel*. I don't know how they got *Jubilee* from that but *Yovel* is the Hebrew word. So all the ancestral inheritance was restored to its original owners at the Yovel, the Jubilee. So when all of Jerusalem, the Old City, the divided part that was part of Jordan, including the Temple Mount, was returned to Israel in 1967, this was a Jubilee for Jerusalem, a Yovel for Yerushalayim. This was a restoration of Jerusalem to the Jewish people.

Now the thing to notice about this, which again I credit Jonathon, is that it came back, but it didn't happen all at once. It happened in stages or steps. Some of it came back. Part of Jerusalem came back in 1948, but the rest of it didn't come back until 1967. So we see that God is restoring the Old City and the Temple Mount to the Jewish people but not all at once.

It seems like there are two big steps that still have to happen for this restoration to be complete. First of all, after 1967, Jordan still administratively controls the Temple Mount where the Muslims worship but Christians are forbidden to worship and Jews were forbidden to enter. However, since 2016 or so, they started to allow Jewish people to go up and visit the Temple Mount, but if you close your eyes and move your lips, they will arrest you and throw you off because you're not allowed to pray on the Temple Mount because that would

19. JERUSALEM JUBILEE

offend the Muslims. So it's not exactly completely restored. Right?

Secondly, none of the nations of the world recognize Jerusalem as Israel's capital. Until 2017, the embassies of all the nations of the world were in Tel Aviv, an hour away from Jerusalem. Some people think that's because of the Palestinians, but it's actually not. This happened because Jerusalem had been seen as a holy city, holy to three faiths. Now you have to understand that in 1947 when the UN was coming up with a plan to partition the land between a Jewish state and an Arab state, it was for Israel and Jordan. It was not for a Palestinian state, but a Jordan one. You see the mandate that Britain had at that time covered all of Jordan and all of present-day Israel and was supposed to be divided into two states with Israel on the west of the Jordan River and Jordan on the east, which is still what's in dispute. The Palestinian state is actually a three state solution. Okay? So in 1947, relevant to what we're talking about, the land was divided between Israel as a Jewish state and Jordan as an Arab state, and Jerusalem was administrated separately by an International Committee. It was not to be part of either Jordan or Israel. It was supposed to be separate because it was seen as this Holy City where all people wanted to come and visit and worship. So this caused all the nations to refuse to recognize Jerusalem as Israel's capital because it was supposed to be a separate, sacred city.

So that didn't change until the 1980s when the Palestinians began saying they wanted Jerusalem for their capital. They didn't even think of that back in 1947. It was supposed to be this separate Holy City. That's even its name, the Holy City! But in the 1980s, it was suddenly supposed to be the Palestinian capital, and they were supposed to decide on the future of it based on the peace negotiations.

But in 1995, the US Congress recognized Jerusalem as Israel's capital and decreed that our embassy must move there. However, Presidents Clinton, Bush, and Obama every six months signed a delaying order to prevent the embassy from moving to Jerusalem. That went on for years because they insisted that Jerusalem's future should be decided through Israeli-Palestinian negotiations.

But on December 6, 2017 in a fulfillment of a campaign promise, former President Trump recognized Jerusalem as Israel's capital, and he ordered the process of moving the embassy there to begin. If he hadn't ordered it, the State Department would never have done it because that's the way the State Department is. That was the first time any nation recognized Jerusalem as Israel's capital in 1882 years going back to 135 when Jerusalem was destroyed. Because the U.S. was the most powerful nation in the world at the time, President Trump's declaration was another step in the restoration of Jerusalem as Israel's capital. It was Yovel Yerushalayim! Do you see that? It was a step.

Other great cities have risen up in the past, such as Babylon and Shushan, and then disappeared, but Jerusalem is back as the capital of Israel, fulfilling prophecy. You're probably familiar with the prophecy in Zechariah chapter 12 about Jerusalem being the center of world affairs.

So the first thing to understand is that President Trump's declaration was monumental prophetically but also I'll coin a new word here: Jubilee-ic. It was a fulfillment of the Jubilee and, of course, it provoked much negative outcry from the Arab world and from many other nations. Their rage at our president was actually fulfilling Psalm 2

> Psalm 2:1-2 *Why are the nations in an uproar, and the peoples mutter vanity? 2 The kings of earth set themselves up and rulers conspire together against ADONAI....*

And just the timing is amazing. During the week before the president's declaration, the UN, if you remember, passed the anti-Israel resolution in the General Assembly. It had been blocked in the Security Council, but it was passed in the General Assembly. So the UN's resolution was in the Yovel Yerushalayim. I actually believe that one of the reasons the president had trouble in the 2016 election was for what he was going to do on December 6, 2017. It was that significant. If you study the Biblical history of Jerusalem, it was similar to how King Cyrus was used to establish God's plan to send the Jews back to Jerusalem to rebuild the Temple, and also in the time of the Maccabees how the restoration of Jerusalem happened at that time. I believe the full significance of this will increase over time. The nations of the world will continue to rage, but Israel will have a capital in Jerusalem. And amazingly, a few nations have followed Trump's lead and have moved their embassy or are planning to move their embassy to Jerusalem also. So can you see that we witnessed a big step in the Yovel Yerushalayim?

So because of that step, Jonathan made a connection between this event and the Jubilee passage that we just read. Let's look back at what happened exactly 50 years before Trump made that declaration. 2017 minus 50. Are you good at arithmetic? 1967. Does that ring any bells? Exactly! 50 years before Trump's declaration, there was another step in the restoration of Jerusalem which we just discussed. It was called the Six Day War and Jerusalem was recaptured. So in 1967 there was another step in the Yerushalayim Yovel! Well, finding two Jubilees prompted a search back another 50 years. 1967 minus 50 = 1917. What happened in 1917? The Balfour Declaration concerning the restoration of Israel!

This is what happened. Because Britain controlled that land at that time, they issued a declaration that created a nation for the Jewish people. Britain owned and controlled it because they had taken it from the Ottoman Empire during World War I. So they issued this declaration saying that there would be a land for the Jewish people.

So we've got 2017, 1967, 1917. Ready for another one? 1917 minus 50 is what? 1867. Well, if you look through history nothing physical like the Balfour Declaration or the Six Day War happened, but the Prophet Hosea spoke this:

> Hosea 3:5 *Afterwards, Bnei-Yisrael will return, and they will seek A<small>DONAI</small> their God and David their king. Then they will turn in awe to A<small>DONAI</small> and to His goodness in the last days.*

So first of all, he is speaking about the Jewish people. Right? B'nei Yisrael, sons of Israel. When Hosea wrote this, King David was long dead, so what's he talking about? Well, he's speaking in a poetic way of the prophets speaking of the son of David, the descendant of David and who is that? The Messiah Yeshua! So Hosea was predicting here that there would be a return to the Land and a turning to the Messiah. So he made a connection between the Messiah and the physical restoration of Israel.

So this is very important to grasp. He was predicting what we would call a Messianic restoration of Jewish people believing in their Messiah, not just a spiritual restoration of the Jewish people like the Hasidic movement or the modern Orthodox movement or something like that, but specifically because he's referring to a descendant of David, a turning of the Jewish people to seek the Messiah.

So was there a Messianic restoration, a Messianic revival in 1867? Well, all you have to do is go to Google, say 1867 what happened. Actually don't go to Google. Go to the Messianic Jewish Alliance website, mjaa.org, and you will find that in 1867 an organization called the International Hebrew Christian Alliance was founded in Great Britain. It was the first organization of Jewish believers in Yeshua since our disappearance sometime between the Year 100 and 325 CE. This was the forerunner of the Messianic movement.

I will explain the difference. The Hebrew Christian Alliance is non existent today. It became the International Hebrew Christian Alliance, and then it was changed to the International Messianic Jewish Alliance, and Paul Wilbur became the president of it. Then Joel Chernoff became the president. So 1867 was a step in Jerusalem's restoration on the spiritual side. You see that? That Jubilee year was part of the spiritual return of the Jewish people to our Messiah.

This return was then accompanied by a revival among Gentile believers who began to understand that Scripture predicted the restoration of the Land to the Jewish people. As we learned in the last chapter, these people were called

Christian Zionists, Christians who believe that Israel should get back its Land. The thing to remember is they encouraged Jewish leaders to begin working and praying and moving toward the possibility of regathering in the Land. The Jewish leaders were scattered in the Diaspora and weren't even thinking about going back to the land up to that point in time. So the Christian Zionists were the instigators of the Zionist movement amongst Jewish people.

So in 1887 only 20 years later, there was a physical restoration. One of the first groups of Jewish pioneers went to the Land of Israel and began restoring the Land. (This First Aliyah actually started in 1882 but this group didn't arrive until 1887 after the Rothchilds stepped in to finance the efforts.) So the 1867 rebirth of the International Hebrew Alliance was a step in the restoration of Jerusalem, of the Jewish people coming to the Messiah and coming back to the Land of Israel. It was a step in the Yovel Yerushalayim.

So we see four Jubilees! Amazing! Every 50 years something significant happened. Now the first Jubilee in 1867 started with a spiritual return to the Messiah which was followed by the physical return. Was there a spiritual component to the other Jubilees? Well 1917 was preceded by the Pentecostal revival in Britain in 1904 and then the Azusa Street revival here in America in 1905, which awakened British believers to God's promises to Israel. So that was a Messianic revival.

What most people don't know is that Lord Balfour was a Bible-believing Christian. That's why he wrote the Balfour Declaration and pushed Britain to open this homeland for the Jewish people. In addition, the person who conquered Jerusalem from the Ottoman Turks was General Allenby for whom streets in Israel are named. He was a strong Bible-believing Christian, and when he walked into Jerusalem, he talked about the fact that he was fulfilling prophecy by liberating Jerusalem from the Muslims. You can read his writings.

So we see that pattern of spiritual then physical. What about 1967? Was there a return of Israel to the Messiah, a Messianic revival? Well, there was something called the Jesus

Movement around then. It actually started in June of 1967 and was called the summer of love. People think of it as the start of the Hippie movement. Interestingly it was the same month as the Six Day War. Many Jewish young people joined the Jesus Movement that summer.

Personally, my life followed this pattern. That was the summer I graduated from college. I got a job in California, and a co-worker, a young man, and I went camping along the coast of California. We were sitting around a campfire, and all these hippies were there smoking stuff. It was the first time in my life that I started to seek something spiritually because I saw something happening there that was beyond what I had ever experienced before. It took ten years from then to when I actually came to the Lord, but I remember it very distinctly, sitting around that campfire, watching all the other people, and experiencing what was going on, the drugs and everything. So it was the beginning of my personal revival. And if you talk to the Messianic rabbis who are leading many Messianic congregations today (or were for decades, but are stepping down now because of their age), almost every one of them got saved during this Jesus Movement time, not necessarily in 1967 but in the next years after that.

So if you look on the MJAA website once again, which is a great source for this information, it will tell you that something happened in 1967 that transformed the Hebrew Christian Alliance into the YMJA, the Young Messianic Jewish Alliance. Those leaders of the Messianic movement, Joel Chernoff and Paul Wilbur and others whom you may know, had become believers in the Messiah and got the revelation in 1967 that they were supposed to continue living as Jews. The Hebrew Christian Alliance didn't believe that.

Let me explain. The Hebrew Christian Alliance was an organization for Jewish people who had come to believe in Jesus. But at that time they were taught that they had to give up their Jewish identity and assimilate into the church. They lived according to the church rules at that time. They were not allowed to live a Jewish lifestyle. There are still lots of Hebrew Christians in the churches today, including in my city of Rochester, NY. They're Jewish by birth. They found the Lord, but they live like the rest of the Christians. They give up all things Jewish, so as not to be accused by Christians of living "under the law."

Messianic Jews, on the other hand, are ethnically Jewish people who believe in Yeshua, the same as the Hebrew Christians, but who have returned to their Jewish identity and continue to live the Jewish lifestyle. So do you understand the difference? So 1967 was critical because that was when the young people in the Hebrew Christian movement got the revelation that we don't have to chop off all of our Jewish upbringing. We can live as Jews. It happened at a prayer meeting at Joel Chernoff's parents' home in 1967. They were filled with the Holy Spirit and got this revelation. And that was the beginning of the Messianic Jewish Alliance of America with the Young Messianic Jewish Alliance of America.

So that was 1967. Have there been restorations of other things because of the Messianic Movement? Well, there's worshipping on Shabbat, keeping the Moadim (Appointed Times), wearing prayer shawls, Davidic dancing, Messianic worship, the sounding of shofars, and more! There are also many more Messianic congregations. There were none of these things before 1967. Interest in the Jewish roots of our faith has taken off since then. So we have been building up the spiritual inheritance since then. So in 1967, there was a physical return of Jerusalem and a spiritual return of Jewish people to the Messiah, a Messianic and spiritual revival worldwide. The Jesus Movement was much bigger than just Jewish people. There was a huge revival all around the world.

So we see the pattern every fifty years. 1867 the Hebrew Christian revival, 1917 the Balfour Declaration, 1967 the Six Day War and the Messianic Jewish revival, 2017 Jerusalem declared Israel's capital. The first three included Messianic revivals along with the physical restoration.

So was there a Messianic revival following president Trump's 2017 declaration? I believe there was. The pattern predicted it. We have seen many Jewish people coming to the Lord in our congregation since 2017 and the number of Messianic congregations in Israel has greatly increased. This declaration is enormously significant, concerning Yeshua's return because in Matthew 23, Yeshua was speaking to the crowds of Jewish people in the Temple courts just two or three days before His crucifixion:

> Matthew 23:37-39 (TLV) *"O Jerusalem, Jerusalem who kills the prophets and stones those sent to her! How often I longed to gather your children together, as a hen gathers her chicks under her wings, but you were not willing! 38 Look, your house is left to you desolate! 39 For I tell you, you will never see Me again until you say, 'Baruch ha-ba b'shem ADONAI. Blessed is He who comes in the name of the Lord!'"*

So He's telling us He will return to where? Jerusalem! We know He'll land His feet on the Mount of Olives. That's part of Jerusalem. And He's telling us the people of Jerusalem will welcome Him. So who will those people be? Will it be the Orthodox Jewish people? Do you think they'll welcome Him? Will the Palestinian Muslims welcome Him? Will it be the Christian tourists? If Israel is open to tourists then, they will welcome Him, yes. But who are the people living in Jerusalem who will welcome Him? Messianic Jewish people! They will definitely welcome Him! So I get this FAQ, frequently asked question, "Which causes the other to happen, the physical return to the Land or the spiritual return to the Messiah? Which do you think is first?" Well, look at this.

> Ezekiel 11:17-18 *Therefore say, thus says ADONAI Elohim, "I will gather you from the peoples and collect you out of the countries where you have been scattered, and I will give you the land of Israel. 18 When they come there, they will remove all of its detestable things and all of its abominations."*

It's describing the return to the physical Land there, right?

> Ezekiel 11:19-20 *"Then I will give them one heart. I will put a new Spirit within them. I will remove the heart of stone from their flesh and give them a heart of flesh, 20 so that they may follow My laws, keep My ordinances and practice them. They will be My people and I will be their God."*

19. JERUSALEM JUBILEE

So first physical and then spiritual. Do you see that? Now actually some people in the church have embraced this prophecy in Ezekiel and have said, "Well, we don't need to share the Gospel with Jewish people until they go back to the Land because Ezekiel predicts that the Spirit is going to be poured out there. So there's no need for expanding the effort to reach Jewish people anywhere else. It's only back in the Land." Believe me there are many groups who take that position. However, Moshe (Moses) predicted just the opposite.

> Deuteronomy 30:1 *Now when all these things come upon you—the blessing and the curse that I have set before you—and you take them to heart in all the nations where ADONAI your God has banished you,*

Who is that speaking to? Israelites. Where? In the Diaspora, scattered all around the world. Right?

> Deuteronomy 30:2 *and you return to ADONAI your God and listen to His voice according to all that I am commanding you today—you and your children—with all your heart and with all your soul,*

When you return to the Lord in the Diaspora. Do you see that?

> Deuteronomy 30:3 *then ADONAI your God will bring you back from captivity and have compassion on you, and He will return and gather you from all the peoples where ADONAI your God has scattered you.*

Do you see how this is the exact opposite of what Ezekiel said? There will be revival in the Diaspora, and then He will bring them back.

> Deuteronomy 30:4-6 *Even if your outcasts are at the ends of the heavens, from there ADONAI your God will gather you, and from there He will bring you. 5 ADONAI your God will bring you into the land that your fathers possessed, and you will possess it; and He will do you good and multiply you more than your fathers. 6 Also ADONAI your God will circumcise your heart and the heart of your descendants—to love ADONAI your God with all your heart and with all your soul, in order that you may live.*

So what are we seeing here? Jewish people revived, believing in the Messiah where? In the Diaspora, and then they return to Israel and are blessed and multiply. See that? So Moses predicted the Messianic revival in the Diaspora first then the return to Israel, while Ezekiel predicted the return to Israel and then the revival. You see that?

Now this is a great lesson. Greek thinkers would say, "Well, the Bible is contradicting itself." It's got to be one or the other, either/or. Right? But what will Hebrew thinkers say? "He could do both!" Why can't He do both? He can! He can bring revival in the Land and then bring people back. And He can bring revival in the Diaspora and then gather them in. It's both. There's no problem.

And today, since 2017, we're seeing both: Jewish people coming to believe in Messiah in the Diaspora and in Israel. So three times Messianic revival and physical return to Israel have been connected in these 50-year Jubilees 1867, 1917, and 1967. So in 2017, we are seeing the same pattern.

Now that's all great, but what should this all mean to you and me? How should it affect us? I saw two ways. First, you should just be so thankful to be alive at this time in history. It is amazing! Yeshua was referring to Himself when He said this, but as I said before, I think it applies to us today.

> Matthew 13:16-17 *But you, how blessed are your eyes... and your ears...! 17 Yes indeed! I tell you that many a prophet and many a tzaddik* [righteous person] *longed to see the things you are seeing but did not see them, and to hear the things you are hearing but did not hear them.*

Many prophets and righteous men desired to see the restoration of Jerusalem, but never saw it, but you and I are seeing it. Amazing! It applies to those of us who are alive today to see this Bible prophecy coming true. I am old enough to have seen both 1967 and 2017. I remember in 1967 my whole attitude and atmosphere, everything changed! The whole world changed in 1967. All kinds of negative things started happening but positive things also. You know the Scripture says that *where sin abounds grace does much more abound* (Romans 5:20).

So whatever you're going through in your life today, these revelations should greatly increase your faith that God's Word is true, and that His plan will be carried out. Secondly, if you are involved in the Messianic Movement or are being drawn to it in some way (perhaps this book is your first taste of It), the Holy Spirit wants you to receive a greater appreciation for the eternal cosmic world-changing, earth-shaking consequences of what's happening, and to know the significance of what you are doing in supporting the Messianic revival, in working toward it, and praying for it. If God is calling you to come alongside the Messianic Movement, to be part of it, to love, to serve, to witness, to pray, to give, all to help bring the Good News to the Jewish people, He's calling you into the forefront of what He's doing in His prophetic plan. It's as significant as that.

Restoring the Jewish people to our Messiah is a critical step in restoring the Land and Jerusalem to the Jewish people, and the critical step in bringing to pass all of the End Time plans of God. As followers of Yeshua, we're called to share the Good News with everyone, everywhere around the world. But as we've seen, bringing Jewish people to the Lord is on the critical path of the Lord fulfilling His End Time plan for the earth. Jewish revival is linked to the restoration of Jerusalem and the return of the Lord.

So as my wife Diane said to me 45 years ago, if you want to see the Lord return, help to restore His brothers and sisters after the flesh to Him because that's what has to happen before He'll come back.

This is why we see opposition. This is also why even if you're not ethnically Jewish, we need you because we need your prayers and support and faith to join with ours. I try to bring this out frequently because sometimes people think, "Well, it's just all about those Jewish people." Yes it's all about the Jewish people because God has chosen them to fulfill His plan. But for His plan to be fulfilled with all the opposition, God is expecting other followers of Yeshua to come alongside and work with Him to see that fulfilled.

Let's pray.
Father, thank You for Your patterns. Thank You for opening our eyes to see these patterns in history. They are amazing!

Thank You for the revelation that the Jewish people are a critical part of Your plan for the End Time. You are working in and through the Jewish people, and we thank You, Lord, that we get to see your prophesies coming to pass.

We pray in agreement, Father, for Your Spirit, Your Ruakh to be poured out on our Jewish people in the Diaspora, all of the cities to which they're scattered all around the world, Lord, and in Israel. And we pray that we would see You bring us back to the Land in fulfillment of Your predictions. And we thank You, Lord, for the honor of being called to be involved in Your End Time plan. It is amazing, Lord

I pray, Father, for everybody reading this that You would show us our role in what You are doing, whether it's in serving, witnessing, working, giving, and praying in spiritual warfare. Show us our role, Father. Show us what our part is. Make us a light to God's people Israel and to the nation Israel.

[I believe the Lord is saying to you, "Arise and shine for your light has come." Arise and shine as you walk in the place where God has you. "My Light will shine through you," says the Lord. "My Light will reflect off you. My light will illuminate you, and you will be a light to the nations as you walk in the paths that I have called you to walk in."]

Thank You, Father. Thank You, Lord.

And Father, bless Rabbi Jonathan Cahn, It is amazing the doors that You have opened to him, government doors, media doors, publishing doors. We pray for You to continue to anoint him. Continue to protect him and his wife Ranade and his two boys, Father. Protect his congregation and his ministry. Protect the publisher, Stephen Strang, that publishes his books, and the publishers of *Charisma Magazine.* Protect them, oh God. Continue to open the doors for Jonathan, Father, especially in government, especially in Washington, I pray, Father. In Yeshua's awesome Name. Amein.

CHAPTER 20
THE STRANGER, THE SURVEY, THE SALE, THE DEED, AND POSSESSION

So we learned that Yovel, Jubilee is about the return of possessions to their original owners. It is commanded to be observed every 50 years to keep property within families. The possessions, as we learned, can be physical, like land, or spiritual, like the Messiah.

The people of Israel were separated from our land since 70 AD when the Romans conquered us, destroyed Jerusalem, and exiled us to all the nations of the world. Moses also prophesied our return.

> Deuteronomy 30:3 *then ADONAI your God will bring you back from captivity and have compassion on you, and He will return and gather you from all the peoples where ADONAI your God has scattered you.*

While we were separated from the Land. Moses prophesied it would become desolate. Nothing would grow. In the prophesy about the desolation, there is an additional prediction.

> Deuteronomy 29:21-22 (22-23) *"...**the foreigner** who comes from a distant land will say, when they see the plagues of that land and the sicknesses ADONAI afflicted on it: 22(23) 'Sulfur and salt, the whole land burnt! It cannot be planted, it cannot sprout, no grass can grow up on it….*

The word *foreigner* there (*stranger* in some versions) is the Hebrew word נכרי nakri. Notice that it's singular. So here's the first amazing God-incidence. The stranger, foreigner who came was Mark Twain who traveled to Israel in 1867 and wrote about it in his book, *Innocents Abroad*. Here is a comparison between Moses' prophesy and what Mark Twain wrote:

Mark Twain wrote "lepers, cripples, the blind, maimed, malformed and diseased"	Moses predicted sicknesses
Mark Twain wrote "it is a scorching, arid, repulsive solitude"	Moses predicted "the whole land burnt"
Mark Twain wrote "all desolate, unpeopled"	Moses predicted "It cannot be planted, it cannot sprout, no grass can grow up on it"

Moses predicted in verse 26 (27) *"So Adonai's anger burned against that land, bringing on it every curse written in this scroll."*

Mark Twain wrote that the land "is desolate and unlovely. And why should it be otherwise? Can the curse of the Deity beautify a land?" This is all the more remarkable because Mark Twain was not a Bible-believer.

Mark Twain traveled to the Holy Land in 1867. His visit marked the beginning of the restoration of the land to Israel. At that time, the Land belonged to the Turkish Ottoman Empire. When there is to be a transfer of land ownership, **there must be a survey**. **Charles Warren**, a British officer, was sent to Jerusalem **to draw a map** of it as it was in ancient times. Warren excavated its foundations working in secret from the Turks. His work ushered in Biblical archaeology. Warren was in Jerusalem at the same time that Mark Twain was there. Twain's last full day in Jerusalem was 9/28/1867, a Shabbat. The Parashah for that Shabbat included Deuteronomy 29:22-33, which speaks of the foreigner coming. So, while he was there, Jewish people all around the world were reading that he would come.

In order for there to be a **transfer of land, the current owner has to be willing to sell**. The Ottoman Turks were not willing to sell, especially to Jews. However, from 1853-56 the

20. THE DEED

Turks fought the Crimean War with France and Britain against Russia. The Turks went into great debt to finance the war. In 1858, the Turks enacted the Ottoman Land Code to raise money from taxing the land, but still would not allow any of the Land to be sold to foreigners. However, taxation didn't raise much, so the Code was changed to allow foreigners to buy the Land. When Jewish people learned of this, they began buying the Land through third parties to conceal their identity. This happened in late 1867.

Let's move to the next Jubilee, 1917, three years after the start of WWI. The Ottoman Empire had sided with Germany against Britain, France, and the U.S. Germany blockaded England and prevented importation of a key ingredient in manufacturing acetone used in making gunpowder. A Jewish chemist, **Chaim Weizman**, invented a way to make acetone and saved England.

Weizman also met **Arthur Balfour** and Lloyd George, both Bible believers and imparted to them his beliefs that it was time for Jewish people to return to the Land. **Lloyd George** became Prime Minister of Britain in 1916 and appointed **Balfour** his foreign secretary. Lloyd George made this proclamation on 10/12/2017 in the Jubilee year:

"His Majesty's Government view with favour the establishment in Palestine of a national home for the Jewish people and will use their best endeavours to facilitate the achievement of this objective" Immigration to Israel increased dramatically. The Parashah for the Shabbat before that included Genesis 12.

> Genesis 12:7 *Then ADONAI appeared to Abram, and said, "I will give this land to your seed."*

Isn't that amazing? And God kept that promise. He gave the **title deed to the Land** to Israel, but they had lost it due to idolatry. Now they were getting it back. While WWI was raging, the Land deed was still in the Ottomans' hands, so the British Empire still didn't own the Land. On 12/9/1917 British General Edmund Allenby captured Jerusalem from the Turks. He was able to take it because he had built up Britain's air force, and it controlled the air over Jerusalem in fulfillment of this verse:

Isaiah 31:5 *Like hovering birds, so Adonai-Tzva'ot will protect Jerusalem. By protecting, He will deliver. By passing over, He will save [NKJV: preserve it]."*

Air power miraculously preserved Jerusalem from destruction in the fighting. This happened on 12/9/1917, the eve of Hanukkah the celebration of Maccabees liberating Jerusalem, but the liberation was not complete.

After the war, under pressure from the surrounding Arab nations, Britain began restricting Jewish immigration to Israel, blocking ships. This was especially tragic during the years when the Nazis persecuted us, starting in the 1930s when millions of Jewish people were seeking refuge and were very willing to find that refuge in Israel. This led to the near collapse and destruction of Britain in the years leading to and during WWII.

We already looked at the next Jubilee in 1967 in the last chapter. Now we need to look at another set of Jubilees. **Theodor Herzl** convened the **first Zionist Congress** in Basel Switzerland to begin the political movement to establish a Jewish state in 1897. Shortly after the end of the Congress on 8/31/1897, Herzl wrote: "At Basel, I founded the Jewish State. If I said this out loud, I would be answered by universal laughter. Perhaps in five years, certainly in fifty years everyone will know it." Fifty years was a Jubilee prophesy.

What happened fifty years later in 1947? After WWII, Britain turned the issue of Palestine over to the UN, and the UN set up a committee, which developed a **Partition Plan**. The Plan was that British occupation would end, and the Land would be divided into a Jewish state and an Arab state.

The American State Department was against it, but President Truman was for it. Truman had deep sympathy for the Jewish people. The Plan was completed on 8/31/47, fifty years to the day from the end of the first Zionist Congress!

The Plan was officially received and recorded by the UN General Assembly on 9/3/47, fifty years to the day from when Herzl wrote his prophesy. The UN vote on the Partition Plan was on 11/29/47, a Shabbat. The Parashah for that Shabbat contained this command from God to Jacob:

20. THE DEED

Genesis 32:10(9) *Then Jacob said, "O God of my father Abraham, and God of my father Isaac, ADONAI, who said to me, 'Return to your land…"*

Five and a half months later in May of 1948 a new nation was formed on that Land and was given the name Israel. That was the name Jacob received when he returned to the Land.

Then we know that as soon as Israel was declared a nation, it was attacked by the surrounding Arab countries, and it took their war of independence against those countries before they could have final possession. And remember how the Israelis had amazingly produced weapons in secret underground under the nose of the British, which is why they were even able to fight the Arabs. (See Chapter 18, p. 217.)

And I hope you know about all the miracles of Biblical proportions that God did for Israel to win that war against all odds. For example, at a time of year when it never rains in one area, God made it rain right after Israel launched a bomb, making the Arabs think it was an atomic bomb because what else could cause it to rain, and they fled! (Read about that miracle and a few of the other miracles here: https://www.jewishhistory.org/miracles-during-the-war-of-independence/)

Let's pray.

Father, we thank You that You are in control of time! It is so amazing!! This inspires us to pray for Israel and the world! We pray, Father, that Your will be done on earth as it is in Heaven. We pray Your plan for the timing of world events and happenings in Israel would always work out perfectly. Help us to listen to You in how to pray for Israel and the world.

Help us to apply this to our lives to realize that You have the timing in our lives planned also. Help us, Lord, to stay submitted to you and sensitive to Your Ruakh, that we would follow Your lead in all that we do and say, so that we do not mess up any of the timing You have planned in our lives or in the lives of those around us. In Yeshua's Name. Amein.

Section 6

SIMCHAT TORAH

Let's Pray
We just pray, Father, that each of us would truly have joy, thankfulness, gratitude for Your Word and for You giving it to us, and opening our eyes to it. Open our eyes to what You want to give us today. In Yeshua's Name. Amein.

CHAPTER 21

HONORING GOD'S WORD ON SIMCHAT TORAH

Simchat Torah is the day after the eighth day, the last day of Sukkot. It is a day to honor the Word of God. The Torah Scroll contains the five books of Moses. Jewish tradition is to read and study through that whole Torah Scroll each year. It is divided up into weekly readings called Parashot, which is plural. The singular, one week's reading, is called the Parashah.

At the end of Sukkot, the Parashot (Torah readings) come to the end of Deuteronomy, which is the end of the Torah Scroll. Then it is time to roll the Scroll back and start at the beginning again in the weekly Parashah (Torah reading) the week following Sukkot. Because of this, it has become the tradition to celebrate the Torah at the end of Sukkot. We call it *Simchat Torah*, which means *Rejoicing in the Torah*. We are celebrating the completing of the reading cycle of the weekly Parashot, reading through the five books of Moshe each year.

So traditionally, Simchat Torah is a time to honor God's Word. How much did God want His Word to be remembered and honored by the people? Well, just look at this Sukkot command:

> Deuteronomy 31:10-13 *Then Moses commanded them saying, "At the end of every seven years, in the set time of the year of cancelling debts* [the Shmitah year], *during the feast of Sukkot, 11 when all Israel comes to appear before* ADONAI *your God in the place He chooses, you are to read*

this Torah before them in their hearing. 12 Gather the people—the men and women and little ones, and the outsider within your town gates—so they may hear and so they may learn, and they will fear ADONAI your God and take care to do all the words of this Torah. 13 So their children, who have not known, will hear and learn to fear ADONAI your God....

These times would've been very memorable having it occur only at the end of every seventh year. (And it looks like the Shmitah year was supposed to start on Sukkot!) This was before synagogues and before the practice of parashah readings. Back then it was possibly only the Tabernacle, the kohanim, and the king that had a Torah Scroll, so it looks like the only way to know it was to hear it read aloud by a kohane or Levite or to hear it recited orally from memory by one of them.

Understand that hand copying Torah Scrolls was the only way that God's Word could be preserved and spread and read and listened to from the time when Moses wrote it, 1500 years before Yeshua, until about the year 1500 CE (AD) when the printing press was invented to print books. Isn't that incredible that for 3000 years the Bible on scrolls was all people had?

So, in our meetings, when we take the Scroll out to honor it, we need to understand that in addition to honoring the Word of God, we are honoring all the people over the centuries who helped preserve it and pass it on accurately to us, including the scribes who meticulously copied it. Also note that we're not just honoring the five books of Moses, we're honoring the entire Word of God, the Tanakh (which is the books of Moses plus the prophets, the history books, and the writings—the Old Testament), and the New Covenant, the Torah of the Messiah (as David Stearn terms it, which is a great term for it).

How the Word came

So, let's start out this chapter by looking at a few things about the Word. First of all, where did God's Word come from? Well, Peter tells us this.

> II Peter 1:21 *for never has a prophecy come as a result of human willing — on the contrary, people moved by the Ruach HaKodesh* (the Holy Spirit) *spoke a message from God.*

So, prophesies are Words from God, spoken or written by people moved by the Holy Spirit. So what did he mean by *"moved by the Holy Spirit"*? The NIV says, *"carried along by the Holy Spirit."* The Amplified Bible says, *"borne along, moved along, or impelled."* The Contemporary English Version says, *"guided by the Spirit."* So, really what this says is that the Holy Spirit gave the prophets Words from God to speak and to write. So that's where it came from.

Now, it's also very interesting for those of us who are reconnecting with our Jewish roots because we've been taught a lot of other interesting things about this. What prophesies is Peter referring to here at the time he wrote this? The Old Testament! The New Covenant hadn't been written yet. So he's saying the Tanakh was inspired by the Holy Spirit, the Ruakh HaKodesh who moved on all the authors, on Moses through Malachi, to write messages from God to the people of Israel. Later, the same Ruakh HaKodesh moved on the authors of the New Covenant to write messages from God to people.

But where does the Ruakh HaKodesh come from? Well, Yeshua promised something interesting about this.

> John 15:26 *When the Counselor comes, whom I will send you from the Father — the Spirit of Truth, who keeps going out from the Father — he will testify on my behalf.*

So Yeshua's saying He's the sender of the Ruakh HaKodesh who goes out from the Father. Now it's a little bit confusing because in the preceding chapter in John 14, Yeshua says the Father will send the Spirit in Yeshua's Name. So some people get all twisted in a knot about that, but there's something that clears that up very easily. Yeshua says this.

> John 10:30 *I and the Father are one.*

So Yeshua sends the Holy Spirit. The Father sends the Holy Spirit. The Holy Spirit is sent from God. So here's the thing that might be a little bit strange to your thinking. The

21. HONORING GOD'S WORD

Ruakh HaKodesh is sent out to move on the authors of both the Old and New Covenants to give them Words from God to write. But if Yeshua and the Father are one, who gave the prophets the Words of the Old Covenant? Yeshua! Right? He and the Father are one. So here's the thing that could be a real revelation to you. Yeshua wrote the Old Testament!! Not just the New Covenant. He inspired the Old Covenant, too!

Now there's another way to look at this. Here again is this very familiar verse:

> John 1:14 *The Word became a human being and lived with us, and we saw his Sh'khinah, the Sh'khinah of the Father's only Son, full of grace and truth.*

So let me ask the same question again. What was the written Word when John wrote that? The Tanakh, the Old Testament! So it's saying Yeshua is the Living Tanakh or Old Testament or Old Covenant!! You got that? The New Covenant hadn't been written yet. So John couldn't be saying He was the living New Covenant. He later became the Living New Covenant, but He wasn't yet because it hadn't been spoken or written yet.

So Yeshua is the Living Word. We could say it this way. The Tanakh became a human being, became flesh and dwelt among us because the New Covenant wasn't there yet. Right?

So Simchat Torah is a day to honor God's Word. And Scripture actually tells us how much God honors or esteems His Word:

> Psalm 138:2 (NKJV) *... For You have magnified Your word above all Your name.*

Other translations say, *"You have exalted Your Word above Your Name."* So it's saying here that God considers His Word to be even higher than His Name. Remember, *"at the Name of Yeshua, every knee will bow and every tongue will confess that Yeshua is Lord,"* but God says the Word is higher, but, of course, the Word is Yeshua! He's the Living Word! Right?

Now, in the Hebraic culture, a person's name represented the person. So to say His Word is above His Name means it's really, really important. His Word is really important:

Acts 4:12 *There is salvation in no one else! For there is no other name under heaven given to mankind by whom we must be saved!*

What Name is that? The Name of Yeshua. We're all saved by putting our trust in the all powerful Name of Yeshua. We're not saying that His Name is a magical incantation or a magical charm. Remember the Hebrew concept that the name represents all that the person is. So the Name is about the Person who made the atoning sacrifice for our sins. So putting our trust in His Name means we're putting our trust in Him.

But God's Word is what reveals Yeshua and His saving power to us. It reveals our need for salvation from sin. That's why God says, "I magnify My Word above My Name." Do you see that? Without the Word, we would not understand the power of His Name. We wouldn't see the power of His Name. That's why He has magnified His Word above His Name.

Again, I'll ask the same question. What did God's Word consist of when David wrote this? No, not even the Tanakh (Old Testament)! This is David. He was before all of the prophets, right? It was not the entire Tanakh. It was the Torah (the five books of Moses) and Joshua and Judges. Job is a very old book, so probably Job, and possibly the beginning of I Samuel, which is about Samuel, King Saul, and David. We don't know exactly when David wrote this Psalm, so it could've been some of I Samuel, and also some of the Psalms because David was writing the Psalms, but Moses and a couple of others also wrote a few Psalms. So even just that part of God's Word is exalted above His Name!

My testimony

I have a particular, special place in my heart for God's Word. You might have heard the story of how I came to the Lord. You know, we have altar calls and we have people going out and sharing the Good News and stuff, but I didn't come to the Lord in either of those ways or any of the other conventional ways. Although I think it is actually a conventional way because I think it is probably the way that most people in history came to the Lord.

21. HONORING GOD'S WORD

All that happened to me is I began to read the Bible. I was inspired to read the Bible by the changes I saw in Diane as she began to study the Bible. So I read through the book of John (because when I asked, Diane had suggested starting there). I was thirty-one years old at the time, but I didn't know the story. If you were raised in a believing home, this is probably hard to grasp. But if you can imagine getting toward the end of one of the Gospels and not knowing how it ends. That was me! I wondered, "What's going to happen here?!" At the end of the book of John, I was like, "I really want to follow this Man." I had been searching for years, but because I was Jewish, it took nine years before I searched in the New Covenant because of all the lies I had been taught about it being a non-Jewish book and being a book of anti-Semitism, and other lies.

So in just reading John, my heart was moved to be a follower of Yeshua, but I didn't have enough revelation to truly follow because I didn't think I was a sinner. I didn't know the Law of God, so I didn't know that I needed salvation. I thought I could just get up and just start following Him.

Then I asked Diane, "What should I read next?" She said, "Well, try the book of Matthew." So I read Matthew, and if you're familiar with Matthew, you know you don't get very far in it before you get to the Sermon on the Mount. That's when I found out that I was a sinner. The revelation was astounding! I was like, "Oh, I've been doing these things all my life! I've been blaspheming! I've been lusting! I've been lying!" I had been doing all of those things, and I didn't even know they were wrong because I was ignorant of the Word. But once I became aware, Scripture did that thing that Rabbi Sha'ul says it's supposed to do. It convicted me of sin. That's when I got down on my knees and said, "Lord, I need Your forgiveness."

See, I couldn't follow Yeshua until I recognized Him as the atoning sacrifice for my sin. That was when my life radically changed. Nobody witnessed to me. Nobody handed me a tract. I didn't go to any Messianic congregation or to any church. It just happened in my bedroom.

So when I get up to Heaven, I'm going to go see John and Matthew and say, "Thank you!!" But there are a lot of other people we're going to say thank you to.

So can you see why He says His Word is exalted above His Name now? Because we need the Word to understand the power and to appreciate His Name, His character, His atoning sacrifice, etc.

Confidence the Word is complete

God's Word also gives us reasons to be confident in its completeness, to be confident that we have all of it that God wants us to have. There are a lot of people around now who are looking for the Gospel of so and so, and wanting to read the Gospel of another so and so—all these hidden Gospels and other extra-Biblical books, trying to find some other revelation. But the Bible clearly states its completeness.

Exodus 24:4 *So Moses wrote down all the words of ADONAI....*

But, if you interact with Jewish people who are not Messianic, you will find this very interesting thing: non-Messianic Judaism magnifies the Talmud up to the level of God's Word. The Talmud is a large collection of commentaries by all the esteemed rabbis over the past couple of thousand years. It has commentaries on Scripture, commentaries on those commentaries, lots of interesting stories and allegories that sort of teach a lesson, and rulings from the rabbinical courts. People would wonder, "Can I do this on Shabbat? Is this allowed?" And then the courts would meet and they would decide and then they would write that down in the Talmud.

Now, here's the interesting thing about this though. Non-Messianic Judaism teaches that God spoke the words of the Talmud to Moses, and Moses passed them down orally, and they weren't written down until somewhere between the first and the fourth centuries CE. So, in this way, non-Messianic Judaism exalts the Talmud up to the level of the Tanakh. They're giving it as much authority, if not more, than the Bible. According to traditional Judaism today, those decisions that are recorded in the Talmud by the Rabbinical courts, by the rabbis who served as judges in the Beit Din, have a higher authority than the Scripture. So, they're the counsel of men over the Word of God.

However, so we don't get too down on our Jewish brethren, we all should understand that the Catholic church and, I believe, other churches have done the exact same thing. They've given the authority of what they call the church counsel higher authority than the Word of God. Why would they do that? Well, there are times when they don't want to obey the Word of God, so they make a decision in the counsel not to do it, and then that has higher authority than Scripture.

That's how some denominations today justify ordaining practicing homosexuals and those who are in same sex marriages. So to them the counsel has a higher authority than the Word of God.

But God's Word, interestingly, specifically tells us never to change it. Moses says this.

> Deuteronomy 4:2 *You must not add to the word that I am commanding you or take away from it....*

Now, this has always been kind of a surprise to me when I've looked at this because I would think that what people would do is take away from the Word of God. "It's got all these commandments. I don't want to obey that one, so I'll take it away." But only God would be wise enough to realize that people would not only try to take things out of His Word, but would also try to add things to it. And we have some pretty large influential groups in the world today that have added to the Word of God. Specifically, Islam claims it has a further revelation that contradicts the Bible. The Book of Mormon is a further revelation beyond the Bible. And we just noted that the Jewish leaders added the Oral Torah, and the Catholics have added non-Biblical rules, doctrines, and traditions, etc.

God commanded also that His Word be guarded and that it be preserved. Remember that Moses stored it beside the Ark of the Covenant, and he wrote it on stones. And remember this:

> Deuteronomy 17:18-19 *Now when he sits on the throne of his kingdom, he is to write for himself a copy of this Torah on a scroll, from what is before the Levitical kohanim. 19 It will remain with him, and he will read in it all the days of his life, in order to learn to fear ADONAI his God and keep all the words of this Torah and these statutes.*

God commanded that every king of Israel make a copy, not to have somebody else make a copy, but make a copy himself of the five books of Moses and read it every day. This also speaks to the fact that it was all written down.

> Exodus 24:4 *So Moses wrote down all the words of ADONAI....*

> Deuteronomy 29:28 *The secret things belong to ADONAI our God, but the things revealed belong to us and to our children forever—in order to do all the words of this Torah.*

So what this is saying to me, and I hope it says it to you, is that we can be confident that God has given us all His Word. He has revealed Himself to us through the Word. We need His written Word. We're to live our lives based on what He has revealed to us through His Word!

In our culture today, as I said, some people are constantly trying to find greater revelations, other Gospels, hidden meanings, angelic revelations, and direction for the future when all they need, really, is direction for today from the Word.

I don't know about you, but to me it's a challenge and takes great discipline, commitment, courage, prayer, and help from others to live out what He has already given us. Paul, Rabbi Sha'ul, writes this:

> II Timothy 3:16a *All Scripture is God-breathed....*

That means inspired by God.

> II Timothy 3:16b-17 *...and is valuable for teaching the truth, convicting of sin, correcting faults and training in right living; 17 thus anyone who belongs to God may be fully equipped for every good work.*

So what Paul is saying there is the Scriptures fully equip us for every good work. We don't need something more. And actually, think about it, what was the Word when Rabbi Sha'ul wrote that? Same answer. The Tanakh (Old Testament) again. It wasn't the New Testament because it wasn't written yet.

21. HONORING GOD'S WORD

God also commanded that His Word be heard by all His people. Here's an example. Joshua read what Moses had written.

Joshua 8:34-35 *Then afterward he read all the words of the Torah—the blessing and the curse—according to all that is written in the book of the Torah.* **35 There was not a word of all that Moses commanded that Joshua did not read** *before all the assembly of Israel, including the women and the little ones and the outsiders walking among them.*

God wanted His Word to be communicated. So He had Moses write it all down. He wanted all people to know it, so that they could know Him.

How the Word was preserved in ancient times

So, how was God's Word preserved for us from those days so long ago? Well, there were a couple of very important things that I'm not sure everyone realizes. One of the biggest preserving factors was that when the Temple was destroyed and the Jewish people were exiled far away in Babylon around 500 years before Yeshua, the leaders at the time set up the synagogue system. These small synagogue groups meeting in the different cities of Babylon began to study the Word written on scrolls.

And what developed out of that, after they came back, is that cities in Israel and cities in the Diaspora where the Jewish people were scattered always organized themselves into local synagogue congregations. After they got to a certain point where they had some resources, they got hold of a Torah Scroll—a used one or one bought from a special group of scribes specifically trained and commissioned for copying the Torah Scroll and checking it, making sure there were no errors.

These congregations all around the Roman Empire and in Israel met on Shabbat in obedience to Leviticus 23:3, which says that we are to have a holy convocation every Shabbat. They listened to the Torah, and they studied it. This was so important because by the time it came for Messiah to be revealed to Israel, this practice of everybody going to the synagogue every Shabbat and studying the Word resulted in a highly Biblically literate Jewish population in the Land of Israel and in all the cities of the Roman Empire. They were a people prepared to recognize and receive the Messiah. Otherwise, they would've been like, "Oh, what's a Messiah? Who are you? Who do you think you are?" But as we read through the Gospels, and if you look for it, you will see that the people were waiting and looking for the Messiah. And they were taught how to recognize the Messiah. Now that doesn't mean they all accepted Yeshua as the Messiah, but many did.

Honor those who wrote the Word

Simchat Torah is also a day to honor the people who were moved on by God to write His Word. So here is the list of the ones that we know the names of in the Bible. I'd like you to read this list. As you read it, think about how much you owe those who wrote each of these books of the Bible.

Moses, Joshua, Ezra, Nehemiah, David, Solomon, Isaiah, Jeremiah, Ezekiel, Daniel, Hosea, Joel, Amos, Obadiah, Jonah, Micah, Nahum, Habakkuk, Zephaniah, Haggai, Zechariah, Malachi, Matthew, Mark, Luke, John, Paul, James, Peter, Jude. Thank you to all of you!

Aren't you glad I didn't do that in Hebrew Names? Then there are books in the Bible that we don't know who wrote them. So here's a list of those writers. We can thank them, too.

Judges, I & II Samuel, I & II Kings, I & II Chronicles, Job, Ruth, Esther, and in the New Covenant, Hebrews.

So we want to honor these people. I hope that when you get to Heaven, you will look up each one of them and say thank you. Thank you for hearing from God and putting it down in writing.

We are also going to honor people who preserved and translated the Word. But to appreciate their efforts and their sacrifices for our sake, we need to be aware of those who opposed the spread of the Word.

First of all, Let's list the ones in Jewish history. Of course, there's Haaman. He wanted to destroy the Jewish people.

Why? Because they had other laws, not those of the Persian Empire. What were those other laws? The Laws of Moses, which has laws against bowing down to other gods or to people. Then there are the Greeks when they ruled the world and were trying to convert all the Jewish people to being Greek. Many people gave up their lives rather than abandon Judaism. Then after Yeshua came, we know that the Romans persecuted many, many believers, fed them to lions, crucified them, burned them. It was always for them keeping the Word. There were many such martyrs.

Opposition to translating the Word

But it was surprising to me as I dug into this where the greatest opposition to translating and spreading the Word came from. You'd think it was the Romans, the Muslims, or the pagans, but it was actually the Catholic church when the only Bible available to the people was in the dead language of Latin. Seven times from 1215 to 1546, Popes or Catholic counsels passed laws forbidding the translation of the Bible into the languages the people could understand. In fact, one of those edicts from one of the Popes, as I read it, actually banned the publication of any book not approved by the Pope.

These laws were re-affirmed by the Catholic church between the 16th and the 19th centuries over and over again. From 1816 to 1897 when Bible societies began publishing Bibles, five Popes publicly condemned them. During all those years, the Catholic church did not make its version of the Bible available either.

In the research I was doing, there was an account of someone who went to Ireland, a very Catholic country, to bookstores, trying to find a Bible. No Bibles at all.

From the 12th to the 17th century, the church persecuted a group called the **Waldenses**. They were a group of people who lived in the hills of France. They refused the church's authority and claimed the Bible as their authority. The Catholic leaders' response blew my mind. The church sent armies and inquisitors against them, killing more than 200,000 of them!

In the 14th century, **John Wycliff** was the first to translate the New Covenant in English. He was persecuted by the church, and only survived because the Queen of England protected him. After his death, the church dug up his bones and burned them!

In the 16th century, **William Tyndale**, who tried to translate the entire Bible, was executed, and his body was burned on the stake because he translated the Bible into English.

The church persecuted people who read Luther's Bible. **Luther** had translated it into German. The church imprisoned a man named **De Enzenes**, who was the person who first translated the Bible into Spanish.

So this was all just shocking to me. It's senseless! I mean, these Catholics were the people who were supposed to be spreading God's Word, and they were keeping God's Word from being spread. It's just so wrong.

But, of course, there were others who opposed the spread of the Word of God in our own time. Communists: the former USSR, and China. (The Word was allowed for a short while in China, from 2014 or so to 2019. Then it was cracked down on again.) And, of course, Muslim countries don't allow the Bible to be around at all. In fact, you may remember when the United States' troops went into Saudi Arabia in 1990, the commanders had to confiscate all the Bibles of our troops! The Saudis would not allow the American troops on their soil because they had Bibles with them. Amazing!

Now also, we should understand that Jewish religious authorities behaved in ways similar to Catholic leaders. In fact, even to today, Jewish religious leaders will teach that you really can't understand the Bible until you learn what all the esteemed rabbis, the Sages, have said about it in the Talmud and after it. And, of course, that takes forever to learn. So most people won't ever get through it. But as we just read, Joshua read it to who? To the women, the children, and to the outsiders among them because we can all understand it.

Honor those who preserved the Word

Now that we've understood the opposition, let's honor the people who have preserved God's Word. I thought of the developers of the Parashot, the Torah reading plan in Babylon, Ezra and the men of the Great Assembly, who also organized the synagogue system that honored the Word and kept the Scrolls, and Ezra read the Word to the exiles who returned. And then those from around 150 years before the time of Yeshua, the Maccabees, who defeated those Greeks who had outlawed the reading of the Word!

Then in the New Covenant, in the Gospels, we read about the scribes. What were they doing? They were carefully hand copying the Word, preserving the Word. And, of course, the Messianic Jews and the Gentile believers who gave their lives to preserve and spread the Word, especially during the time of Roman persecution.

Then later on, there were monasteries established, and when the Word wasn't going out to the people, the monks had the Word, and they preserved it. They copied it, and they kept it.

Beyond the preservers, there are the translators. Thank God for the translators who made the Bible available to people in their own language.

There were some Jewish translators 500 years before the time of Yeshua, who translated the Tanakh from the Hebrew into the Aramaic because the people of Israel had stopped speaking Hebrew and were speaking mostly Aramaic. Those are called the Targums. You can find them online, and can read the ones translated into English. They are very close to our Old Testament.

300 years before Yeshua, Jewish translators translated the Hebrew Tanakh into Greek in something called the Septuagint. We still have that.

Then another group that we owe a great debt to from the 9th century to the 15th century, was a group called the Masorites. They were Jewish scholars, and they gathered together the various manuscripts of the Tanakh. The manuscripts didn't all agree with each other. So they sorted through them and they created one unified text of the Tanakh. They are the ones that added the vowel points to the Hebrew so we know how to pronounce the words. They basically preserved the Scriptures from around the year 900 right up till 1500 when the printing press was developed, and the Word began to be available to all people, instead of just having one Scroll per congregation.

Finally, the Christian translators. I didn't think Christian translating had happened very early, but it actually started way back in the 4th century when the Scriptures were translated into Gothic. Then Jerome translated it into Latin, called the Latin Vulgate, around the year 400. He had a lot of resistance, by the way, in doing it.

In the fifth century, someone named Resperob translated it into Armenean, but then there were other translations: Syrian, Coptic, Nubean, Ethiopian, and Georgian translators in the fifth century!!

Then there was the long period of the Dark Ages. Then in the 13th century there was a translation into French, and in 1360 into Czech. Then in 1383, John Wycliffe translated the New Testament into English from the Latin Vulgate. (His assistant did the Old Testament, which wasn't as readable, Wikipedia says.) In the 15th century, it was translated into Hungarian and Spanish. In 1522 Luther translated it into German. In 1526, Jacob van Liesvelt translated it into Dutch. Tyndale spent eight years from 1526-1534 translating the Bible directly from the Hebrew and Greek texts into English, for which we noted he was executed, burned at the stake. Myles Coverdale completed Tyndale's work in 1537, which was the first complete printed English translation of the whole Bible. In 1563, it was translated into Polish and twenty years later in 1583 into Slovene. Finally in 1611, the King James Version came out, and it became widely distributed. Here is the list again for your reference.

    4th Century - Ulfilas - Gothic
    400 - Latin Vulgate - Jerome

5th Century - Mesrob - Armenian, also Syriac, Coptic, Nubean, Ethiopian, Georgian translators
13th Century - French
1360 - Czech
1383 - Wycliffe - English
15th Century - Hungarian
1478 - Spanish
1522 - Luther - German
1526 - Jacob van Liesvelt - Dutch
1526-34 - Tyndale - English - for which he was executed. Coverdale completed Tyndale's work, the first complete English Bible
1563 - Polish
1583 - Dalmatin - Slovene
1611 - KJV

There are others who contributed to translating and preserving and spreading the Word. I just want to mention and honor some of them. You remember reading about people smuggling Bibles into Russia. Brother Andrew is one. Others, some I know personally, smuggled Bibles into China before China was willing to open up.

In 1899, the Gideon society started. They've done an incredible work. Every time you go to a hotel or a motel, just open the desk drawer, what's there? A Bible! Around that same time, other Bible societies started. In many countries of the world, there are Bible societies just publishing Bibles in their languages.

I also think we ought to be thankful for the significant number of people who have made the Bible available on the internet for free! For nothing! You can just go to some websites, like *YouVersion*, and they've got around 50 versions and 200 languages you can read the Bible in. It's just amazing! Somebody had to put those all in, you know. I don't know who they are, but somebody had to take the time to do all that. Amazing!

I want to give a special thanks to David Stearn who did the *Complete Jewish Bible*, an amazing work! Also the *Tree of Life* version team. We now have two Messianic Jewish translations of the Scripture, for which we Messianics are grateful.

And I want to honor and say here that there have been men and women, all through this period of time, who preached the true Word of God with no recognition. They may have preached in smaller congregations, but they are heroes in my mind.

So, just to give you a little summary of where it is right now. As of 2022, the complete Bible is now available in 704 languages! The New Testament is available a total of 1551 languages. More than 98% of the world's population now have a Bible in their language. Isn't that amazing?!! Look where it has come with all that resistance! So, praise the Lord!!!

CHAPTER 22
JOSIAH'S LEGACY

I want to share in this chapter from an amazing story that just so intrigued me. As I was thinking about Simchat Torah and about honoring the Word on this special day, this story came to my mind. You may know it. It is a time when the Torah got lost. We're talking about the actual Torah scroll with the five books of Moses written on it! No other Bible scrolls existed then. At the time of this story, all the Bible they had was what Moses had written down. Some of the prophets had written things that had not been declared Scripture yet, but pretty much it was just the books of Moses. We'll see, as we get to the end of the story, how it relates so well to our time in history.

So we'll go back to the time when the Kingdom of Israel had been divided after King Solomon. Many years had passed, and many kings had reigned. Finally the Northern Kingdom, which was called Israel, was conquered by the Assyrians, and those people, the ten tribes (actually only nine tribes because most priests and Levites had moved south to Yehudah) were taken into exile into various parts of the Assyrian kingdom. But Yehudah (Judah), the Southern Kingdom, remained as a kingdom for many years after that, and several more kings reigned.

In II Kings 21, we have the account of King Manasseh, an awful, terribly evil king who sinned horribly. He got involved in idolatry. He shed innocent blood. He sacrificed children to pagan gods. The prophets spoke against what this King was doing. They spoke judgment on Judah, that Judah is going to be destroyed because of the sins of King Manasseh.

When King Manasseh died, his son Ammon followed him and also did evil. After reigning only two years, he was assassinated, and his eight-year-old son became king. This boy king's name in Hebrew was Yo-shi-ya-hu, but we will use the English name, Josiah. So we're going to pick up the story there. It's in both II Chronicles and in II Kings, so we'll be going back and forth for different details.

> II Chronicles 34:1 (CJB) *Yoshiyahu was eight years old when he began his reign, and he ruled for thirty-one years in Yerushalayim.*

Before we go on, let me explain his Hebrew Name. Yoshiyahu, pronounced Yoh-shee-yahoo, actually means *Yah* (God) *supports him*. *Yoshi* is *support,* and *Yah* is an abbreviation of God's Hebrew Name. *Hu* is *he*. So *God supports him*. And we'll see how God supported him.

> II Chronicles 34:2-3 *He did right in the eyes of Adonai, and walked in the ways of his father David. He did not turn aside to the right or to the left. 3 In the eighth year of his reign, while he was still young, he began to seek after the God of his father David.*

So this young man turned to the Lord, not when he first started his kingship, but when he turned 16 years old. Then during the 12th year of his reign when he was 20 years old, he began to cleanse the Temple, which was in great need of cleansing because of what the previous kings had done in it. When he was 26, we find this amazing passage. One of his servants, named Shaphan, came to him from the work that was going on, cleaning out the Temple and repairing and refurbishing it.

> II Kings 22:9 *Then Shaphan the scribe came to the king and brought back word to the king and said, "Your servants have emptied out the silver that was found in the House and have given it into the hand of the workmen appointed to oversee the work on the House of Adonai."*

> II Chronicles 34:14-15 *While they were bringing out the silver that had been brought into the House of Adonai, Hilkiah the kohen found a Torah scroll of Adonai given by Moses.*

15 Hilkiah responded by telling Shaphan the scribe, "I have found a scroll of the Torah in the House of ADONAI." Hilkiah gave the scroll to Shaphan.

II Kings 22:10-11 (CJB) Shafan the secretary also told the king, "Hilkiyah the cohen hagadol [high priest] gave me a scroll." Then Shafan read it aloud before the king. 11 After the king had heard what was written in the scroll of the Torah, he tore his clothes.

Not the reaction you would expect! Tearing your clothes in Judaism, as you might be aware, is a sign of grieving. So he was very grieved. Why? Let's read on to find out:

II Kings 22:13 (CJB) "Go; and consult ADONAI for me, for the people and for all Y'hudah in regard to what is written in this scroll which has been found. For ADONAI must be furious at us, since our ancestors did not listen to the words written in this scroll and didn't do everything written there that concerns us."

That's why he was grieving. He realized that they had not been obeying what was written in the scroll. Now what I believe the Holy Spirit wants us to grasp here is how amazing these circumstances are. Josiah had been raised in the household of the king. He had already, at this point, reigned as the king in Yerushalayim near the Temple for 18 years. He had been seeking the Lord for ten of those years, and he had never seen or heard the Bible read?! Isn't that shocking?! I mean, when you first read it, you don't grasp that, but that is the situation here. He had never heard it, not because God had forgotten to remind him to read it, but because it wasn't there. They didn't have it. It had been lost for a long time!

This is even more shocking when you realize that in the Torah, there are three verses that tell every king what he's supposed to do with the Torah. Copy it and read from it daily, remember? Then God gives the reasons why:

Deuteronomy 17:18-20 (CJB) "... he is to write a copy of this Torah for himself in a scroll, from the one the cohanim and L'vi'im [priests and Levites] use. 19 It is to remain with him, and he is to read in it every day, as long as he lives; so that he will learn to fear ADONAI his God and keep all the

> words of this Torah and these laws and obey them; 20 so that he will not think he is better than his kinsmen; and so that he will not turn aside either to the right or to the left from the mitzvah. In this way he will prolong his own reign and that of his children in Isra'el.

So God had given specific instructions of what every king was to do, and it's not just to read it. Do you see what this says? He is supposed to copy it himself! Have you ever seen a Torah scroll and the writing on it? Can you imagine? That would be quite a job to handwrite your own copy! Then he is supposed to be reading it every day.

Obviously Josiah hadn't done that, nor had his father or grandfather for sure. His great grandfather Hezekieh probably had because he also followed the Lord and cleansed the Temple. We know for sure that David did because he writes in the Psalms many songs about the Word of God. Just look at Psalm 17. So David knew the Word of God. Solomon wrote in Proverbs 3 about the Word of God, but 340 years had passed, and fifteen kings had reigned in Yehudah since the time of Solomon. There are lots of records in the books of Kings and Chronicles of battles, court intrigue, and assassination, but there's no record in the Bible of any king copying the scroll and reading it every day. Pretty sad, huh?

So evidently no one had read the Torah for a long time, not even the priests or scribes, and no one knew where one was. Josiah had been walking with the Lord for many years. Surely, he would have been asking, "Is there a copy of the Torah Scroll around somewhere?" But it looks like they found the only known Torah Scroll in all of Israel. Otherwise if another one existed, then Josiah, being the king and a Godly man, would have found it. So he sent his servants to a prophet, actually it was a prophetess. Her name was Hildah, and this is what she told them:

> II Kings 22:16 *Thus says Adonai, behold, I am bringing disaster on this place and on its inhabitants, as in all the words of the scroll that the king of Judah read.*

I believe that what he would have read in the Scroll was the consequences for disobedience. One place where terrible

22. JOSIAH'S LEGACY

judgments for disobedience are listed is in Leviticus 26, but the most powerful set of judgments for disobedience is in Deuteronomy 28. You may remember that it's got the blessings and then the curses. That's almost at the end of the Scroll. So if he heard that part, Shaphan must have read through the entire Scroll to him. That would have taken at least half a day!

> II Kings 22:17 *For they have forsaken Me and burned incense to other gods, in order to provoke Me with all the work of their hands. Therefore My wrath has been kindled against this place and it will not be quenched.*

This is not good news for Josiah. It's basically saying that the judgment is coming, not just because of Manasseh, but because of the many kings that were evil and the people who went along with the kings. But then she went on.

> II Kings 22:18-19 *"But to the king of Judah who sent you to inquire of Adonai, thus will you say to him: 'Thus says Adonai, God of Israel. As for the words that you have heard, 19 because your heart was softened and you humbled yourself before Adonai when you heard what I spoke against this place and against its inhabitants—that they should become a desolation and a curse—and because you have torn your clothes and wept before Me, I also have heard you,' declares Adonai."*

So because of how Josiah had a contrite heart and a humble spirit, the Lord God says, "I've heard you." This is a beautiful example here of the grace of God. There's been all this evil but because you have turned, because you are sorry, I have heard you. She went on to say:

> II Kings 22:20 *"'Therefore behold, I will gather you to your fathers and you will be gathered to your grave in shalom. So your eyes will not see all the disaster I am bringing on this place.'" Then they brought back word to the king.*

So this is a very interesting promise. "I will not bring destruction in your lifetime, Josiah. It'll still come, but it won't be in your lifetime." Now if that were you, how would you handle something like that? I mean this could be very depressing. In other words, nothing that I do is going to help. Right? I'm not going to be able to stop this. The tendency might be to go off and sulk about it or to get angry. There's no way that Josiah can prevent what's going to happen to his nation. But look what Josiah did.

> II Kings 23:2 *The king went up to the House of ADONAI and all the men of Judah and all the inhabitants of Jerusalem with him—the kohanim and the prophets, all the people, young and old—and he read in their hearing all the words of the Book of the Covenant which was found in the House of ADONAI.*

I want you to picture this. This is the king himself, not a servant. He's reading all the way through the Torah Scroll to all the people. Now how many people were there? Thousands! I mean just for everyone to be able to hear, he would have had to be shouting, and he went all the way through that Scroll! And he did more!

> II Kings 23:3 (CJB) *The king stood on the platform and made a covenant in the presence of ADONAI to live following ADONAI, observing his mitzvot, instructions and regulations wholeheartedly and with all his being, so as to confirm the words of the covenant written in this scroll. All the people stood, pledging themselves to keep the covenant.*

So the people were so inspired by Josiah that they said, "We'll keep that covenant too." Now I'm going to go through the rest quickly because there's a lot here. I recommend you read chapters 4 through 9.

Josiah began to destroy the idols that were in the Temple area, lots of them, and he deposed the idolatrous priests that had been appointed by previous kings. Then he completely destroyed all the idols all through the Land and destroyed the houses of cult prostitutes because the ancient pagan cultures mixed fornication in with their religion and their worship. So he destroyed all of that. He removed men who were supposed to be Temple priests but were serving in high places and destroyed those high places because the Scroll said you weren't supposed to worship in any place else but the Temple, not in any other places, only in Jerusalem in the Temple.

Then this one was very interesting. Let's just read this to see how bad it was there:

22. JOSIAH'S LEGACY

II Kings 23:10 *He desecrated the Tofet fire pit in the Ben-Hinnom Valley, so that no one could cause his son or daughter to pass through fire* [as a sacrifice] *to Molekh.*

See what they were doing? Child sacrifice! In verses 11 through 20 he ordered one more cleansing, and then in verse 21, he commanded Passover to be kept.

II Kings 23:24 (CJB) *Yoshiyahu got rid of the mediums and the people using spirit guides, as well as the household gods, the idols and all the disgusting things spotted anywhere in Y'hudah and Yerushalayim. He did this in order to establish the words of the Torah written in the scroll Hilkiyahu the cohen had found in the house of ADONAI.*

So he destroyed the people that were doing occult practices: fortune tellers, mediums, spiritists, etc. He was thoroughly cleansing the Land of all evil and setting the Temple services back in order. He reorganized the kohanim and Levites, and the singers and musicians to serve in the Temple and then did something very important, which brings me to my main point.

II Chronicles 35:3 *He said to the Levites who taught all Israel and who were consecrated to ADONAI, "Put the holy Ark in the House which Solomon the son of King David of Israel built. Since it is no longer a burden on your shoulders now, serve ADONAI your God and His people Israel."*

The word used there for *taught*, is המבונים *hmbvnym*. It doesn't have any vowel markings in the Hebrew text, which is highly unusual, and apparently indicates that no one knows for sure what it means. The interlinear Bibles record it with vowel markings, but spelled slightly different: המבינים *hambinim*. *Strong's Concordance* and BlueletterBible.org give the root word as בין *bin* (pronounced "bean") meaning *understand, understanding, consider,* etc. One online Hebrew Interlinear Bible (at scripture4all.org) translates it *the ones-explaining.* I think King Josiah was telling the Levites that they need to start serving God and His people by doing what they were supposed to be doing, teaching and explaining the Torah to the people. They obviously had not been doing that at all for a generation or two since no one seemed to know what was in the Torah. I believe he did the awesome thing of sending the Levites out to the people all around the Land of Israel to diligently teach them the Word. He was trying to make sure there would never be another day when the Torah would be lost either literally or spiritually. The author of II Kings then sums up all that Josiah did:

> II Kings 23:25 *Before him there had never been a king like him, who turned to ADONAI with all his heart and with all his soul and with all his might, according to all the Torah of Moses, nor has any king like him risen since him.*

What better thing could be said? That's what you would want to have said about you! Yet with all Josiah's righteousness and accomplishments, he was not able to prevent the judgment that was coming on Israel.

So how did it come? Well, read on in II Chronicles 35. Josiah picked a fight with Pharaoh Nico, the king of Egypt. He didn't have to, but he decided to go out and fight with him and was mortally wounded in the battle and died. As I read this, I thought, "You know, if I were Josiah and I understood that judgment wasn't going to come until I died, I'd be real careful with my life. I would keep away from anything dangerous." I don't know why he insisted on fighting that pharaoh. The only thing I could think of was that he didn't trust the Lord to protect Judah. Maybe it was pride. Maybe he thought he could defeat him or something, but it was a fatal mistake that Josiah made, and he died, which fulfilled the prophecy that he would die before the judgment came.

But before he died, he made two other mistakes that might have kept the judgment from coming a little while longer and maybe for a long time longer. He didn't disciple his two sons in the way of the Lord because we read that they both did evil in the sight of the Lord when they reigned after him. Somehow all his reformations didn't reach them. The evil seed of Josiah's grandfather was still in them. We don't know how long the judgment would have been delayed if they had been good kings, but they weren't, so eventually the judgment had to come.

> II Kings 23:26-27 *Nevertheless, ADONAI did not turn from the fury of His great wrath which burned against Judah, because of all that Manasseh had provoked Him. 27 ADONAI*

said, "I will banish Judah also from My presence as I banished Israel, and I have spurned this city, Jerusalem, which I chose, and the House about which I had said: 'My Name will be there.'"

So II Kings 24 records the invasion of Yehudah (Judah) by the Babylonians under Nebuchadnezzar. It records the exile of the people, the destruction of the city and the wall, and finally the destruction of the Temple itself in fulfillment of the prediction by the author of II Kings that the evils of Israel before Josiah had been too great for the Lord to allow the nation to continue to exist. So, except for the sad ending, it's a great story, isn't it?

Now how does it apply to us? The Spirit of God led me to this story, and I was like, "Okay, it's a wonderful story. Somebody should make a movie out of it, but what has it got to do with us?" Then the Spirit began to reveal some things to me that I hadn't really grasped before. I hope that you can grasp this, too.

First, we have to understand that this was not the end of the story. This was not the end of what God was doing through the people of Israel. After 70 years in exile in Babylon, the Lord spoke to Cyrus, the king of Persia, who was over them at that time, and he sent the people of Israel back to Jerusalem to rebuild the Temple and the wall. You can read about that in the books of Ezra and Nehemiah. Three hundred years later, God-fearing values were preserved through the courage of the Maccabees and their followers. So 600 years after the Babylonian conquest, Israel was still a nation when it was time for the coming of the Messiah and the pouring out of the Spirit! Then came the establishing of Messianic Judaism and the spreading of the Good News throughout the entire world.

So the destruction of Jerusalem wasn't the end of the story. Perhaps as Josiah studied Moses' writings, he gained some hope for what was to come, specifically that God promised in Deuteronomy 18 that He would raise up another prophet like Moses, the Messiah, and He also promised that when the people were exiled, He would bring them back some time later.

Then the Spirit revealed something new to me in studying this, which was that Josiah played a critically important role in God's plan to bring the Messiah. What was that role? Well, I have to give you the background setting first to be able to explain it. Earlier we learned that neither the kohanim, nor the people, nor the king were knowledgeable of the Torah in the time before Josiah. All Torah Scrolls had been lost somehow, even the one in the Temple. Some may have remembered some of it by heart, especially any faithful kohanim, Levites, and scribes that were left. They would have maybe been reciting parts of it, but it seems nobody knew any of it. If anybody had memorized part of it, they definitely didn't know the parts about the curses for disobedience! And they certainly had not memorized the part that said King Josiah was supposed to copy it and read it every day. Josiah had never heard any of that stuff, and that's why he mourned.

After he heard the Scroll read for the first time, he personally read it to the people, as we saw, and then he led them to make a covenant to begin obeying it. He led them to keep Passover, which means he would have had them keep the other Appointed Times, and he sent kohanim out to teach the Torah to all Israel. So he did all that.

Eleven years after his death after his two sons had reigned wickedly, Yehudah (Judah) was carried away into exile to Babylon. Here's some more history about their exile in Babylon that we touched on in the last chapter. Historians tell us that it was during their Babylonian captivity when there was no longer a Temple, under Ezra's leadership, that they set up the synagogue system, so that each town of the Jewish people had a synagogue in it, and each town would have a Scroll, and they would come to the synagogue, and the leaders would read the Word publicly every Shabbat. That was the plan at least. We don't know how slow the process was nor what percentage of the towns were reached.

Simchat Torah celebrates the beginning of the Torah reading cycle. We understand that the reading cycle was actually developed and put into practice during the Babylonian captivity. That's when it actually started. So when the people returned to Jerusalem seventy years later, we have evidence in the Bible that they wanted to hear the Scripture read. You may have seen this verse in Nehemiah, which shows, to me, that it was the custom by this time to study the Word. This is after the people of Israel had returned from exile, were settled, and had gathered in Jerusalem for the Appointed Time of Rosh Hashanah.

> Nehemiah 8:1 (CJB) *When the seventh month arrived, after the people of Isra'el had resettled in their towns, all the people gathered with one accord in the open space in front of the Water Gate and asked Ezra the Torah-teacher to bring the scroll of the Torah of Moshe, which ADONAI had commanded Isra'el. ...*
>
> Nehemiah 8: 8-9 (NRSV) *... They gave the sense, so that the people understood the reading. 9 ... all the people wept when they heard the words of the law* [Torah].

Notice that the people asked Ezra to read from the Torah scroll. They had become accustomed to reading the Word during their time in Babylon captivity. Or at least they knew there were towns that had a Scroll and looked forward to the day when their community would have one, and longed to hear it read. Maybe many had never heard it read yet. What else would cause them to weep? I guess they could've been weeping tears of joy because they are now in a land where the Torah can more easily be followed, and now they can build the Temple again. But the Levites thought they were sad and repenting, as we can see in their reaction in a later verse (which we will talk about in chapter 27). And notice that even Ezra and the Levites didn't know the whole Torah:

> Nehemiah 8:13-14 *On the second day, the heads of the families along with the kohanim and the Levites gathered around Ezra to ponder the words of the Torah. 14 They found written in the Torah that ADONAI had commanded through Moses that Bnei-Yisrael should dwell in sukkot during the feast of the seventh month.*

The Jewish leaders didn't even know about Sukkot! That's hard to fathom! So apparently Ezra and the Great Assembly of leaders weren't able to completely fulfill their plan in every town and community. You know how people are and how hard it is to change a whole society, especially when you're a minority people living in a foreign land as exiles under a foreign government. Perhaps some of the local Babylonian leaders didn't allow such things in their regions. So there would've been lots of hurdles there.

But with their own people, there was a lot that had to be accomplished. First, all the kohanim and Levites had to be taught to reverence the Torah and learn it and memorize it. And to do all that, they had to stay fluent in Hebrew while needing to learn and become fluent in the Babylonian languages where they now lived.

Scribes also had to know Hebrew and learn Torah, and then be taught how to copy it meticulously and perfectly with great reverence and awe and worship. They had to be pious men of honor with total integrity, and be given a special title that indicates all of that, like today's title, **sofer** (scribe who hand writes the scroll). So the training had to be official and certifiable. Rules and rituals had to be set in place to help the scribe be reverent and focused so there would be no sloppiness or copy errors and no creativity. For example, today, before beginning, the **sofer** has to be cleansed in a mikveh. Then he has to carefully check all his writing instruments and replace any flawed ones, and then recite a declaration that he is copying the Holy Torah for a holy purpose.

The Torah had to be copied exactly with no personal flare added in handwriting style or anything. Today, according to "Torah Scroll Facts" on the Chabad.org website (chabad.org/library/article_cdo/aid/351655/jewish/Torah-Scroll-Facts.htm), "A sofer must know more than 4,000 Judaic laws" before he is qualified!! So it would've taken a whole generation possibly to get this special cultural office of the scribes established and properly honored. And this was hand copying, of course. It takes nearly a whole year to hand copy just one scroll.

Here are some facts to show you how difficult the whole procedure is. A Torah scroll is made of parchment sections made from the skin of a kosher animal. The **sofer** does one section at a time. When all the sections are finished, they are sewn together (from: myjewishlearning.com/article/torah-scroll/). If any mistake at all is made, that whole section of the scroll cannot be used. If any mistakes are found after it is sewn together, chabad.org says: "Even a single missing or misshapen letter invalidates the entire Sefer Torah" (chabad.org/library/article_cdo/aid/351655/jewish/Torah-Scroll-Facts.htm). Then the scribe would have to start over with a new scroll.

So you see how long it took and how involved King Josiah's and later Ezra's implementations were. But notice that because of them, the people had great reverence for God and for the Torah:

> Nehemiah 8:5-6 *Ezra opened the scroll in the sight of all the people for he was above all the people. When he opened it, all the people stood up. 6 Ezra blessed A<small>DONAI</small>, the great God, and all the people answered, "Amen, amen!" as they lifted up of their hands. Then they bowed down and worshiped A<small>DONAI</small> with their faces to the ground.*

And they listened intently, even for several hours, from sunrise to noon!!! It says so here:

> Nehemiah 8:3 *So he read from it before the plaza in front of the Water Gate from first light until midday, in the presence of the men and women, and others who could understand. And all the people listened attentively to the scroll of the Torah.*

Now look at this next verse:

> Nehemiah 8:7-8 *The Levites — Jeshua, Bani, Sherebiah, Jamin, Akkub, Shabbetai, Hodiah, Maaseiah, Kelita, Azariah, Jozabad, Hanan and Pelaiah — instructed the people in the Torah while the people were standing in their place. 8 They read from the Torah scroll of God, distinctly explaining it and giving insight.*

Notice that the thirteen Levites named there knew at least some of the Torah well enough to teach it. So surely many kohanim did also. Then as we saw in 8:13-14 (p. 281), the leaders with Ezra spent time meditating on the Torah and discovered the Sukkot commandments for each family to make a sukkah, and if you read on, you will see that the people all excitedly obeyed and fully celebrated Sukkot.

The returning exiles then, under Ezra's leadership, established synagogues all around Israel, so that by the time Yeshua came, there were synagogues in every city and village. We read about Him going into them and reading from the Scroll. So what the Spirit is trying to get us to see is that, before Josiah, none of that was in existence. They didn't even know where the Scroll was for probably hundreds of years. So Josiah deserves some credit for the Jewish people as a whole never being Torah illiterate and without a Torah Scroll ever again.

Three hundred years after their resettling from exile, we have the time of the Maccabees, which is what we celebrate at Hanukkah. If you remember the evil king of Syria, Antiochus Epiphanes, what did he do? In his decree, he forbade Torah study, and he forbade obedience to God's Word: no circumcision, no keeping the Moadim, no keeping kosher. That decree resulted in the Maccabean revolt. What does that show? It shows how committed the people were to studying and obeying the Word by that time. Do you see the contrast there? Before Josiah, there were idols all over the place, mediums, and spiritists, and high places where they were worshiping God in an un-Scriptural way, even burning children in the fire as a sacrifice. But by the time of the Maccabees, people were fighting and risking their lives to be able to keep the Word. What a contrast!

And 150 years after the Maccabees, in the time of Yeshua, the Gospels paint a picture of a culture with an extremely high level of Biblical knowledge. Have you ever thought about that? The people all knew the Messianic prophecies. They were praying for and expecting the Messiah! Fishermen, like Peter and James and John, were quoting Scripture all over the place. Even a tax collector like Matthew quoted Scripture. If you read their writings, every few sentences they quote from the Tanakh, the Old Testament. They knew the Word! So we see a drastic contrast between the time before Josiah and afterward, even up to the time when Yeshua came on the scene.

So here's the thing. Why was this Biblical literacy and obedience so important to God's plan? It's really important to the spiritual history of the world and to us. Why? Well, in the New Covenant in the book of Galatians Paul says this about the Messiah:

Galatians 4:4 (NKJV) *But when the fullness of the time had come, God sent forth His Son, born of a woman, born under the law,*

What does this mean? In God's plan for redemption, there was a specific time when the Messiah was to come and that time had to meet certain requirements.

First, it had to be when the Messiah could be born under the Law. What does that mean? It means it had to be a time when His parents could live according to the Law, the Torah, and do the things that were required to be done to a child born according to the Torah, like circumcision and Pidyon HaBen (redemption of the first born). And then as He grew up, He had to be able to live in obedience to the Laws of God, keeping all the Moadim, going to Jerusalem three times a year, all the things required of all men in the Torah.

Why? What would have happened if He didn't do those things? Could he have been the Messiah? No because not keeping the Torah would have been sin, and He had to be without sin to be the spotless Lamb. So He had to perfectly obey all of God's Torah. If not, His sacrifice would not have been able to pay the price. Do you see that? It would not have been the perfect sacrifice to pay the price for all sin for all time for all people. Living under the Law could not have been accomplished if He was living all by Himself in a vacuum. There had to be a Temple. There had to be a functioning priesthood. He had to be living in a Biblically literate and Biblically obedient culture to be the Messiah. You see that now, right?

Okay, but here's another thing. What would have happened if He had come to a culture that was Biblically obedient, but not literate? "We're doing all these things that God commands, but we don't know the Bible." Only if the people were Biblically literate would they have been expecting the Messiah, able to recognize the Messiah, have faith in Him, and be willing to follow Him and even give their lives for Him. If they hadn't known all the prophecies and what this was all about, they wouldn't have been expecting Him. Remember there were no New Covenant Scriptures. All they had was the Torah, the prophets, and the writings, i.e., the Tanakh. If they hadn't known, even if He came, nobody would have followed Him because they wouldn't have been prepared for Him.

So here's the question that ties Josiah together with the reading plan and the Messiah. How did Israel go from a nation that had lost the only copy of the Bible they had—from a completely Biblically illiterate and disobedient nation, filled with idolatry, witchcraft, and child sacrifice—to a nation described in the Gospels where nearly everyone knew the Scriptures? I mean they weren't perfect in the time of Yeshua, but it's obvious that they were trying their best to keep all the Laws of God. Right? How did they get there? Where do you see the drastic change?

Well, we just read the account of one man who turned that tide. If not for Josiah, none of that would have happened. He caused the change. His contrite heart caused it. When he heard the Word read for the first time, he repented. He sought the Lord. He restored the Appointed Times. He had the Temple cleansed and restored the priesthood. He taught the people the Word. He sent the priests out throughout the land to teach the Word.

And here's the amazing thing. Even though the nation was destroyed by the Babylonians, the people just from that one period of time changed! I mean it was just from his 18th year to when his reign ended at 31 years. So it was about 12 or 13 years that he was able to oversee the whole nation obeying the Scriptures. After that his evil sons took over. After their short reigns, the nation was destroyed, but that was enough to make the people want to stick with the Word all the way through the Babylonian captivity, all the way through the time

22. JOSIAH'S LEGACY

before the Maccabees, through the battles and then the reign of the Maccabees, all the way until after the Romans invaded, and up to the point where Yeshua became the Messiah. Isn't that amazing? That was Josiah's contribution. His example and his reforms led to many who actually lived righteously even through the judgment of being exiled. They were sent to Babylon, yet they still walked with God through those times. They wouldn't have if it wasn't for Josiah.

Who are they? Daniel. How did Daniel know all that he knew about Torah? Well, he had started reading the Word when Josiah did. The same with Ezekiel and Jeremiah. How about Ezra, Nehemiah, Mordecai and Esther, the Maccabees and all their descendants? How did they know? For all of them, it was passed down because of Josiah's reforms. And they clung to that commitment to being people of the Word. Without Josiah's example and reforms, Israel would have remained illiterate and disobedient.

Here's another thing. The appointed time for the Messiah to come could not have come. Well, we know God would have had another way, but I realized that we all owe a big debt of gratitude to Josiah. I want to see him when I get to Heaven and thank him for this. He had a big part in the blessing of us being able to be here today, rejoicing in the Word. Do you see that? This culture that we have, which was transmitted from Judaism to Christianity, of loving the Word and of following the Word, or used to have, maybe I should say, we can trace it back to Josiah.

You know, many denominational churches read through the New Testament yearly. Where did they get that from? From the synagogues where they read through the five books of Moses every year. We owe all of that to this one man who had a contrite enough heart to say, "Oh no! We haven't been doing it right. Let's start now!" I believe he's a Biblical hero. I've never thought of him this way before, but he's up there with David and Moses in my mind now. He is amazing.

So how does this apply to us and our lives and where we live today? Well, as I thought about this, I saw that we live in similar times to Josiah and in a similar nation to Josiah's nation. We know our nation is rapidly becoming Biblically illiterate and is rapidly disregarding God's Laws all the time. And we know from Bible prophecy that destruction is coming, right? Judgment is coming. It's coming on the entire world. The Great Tribulation, the "time of Jacob's trouble" is coming.

And you know what? We can't stop it. There's no way we can stop it. We can't prevent that judgment from coming. I believe this is the message to us. We must follow what Josiah did. He knew he couldn't stop the judgment, but from his example, we can draw hope that we can reach our generation as he did, or at least part of our generation, people put in our path. And if that judgment comes, some people will go through that judgment—maybe we'll go through that judgment, but they and we will be walking with the Lord through that judgment like Daniel, Ezekiel, Ezra, and Nehemiah.

You might believe in a pre-tribulation rapture, that we're not going to have to go through the judgment. I always say I'm not sure. I don't know whether it's going to be pre- or mid- or post-. So we may have to go through that judgment, but we need to go through it with commitment to the Word and following the leading of the Spirit of God.

The other thing is that we can't know, you can't know how great an impact you can have on the world. This man. I mean he was a king, but look at the impact he had! Look at the fruit that he bore. Each of us can influence people that God brings across our path. We can bring them to salvation, so they won't be destroyed in the coming judgment. They'll be able to walk through it, your loved ones, your descendants. How? By turning them to the Book the same way Josiah did. We mustn't give in to discouragement about the approaching judgment. Instead, we should be more zealous to reach as many as we can before the judgment comes, so that people will be prepared.

So let's pray.

Father, we thank You for Josiah. Thank You for his amazing example and the enormous effect of what he did. Thank You for the people who followed his lead and continued to treasure, protect, and spread Your Word for those six hundred years until Messiah came, and for the two thousand years since. So I pray, Father, for myself and for everyone who's reading this that You would give us courage and strength to stand up for Your Word against all the forces that are trying to destroy it and those who spread it right now, and trying to destroy its influence in our world. Show us our part as individuals in spreading Your Word, Father. Show us how to be examples of its power in our lives, Father. May we all have testimonies of Your Word leading us.

Help us to communicate, Lord, the power to those who don't know it, especially to the Jewish community. Keep us from fear of persecution, which is rising now toward those who would spread Your Word. May we see many Jewish people saved from the coming judgment.

I pray, Lord, that we would be able to pass Your message on to those whom we disciple, especially our children, Father, but to all whom You bring across our paths, that they would be able to carry it on and pass it on to their children and to others. We want to make disciples who make disciples. Help us teach others to make disciples so that this treasuring of Your Word and obedience to it would go on even through the tribulation and the judgment that we know is coming. We thank You once again in Yeshua's Name for Your Word. Amein.

CHAPTER 23
THE POWER OF THE PARASHOT

For this chapter, I decided to take a look at the history and purpose of the Parashot. This led me to looking at God's purposes for Israel, how He accomplished and is still accomplishing those purposes, what that teaches us about Him, why there has been so much opposition to His plan for Israel, and the importance of this understanding to our lives.

We just learned in the last chapter how Josiah's reforms caused Israel to be a Biblically literate nation. Well, it was his reforms that led to the Parashot being developed years later during the exile. So let's look into the history of the Parashot from a little different angle this time, starting with Moshe and then jumping ahead to Ezra and then to after Yeshua and up to today to see how the Parashot have affected the whole world. We will see that the Parashot has been one of the most important things in making the Word of God have greater effect.

History of the parashot

> Deuteronomy 31:9 (CJB) *Then Moshe wrote down this Torah and gave it to the cohanim, the descendants of Levi who carried the ark with the covenant of ADONAI, and to all the leaders of Isra'el.*

So Moshe wrote down the Torah. Again this contradicts Rabbinic Judaism's claim that the Oral Law was given to Moshe to transmit orally, that he didn't write it down.

> Deuteronomy 31:10-11 (CJB) *Moshe gave them these orders: "At the end of every seven years, during the festival*

23. THE POWER OF THE PARASHOT

of Sukkot in the year of sh'mittah, 11 when all Isra'el have come to appear in the presence of ADONAI at the place he will choose, you are to read this Torah before all Isra'el, so that they can hear it.

The Torah commands us to read the whole Torah scroll to all the people every seven years in the Shmitah year. That is not very frequent, but during the Shmitah year lots of different things happen, like the land resting, so no farm work was to be done. So it was like a vacation year. So the Torah also being read that year would have been quite a memorable event!!

Ezra fulfilled this command, though not at Sukkot the first time but at Rosh Hashanah:

> Nehemiah 8:2-3 (CJB) *Ezra the cohen brought the Torah before the assembly, which consisted of men, women and all children old enough to understand. It was the first day of the seventh month. 3 Facing the open space in front of the Water Gate, he read from it to the men, the women and the children who could understand from early morning until noon; and all the people listened attentively to the scroll of the Torah.*

"Early morning until noon!" That's 5-6 hours of listening. The Torah was being read and explained. They also did this at the correct time at Sukkot:

> Nehemiah 8:17-18 *The entire assembly who had returned from the captivity made sukkot and dwelt in the sukkot. Since the days of Joshua the son of Nun until that day Bnei-Yisrael had not done so—and the joy was very great. 18 Day after day from the first day to the last day, he* (Ezra) *read from the scroll of the Torah of God. So they kept the festival for seven days, and on the eighth day, according to the regulation, there was a solemn assembly.*

So God commanded that the Torah be read to everyone once every seven years. But, in Acts we find the custom of reading from it every week.

> Acts 15:21 *For from the earliest times, Moshe has had in every city those who proclaim him, with his words being read in the synagogues every Shabbat."*

So by this time in Israel's history, in addition to reading all of the Torah every seven years, they were reading part of Moshe every seven days. When did this custom start? As you know by now, it was Ezra who initiated it. He started the weekly Parashah readings along with synagogue movement while they were still in exile in Babylon. So this custom was in place 600 years before Yeshua!

The reading of the Parashah was always the focus of Shabbat assemblies in the synagogues. The Brit Hadashah tells us in Luke 4:17 that Yeshua went to the synagogue in His hometown of Nazareth and read from Isaiah, which would've been the Haftorah reading, which is selected readings from the prophets and the wisdom books to go with the Parashah reading. (The word *haftorah* means *conclusion.*) So this was also in place in Yeshua's time.

The Effect of the Parashot

The Weekly Parashot made the Word of God have greater effect. How? It kept the Torah's teachings before the people. And thankfully this custom is still with us today. Moshe is read weekly in every synagogue all around the world, orthodox, conservative, reformed, and Messianic.

This custom also affected the Gentile world. When the church separated itself from its Jewish roots, it retained the custom of meeting weekly to read from the Word. Most evangelical churches no longer read according to a schedule, but, I visited Catholic services a few times and was amazed how similar their tradition is to Jewish traditions. They say a blessing and kiss the book, as one small example, and they have a weekly Bible reading plan. However, their plan doesn't cover the entire books of Moshe, just selections connected with Brit Hadashah passages.

This periodic reading was instrumental in fulfilling God's purposes for the world. Obviously it's an important part of God's plan to grow His Messianic Body, but it also had a vital, miraculous effect on non-Messianic Israel. It kept us distinct as a people even when scattered among the nations in the face of incredible opposition inspired by ha-satan.

How did the Parashot contribute to our miraculous survival? Well, it unites us by hearing our story every year, so we never forget our origins and the God who chose us. It also reminds us of God's commandments, so we know how we are required to live. These weekly Parashot cause us to read over and over how God has a high standard of obedience that He requires of us. In the Torah, Moshe makes many amazing prophesies that are warnings concerning disobedience to give us a healthy fear of disobeying.

> Deuteronomy 28:58-59 *If you do not take care to do all the words of this Torah, the things written in this scroll, to fear this glorious and awesome Name, ADONAI your God, 59 then ADONAI will make your plagues and the plagues of your descendants extraordinary—terrible and prolonged plagues, severe and prolonged illnesses.*

There is a price to pay for not obeying the Lord.

> Deut. 28:63-64 *Now just as ADONAI rejoiced over you to do you good and to multiply you, so ADONAI will rejoice over you to ruin and destroy you; and you will be uprooted from the land that you are going in to possess. 64 "ADONAI will scatter you among all peoples from the one end of the earth to the other, and there you will serve other gods—wood and stone—that you and your fathers have not known.*

We know that Israel was divided following King Shlomo's (Solomon's) death; that in 700 BCE the Northern Kingdom of Samaria was exiled to Assyria and scattered, and then around 600 BCE the Southern Kingdom of Yehudah (Judah) was exiled to Babylon. But, the scattering among all nations is not recorded in the Bible. That happened after the destruction of Yerushalayim in 135 CE when Israel was scattered by Rome. Since then Jewish people have lived in every country of the world in fulfillment of this prediction. It even has a name—The Diaspora. It began 1500 years after Moshe's prophesy.

Moshe also predicted in the same Parashah what life would be like in this Diaspora as a further incentive to follow the Lord.

> Deut. 28:65 *Among these nations you will find no rest, and there will be no rest for the sole of your foot. But there ADONAI will give you a trembling heart and failing eyes, and a despairing spirit.*

From 414 CE to 1918 CE Jewish history records entire populations being evicted from 70 cities and nations.

> Deut. 28:66-67 *Your life will hang in the balance before you; you will be afraid night and day, and you will have no assurance of your life. 67 In the morning you will say, 'If only it were evening!' and at evening you will say, 'If only it were morning!'—from the fear of your heart that you will fear and the sight of your eyes that you will see.*

There are 118 historically recorded killings of Jews from 414-1918. At some of them, tens of thousands were killed. The 119th killing is the Holocaust when 6 million Jewish people were killed. Moshe's words are so accurate—terror your eyes will see.

To understand Jewish attitudes today, it is important to know who carried out these persecutions. Almost all of them happened in Christian nations incited by ha-satan, and were carried out by the Catholic church or under their averted eyes. It was often carried out by those professing to be Christians based on many false accusations of the Jewish people.

We understand that in those days most who professed to be Christians were ignorant of the Word. Although parts of the Word were read in Catholic churches every week, it was not read in the common languages, and only priests could interpret it. But, some, like Martin Luther, were believers and knowledgeable. Later we'll see why ha-satan continually incited these persecutions.

Keeps our purpose before us

The Torah's warnings of being expelled come along with instructions on how to live in the Land given to us by God for a great purpose. Let's look at what that great purpose was:

> Exodus 19:6a *So as for you, you will be to Me a kingdom of kohanim and a holy nation. ...*

We were to be a kingdom of kohanim, all priests. Kohanim speak to God for the people and to the people for God. But, if we were all to be priests, who would we be speaking for or to? The nations! Israel received a great mandate from God to bring His revelation to all nations, so the nations would turn from false god's and worship Him.

> Genesis 12:3 (CJB) *I will bless those who bless you, but I will curse anyone who curses you; and by you all the families of the earth will be blessed.*

We were to be a blessing to all the families of the earth. How? By bringing the revelation of God through the Scriptures, and then for Him to bring forth Mashiakh from among us. His plan was to make us distinct from other nations (Exodus 19:6, above), for us to demonstrate God's holy character:

> Leviticus 19:2 *"Speak to the entire community of Isra'el; tell them, 'You people are to be holy because I, ADONAI your God, am holy.'"*

Our living according to God's Law was to be a testimony to the nations to lead them to Him. Speaking of His commandments, God says this:

> Deut. 4:6-7 *You must keep and do them, for it is your wisdom and understanding in the eyes of the peoples, who will hear all these statutes and say, 'Surely this great nation is a wise and understanding people.' 7 For what great nation is there that has gods so near to them, as ADONAI our God is whenever we call on Him?*

We were to shine as lights to the nations that God was with us and helped us. At times we fulfilled this calling. For example, during King Solomon's reign, Queen of Sheba came to see Israel because the word that God's wisdom was present had reached Ethiopia. But, sadly, instead of being an example of Godly living to the nations, we often turned away from His Covenant. Our sin caused nations around us to mock and blaspheme His holy Name.

God pleaded with our forefathers to turn back, but finally His just nature compelled Him to execute judgment, and so we were expelled from the land, twice. We were exiled to Babylon for 70 years, and later to the Diaspora, fulfilling the warnings, that turning away would lead to expulsion, experiencing the awfulness described by Moshe. God was saying: if you will not be a light to the nations in your land, you will live in darkness in their land.

Yet amazingly God used His judgment upon us as a witness to nations.

> Ezekiel 5:15 (CJB) *When I execute judgments and furious punishments among you in anger and fury, [Yerushalayim] will be an object of reproach, derision and horror, and a lesson to warn the nations around you. I, ADONAI, have announced it.*

By viewing our punishment, nations were led to understand that God is faithful to His Word, holding men accountable to keep His Law, and He punishes those who forsake it. So, our obedience in the Land was used by God as a light to the nations and then He amazingly used our punishment for disobedience as warning to nations.

But, Moshe's prophesies are not all about judgment. Moshe also gives hope for restoration upon t'shuvah, which encouraged the Jewish and Christian Zionists to work and pray for restoration.

> Deut. 30:2-4 *and you return to ADONAI your God and listen to His voice according to all that I am commanding you today—you and your children—with all your heart and with all your soul, 3 then ADONAI your God will bring you back from captivity and have compassion on you, and He will return and gather you from all the peoples where ADONAI your God has scattered you. 4 Even if your outcasts are at the ends of the heavens, from there ADONAI your God will gather you, and from there He will bring you.*

The Return of Jewish people to the land started in the late 1800s, and is still going on.

> Deut. 30:5 *ADONAI your God will bring you into the land that your fathers possessed, and you will possess it; and He will do you good and multiply you more than your fathers.*

Just as our expulsion was to be a witness to the nations, so would our restoration be a witness to the nations of God's faithfulness to chastise, cleanse, preserve, and re-instate His people. When Israel was re-established as a nation in 1948, most thought Israel's existence was not of God, a quirk of history. After all, the founders of the nation were not religious people. But, in 1967 after Jerusalem was taken as a result of amazing victories in just six days against overwhelming enemy forces in three separate wars, believers everywhere began to

23. THE POWER OF THE PARASHOT

accept that the modern State of Israel was from God because God's promises of the restoration of Israel were being kept in our time! His faithfulness was being demonstrated to the world, and it was being recorded on the pages of our newspapers and shown on TV!

What was vital to that restoration? We had to still be a distinct people. The Parashot developed during Babylonian captivity was the main reason we obeyed and stayed distinct in Babylon, so it was very effective in Babylon. Then because of it, we kept obeying during the 600 years back in the Land. When we were again scattered due to disobedience, the Parashot were again the main reason some of us obeyed, and we stayed distinct through the 1,813 years of the Diaspora. The Parashot contributed greatly to that miracle of keeping us together as a people through terrible persecution and for such a long time.

The wonderful promises of restoration and return to the Land when we turn back to Him, read yearly in the parashah, have had the enormous, strengthening effect of keeping Jewish people together and keeping us distinct as a people. Many have assimilated, but a large remnant has remained faithful to reading and believing God's promises for us. There's a traditional, non-Messianic Zionist remnant and a Messianic remnant. There's a final stage to this restoration coming that we hope to see.

> Ezekiel 36:23-24 (CJB) *I will set apart my great name to be regarded as holy, since it has been profaned in the nations - you profaned it among them. The nations will know that I am ADONAI,' says ADONAI Elohim, 'when, before their eyes, I am set apart through you to be regarded as holy. 24 For I will take you from among the nations, gather you from all the countries, and return you to your own soil.*

God has been fulfilling verse 24 over the past decades. Some day soon verse 23 will be fulfilled and His great Name will be *"set apart through you to be regarded as holy"* in the Land. This speaks of the revival we're starting to see now in the Land of Israel with significant growth of the Messianic Movement in the Land over the last several decades.

During times of chastisement, we Jewish people experienced great wrath from many peoples. There are **two reasons** for all this persecution and attempts to destroy Israel. Knowing them will help you understand why Israel has experienced so much opposition, persecution, and attempts at annihilation. **First,** as I pointed out, is our great disobedience and falling away as predicted by Moshe. **Second** is ha-satan's continuous, highest priority work to destroy us.

Why does ha-satan want to destroy us so badly? **First**, ha-satan has read the Bible, and he knows that for God to complete His plan for the earth, Israel must be around, and have a role. Ha-satan also knows that the completion of God's plan will result in his destruction. The Bible says he will be thrown into the Lake of Fire. So he has been trying to prevent God's plan from being fulfilled by destroying Israel.

Second, Israel's mandate is to proclaim Yeshua among the nations and turn people from ha-satan, and his false deities, to the Messiah. When the Messianic revival reaches its fullness, Jewish people will fulfill this mandate and bring history's greatest revival. Ha-satan wants to prevent this.

Third, the destruction of Israel will prove God does not keep His promises, that He is not able to keep His people as He promised, that He is not faithful to chastise and restore as He promised. But, Israel's history is a three millennium worldwide drama that demonstrates God's incredible faithfulness.

Why is proving God to be unfaithful so important to ha-satan for him to make it his highest priority? Here's where all this becomes important to every believer. How can anyone, Jew or Gentile, have faith that God will keep any of His promises if God has not kept His many promises to Israel?

> Psalm 98:3 (CJB) *He has remembered His mercy and His faithfulness to the house of Israel; All the ends of the earth have seen the salvation of our God.*

The word, *faithfulness* there is *emunahtekhah*. It means *firmness, security, moral fidelity, faithfulness, stability.* All nations will see *Yeshuat Eloheynu – the salvation of our God.*

23. THE POWER OF THE PARASHOT

Are you depending on God's faithfulness to His promises in the Brit Hadashah? Promises like forgiveness, the Ruakh HaKodesh, and Heaven? If so, then seeing God's promises to Israel fulfilled should strengthen your faith. How could you have faith in those promises in the Brit Hadashah if God had not kept His promises to Israel? Promises to bless our obedience, punish our disobedience, and restore us when we turn back to Him.

This is why today many Christians support Israel in prayer, politics, and finances. The challenge to us today is to be effective and fruitful in doing our part in advancing God's plan for Israel. I'm very thankful we are living in these days, are you?

Here's another challenge. Now that you've seen the power of reading the Word regularly, do you read it faithfully every day? Do you follow the Parashot or are you following some other plan for reading through the Scripture regularly? That's okay, too, but if you have never followed the weekly Torah readings, I challenge you today to follow them. I challenge you to read and study each week's parashah for at least a year. You will be reading the same passages that all the religious Jewish people all around the world are reading. Do that for at least a year. You might be amazed the effect it will have on you and the connection you will feel with Israel and the Jewish people.

Let's pray.

Thank You, Lord, for Your Word. Thank You that You instructed Moses to write it down so it would be preserved just as You spoke it.

Thank You for inspiring the custom of reading Your Word every Shabbat. We are thankful to the Jewish people for continuing this tradition even when scattered all over the world.

Thank You, Father, for showing Moses the future and encouraging us with his predictions. Thank You that we have the honor of being alive to witness their fulfillment in the restoration of the nation of Israel to the Land. Thank You for enabling restored Israel to survive in the face of so many attacks by hostile enemies.

We pray for Your Name to be set apart by Jewish people so the nations will know You are holy. We pray for the Messianic Movement to grow in Israel, for revival, for a great outpouring of Your Spirit. We pray for our Jewish people to understand the spiritual battle that causes so many enemies to come against us.

May our faith in Your promises in the Brit Hadashah be strengthened by Your fulfilling Your promises to Israel.

Give us the discipline to regularly read and study Your Word, the Parashot and all of Your Word and to allow it to change our hearts and grow us in You. In Yeshua's Name. Amein.

CHAPTER 24

STUMBLING STONE

We've learned about the Sukkot traditional Water Drawing Ceremony that was done each day all seven days and how on the seventh, the Great Day, the kohanim marched around the altar seven times with the water before pouring it out with great celebration. We learned that the ceremony included prayers for rain, and that during the prayers for rain, they recited the Great Hoshana, the great "Please save us" prayer. They are praying this verse in Psalms. Remember?

> Psalm 118:25 *Hoshia-na! Please, ADONAI, save now! We beseech You, ADONAI, prosper us!*

Remember that they sang this along with the Ushaftem Mayim song from Isaiah 12:3 about the wells of ha-YESHUAH which together became a calling out for the salvation which only the Messiah can bring. Thus Sukkot became associated with the coming of the Mashiakh and still is today in traditional synagogues.

Did you know that they sang Psalms 113 to 118 as they went up the hill to Jerusalem each year on Sukkot. They did, and also again each day as they followed the Kohane HaGadol carrying the pitcher for water down to the pool and as he carried it full of water back up the hill to the Temple. So now let's look at what else is in Psalm 118, from which the Great Hoshana prayer is taken. I decided to dig a little deeper in this Psalm, and I came upon some interesting, difficult verses.

> Psalm 118:22 (NKJV) *The stone which the builders rejected has become the chief cornerstone.*

This is speaking of a structure that God is building. The chief cornerstone is the stone the builders start with. It must be strong, perfect size, and perfectly square. If not, the building will be weak and crooked. The rest of the structure rests upon it, and is lined up to it. Isaiah describes this chief cornerstone:

> Isaiah 28:16 (NKJV) *Therefore thus says the Lord God: "Behold, I lay in Zion a stone for a foundation, A tried stone, a precious cornerstone, a sure foundation; Whoever believes will not act hastily."*
>
> TLV: *...whoever trusts will not flee in haste.*
> KJV: *... he that believeth shall not make haste.*
> NASB: *...The one who believes in it will not be disappointed.*
> NRSV: *'One who trusts will not panic.'*
> NIV: *...will never be stricken with panic.*
> NLT:*... Whoever believes need never be shaken.*

What are Psalm 118:22 and Isaiah 28:16 saying? The builders rejected a certain stone. It is a *tested, tried, precious stone, a sure foundation*. But that rejected stone became the *precious, chief cornerstone* anyway. And, the building was built on it.

> Psalm 118:23 (NKJV) *This was the LORD'S doing; it is marvelous in our eyes.*

Marvelous means *great, wonderful.* This rejection of the chief cornerstone by the builders was God's plan. It would become the chief cornerstone anyway. But, who are these builders who would reject God's chosen cornerstone? We can learn that from the Brit Hadashah. Yeshua quoted this passage here:

> Luke 20:1 *One day, as Yeshua was teaching the people at the Temple, making known the Good News, the head cohanim and the Torah-teachers, along with the elders, came up to him ...*

It was the religious leaders of His day. Remember they were also political leaders.

> Luke 20:2 *... and said, "Tell us, what s'mikhah* [authority] *do you have that authorizes you to do these things? Who gave you this s'mikhah* [authority] *?"*

24. STUMBLING STONE

The religious leaders were questioning who had ordained Him. They were questioning His authority. He answered by telling them the parable of the vineyard against them, ending it like this:

> Luke 20:15-19 ... *"Now what will the owner of the vineyard do to them? 16 He will come and put an end to those tenants and give the vineyard to others!" When the people heard this, they said, "Heaven forbid!" 17 But Yeshua looked searchingly at them and said, "Then what is this which is written in the Tanakh, '**The very rock which the builders rejected has become the cornerstone**'? ..." 19 The Torah-teachers and the head cohanim would have seized him at that very moment, because they knew that he had aimed this parable at them, but they were afraid of the people.*

Yeshua was quoting Psalm 118:22. So, the builders who rejected the chief cornerstone were the religious leaders of Yeshua's day, who rejected Him as Messiah. That solves that riddle, but it leads us to an even tougher riddle because He went on to say:

> Luke 20:18 *Whoever falls on that stone will be broken in pieces; but if it falls on him, he will be crushed to powder!"*

This is another hard-to-understand saying. Somehow this precious cornerstone, Mashiakh, a great and wonderful thing, will be a stone that does two things: it will cause people to stumble and be broken in pieces, or it will fall on people and crush them to powder. Yeshua is actually quoting Isaiah 8:14, which referring to the Lord, says this:

> Isaiah 8:14-15 *He will be as a sanctuary, but a stone of stumbling and a rock of offense to both the houses of Israel, as a trap and a snare to the inhabitants of Jerusalem. 15 And many among them shall stumble; they shall fall and be broken, be snared and taken.*

This is even harder to understand! Here the Lord is portrayed as not just the cornerstone, but as a sanctuary, and as a stone causing people to *stumble*, to be offended, to *fall*, be *broken, snared and taken*. That doesn't sound like good things that happen due to this stone. It's a riddle. We already concluded that Yeshua is the chief cornerstone, yet it seems like a bad thing to stumble on the stone.

What is the answer to this riddle? There is a very important answer. If we think of our lives as a journey, stumbling over the chief cornerstone is a very necessary step in God's plan for each of us.

Here's how it worked in my life. I was living my life, trying to get along in my own strength, trying to accomplish the things that I thought were important. There were some things I was unable to deal with, like sickness (allergies, my children's health), relationships (marriage, parenting, in-laws). Have you struggled with any of those things? Situations that turn out bad?

Here's a couple of the things the Lord used for me. Mazda came out with a rotary engine, and I bought one. It was the dumbest thing I ever did because that thing fell apart after only 30,000-40,000 miles. I had a guarantee on it. They replaced the engine, but it still didn't work! They replaced it a second time! It still didn't work! I finally had to give up on that car! That was a hard thing for me. Then when we were living in California, I was working for Xerox and they transferred me. They had a real estate company that would take the house off our hands, so we didn't have to worry about selling it. So we were all packed up. Our furniture was all loaded on the moving van. We were going to spend the night in a motel and the next day fly to Rochester where they had transferred me. Then we got a call from that real estate company saying,"We can't take your house." So there we were on our way, and we had to deal with selling that house from 3000 miles away. Those were the kinds of things I just couldn't handle.

Then, five years later, I learned about Yeshua. I learned that He brought the Kingdom of God to this world with power over the physical world and the spirit world. He dealt with sickness supernaturally, and He dealt with the material world supernaturally. It was like I stumbled in broad daylight. I had been trying to deal with life in this world in the natural. I woke up to see how blind I was to the supernatural, spiritual world.

I had tried the supernatural before, but it was through Eastern religions, Hinduism and Yoga. The results had not been positive. When I stumbled over Yeshua, I was able to see my helplessness, my inability to deal with the spiritual.

After stumbling, we usually find ourselves on our knees. My allergy to bee stings brought me to that place, on my knees. So I decided I needed to humble myself, and I acknowledged my need for Mashiakh, first to pay for my offenses against God, then to lead me through the rest of my life.

Something needed to be broken in me when I stumbled. What was that? Pride. My pride needed to be broken in pieces, so I could see that I could not make it on my own. It's hard to maintain that wall of pride when you've just stumbled.

There was also an offense involved. It offended me that the Bible taught that I needed to be dependent on God. I wanted to be able to solve all my problems myself.

Here's the next question. Is this need for humbling an isolated statement by Yeshua or a recurring theme?

> Matthew 18:2-4 *He called a child to him, stood him among them, 3 and said, "Yes! I tell you that unless you change and become like little children, you won't even enter the Kingdom of Heaven! 4 So the greatest in the Kingdom is whoever makes himself as humble as this child.*

Stumbling over any stone usually causes us to fall—on our knees or our faces. Everyone stumbles. If we don't humble ourselves when we find ourselves on our knees and like a child see our need for Yeshua, we won't be able to see the Kingdom of God. If we humble ourselves and are broken and turn to Him, we will be saved, and will not be harmed by the fall.

What about the being *"crushed to powder"* by the chief cornerstone falling on us? We all stumble, but not all of us humble ourselves. If we don't humble ourselves and receive His grace, it's like the stone we stumble on rolls over us and crushes us. We won't receive the gift of eternal life, instead we will be judged on what we want to be judged on. For me it was whether I could handle things myself, whether I could be a good person. And there isn't a person on earth who wouldn't fall short, and then we would receive the punishment we deserve. There is a hell, but walking on this earth without the Lord's help is like a hell on earth. It isn't as bad as what would be waiting for us if we die without Him, but it is awful.

So, how did that stumbling stone get placed in my path? Well, we know that chief cornerstone is a manifestation of Yeshua Himself, so it was moved into my path by the grace of God, and prayers of the people who were praying for me to be saved. After my wife was invited to a ladies Bible study group, they all prayed for six months for me to come to the Lord, and the Lord started moving! He started putting stumbling stones into my path so that I would stumble and be broken. Then in the very next Psalm we have this wonderful verse:

> Psalm 119:105 *Your word is a lamp to my feet and a light to my path.*

Sounds like just the opposite, doesn't it? A light on our path would help us not to stumble. How can He be both my light, and my stumbling stone, the thing that keeps me from stumbling and the thing that causes me to stumble? It doesn't work with our Greek way of thinking. But in the Hebraic way of thinking, you can have "both/and" truths. The Lord can be both the stumbling stone and the light for our path. He is the one we must stumble over for the light to get turned on. And if we humble ourselves, the light does get turned on.

So let me relate this back to Simchat Torah and His Word. Yeshua is the Living Word. His Word brings conviction that causes us to stumble. Then we have that choice. If we humble ourselves when we've fallen to our knees, His Word brings light and salvation—helping us to walk, following Him. Are you with me on that? The stumbling stone and the Light are both wrapped up in the same person.

You might be thinking, because that's how I related it here, that the stumbling stone is only about helping us come to Yeshua, but there's more to it than that. After we turn to Him, we need to follow Him. To keep following Him, we need to be constantly aware of our need for His direction, support, and Love. So I believe He still puts stumbling stones in our paths periodically because we get that independent attitude. Then every once in a while we run into something that we can't handle. So, He continues to come to us as our stumbling stone and rock of offense, not to crush us to powder but to break us, to break our pride.

My wife spoke of something similar once. She said that sometimes people in your lives that offend you, or that get offended by you, can be sent to you by the Lord. You might be thinking, "Oh ... no, that couldn't be!" But I'm saying the same thing here. I've found that I need to be periodically offended by someone to keep me seeking God for my relationships. If everyone just acted nice to me all the time, why would I seek Him for my relationships? We also need to know when we have offended others because otherwise we can go through life thinking we are just such a nice person, I get along with everybody and everyone is okay with me. All of a sudden we find out that someone got offended by us. Then we're like, "Oh dear! I didn't mean to offend! What did I do?!" And we go to the Lord, "Oh Lord! Help me! Change me!" But again, if we are offended or we offend someone, and we don't humble ourselves, we are in danger of being crushed, which isn't good! But if we humble ourselves, God works in us. Now do you think I'm making this stuff up?

> 2 Corinthians 12:7 *Therefore, to keep me from becoming overly proud, I was given a thorn in my flesh, a messenger from the Adversary to pound away at me, so that I wouldn't grow conceited.*

I believe this was a demon assigned to Sha'ul to harass him in many ways. But it was for his good. It kept him humble.

> 2 Corinthians 12:8-9a *Three times I begged the Lord to take this thing away from me; 9 but he told me, "My grace is enough for you, for my power is brought to perfection in weakness."*

That's dependency of God.

> 2 Corinthians 12:9b *Therefore, I am very happy to boast about my weaknesses, in order that the Messiah's power will rest upon me.*

Now listen to this:

2 Corinthians 12:10 *Yes, I am well pleased with weaknesses, insults, hardships, persecutions and difficulties endured on behalf of the Messiah; for it is when I am weak that I am strong.*

Those are those stones in Sha'ul's life that he was stumbling over. These struggles kept him humble. They were stumbling stones. I have stumbled many times. I have offended others. I know that. I'm not going to give any specific incidences here, but through my own shortcomings, often times not really grasping where people were coming from. I have also been offended by people. Sometimes I find out later that it was by a wrong assumption, and it was foolish of me to be offended. They didn't mean what I thought they did. They meant it in a different way. Those things have humbled me.

I have also failed many times. You might be aware that I worked for Xerox for 24 years. And I'm thankful to say that by the grace of God I was instrumental in coming out with one of the most significant products that was on the market for a long time, and another one that was very difficult to come up with. But you know what? I worked on about twenty projects, but only two of them made it to the market. There were 18 failures! If you know about technology, you know that is pretty typical. And we get so distraught when we fail! But we need to fail to learn sometimes. I have come to see that I have needed all those stumblings and failures because they have made me the person I am today.

Our congregation has had successful prayer gatherings in and around our large congregational sukkah during Sukkot to pray for peace for Israel, but early on, one year, we put out the call for prayer for Israel. We had a special speaker come to talk about terrorism in Israel and planned for a great gathering, but only about 40 people showed up. We felt like it was a failure. Yes, we prayed, and the Lord's presence was there, for which we were thankful. But we learned from that how to get the word out better, how to make it known better in the community, and the Lord blessed it in the following years. We have had great turnouts ever since, not counting during the pandemic, of course.

So have you ever failed at anything? You have? Well, I want to end here by encouraging you. God uses every failure. He uses every stumbling stone. Every time we try and yet we fail and we get frustrated and it doesn't work, God will use it later. Don't give up. Don't be discouraged. Don't think, "I'll never make it." God will use what you suffered and what you learned. It might be a year or two later. But suddenly you'll run into a situation, and you will realize, "Oh! I've seen that before. I'm not going that way again. I've been down that road before, and I remember how it turned out." So you handle it better, and this time it's a success! So be encouraged.

Let's pray.

Father, we come to you right now with our minds stretched. We need to humble ourselves like little children. We want to do that, Father. We want to come close to You. We want to listen to You and hang on Your every Word. Help us to learn that Your ways are not like our ways, and to submit to Your ways.

We pledge, Lord to humble ourselves when we stumble on You, to humble ourselves and realize our need for You. Help us to humble ourselves when we are offended; to humble ourselves when we offend; and to humble ourselves when we fail. And help us in that, Father. Keep us from discouragement when we fail, we ask. Help us to trust and believe and see that You will use it all for our good and for Your glory. In Yeshua's Name. Amein.

CHAPTER 25
How the Torah Spoke to Me

Remember, the word *Torah* can mean the Decalogue (10 commandments), the Pentateuch (the five books of Moses), or the Tanakh (an acronym, meaning the whole Old Testament). And to Orthodox Jewish people, when they say the word Torah, they could mean the Tanakh but they could also be including the Talmud.

When I say Torah, I mean the Tanakh and the Brit Hadashah. So for me when I celebrate Simchat Torah, rejoicing in the Torah, I'm rejoicing in the whole Word of God, the Tanakh and the Brit Hadashah. In our synagogue meetings, we do the Torah procession with the Torah scroll. That scroll contains only the Pentateuch, but we are honoring the whole Bible.

Remember, the definition of the word, *Torah*, in Hebrew is *a statute, a law*. The root of the word means *to point the finger, to point out, to show the way, to instruct*. So it doesn't necessarily mean *law*. It means *instruction*, the instruction or direction from God.

The Torah procession seems strange to people new to the Messianic movement. We take out the Torah scroll and carry it around and people touch it with their Tallit or a scarf and then kiss the Tallit or scarf. They can also touch the cover of the scroll with their Bible and then kiss their Bible, and today we even allow people to use their phone because they read the Bible on their phone.

25. HOW THE TORAH SPOKE TO ME

It is an honoring, rejoicing procession, but I've heard new people say, "They're worshiping the scroll." But they are wrong. We are not worshiping it. We are worshiping the God who gave us the Torah and thanking Him for it. Our Torah scroll is an antique. It is over 100 years old. And, again, we need to understand when we look at a scroll that this is how the Scriptures were communicated and preserved for over 3000 years. It's only been the last 500 years that we've had printing presses and books. The Torah was on scrolls all the time before that. It always brings to my mind how ancient the Word of God is and how carefully it has been preserved so that we are blessed to have it still today. That is really something to rejoice about.

Let's pray.
Lord, we thank You for Your Word. We thank You that it is alive. We thank You that it changes lives. I thank You that it changed my life. We pray, Father, that it would continue to change our lives as we continue to read it and study it. In Yeshua's Name. Amen.

Simchat Torah is one of my favorite times of the year because I LOVE the TORAH! As rabbi, I get to talk and write about something I really love. So what could be better? I get invited to speak at other places a lot, especially to teach about the Moadim. One year I spoke at several churches about Rosh Hashanah, a total of six different times. I did Yom Kippur services at other churches twice and Sukkot services three times. The total number of times I was invited to speak that year was around 15-20 times! I love teaching the Word and teaching on the Moadim.

The Word of God has had a monumental, life-changing, earth-shaking effect on my life, personally. I suspect it has had that kind of effect on your life also. I was raised in a Jewish home. I had read part of the Tanakh for my Bar Mitzvah. My parents, though, were atheists. So they gave me the attitude that it was just a bunch of myths, that it was good for culture, but it wasn't really the truth. You might not be aware of this, but there are a lot of Jewish people who are not believers and are very secular. My parents and most of their friends were like that. I didn't know many people at all who were serious about their religion.

So that was my first exposure to the Bible. But things got really interesting in 1977. After we had been married for nine years, my wife Diane suddenly developed an interest in the Bible. She's not Jewish and she wasn't a Christian at the time. She had gone to church as a child and had given her heart to the Lord. But when we met, religion wasn't important to either of us. So we never went to services anywhere.

Diane's interest in the Bible, I am sure, and she agrees with me, arose out of the fact that she was going through some hard times in raising a family and dealing with me! So she turned for help to what she had been raised in. We had moved from California to our hometown, Rochester, New York into a new neighborhood where we didn't know anyone. So we were very lonely, and some of our neighbors reached out and invited Diane to a Christian women's Bible study. Diane says the only reason she went was because they offered free babysitting.

As she began to study the Bible with these ladies, I began to see a tremendous change in her. She began to have a peace that she didn't have before and wisdom and a purpose in her life. She began to be easier to get along with. She wasn't as depressed as she had been, and she began to forgive me quicker than she had before, which was a real benefit!

I saw all these positive effects, and in the natural, it should've made me want to read the Bible, too. But I wanted nothing to do with it. I was resistant particularly to the New Testament. The reason is very common amongst Jewish people. It was because I knew Jewish history. So I knew all the persecution that we Jewish people had suffered at the hands of Christians! So I wouldn't have anything to do with it. What I had heard from it at different times in my life just wasn't meaningful to me at all.

25. HOW THE TORAH SPOKE TO ME

There is a very important passage written by Rabbi Sha'ul, talking about his people. He was a Jew:

II Corinthians 3:14 *What is more, their minds were made stonelike; for to this day the same veil remains over them when they read the Old Covenant; it has not been unveiled, because only by the Messiah is the veil taken away.*

So only Messiah can remove this veil from the Jewish people. When the veil is removed, we Jewish people can see in the Tanakh, in the Torah, the arrows pointing to the Messiah, the things that speak of Messiah, the coming of the Messiah.

II Corinthians 3:15 *Yes, till today, whenever Moshe is read, a veil lies over their heart.*

So the veil is not just over their spiritual **eyes**. We can read it or hear it, and even get it into our minds, but the veil is over the heart. And in fulfillment of this, that was me. There was a veil over my heart and it hid the power of the Scriptures from me. The next verse is interesting and so important.

II Corinthians 3:16 *But the Torah says, whenever someone turns to the Lord, the veil is taken away.*

So when someone turns to the Lord, the veil is removed and the Bible reaches their heart. That's what it is saying. It gets to your heart.

I was about 31 years old. We had two kids, and life had brought me to the place of seeing my need for help from a higher source. I had had health trials, marital trials, financial trials, automotive trials, real estate trials, employment trials, unemployment trials, and even draft trials (in the 1960s when the very unpopular Vietnam war was going on and some of us were eligible for the draft and were quite worried about that). So I had all these trials in my life and on top of that the thing that I had struggled with all through my life was trying to find a purpose. Why am I here? What am I supposed to be doing? What is the reason for my existence? I had explored politics. I got involved in it, and discovered that if the people I was supporting got into power, they would be worse than the people we wanted kicked out. It became obvious to me because it happened so many times.

I was a scientist at the time. I had finished my degree in physics and was working as an engineer for Xerox. So as we said at Xerox, we were making the world a safe place for laser printing. That was my purpose! I was working for that purpose. But, of course, it wasn't fulfilling enough. So that got me to that place where I was a candidate for turning. Remember the Hebrew word for turning? *T'shuvah!* It's the theme of the Ten Days of Awe and of Yom Kippur. (Learn more about all of that in my two books *Yom Teruah* and *Yom Kippur*.)

Then a little bit more influence happened, which I found out later. Every week Diane went to that Bible study with those women. And what do you think they did? They prayed for me! In answer to those prayers and because I was turning to the Lord, God removed the veil. One day something happened. I like to think of it as a spiritual lobotomy. I had this part in my brain that was resistant to the Bible, and I can still remember this. I came home from work one day, and I heard these words come out of my mouth, "You know, Diane, you're so interested in the Bible..." She was studying the Bible all the time at this point. "I think I'll read it, so we have something to talk about." And I looked around thinking, "Who said that?" But really! How could that person who was so resistant say that? But I said it, and now I was stuck with it! I had to do it!

So I asked her where to start, and she told me to read the Book of John. You know, I thought about this later. I was 31 years old with four years of college and three years of graduate school. I considered myself to be pretty intellectual, and yet I had never read the most influential book in the entire history of the human race! Why? Well, there was a veil, a misconception of what it was about.

Before this I had searched Eastern religions for truth. I had gotten involved in Yoga and had read books on Hinduism, very mystical, mysterious books. I thought the Bible would also be a mystical book, but I thought the Brit Hadashah would be an instruction book on anti-Semitism. Really, I thought that's what it would be. Because the people who followed the Brit Hadashah persecuted my Jewish people, I thought there would be instructions in there on why we should hate Jewish people. But what I found was amazing! The Gospel of John was a biography! (Gospel means Good News.) It was the story of this man Jesus. It is amazing that no one had witnessed to me, yet I found Him. Diane would answer the questions I had, but she didn't preach at me. After I finished reading John, I asked Diane what to read next. She suggested I read Matthew. She didn't say anything else. She just let me read the book. And what was the effect of that book on me? The only thing I can say is I fell in love with the man this book was about! I fell in love with His integrity, with the wisdom that came from His mouth, and with the incredible things He did. What really got me was that the things He said about life were so wonderful! I was just grabbed by them. They just kind of reached off the page and grabbed me.

I want to show you the ones that really spoke to me. Maybe you've never heard of them. Maybe you have, but you never realized that these are things Yeshua said. These particular ones are from the Sermon on the Mount which blew me away!

> Matthew 5:28 *"But I tell you that a man who even looks at a woman with the purpose of lusting after her has already committed adultery with her in his heart."*
>
> Matthew 5:43-46 *"You have heard that our fathers were told, 'Love your neighbor — and hate your enemy.' 44 But I tell you, love your enemies! Pray for those who persecute you! 45 ... 46 What reward do you get if you love only those who love you? Why, even tax-collectors do that!"*
>
> Matthew 7:1-2 *"Don't judge, so that you won't be judged. 2 For the way you judge others is how you will be judged — the measure with which you measure out will be used to measure to you."*
>
> Matthew 7:3-5 *"Why do you see the splinter in your brother's eye but not notice the log in your own eye? 4 How can you say to your brother, 'Let me take the splinter out of your eye,' when you have the log in your own eye? 5 You hypocrite! First, take the log out of your own eye; then you will see clearly, so that you can remove the splinter from your brother's eye!"*

I remember reading those Words and saying, "This man has the Words of life. These are the most incredible Words being said here." They were grabbing at my heart. The veil was being taken completely away.

One thing I realized in reading those Words was that I was falling far short of His standards for life on this earth. I certainly was not measuring up. Not judging. Whew! That was a tough one for me. Not lusting was another tough one for me. Loving your neighbor? Hmmm, another tough one.

I began to see that I was guilty of many of the things that He called sin. I had never seen myself as a sinner before. It really opened my eyes.

A little bit later, I had a friend, a Jewish guy named Mark, a co-worker at Xerox, who helped me understand how this worked for me. He began to have the same thing happen to him. He became enthralled with the Word. We were studying the Bible together, and I remember I bumped into him in the hall one day. I said, "Hey, Mark, how's it going?"

He looked at me and said, "I'm reading Luke!"

I said, "Oh! Okay, that's good."

He said, "Yea! And he's shaking me." He motioned as if Luke had him by the lapels of his jacket and was actually shaking him, saying "Mark! Wake up! Wake up!"

That was what was happening to me. I was being shaken to my foundation! What I believed and what I thought of myself as a person was being shaken. Then I came across this verse in John again that was very interesting. Yeshua says to the people who were following Him and listening to His teachings:

> John 3:12-13 *If you people don't believe me when I tell you about the things of the world, how will you believe me when I tell you about the things of heaven? 13 No one has gone up into heaven; there is only the one who has come down from heaven, the Son of Man.*

So in other words, He knew about the things of Heaven, about the Laws of the Kingdom of God, basically, because He had been there. I realized that I believed Him about the things of this world in the Sermon on the Mount. It was true what

25. HOW THE TORAH SPOKE TO ME

He said. It's true that if you lust, it's just as bad! It's true that you should love your neighbor as yourself. It is true that if you judge, you will be judged. So the question came to me. "Okay, I believe Him about these earthly things, why don't I believe Him about the Heavenly things?"

What are some of those Heavenly things that He was telling them about? Well, He says this about Himself, about why He came.

> Matthew 20:28 *"For the Son of Man did not come to be served, but to serve—and to give his life as a ransom for many."*

So I decided to believe that! I decided, "Okay, if He has so much wisdom about this world, that's a spiritual thing—He's talking about why He came. I can believe that! I can believe He came to this world to die to pay a ransom to set people free from being held hostage." Hostage to what? Well, I knew what it was. It was hostage to sin! It was hostage to going my own way and not obeying God. Then I came to another one of those Heavenly things.

> John 14:6 *Yeshua said, "I AM the Way — and the Truth and the Life; no one comes to the Father except through me."*

Whoa! I had a struggle with that one! Maybe you did too. That was a tough one. "You mean there's no other way? What about all those Hindu people? What about the people who've never heard?" Those are tough questions, but I finally came to the place of saying, "I believe it! I believe He's telling the truth here." So I found myself wanting to follow this man who was so powerfully speaking to my heart through the pages of this book! But I still struggled with one of those Heavenly things He said.

> Luke 14:33 *So every one of you who doesn't renounce all that he has cannot be my talmid* [disciple].

Now I read that word "all," and I said, "Oh. Oh! What does He mean by 'all'?" You know, there were things I was willing to renounce. I could renounce some of the sinful things that I knew I shouldn't be doing. I could renounce the drinking and the drugs and things like that. Those were things I knew I could eventually renounce. But I knew that this meant, really, giving up control of my life. Who was going to be the boss? Who was going to be the one in control of what I did? Was it going to be my will or His will? I really struggled with that.

So that brought me to Labor Day weekend in 1977. In case you haven't heard my story or haven't read it in one of my other books, I will tell it again here. I was on that fence. I was saying, "I want to follow this Man, but I'm not sure I want to give up and make Him my Lord." So I was out driving in my car with my five-year-old son with me. It was a beautiful day. I had the window rolled down. I was driving along Route 104 out in Williamson with my arm leaning out the window, when I felt something hit my arm. A couple of seconds later, I felt a sharp pain. I looked down, and it was a bee. I killed the bee, and then I pulled over to the side of the road. Now, I had a real dilemma because I had a history of having violent reactions to bee stings, so violent that I would be unable to breathe. In fact that was why I didn't go to Vietnam! I was actually given a 4-F because of the record of being rushed to the hospital a half a dozen times as a child when I was stung by bees.

So I was there on the road with my five year old son, stung by a bee, and I had to decide, "What do I do?" I could drive straight to the hospital and hope I got there before the reaction set in. Or I could try to get home, which was closer, and my wife could take me to the hospital. Remember this was before cell phones. "What should I do?" Then all of a sudden, this thought came to my mind, "You know you've been reading the Bible so much. Why don't you pray?" This was a new thought for me. Pray! "Okay. Okay, God. I'll pray!"

Well, you know, I'm a son of Abraham, so when I prayed, what came out was bargaining. Remember when Abraham bargained for Sodom and Gomorrah? Here's what my bargain was. "Lord, if You keep me from having a reaction to this bee sting, I'll do what I know I'm supposed to do here. I will renounce everything and become Your disciple." So I prayed that prayer, and I didn't have a reaction to that bee sting. That was the first time in my life that I did not have a reaction to a bee sting!

25. HOW THE TORAH SPOKE TO ME

Well, I'd like to report that as soon as I got home and realized that I had no reaction, that I fulfilled my part of the bargain. But I have to report that I didn't. The Lord needed to deal with me a little stronger. I really don't know why. It just didn't cross my mind that I had prayed that prayer until the next day. So after the bee sting, I just went on about my business, but God was not going to let me get away with it, though.

The next morning, I was moving some things out of our basement, and when I took the first step out into our back yard, I felt a sharp pain up on my forehead. What do you think it was? Another bee! Two bee stings in two days. And I had not been stung since like five years before this. So I went up to our bedroom, and I sat down, and I said, "I think God is trying to tell me something here!" Naw! (*smile*) "And I think it's getting dangerous." So, at that point in my bedroom, without anyone with me, without any instructions, I just said, "Lord, I surrender to You. I renounce all, and I'm giving my life to you. I'm making You Lord, and You, God, You take care of my life." That was the beginning of my love affair with the Bible. I continued to read it.

Let me tell you what happened. As I prayed that prayer, I was flooded with this incredible joy of forgiveness! I knew that I was forgiven. I knew that I was right with God. I knew that I had been made right by the sacrifice, by the ransom paid by Yeshua, that I was now God's child, and that He had a plan for me. There was peace and joy that just flooded over me. Unfortunately, I was still in this body. So a few minutes later, I decided to look at myself. It was dark, so I turned on a light in the bedroom. I looked in the mirror at myself, and there were big red hives breaking out all over me. God was not going to spare me this time. So I called Diane, and she rushed me to the hospital where I got an adrenalin shot, and I was fine. But my life was radically changed.

I began to devour the Word because it was the Word that had brought this all to me. It continued to keep shaking me over and over again, shaking me and changing me. By the time of writing this book, I have read through the Bible many times, and I want you to see that what was happening in my life was a fulfillment of something that John says about Yeshua. They are familiar verses.

> John 1:1 *In the beginning was the Word, and the Word was with God, and the Word was God.*

Now that is a mystical, mysterious verse. What does that mean? It's like God and His Word are one, all part of the same being. Then verse 14 was what really got me.

> John 1:14 *The Word became a human being and lived with us, and we saw his Sh'khinah* [Glory], *the Sh'khinah of the Father's only Son, full of grace and truth.*

So the Living Word took on the form of a man, and that was Yeshua. Now I don't understand how that can happen, but I do know as I've read the Bible, particularly in the stories in Genesis, Exodus, Joshua, and Daniel, it does tell about God appearing as a man to Avraham, to Moses, to Joshua, and with Daniel's three friends in the furnace. God can do anything. If He decides He wants to come to earth as a man, He can come to earth as a man! And I got to a point where I said, "Okay, that is what He did."

But I want you to see that what John is talking about is the living Word, that Yeshua is called the Living Word, the Word made flesh. Sukkot is all about God's presence among His people. That's what our sukkah represents—God dwelling among His people while they were wandering in the desert.

What I have concluded is that when I encountered Him, I encountered Him as the Living Word. I met Him that way. I met Him out of the Word, the Bible! It wasn't from a movie or from someone preaching. It was purely His Word. The only people who witnessed to me were John and Matthew. They wrote down what they had seen, and it spoke to me! That's why my love for the Word is the same as my love for Yeshua because to me they're one.

What does it mean that Yeshua is the living Word? Well, when you read the Gospels, the biographies of His life, you see that He spoke the Word of God! He spoke from the Old Testament most of the time. Other times He spoke an interpretation of it or a new revelation as the Living Word of God. The Word of God was truly coming out of Him alive.

The things He did were the Word of God doing things. In Genesis, God said, "Light be!!" And light was! So the Word of God is a creative force!! The Word of God does things! So when the Word of God became flesh, it did things in this world. It changed the world! You know if you think about the word, *history*, it breaks down into two words: *His story!* Whose story? Well, in our culture, it's the story of the person whose life starts with the year zero. Before Him and after Him, it's His story. So the whole world changed and history changed by the appearance of the Word of God.

As I sought to be obedient to this Word, my life changed drastically, not just that I stopped certain sins, which I did, but my whole direction changed. One speaker at our congregation once talked about having a picture with God in the center and people are either moving away from God or towards God. That's what happened in my life. It was T'shuvah! I was moving away from God, and then I turned toward Him. The momentum of my life began to go toward Him. I began to walk with Him. And for the first time in my life, I had peace. I had purpose. I had joy.

The love was really life-changing. One of the things that is incredible about coming to the place of knowing the Lord is that we are only able to love others in so far as we can forget about ourselves, and trust that we will be taken care of. In other words, if I have limited resources, how can I help other people if I'm worried about myself? Well, the only way I can quit worrying about myself is if I am convinced that someone is taking care of me. And that's what happened to me! I became convinced that Someone else is taking care of me! So my life changed and I began to be able to give, where I hadn't been able to give before.

So now time has passed, and my relationship with the Word has changed because I've read through it so many times that most parts of it are not new to me anymore. They're not fresh or unfamiliar, yet it continues to shake me and change me. I would say that the greatest honor that I've had in my life is that God has called me to teach His Word. There couldn't be any greater honor to me than that.

Three sets of people

So, now I want to talk about three sets of people in the world. There are more, but I want to talk about these three.

First, there are people who have **never had an encounter with Yeshua** and maybe don't believe that He's the Messiah and thus haven't made Him Lord.

Second, then I think there are those who believe in Yeshua, maybe even have made Him Lord, but they **don't know Him as the Living Word**. In other words, the Word has not come alive to them. They prayed the prayer; they're coming to services; they're doing things for the Lord, but it's not like they take the Bible and read it every day and say, "Wow! Look what it's saying to me!"

Third, I suspect there are some people who came to know Him as the Living Word years ago, but it **has kind of worn off**, to where it's not like you open up your Bible every day and go, "Wow, look what I got from the Word today!"

I want to offer some help to those in these three groups. **First of all to those who've never had an encounter,** you should realize that there's a veil. Sha'ul talks about a veil over your heart. We will pray for that veil to be removed. What we're praying is simply, "God I want to let Your Word speak to my heart." It's not something that you have to worry about whether it's Christian or Jewish. We're speaking to God, asking that His Word move in your heart. Remember that Scripture says that whenever someone turns to the Lord, the veil is removed? So if you turn to the Lord, if you say you want to move toward rather than away from Him, that veil will come off.

I want to give you a couple of interesting verses.

> Luke 18:17 *Yes! I tell you that whoever does not receive the Kingdom of God like a little child will not enter it at all!*

Interesting. We have to come to Him in childlike innocence rather than with preconceived ideas about who He is. You have to set those aside and just ask that the Word speak to you. God's Word is a covenant. A covenant is made between two parties based on trust. The Bible is a covenant between God and people. I believe if you read it that way, "This is my covenant with God, my personal covenant. I'm going to read it, asking, 'What does God expect of me. What is God promising me?'" Then it will open up to you.

> Joshua 1:8 *This book of the Torah should not depart from your mouth—you are to meditate on it day and night, so that you may be careful to do everything written in it. For then you will make your ways prosperous and then you will be successful.*

Have you ever had a piece of equipment, like a computer, that was really difficult to set up? You try, but you can't quite figure it out. And then you remember, "Oh it has an instruction manual! I didn't read it!" Then you read it ,and you have to take it back apart because each piece has to go in the right place. You have to put piece A in place before you can put piece B in place, etc. Well, when I began to read the Bible with the veil removed, that's what it was like. It was like the instruction manual for life! Life had been confusing, and I couldn't make it work quite right. Then I found the instruction manual and it suddenly made sense to me.

> Psalm 119:105 *Your word is a lamp to my feet and a light to my path.*

It's important to read the Word as personal to you, God's love letter to you. When you read it, pray for personal applications to your life. It will be like a light shining on your path.

For those in the **second group**, who need to know Him as the Living Word, you need to do some of those same things.

Those in the **third group,** I have a few suggestions. First, I suggest you read the Word when you are alert. For me that's the first thing in the morning. At night, reading makes me sleepy, so I read the comics in the newspaper. **Second**, use *Strong's Concordance*. That helps you to find things in the Word. Use it to study a concept, like *atonement* or *anger*. **Third**, get a Bible study book. Read someone else's study.

Fourth, most of all, look for applications in your life. And **fifth**, begin to memorize verses. One way to do that is to sing Scripture songs.

Then **sixth**, notice that God told Joshua to meditate day and night. Meditating is important. Think about Joshua. He had direct communication with God. God appeared to him and gave Him incredible revelation. He also had the Kohane HaGadol (High Priest) who had the Orim and Tumim, and whenever Joshua wanted, he could go to the Kohane and say, "We need to know what God is saying about this." (We don't know exactly how they revealed God's answer, but we know they did.) Yet even though Joshua had all this, he was still instructed to meditate on the written Word, night and day. (See chapters 29 and 30 for more on how to meditate on the Word.)

Here's a comment by S.R. Aldridge on Joshua 1:8 (from BibleHub.com/sermons/Joshua/1-8): "Meteor flashes were not to make him careless of the steady light that burns in the lamp of God's truth." In other words,, he was to be grounded in God's Word. That means he wasn't to just go by what people were saying, or just by revelation that he had or the visions that he had. He was to be grounded in the written Word.

Notice it says not to depart out of his mouth. In those days they only had the huge scrolls, so they had to memorize the Word to carry it with them, so that means saying it over and over aloud out of their mouths. That is one way to memorize and to meditate on it. (Again, see chapters 28 and 29 for more on meditating on the Word this way.) And meditating carries with it to understand the meaning. And it also means to obey it. Yeshua made that very clear.

> Matthew 7:21 (TLV) *Not everyone who says to Me, 'Lord, Lord!' will enter the kingdom of heaven, but he who does the will of My Father in heaven.*
>
> Joshua 1:9 *Have I not commanded you? Chazak! Be strong! Do not be terrified or dismayed, for ADONAI your God is with you wherever you go.*

God said this to him to encourage him because Joshua was going to encounter opposition. And you might also encounter opposition. So you need to be strong and to be encouraged that God will be with you all the way.

> Matthew 28:19-20 *Therefore, go and make people from all nations into talmidim* [disciples], *immersing them into the reality of the Father, the Son and the Ruach HaKodesh, 20 and teaching them to obey everything that I have commanded you. And remember! I will be with you always, yes, even until the end of the age.*

Who is supposed to make disciples? All of us. And what are we supposed to do then? Teach them. So we are all supposed to be teachers. And I've found that preparing to teach is a great way to get to know the Bible better.

It is also good to listen to other teachings, but we need to be cautious. Yeshua said to beware of false prophets.

> Matthew 7:15-16 *Beware of the false prophets! They come to you wearing sheep's clothing, but underneath they are hungry wolves! 16 You will recognize them by their fruit.*

The problem with watching teachings on the internet is we can't see the fruits of those teachers. We don't know how they behave off camera.

As you study the Word and begin to teach it, be aware of this. Do you realize this? The more you know, the more will be required of you.

> Luke 12:48 *[H]owever, the one who did what deserves a beating, but didn't know, will receive few lashes. From him who has been given much, much will be demanded—from someone to whom people entrust much, they ask still more.*

You know, we have been given much! We live in an awesome time when the Word is so available to us. Back in old times, they only had the one scroll in their synagogue. So they had to go there to read it. And I don't think you could read any other portion because they had it unrolled to the parashah for that week. Also only certain people were allowed to get it out and handle it. So it would have been very hard to be able to read it for yourself. So I am very grateful for all the access we have to the Word and all the different study tools we have. So Thank You, Lord!

Let's pray.

Father, we pray for that veil to be removed from people who are reading this. We pray simply, Lord, that You remove the veil so Your Word can speak to their hearts. You are the Living Word, so may Your Word come alive in all of us. Grow in us a love for Your Word.

Give us the discipline to study Your Word, to memorize it, to meditate on it, to teach it and most of all to obey it.

Give us discernment so we can discern and stand against the spirits that will try to keep us from being in Your Word; busyness, idolatry, pride, depression and any others.

We pray that you would arrange circumstances in the lives of Jewish people that would cause them to turn to You for help. We pray for Jewish people we know, and that we don't know, that you would remove the veil over their hearts. In Yeshua's Name. Amein.

CHAPTER 26
Torah vs Legalism

We are still in the Simchat Torah section. Remember Simchat Torah means rejoicing in the Torah. As I said, I see it as rejoicing in the entire Word of God, including the Living Word, Yeshua.

When I first became involved in the Messianic Movement, I wasn't so sure we should be rejoicing in the Torah. I had no problem with Genesis. I love Genesis. It's a wonderful book full of stories. But I didn't like the other four books so full of laws. But I was interpreting the word *Torah* as meaning the Law of Moses, or just The Law, and I wasn't comfortable with rejoicing in it! However, I was eventually able to get behind the Simchat Torah celebration when I saw that Torah can mean the entire Word of God.

Why my discomfort? Well, didn't the Law bring a curse? I had been in the church for several years after I came to Yeshua, and I had been taught this verse:

> Galatians 3:10 (NKJV, KJV) *For as many as are of the works of the law are under the curse;…*

And haven't I been redeemed from the curse of the law as I had been taught from this verse?

> Galatians 3:13 (NKJV, KJV) *Messiah has redeemed us from the curse of the law,…*

So, why rejoice in the Law or Torah from whose curse I had been redeemed? I remember my reaction when I first became part of the Messianic Movement at Congregation Shema Yisrael. I came from a secular Jewish background, and had spent seven years as a believer in churches. They were good churches, but they taught very strongly that we were not to be of "the works of the law." Any involvement with the Law of Moses was suspect to being a "work of the law."

But, when God called me to Messianic Judaism to reach my own people, I found that Messianic Judaism has a lot to do with the Law of Moses for several reasons: first, of course, in being obedient to it, but also in making our services "seeker sensitive" to Jewish people; in restoring Jewish believers to their Jewish roots; and in re-connecting the church with its Jewish roots.

I remember visiting other Messianic congregations and thinking they were doing the "works of the law" because they did things more traditionally Jewish than we did. If they seemed to be more into the "Law" than I was, I would look down on them as being in bondage to the law.

One way, back then, I reconciled my struggle concerning **Rejoicing** in the Torah was to see, as I said, that the Torah represents the whole Word of God. When I thought of the Torah scroll as representing the whole Word of God, I didn't think of it as bondage. However, over the years, my attitude has changed. I can now also rejoice in the Torah as the Law of Moses, itself.

Anti-nomianism

My struggle was due to the influence of anti-nomian doctrine. *Anti-nomianism* means *anti-law*. It is a heresy that has permeated the Body. It's a doctrine that disparages the Law, and here by the *Law* I mean the actual statutes. Anti-nomianism teaches that the Law is no longer of any value.

How did it develop? It came about linguistically by faulty translation of the original language of the Bible. Our Scripture was written in two languages, Hebrew and Greek, which most of us don't understand. It was written in the context of two cultures, which are not with us today. Not only was it written

26. TORAH VS LEGALISM

in two foreign languages, but the unfamiliar language of the Brit Hadashah refers to the unfamiliar language of the Tanakh, creating a double difficulty in understanding it.

Due to these factors, the Scriptures sometimes seem to contradict themselves. When they do, we have three choices. 1. We can throw away our belief that the Scriptures are inspired by God. 2. We can ignore the side we don't like or have been taught against, or 3. We can pray for wisdom and attempt to reconcile the seeming contradiction.

> 2 Timothy 2:15 *Be diligent to present yourself approved to God, a worker who does not need to be ashamed, rightly dividing the word of truth.*

Reconciling the contradiction is *rightly dividing the Word of Truth*. In our attempt to understand the culture and the language, we have to accept that translations were not divinely inspired and can be wrong in some places, and that reconciliation of the contradictions is still not always possible.

Let's focus on an apparent contradiction.

> Galatians 3:10 (NKJV) *For as many as are of the works of the law are under the curse;...*

Sounds like the works of the law are not something we should be doing, right? Yet Paul says:

> Romans 3:31 (NKJV) *Do we then make void the law through faith? Certainly not! On the contrary, we establish the law.*

How do we reconcile these two statements? In Greek, *"nomos"* usually means *"law,"* but it is also the New Testament word for the Hebrew word, *Torah*, the *Law of Moses*. In Galatians 3, we have a Greek word being used for a Hebrew word, both from unfamiliar languages. *"Erga nomou,"* literally, *"works of law,"* usually taken to mean "actions done in obedience to the Torah."

C. E. B. Cranfield says in his commentary in Romans, Volume. I, 108 (*The International Critical Commentary*) (T&T Clark, 1979, p. 853):

> " ... Greek language of Paul's day possessed no word-group corresponding to our 'legalism,' 'legalist' and 'legalistic.' This means that he lacked a convenient terminology for expressing a vital distinction, and so was surely

seriously hampered in the work of clarifying the Christian position with regard to the law. In view of this, we should always be ready to reckon with the possibility that Pauline statements which at first sight seem to disparage the law, were really directed not against the law itself but against that misunderstanding and misuse of it for which we now have a convenient terminology," i. e. legalism.

David Stern, in his *Jewish New Testament Commentary* commenting on Galatians 2:16b, says this:

> "erga nomou" usually translated "works of the law" not deeds done by following His Law, the Torah, in the way God intended but deeds done as a result of perverting the Torah into a set of rules obeyed mechanically, automatically, legalistically without having faith, without having trust in God, without having love for God, and without being empowered by the Holy Spirit.

Once we rightly divide the Word this way, we see that Sha'ul wrote against the sin of perverting the Torah into legalism, but he had nothing but good to say for the Torah itself. The contradictions, in his view of the Torah, vanish, and then other verses make sense, for example, this one where the Apostles are speaking to Sha'ul:

> Acts 21:24 ... there is nothing to these rumors which they have heard about you; but that, on the contrary, you yourself stay in line and keep the Torah.

> Matthew 5:17-19 *Don't think that I have come to abolish the Torah or the Prophets. I have come not to abolish but to complete. 18 Yes indeed! I tell you that until heaven and earth pass away, not so much as a yud or a stroke will pass from the Torah—not until everything that must happen has happened. 19 So whoever disobeys the least of these mitzvot and teaches others to do so will be called the least in the Kingdom of Heaven. But whoever obeys them and so teaches will be called great in the Kingdom of Heaven.*

So in rightly dividing the Word, we need to determine when the Greek word *"nomos"* means *God's Torah*, and when it means *legalistic perversion of God's Torah*. Most translations fail to make this essential distinction and misrepresent Sha'ul and foster anti-Semitism and anti-nomianism.

26. TORAH VS LEGALISM

With this understanding, let's look at Galatians 3:10-12 in the NKJV to see how it fosters anti-Semitism and anti-nomianism:

Galatians 3:10 (NKJV) For as many as are of the works of the law are under the curse; for it is written, "Cursed is everyone who does not continue in all things which are written in the book of the law, to do them."

The false meaning that comes across here is that imperfect human nature is incapable of keeping all the commands of the Torah. Everyone who tries, fails and is therefore cursed. How does it foster anti-Semitism? Well, since the Jewish people attempt to obey the Torah and are not capable of doing everything written in it, then they all live under God's curse.

This became a doctrine of the church. They saw the Jewish people as also being cursed because they saw them as connected to the death of Messiah. The church saw the evidence of that curse in the destruction of the Temple and the scattering of the people of Israel. This led to the church participating in the carrying out of the curse, either by standing by while others persecuted the Jewish people or by actually doing the persecuting.

Historically, once the church began to curse Israel, it had the effect promised in Genesis 12. Look at church history after 325 when it broke from its Jewish roots and began believing Jews were cursed. The church gained political power, but then we had the Dark Ages, the Crusades, and the Inquisition.

The false meaning of Galatians 3:10 also fosters anti-nomianism, anti-law because it seems to say that if we do things out of obedience to the Law, we are cursed. This causes us to become less committed to obeying God's Laws. Historically, this is what happened. The Church separated itself from its Jewish roots and rejected Jewish law. However, laws were needed, so the Church replaced God's Laws with its own laws. The Church then became legalistic, for example in selling indulgences. The Reformation turned people back to a relationship with God. But it was like a pendulum. Anti-nomianism became legalism. Then the reaction to legalism caused anti-nomianism.

> Galatians 3:11-12 (NKJV) *But that no one is justified by the law in the sight of God is evident, for "the just shall live by faith." 12 Yet the law is not of faith, but "the man who does them shall live by them."*

This seems to say the Torah itself is defective, because it is not based on faith. Let's look at this whole passage in David Stern's translation.

> Galatians 3:10 *For everyone who depends on* [erga nomou] *legalistic observance of Torah commands lives under a curse, since it is written, "Cursed is everyone who does not keep on doing everything written in the Scroll of the Torah."* (Sha'ul is quoting Deuteronomy 27:26.)

So now it is saying, legalists, by being legalists, do not keep all of the Torah's commands. Therefore, they come under a curse. Which command does the legalist violate?

> Galatians 3:11 *Now it is evident that no one comes to be declared righteous by God through* [erga nomou] *legalism, since "The person who is righteous will attain life by trusting and being faithful."* (Habakkuk 2:4)

The command legalists violate is Habakkuk 2:4, which commands us to base all our actions on trusting God and being faithful to Him, being in a relationship with Him.

> Galatians 3:12 *Furthermore,* [erga nomou] *legalism is not based on trusting and being faithful, but on a misuse of the text that says, "Anyone who does these things will attain life through them."* (Leviticus 18:5)

Sha'ul is saying that legalists take that one verse, Leviticus 18:5, out of context and say that anyone who does "these things," the things commanded in the Torah, who mechanically follows the rules for Shabbat, kashrut (kosher), etc., will attain life through them, will be saved, will enter the Kingdom of God, will obtain eternal life, implying there's no need to trust God. Just obey the rules!

Legalists ignore the "law" in verse 3:11 (above), that faith and relationship must underlie all rule-following. This is what God finds acceptable. So here's the conclusion: "legalistic obedience to Torah commands" (erga nomou, "works of law") is actually **dis**obedience to the Torah!

In other words, we could be obeying every single mitzvah (commandment) (except, by assumption, the mitzvah of trust), but if we are obeying without heartfelt trust in God, without a relationship with Him, then our obedience has no value. God actually hates outward-only, surface-only obedience (Isaiah 1:14). The person doing it, the legalist, "lives under a curse." Sha'ul once believed this false doctrine himself. See Romans 7.

He was not alone. Not all first century non-Messianic Jews were legalistic, but legalistic heresy was a major way of relating to the Torah. It remains a heresy sometimes seen within non-Messianic Judaism today. But it is not only a Jewish heresy; it is also a Christian heresy, "If I do this, this, and this (some self-determined agenda, even based on Scripture), God will accept me, He will applaud my deeds and be obligated to reward me for them, whether I trust Him, or am faithful to Him or not."

> Galatians 3:13 *The Messiah redeemed us from the curse pronounced in the Torah by becoming cursed on our behalf; for the Tanakh says, "Everyone who hangs from a stake comes under a curse."*

The curse spoken of here applies to legalists and the disobedient, but the redemption covers all curses. Those who have faith are not under the curse. Messiah redeemed those who trust in Him from the curse. How? By becoming cursed on our behalf, in our place. He did this by His own choice, at the cost of His great suffering, out of His Love for us, and while we were yet sinners. His willingness to suffer for us causes us to obey out of love and not legalism.

> Galatians 3:14 *Yeshua the Messiah did this so that in union with him the Gentiles might receive the blessing announced to Avraham, so that through trusting and being faithful, we might receive what was promised, namely, the Spirit.*

Why did He do this? So that the Gentiles might receive the blessing announced to Avraham, promised in Genesis 12:1–3, and not only the Gentiles, but also "we," which includes Jewish believers. Now that we see that being obedient to the Law does not bring a curse unless we do it legalistically, what Law are we talking about?

Well, there's a bit of a misunderstanding in it being different for Jews and Gentiles. The misunderstanding of this verse makes it seem there is no law for Gentiles.

> Acts 15:28-29 *For it seemed good to the Ruach HaKodesh and to us not to lay any heavier burden on you than the following requirements: 29 to abstain from what has been sacrificed to idols, from blood, from things strangled, and from fornication. If you keep yourselves from these, you will be doing the right thing.*

If we take that verse alone as the whole council of God, it could mean that Gentiles can murder, steal, and lie. But, there are over 1,100 commands in the Brit Hadashah. Nine of the Ten Commandments are repeated in the Brit Hadashah. Only the Shabbat is missing. That's a significant legal code for anyone. For Jewish believers, the Law of God is all 613 commandments that still apply. That rules out Temple worship and slave ownership, for example. But, they need to be studied and applied as led by the Ruakh, not necessarily as the Orthodox have applied them. In fact it is impossible to obey them plus the laws given in the Brit Hadashah without the help of the Ruakh HaKodesh. For example: How do you "love your neighbor as yourself" without faith in God?

Are these laws of God or just suggestions? When we obey them, are we putting ourselves under a curse? No. Are we saved by obeying these laws? No. The laws are not to be obeyed legalistically, but out of a trusting, faith, relationship with God. But, they are to be obeyed.

Why is all this important? Misinterpretation leads to anti-Semitism. Misinterpretation also leads to anti-nomianism, being against the law, which leads to disrespect for the law, which then weakens our ability to walk in righteousness. When we are tentative about obeying the law, we are easily swayed to compromise with the law, and easily swayed by peer pressure. The end result is a lack of holiness.

One of the problems the church encountered when it cut itself off from its Jewish roots and rejected the law, the Torah, is it led to a disrespect for law. We see much of this in the Body today. Here's one example of the Body's lack of obedience. Divorce is allowed by the laws of our land, but, the Bible says:

> 1 Corinthians 10:10-11 *To those who are married I have a command, and it is not from me but from the Lord: a woman*

is not to separate herself from her husband 11 But if she does separate herself, she is to remain single or be reconciled with her husband. Also, a husband is not to leave his wife.

This commandment is not from the Tanakh. It's from the Brit Hadashah, so it applies to Believers. It's not from Paul, it's *"from the Lord."* Now Believers know we have this law, yet, the divorce rate among Christians is equal to the divorce rate among non-Christians. Is there a lack of respect for the Law of God? We have all been infected by this doctrine.

What should our attitude be toward God's Law, toward His Torah? May our attitudes become more like this:

> Psalm 119:72 (NKJV) *The law of Your mouth is better to me Than thousands of coins of gold and silver. ... 77 Let Your tender mercies come to me, that I may live; For Your law is my delight. ... 97 Oh, how I love Your law! It is my meditation all the day. ... 163 I hate and abhor lying, But I love Your law. 164 Great peace have those who love Your law, And nothing causes them to stumble. ... 174 …Your law is my delight.*
>
> Proverbs 6:23 (NKJV) *For the commandment is a lamp, And the law a light; Reproofs of instruction are the way of life,*
>
> Proverbs 29:18 (NKJV) *Where there is no revelation, the people cast off restraint; But happy is he who keeps the law.*

Let's pray.

Father, we pray against the effects of anti-nomian doctrine in us personally. We pray that we can truly rejoice in the Law

Thank You, God, that there is a provision for when we disobey which is that Yeshua died for our sins.

We pray against the effects of anti-nomianism in the Body and in our nation. In Yeshua's Name. Amein.

CHAPTER 27
THE TORAH ON RELATIONSHIPS

The Bible, the Torah is God's instruction. It's the instruction manual for life. Alright? As I was praying about this, the Spirit of God brought before my mind how the Torah is specifically a manual on how to maintain healthy personal relationships, and how to repair those relationships when they've been damaged. Have you ever had a damaged relationship? You might not want to admit it, but yes? Yes, we all have! So if you think about it, this historic instruction on relationships is given in the Bible in many forms. It's in the form of commands given by Moses, by the prophets, by Yeshua, and by the Apostles. It's in the form of wise sayings in Proverbs, in Psalms, and by Yeshua. It's also in the form of stories in the accounts of real people and the conflicts and broken relationships they had. And finally, it's in the parables given by Yeshua and the prophets.

So instructions on relationships are all through the Bible, and if I went through all of them, I would end up with an encyclopedia size volume of books! So I just chose a few. I believe the Spirit guided me as to which ones to choose, and I believe the Spirit wants you to read this instruction, not just with interest, but to apply it to your own life because we all struggle with relationships.

So we're going to look briefly at a few stories about relationships, and I want to suggest that you go get your Bible and re-read these stories as we go along. We will see how they apply to relationships.

Relationship destroyers

So let's start in the Garden. The message it brings is that actions and words have consequences that effect relationships and lives in significant ways. The first part of the Bible deals with Adam and Eve's relationship with God, but it's also applicable to a relationship with anyone in authority over you or anyone you have authority over. If you are working on a job, you have somebody in authority over you, right? If you are a parent, you are in authority over someone. So God told Adam not to eat of a certain tree, but ha-satan said this to Eve:

> Genesis 3:5 *For God knows that when you eat of it, your eyes will be opened and you will be like God, knowing good and evil.*

Some translations say like gods with a small g, which are demons, but, either way, she was being tempted to be more than she was. So I put together a couple of lists. The first is a list of relationship destroyers. The second is a list of relationship restorers. **The first relationship destroyer is pride**, and this is especially dangerous if you have a person in authority over you. If you have too much pride, it's really hard to be able to submit to that authority.

> Genesis 3:6 *Now the woman saw that the tree was good for food, and that it was a thing of lust for the eyes, and that the tree was desirable for imparting wisdom. So she took of its fruit and she ate. She also gave to her husband who was with her and he ate.*

This was a clear act of disobedience to the authority of God, instigated by pride. **The second relationship destroyer** after pride **is disobedience to authority**. After Adam ate the forbidden fruit, God confronted him.

> Genesis 3:12 *Then the man said, "The woman whom You gave to be with me—she gave me of the Tree, and I ate."*

When disobedience to authority in a relationship happens, it can be repaired by repentance, but what did Adam do? He blamed Eve and who else? He blamed God because God had given Eve to him. And that didn't help at all. So reacting to being caught in sin by shifting the blame and denying responsibility never leads to reconciliation. In verse 13 we see some more of it.

> Genesis 3:13 A͟DONAI E͟LOHIM said to the woman, "What did you do?" The woman said, "The serpent deceived me and I ate."

So she shifted the blame, too. This is a common way of shifting the blame. The forces of evil, the devil made me do it. So **the third relationship destroyer is shifting the blame, not accepting the responsibility**. So in verses 16 through 19 God decreed punishment for Adam and Eve, and a curse on each of them. And then He banished them from the garden:

> Genesis 3:24 And He expelled the man; and at the east of the Garden of Eden He had cheruvim dwell along, with the whirling sword of flame, to guard the way to the Tree of Life.

So the consequences of this disobedience of eating the fruit and trying to usurp authority, and blaming others was pretty serious. It brought a curse, the destruction of their relationship with God, no longer having that face-to-face fellowship with Him, and being kicked out of the Garden. They were now far away from all the benefits of that relationship they had been so privileged to have with God. So there's a pretty good lesson here.

The next account shifts to the consequences of peer relationships, and how we can keep peer relationships. For this, we are going to look at the story of Cain and Abel. So in this story, God complimented Abel for the offering he made that was his way of worshiping God. But God corrected Cain for an unacceptable offering, and Cain pouted. Then God warned Cain about the sin:

> Genesis 4:6 Then A͟DONAI said to Cain, "Why are you angry? And why has your countenance fallen?"

Cain's "countenance fallen" means he was depressed, bitter, angry.

> Genesis 4:7a "If you do well, it will lift. ..."

God was saying, if you follow Abel's example and bring an acceptable offering your depression will lift.

> Genesis 4:7b "... But if you do not do well, sin is crouching at the doorway. Its desire is for you, but you must master it."

Do do you know what the sin was? Jealousy. **Envy and jealousy** were crouching at the door, and Cain needed to resist it. Now we're all tempted by this. Can you say that you have not been tempted by envy or jealousy at some point in your life? We all are, but we see here that there is a great danger in entertaining it. **It's the fourth relationship destroyer**, not only of the person that you're envious or jealous of, but also other people will pick it up, and it can destroy many relationships.

So Cain did not master the spirit of envy. Instead he obeyed it and what did he do? He murdered his brother Abel! Then God confronted Cain:

> Genesis 4:9-12 *Then Adonai said to Cain, "Where is Abel, your brother?" "I don't know," he said. "Am I my brother's keeper?" 10 Then He* [God] *said, "What have you done? The voice of your brother's blood is crying out to Me from the ground. 11 So now, cursed are you from the ground which opened its mouth to receive your brother's blood from your hand. 12 As often as you work the ground, it will not yield its crops to you again. You will be a restless wanderer on the earth."*

So here are the lessons of the destructive effects of entertaining envy and jealousy. They lead to resentment, hatred, and eventually they can lead to murder. And the consequence of murder was to be exiled from God's presence. So we see here not only envy and jealousy, but also **hiding sin destroys relationships**. God knows everything. We cannot hide anything from Him and yet people try. **So the fifth relationship destroyer is hiding sin**.

The next account is from the story of Abraham, and it reveals immense blessings for obedience. Abraham was a model of obedience. He obeyed God's instructions even to his willingness to sacrifice his beloved son in chapter 22 of Genesis. His blessings were many descendants, the Land, and that he'd be a blessing. But Abraham messed up some relationships. He moved to Egypt during a famine and was welcomed by Pharaoh, but then he lied to Pharaoh, and his lie was uncovered.

Genesis 12:20 *Then Pharaoh instructed men concerning him, and they expelled him, with his wife, and everything that belonged to him.*

So there's another lesson **lying and deception destroys relationships. So the sixth relationship destroyer is lying and deception.** You can only have a healthy relationship with someone who trusts you and once you're caught in a lie, there goes the trust.

Now we'll go on with the family of Abraham. Abraham's son Isaac and his wife Rebecca had ungodly favoritism concerning their sons. Isaac favored Esau and Rebecca favored Jacob. It resulted in Jacob stealing Esau's blessing by deceiving their father Isaac, and he did it at his mother Rebecca's instruction. She was the one who put him up to it. That resulted in Jacob being exiled from his family because his brother wanted to kill him. So this is a big one, especially for those of us who are parents. **Parental favoritism is destructive and cannot be entertained.** So parental authority or any authority figure, anybody who's in authority that shows favoritism to someone is being destructive. **So showing favoritism is the seventh relationship destroyer**.

Jacob moved away to get away from his brother, and he was cheated several times while living with his uncle Laban, but remember what he did to his brother Esau. He cheated him, and so we see the reaping of what we sow. **If we cheat, we will be cheated. Cheating someone is a big-time relationship destroyer. It's the eighth one.** This one brings consequences and, without God's intervention, is almost irreparable.

Jacob's cheating resulted in him being cheated into having two wives who were sisters and two more wives who were the sisters' servants, and guess what that caused? Jealousy all over the place and favoritism. Jacob favored one wife over the others. It ran through that family, and it was passed down to their children. We'll read about that in a minute with the story of Joseph and his brothers, but notice, and this is interesting to me, all the way up to here (we are in the 32nd chapter in the Bible), there has been nothing so far about how to restore a relationship. All that's there before this point is how to break relationships, how to mess them up. The account of Jacob's return to be back with his estranged brother Esau is the first account of there being any reconciliation in the Bible.

Esau had stayed in the same place. Jacob moved away, and because Jacob had cheated him, Esau wanted to kill him. So Jacob was directed by God to return, but he was very afraid of encountering his brother Esau after what he had done. So what did Jacob do? He fell on his face and prayed, and it says he wrestled with God, but, I believe it was mostly that he just clung to the Lord, begging Him for favor with his brother.

Relationship restorers

There's a really significant lesson here about restoring relationships. Most times **restoring a relationship, requires God's favor and His intervention**. If you've been trying to restore a relationship with someone and it hasn't been working, there's a lesson for you here. Go before the Lord and cry out to Him, begging for His favor. I've seen this happen several times because you get to a point where there's nothing more you can do. We're going to list some of the things you can do, but when you've done everything possible, then all you can do is say, "God, I need You to intervene here." So **God's help and grace** is needed to restore relationships. **That's the first relationship restorer, God's help and grace**. So God gave Jacob favor with Esau, but then we see some other things.

So what did Jacob do? He took some actions himself to try to restore the relationship. First of all, when they met, Jacob bowed before Esau, showing his submission to his older brother. I didn't see this before until I studied it again this time, but understand that Jacob could have told Esau, "You bow to me! You sold me your birthright. I have the headship of the family now because I have the firstborn birthright. That means I have the place of the older brother." But he didn't do that. Instead, if you read the story, what did he do? He bowed before Esau seven times (Gen. 33:3). He humbled himself. So **the second relationship restorer is humility**. Humility is one of the traits that's needed to restore relationships.

Then we also read in the story that Jacob gave Esau bounteous gifts. Proverbs also speaks about this, that a gift will turn a relationship.

Proverbs 18:16 *A man's gift makes room for him....*

Sometimes a gift will do that, but why did he give gifts? Remember Jacob had cheated Esau out of his birthright, and what that meant was a double portion of his father's inheritance. Jacob was going to get that double portion because Esau had sold him his birthright. Alright? So now he is reimbursing Esau. He gave him an abundance to make up for what he had cheated him out of. So **giving gifts is the third relationship restorer**.

But if you read further through that story, you find that Jacob did not move in with Esau or live near him. Understand that in that culture that's what families usually did. All the brothers stayed together, and they became like a tribe or a clan, and the father was the head of the clan until he died. Then the oldest brother become the head of the clan. But in this story, you find that after Jacob and Esau reconciled, Jacob went to live somewhere else. That's because there's a step in maintaining relationships beyond reconciliation, and that's restoration.

Restoration takes time because what needs to be restored is trust. So you can have a relationship reconciled, but you don't trust the person yet who hurt you, and that's okay. That's what Jacob was doing. It was like, "Okay, we're reconciling, but I'm not going to hang out with him because I don't really trust him yet. I'm going to move over here, so we have a little distance between us, and we'll see if we can get along, and trust can be restored."

This is very important to understand. It always takes time to restore trust. It doesn't happen quickly. It doesn't happen just because you say, "I'll be nice to you from now on, I promise." It doesn't happen because if you've hurt someone or if someone has hurt you, you're going to have a little bit of mistrust. And like I said, that's okay. So we've got the understanding that **restoration takes time, the fourth relationship restorer**.

Now the iniquity of Isaac's favoritism, remember, was visited upon Jacob, and he favored one of his four wives, Rachel, and therefore favored her son, even though he had eleven other sons. He had two sons by Rachel, and he favored the eldest one. I'm sure he favored the youngest one also a lot. But his favoring of Joseph caused what? Jealousy and envy in his nine older sons. This jealousy resulted in them selling Joseph into slavery into Egypt. Then those nine brothers lied to their father, Jacob, telling him that Joseph had been killed by a wild animal, which resulted in the father suffering great grief, and the nine brothers suffering guilt for many, many years.

So whether you are familiar with the story or not, you should read it. It's one of the best stories in the Bible. Joseph came into great power. He became the prime minister of Egypt by predicting a coming famine and directing the Egyptians in preparing for it by storing up food. His brothers came down to him in Egypt from Canaan to buy food during the famine, but they didn't recognize him. Joseph recognized them, and in a great lesson on reconciliation, he did not punish his brothers who deserved it. Instead he manipulated circumstances to test his brothers to see if they had become truly sorry for what they had done to him.

This very important lesson is that **reconciliation can only happen when there's true repentance**, not just shallow repentance but sincere, deep repentance for whatever offense happened that caused the broken relationship in the first place. So **the fifth relationship restorer is true repentance. True repentance restores relationships.**

So when Joseph was sure that they had sincerely repented, he revealed himself to his brothers, and we find that immediately after he revealed himself, he comforted them.

> Genesis 45:5 *"So now, don't be grieved and don't be angry in your own eyes that you sold me here—since it was for preserving life that God sent me here before you."*

This is something that I believe is very valuable. Do you find it hard to forgive? Sometimes it helps to forgive when you can see that God's purposes are behind what happened.

Okay? Joseph was seeing here that God's purposes were behind what his brothers did to him. So he was like, "Yeah, you guys did a terrible thing to me, but you know what? God was behind it, and I forgive you."

So **the sixth relationship restorer is seeing God's hand on the situation.** In this case, God's purpose was for Joseph to save the people of Egypt from famine, preserving many lives. And God's purpose was also to put his brothers through circumstances that brought them to true repentance and changed them.

But even though reconciliation had happened, full restoration had not come to this family. In that culture, the head of the family who was now clearly Joseph was responsible for providing and protecting the rest of the family. Obviously, Joseph, as the prime minister of Egypt, was well capable of doing that. But yet we find this attitude in the brothers years later:

> Genesis 50:15 *When Joseph's brothers saw that their father had died, they said, "Maybe Joseph will be hostile towards us and pay us back in full for all the evil we showed him."*

You see that they were reconciled, but they didn't trust him.

> Genesis 50:16-17a *So they charged Joseph saying, "Before his death, your father gave a command, saying, 17 "Thus you must say to Joseph: 'Please forgive, I beg you, the transgression of your brothers and their sin because they treated you wrongly.' Therefore, please forgive the transgression of the servants of the God of your father."*

This was an outright lie! Their father never said that, but it shows something very interesting here. It shows how guilty the brothers still felt, and how they didn't trust that Joseph had actually forgiven them. They still were not fully restored. The rest of verse 17 is very interesting.

> Genesis 50:17b *Then Joseph wept when they spoke to him,*

I believe he wept because he had been so good to them. He had given them homes, provided for them, and protected them. He had shown them love, and yet they were still not trusting him and still believing that he would hurt them. Then he says this:

27. THE TORAH ON RELATIONSHIPS

Genesis 50:20-21 *"Yes, you yourselves planned evil against me. God planned it for good, in order to bring about what it is this day—to preserve the lives of many people. 21 So now, don't be afraid. I myself will provide food for you and your little ones." So he reassured them, speaking kindly to them.*

What this speaks to me is that restoration of trust really is not easy. It's very difficult. It takes time, and it takes effort. It's best to pray and ask God for grace to help us restore trust. **Restoration requires evidence to trust. So evidence that you can be trusted again is the sixth relationship restorer.**

So those were stories. Now we want to take a look at some actual instructions or commands from God. They give another requirement and another insight into this whole area of reconciliation.

In Leviticus chapters 1 through 6, there are instructions on all of the animal sacrifices required by God. If you read it carefully, you will see that most of the sacrifices for atonement for sin, were for unintentional sin, not for intentional sin. However, when you get to chapter 5, there's one sacrifice that deals with a few intentional sins. In Hebrew, intentional sins are called *pesha*, which means *trespasses against God's laws*. We're going to read through them. Take note that they're in chapter 5 in Jewish Bibles, but they're in chapter 6 in English Bibles (given in parenthesis).

Leviticus 5:21-22 (6:2-3) *Suppose anyone sins and commits a faithless act against ADONAI by dealing falsely with his neighbor in a matter of a deposit or a pledge of hands, or through robbery, or has extorted from his neighbor, 22 or has found what was lost and lied about it, swearing falsely—so sinning in one of any of these things that a man may do.*

Now do you see that these would be intentional sins? You know, you can't rob unintentionally. You can't extort unintentionally. Right?

Leviticus 5:23-24 (6:4-5) *Then it will be, when he has sinned and has become guilty, that he must restore what he took by robbery, or what he got by extortion, or the deposit that was committed to him, or what was lost that he found, 24 or any thing about which he has sworn falsely, he is to restore it in* full, and add a fifth part more to it. He must give it to the one to whom it belongs on the day of presenting his trespass offering.

So what Moses is teaching here is that reimbursing is also required for there to be reconciliation and restoration. **Reimbursing is powerful evidence of true repentance and change.** Reimbursing more than what you stole, more than what you cheated the person, at least one-fifth more is even better convincing evidence. **So the seventh relationship restorer is full plus one-fifth more reimbursement.**

This is something that I don't think many people realize. Intentional sins for which there was no atonement that can be made for them were sins for which no reimbursement could be made, like murder. How can you reimburse for murder? You can't reimburse it. The person is gone. How about adultery? You can't reimburse a married couple if you commit adultery with one of them because it has done such damage to the marriage. You can't possibly make up for it. So there is no atonement for intentional sins unless there's possible reimbursement. Do you see that? Okay.

But this passage raises another related necessity for reconciliation, and it's very interesting. Let's read verse 21 again.

> Leviticus 5:21 (6:2) *Suppose anyone sins and commits a faithless act against Adonai by dealing falsely with his neighbor....*

Notice it is saying that these intentional sins—lying, cheating, stealing, and extortion—are against who? Against the Lord! And we find this in Psalms 51 when David confesses his sin, he says, "Against you and you only have I sinned." So we begin to see that when we sin against each other, who do we also sin against? God! So here's the $64,000 question. We learned that intentional sins can only be forgiven if there is reimbursement. How do you reimburse God? How can He be reimbursed when you've committed sin against Him? Here's the answer.

> Leviticus 5:25-26 (6:6-7) *He is to bring his trespass offering to Adonai, a ram without blemish from the flock, according*

to your value, for a trespass offering, to the kohen. 26 The kohen shall make atonement for him before ADONAI, and he will be forgiven concerning whatever he may have done to become guilty.

So the unblemished ram of the trespass offering paid the penalty for the trespass sin against God. See, the person whom they cheated they had to pay back, but to pay back God, they had to offer an innocent animal, an unblemished ram. This is why the Torah says this:

Leviticus 17:11 *For the life of the creature is in the blood, and I have given it to you on the altar to make atonement for your lives—for it is the blood that makes atonement because of the life.*

Hebrews 9:22b *... [I]ndeed, without the shedding of blood there is no forgiveness of sins.*

So **the eighth relationship restorer is that God must be reimbursed.** You see that? We must reimburse people for our sins against them, plus we must reimburse God. There's a penalty that must be paid.

Now this leads us to something you're probably thinking about already—what Yeshua did. Right? We're going to get there, but I want to first cover a couple of things that Yeshua said about relationships because they're so powerful.

Matthew 5:23-24 *So if you are offering your gift at the Temple altar and you remember there that your brother has something against you, 24 leave your gift where it is by the altar, and go, make peace with your brother. Then come back and offer your gift.*

Now understand God's presence was in the Temple at this time, and offering a gift was the main form of worship. So Yeshua is saying, "Don't try to come into God's presence if your brother or your sister has something against you." It's not if you have something against them, but if they have something against you. So this teaches the importance of maintaining healthy relationships, and seeking reconciliations because if we don't, it breaks our relationship with God. So **we must reconcile with people to reconcile with God.**

Now this is important to understand. There are times when your brother or sister will have something against you even after you've done all you can to reconcile. You can't force anybody to forgive you. You know that, right? You can't force them. The more you try, the worse it'll be. But you can pray and ask God to intervene in that situation, and I believe very strongly that if you've done your part, if you've done everything you can, God will honor your sincere effort and hear your prayers and welcome you into His presence once again.

So that verse spoke about somebody having something against you, but Yeshua also said this:

> Matthew 6:14-15 *For if you forgive others their offenses, your heavenly Father will also forgive you; 15 but if you do not forgive others their offenses, your heavenly Father will not forgive yours.*

So this is the inverse of chapter five. You see that? Chapter five was about somebody having something against you. This is about you having something against somebody else. So this teaches the importance of forgiving and reconciling, teaching you that your prayers won't be answered unless you forgive. In fact, we won't receive forgiveness from God, if we don't forgive! So **forgiveness is relationship restorer number nine**. (For an in-depth study on how to truly forgive see my *Counting the Omer* book, "Resurrection to Ruakh," Week 4, pages 345-351.)

Now, in addition to Yeshua's teachings on maintaining and restoring Godly relations, we have His actions—His atoning sacrifice—which is the most important part of all this. Yeshua came to earth as a human being; lived a life without sin; taught God's Word; performed countless amazing miracles; and allowed Himself to be falsely accused, arrested, tried, beaten, whipped, condemned to death; and sacrificed His life as a trespass offering to make atonement. Remember, trespasses are intentional violations of God's Law. He offered Himself as a trespass sacrifice to make atonement for all sins for all time. So we can all be forgiven concerning—that phrase that was used in that verse—*"concerning whatever you may have done to make yourself guilty."* Every person who puts their trust in

Messiah's sacrifice will be reconciled with God whom they have sinned against. Rabbi Sha'ul (Paul) writes about this:

> II Corinthians 5:20-21 *Therefore we are ambassadors of the Messiah; in effect, God is making his appeal through us. What we do is appeal on behalf of the Messiah, "Be reconciled to God! 21 God made this sinless man be a sin offering on our behalf, so that in union with him we might fully share in God's righteousness."*

So God's greatest desire is for every individual person to be reconciled with Him. You may be thinking, "Why do I need to be reconciled with God?" Well, Solomon in the book of Ecclesiastes tells us why.

> Ecclesiastes 7:20 *Surely there is not a righteous person on earth who does what is good and doesn't sin.*

Now that tells me that if you've never sinned, you must not be living on earth, right? Perhaps you don't think you've ever sinned because you don't know all of God's commandments. I've talked to a lot of people who think, "Oh yeah. I'm fine. I never do anything wrong." Then I start reading them the Ten Commandments and their countenance falls because they realize, "Oh yeah, I do that and I do that." Here's one. How about the one that we recite in every Shabbat meeting? *Love your neighbor as yourself.* How many people have been able to always obey that one? Have you?

So as we learned from the account about Adam and Eve, disobedience to God destroys your relationship with Him, and **Yeshua's atoning sacrifice is the final relationship restorer**.

So we're going to pray now to be reconciled with God, but also this is a time to pray for reconciliation with other people. And I have to say I have been blessed. I've had a couple answers to that prayer. A few years ago I had somebody come up to me who had been estranged from me for awhile, and say, "You know, I've realized that I was wrong, and we need to be close again. We need to be friends." It was so awesome! I told him he made my day! He said he expected me to say something like, "Well, I'm not sure. You know, you really offended me." Instead I just was like, "Wow! I'm sorry for anything I did that broke our relationship." It was amazingly wonderful!

Then right before I taught this message to my congregation, somebody else said something similar to me that morning! Whenever those things happen, they are so tremendous and healing!

Let's pray.

Father, we thank You that You desire to be in a healthy relationship with every one of us and for us to be in healthy relationships with each other. We recognize that we have disobeyed Your Laws. We take responsibility for our disobedience. We won't shift the blame. We repent and ask You to count Yeshua's atoning sacrifice to pay the penalty and the reimbursement for our sin against You, and we receive Your forgiveness. We ask that You give us assurance that we're right with You and fill us with Your Spirit.

We ask that You would help us, Lord, to maintain healthy relationships. We repent of any pride that has caused broken relationships and disobedience. We repent of jealousy. We repent of any deception we used. We repent of any shifting of the blame when we've messed up. We repent of hiding anything we've done that has harmed someone else. We repent of any favoritism that we showed.

Those are the things we covered here, Lord, but we know there's a whole lot more stuff.

For our broken relationships, Lord, we need Your grace, whether they are with family members, with coworkers, with fellow students, with neighbors, employers, employees, or others in the congregation, we need Your grace to restore those relationships. We repent of our part in any break that has happened. We humble ourselves. Help us to reconcile. We recognize that we need Your grace. If we're to give gifts to encourage reconciliation, Lord, show us what we're to give. Show us what we're to reimburse for what we've done.

Help us to be patient, Lord, because we understand that restoration of trust takes time. Give us wisdom to not put ourselves in danger if that person is not trustworthy yet. Lord, in whatever broken relationship, let there be true repentance. If we need to truly repent, show us!

Help us to see Your hand in any relationship that's been broken that You may have some purpose in it. Thank You, Lord, that You made a way that we can reimburse You. The penalty must be paid, and You paid it! You paid it by going to the Cross, by being beaten, by being whipped, by being humiliated by all the things that were done, being falsely accused, and the terrible, terrible pain that You suffered. We thank You so much, Lord, that You paid the price so that we can be right with You!! The penalty can be paid. The reimbursement can be made because You are a God of justice, and there always needs to be a paying back for what has been done. So we just thank You for that revelation.

And Father, I just pray for all the readers of this book that in the days to come, they would see breakthroughs in broken relationships, whether they're within families or friends or ex friends or the congregation, that they would see breakthrough, Father, that they would be guided by Your Ruakh, by Your Spirit, and would see reconciliation and restoration of those relationships, a coming together where there's been separation. What a wonderful thing it will be! So we just commit this to You in the awesome, wonderful Name of our Lord, Yeshua HaMashiakh. Amein. Amein.

CHAPTER 28
RIGHTLY DIVIDING THE WORD

In these End Times, the closer we get to the day of Yeshua "*coming in the clouds with power and great glory,*" the more we need to know His Word! Why? Because here is what the Holy Spirit says about how to live in these End Times.

> I Timothy 4:1-2 *The Spirit expressly states that in the acharit-hayamim* [last days] *some people will apostatize from the faith by paying attention to deceiving spirits and things taught by demons. 2 Such teachings come from the hypocrisy of liars whose own consciences have been burned, as if with a red-hot branding iron.*

So Rabbi Sha'ul writing to Timothy here is giving a very strong warning that there will be false teachings inspired by deceiving spirits in what? The last days. We need to know God's Word to protect against these false teachings and because it is His Word that feeds us.

> Deuteronomy 8:3 ..*He afflicted you and let you hunger, then He fed you manna—which neither you nor your fathers had known—in order to make you understand that man does not live by bread alone but by every word that comes from the mouth of ADONAI.*

His Word is how He feeds you, how He refills your tank. Your spirit needs His Word like you need physical food every day. And what is the source of His Word. The Bible. Not only is the Word our food, it is also our tool for building the Kingdom and our weapon against the enemy. In his second letter to Timothy, Sha'ul writes this:

28. RIGHTLY DIVIDING THE WORD

II Timothy 2:15 (NKJV) *Be diligent to present yourself approved to God, a worker who does not need to be ashamed,* **rightly dividing** *the word of truth.*

II Timothy 2:15 (NRSV) *Do your best to present yourself to God as one approved by him, a worker who has no need to be ashamed,* **rightly explaining** *the word of truth.*

II Timothy 2:15 (TLV) *Make every effort to present yourself before God as tried and true, as an unashamed worker* **cutting a straight path** *with the word of truth.*

II Timothy 2:15 *Do all you can to present yourself to God as someone worthy of his approval, as a worker with no need to be ashamed, because he* **deals straightforwardly** *with the Word of the Truth.*

So what the Spirit is saying is that especially in these days, you need to know how to *rightly divide* and *explain* and *deal straightforwardly* with the Word. That means you need to know how to understand the Word, interpret the Word, and apply the Word of Truth, which is the Bible. And you must be able to discern false teachings from the true teaching of the Bible.

Because many of us think that we can't possibly be deceived, I want to share some examples of the Word of Truth being wrongly divided today, that are widely accepted. If you're deceived, you won't know it. Right? That's the definition of being deceived. You don't realize what's happening, so you're deceived.

So we're going to look at some of these misapplications or wrongly dividing of the Word of Truth today. I think they will be kind of shocking. Are you ready to be shocked?

Have you ever said this or heard it said: God inhabits the praises of His people? Have you prayed it? Here's the shock. That phrase is not in the Bible. Not in the Bible. Now just so you know, I'm not just using a Jewish-friendly translation. You can see first here the King James and the New King James, then the NIV, then the Jewish versions:

Psalm 22:3 (KJV) *But thou art holy, O thou that inhabitest the praises of Israel.*

Psalm 22:3 (NKJV) *But You are holy, Enthroned in the praises of Israel.*

> Psalm 22:3 (NIV) *Yet you are enthroned as the Holy One; you are the one Israel praises.*
>
> Psalm 22:4 (3) (TLV) *Yet You are holy, enthroned on the praises of Israel.*
>
> Psalm 22:4 (3) (CJB) *Nevertheless, you are holy, enthroned on the praises of Isra'el.*

Do you see that all except the NIV say basically the same thing? So, first of all, why would people quote this verse? Well, it's a great verse to encourage people. Right? Praise Him and God will inhabit your praises. Right? He'll be in your midst. So it's a great verse or pseudo verse, right? Why is it almost always quoted incorrectly with "His people" substituted for "Israel"?

Well, you could take two stands on that. It's a well-meaning error. It helps all believers trust that God inhabits their praises no matter what their ethnic background is. Right? That's good. But if you look at it from a not-so-good reason, it's the result of Replacement Theology teaching that the church has replaced Israel, rather than that believers in Yeshua—who are not Jewish ethnically—become part of Israel when they become believers. Big difference there, right?

So let me just show you a little bit about that because that's something that everybody should understand. Writing to Gentile believers about their situation before they became believers, so before coming to the Lord, this is what Rabbi Sha'ul wrote:

> Ephesians 2:11-12 *... you Gentiles by birth — ... 12 at that time had no Messiah. You were estranged from the national life of Isra'el. You were foreigners to the covenants embodying God's promise. You were in this world without hope and without God.*

Then describing the status of Gentiles after becoming believers in Yeshua:

> Ephesians 2:19 (TLV) *So then you are no longer strangers and foreigners, but you are fellow citizens with God's people and members of God's household.*

28. RIGHTLY DIVIDING THE WORD

So what does this tell us? Gentile believers have been made fellow citizens with fellow Jewish people. What are they citizens of? The Commonwealth of Israel, God's household.

But Replacement Theology has taught that the church has replaced Israel as God's chosen people, and that Israel is under a curse. So they see the verse as saying, *God inhabits the praises of* His people, the church, but not Israel anymore. That's the error there.

So let's *rightly divide* and *deal straightforwardly* to correctly understand Psalm 22:3. *God inhabits (or is enthroned upon) the praises of Israel*, and you, Gentiles, are now citizens of the Commonwealth of Israel, so He also inhabits your praises. Got that? That's what it actually says. That's good! Right? But I can't tell you how many times I've heard people say, "God inhabits the praises of His people," and they all believe they're quoting the Bible.

So that's one example of a passage that has been wrongly divided. Here's another example that has been wrongly divided or incorrectly understood. In this case, the understanding of the passage is misunderstood because it's not looked at in context of what comes before and after it.

How many have sung or quoted this one? The joy of the Lord is your strength. We all quote that. In fact, we have the song, "The Joy of the Lord is My Strength" and another verse of it, "If You Want Joy You Must Dance For It." Do you know that song? Good old songs, right? I always understood the meaning as joy that comes from God gives us strength, which is true! Right? In fact, one of the fruits of the Spirit is joy. And there's the joy of salvation that David speaks about in Psalm 51.

So what's the problem? Well, this statement, "The joy of the Lord is your strength," does appear in the Bible in Nehemiah 8:10, but what's the context? Is it that, "Oh, you should have strength because you've got God's joy in you"? We'll see.

The setting is just after the Torah was read to the exiles who had returned to Jerusalem from 70 years of captivity in Babylon. As we saw in chapter 21, many of them had no access to the Torah—to reading it or hearing it read. No one had been able to obey it because there was no Temple, so they couldn't do a lot of the things that had to take place there. So let's look at the verse immediately proceeding that statement.

> Nehemiah 8:9-10 *Then Nehemiah the governor, Ezra the kohen-scribe, and the Levites who were teaching the people said to all the people, "Today is kadosh [holy] to ADONAI your God. Do not mourn or weep!" For all the people had been weeping when they heard the words of the Torah. 10 So he said to them, "Go! Eat choice food, drink sweet drinks, and send portions to those who have nothing ready. For today is kadosh to our Lord. Do not grieve, for the joy of ADONAI is your strength."*

So the context is that they began to weep in repentance as the Torah was read to them because they had not been obeying God's Word. Then the priests tell them not to grieve because God's joy in your repentance is your strength. So what did their repentance, their turning from sin to God, produce in the Lord? Joy! God was rejoicing over their repentance because He could see people truly repenting with true hearts. They were sorry for having disobeyed Him. Nehemiah was saying, "God is pleased by your repentance. He's so pleased that He's rejoicing over you about it. Therefore, don't grieve, for God's joy at your repentance is your strength." Is that a little bit different meaning? Yea!

Now, I don't know if you can get the other part, but why was the day holy to the Lord? It's because it is a feast day, an Appointed Time.

> Nehemiah 8:2b ... *This happened on the first day of the seventh month.*

Which Appointed Time is that? Yom Teruah, Rosh Hashanah! Is it a Shabbat? Yes. So it is a Holy Day. One of God's instructions for Yom Teruah is that we are to rejoice. They were repenting on that day after hearing the Torah read. So that's why Nehemiah and the priests are telling them to rejoice. (To find out more about that day, read my *Yom Teruah* book.)

So, Nehemiah encouraged them by telling them that their repentance as evidenced by their weeping has brought joy to the Lord, and that His joy was their strength. Why would they need strength at this point? Because they were committing themselves to obey His Word now, and they needed the strength to go ahead with that turn. It's one thing to say, "Oh, I'm so sorry I disobeyed You, Lord." But what takes strength? To now obey! So to understand that God was happy, that God was rejoicing that they had repented, now he was saying that should be your strength. Now go and obey and rejoice in that. That's quite different from just saying to someone who's down, "The joy of the Lord is your strength!" Right? The admonition is actually to repent. It should be spoken to people in context when people are repenting and weeping in repentance.

Ready for another one? Okay. This is another one taken out of context. Do you know the popular worship song, "Sound the shofar in Zion" ("Blow the Trumpet in Zion"[10])? It's sung as a victorious song with shofars sounding! We will have victory! Let me give you some of the other lines in the song.

Sound the alarm on My Holy Mountain!
They rush on the city, they run on the walls. Great is the army that carries out His Word!
The Lord utters His voice before His army!

Are you familiar with that song? How do we sing it? We are the army. We're going to take on the evil. We're going to break the gates of hell. Right? But what's the context? Do you know? Let's look at Joel 2.

> Joel 2:1 *Blow the shofar in Zion! Sound an alarm on My holy mountain! Let all living in the land tremble—for the day of A<small>DONAI</small> is coming—surely it is near!*

Sounds okay so far. I'm now going to pick phrases out because it is a long passage.

> Joel 2:2, 3, 5 *... A great and mighty people— ... 3 A fire devours before them and behind them flame blazes up. Like the Garden of Eden is the land before them, and behind them a desolate wilderness. Nothing at all ever escapes them. ... 5 Like the clatter of chariots, they leap on the tops of mountains, like crackling flame of fire devouring stubble, like a mighty horde in battle array.*

---

10 Craig Terndrup © 1983 Sounds Of Vision (Admin. by Integrity Music)

What is this describing? An attacking enemy but, literally, a plague of locusts.

> Joel 2:6, 9 *Before them peoples are in anguish. All faces become ashen gray. ... 9 They rush on the city, they run on the wall, they climb up into the houses, coming through the windows like a thief.*

It's talking about insects!

> Joel 2:10 *Before them land quakes, heaven trembles, sun and moon become dark, stars withdraw their brightness.*

The cloud of insects darken the sky, which is exactly what happens in a plague of locusts.

> Joel 2:11a A*DONAI* *utters His voice before His army.*

This is the Lord's army.

> Joel 2:11 *... For His camp is very vast—for mighty is it that carries out His word. For great is the day of A*DONAI*—very terrifying! Who can endure it?*

So is this a rejoicing song? No way! It's about an attack on Zion!—on Jerusalem by a destroying army! So what is the purpose of this passage? It actually has a very good purpose. Joel is calling the people to repentance:

> Joel 2:12-13 *"Yet even now"—it is a declaration of A*DONAI*— "turn to Me with all your heart, with fasting, weeping and lamenting." 13 Rend your heart, not your garments, and turn to A*DONAI*, your God. For He is gracious and compassionate, slow to anger, abundant in mercy, and relenting about the calamity due.*

In other words, you deserve calamity.

> Joel 2:15a *Blow the shofar in Zion!*

Here's what it's to be blown for:

> Joel 2:15b *Sanctify a fast; proclaim an assembly.*

Do you see what this is about? The prophet is sounding a warning, calling for repentance, calling for a fast because the Lord's army in the form of locusts is attacking Zion because of their sin! So that's a little bit different from how we have sung it, right? Now there's another shofar song that is great. "In the Year of Jubilee, Sound the Shofar." That song is great, but not this one.

So we have seen three examples of **wrongly** dividing the Word. Now I'm going to give some really practical suggestions on how we can **rightly** divide the Word.

Nine techniques for rightly dividing the Word

Technique one: Always look at the context to understand the text. The Holy Spirit inspired the Word in the context of what was happening at the time. Without knowing the context of the Word, it can be misused and misappropriated. So we need to know what His Word says and what it means in the context in which it was written. Usually you can get the context by reading a few verses before and after. Usually that's all you have to do, but sometimes you need to read a few chapters before to understand the situation leading up to that passage. So that's number one.

Technique two: Think about what you read when you read the Bible. I want to introduce this second technique by talking about a very interesting experience I've had while teaching our Messianic Judaism class. In case you haven't taken the class, the format is that we go around the room and each person has to read a Scripture passage. Then there's a question that they have to answer that the passage clearly answers. But guess what happens when people first join the class? They hem and haw and have a really hard time answering correctly. So let me give you an example.

> John 16:13 *However, when the Spirit of Truth comes, he will guide you into all the truth; for he will not speak on his own initiative but will say only what he hears. He will also announce to you the events of the future.*

So a person in the room reads that passage and then they have to answer this question: What role of the Holy Spirit in our lives is described here in this passage? People give answers like, "The Holy Spirit gives gifts of the Spirit." or "The Holy Spirit gives the fruits of the Spirit." "The Holy Spirit gives power." "The Holy Spirit enables us to hear from God." And I have to stop them and say, "That's good, but what does the verse say?" Obviously the verse says what? He will guide you into all truth. He will reveal the truth to you. And? Tell you about the future. Here's another example. Here's the verse:

> Romans 15:4 *For everything written in the past was written to teach us, so that with the encouragement of the Tanakh we might patiently hold on to our hope.*
>
> Romans 15:4 (TLV) *For whatever was written before was written for our instruction, so that through patience and the encouragement of the Scriptures we might have hope.*

Then the question is: What purposes of the Scripture are given here? You might easily see the answer right there, right? It's not a hard question. The purposes are endurance, encouragement, and hope. They're all there. But if you've taken the class, you can testify to how hard it is for people to catch on to this.

So after teaching this class for awhile, I began to pray and ask God why people have such a hard time. If you've taken the class, you've seen it. Their answers are true, but they're not doing what they're told to do, which is to look at the verse and say what the verse says. So I prayed about this, and I realized that most of us, who've been believers for awhile, have received lots of teaching. When people are asked about a particular Bible verse, they typically respond with what they've been taught without looking at the verse. So they read a familiar verse, thinking, "Oh, I know this verse. I heard somebody teach this on it, so I know what it means, and I can impress everybody." Rather than looking and saying, "Oh, what does it actually say?"

I also think our education system doesn't really teach people to comprehend what they're reading. They read it, but it doesn't go in. So, I personally believe that the greatest fruit from that class is that people learn, after making that mistake a few times, to actually look at the verse and see what it says. It sounds like such a simple thing, but most people don't do it. And that is so important to do, to actually look at the verse.

So again technique two is: when you read the Bible, pay attention to what you are reading. Don't just think about what you've been taught about it, but think about what it actually says. This is called inductive study, meaning you're not trying to find things in the Bible to support your doctrine or belief, but you're trying to understand what the Bible says.

Now good Bible teachings are great when they are truly based on what the Bible really says. I'm not against listening to Bible teachers, of course. But if you can read the Bible and actually comprehend it for yourself and actually see what it's saying, not having to have somebody to tell you what it says but actually grasp it for yourself, that is a tremendous gift that I've seen many gain over the course of taking the class. To me it's the most important thing you could have learned in that class really. The class is pretty long. It takes about nine months to get through the whole book. By the time you get into that ninth month, it's like, "Oh yeah, I can do this."

So put aside how a verse will support what you believe, and ask yourself, "What does it actually say?" Then let God's life-changing Truth sink in. So that's technique two.

Technique three: Check out other translations when you're reading your Bible. This is really quite important. The translations that we use is another area of potential for misunderstanding. Let me give you an example here. This passage is from the writings of Rabbi Sha'ul (Paul), and he's speaking about how God sees unbelieving Jewish people. I will give it in a couple different translations.

> Romans 11:15 (NKJV) *For if their being cast away is the reconciling of the world, what will their acceptance be but life from the dead?*
> Romans 11:15 (KJV) *For if the casting away of them be the reconciling of the world, what shall the receiving of them be, but life from the dead?*

You might be familiar with that verse. So who has been cast away or rejected according to what it says there? Jewish people! He is writing about them in this chapter. Who has cast them away? God. That's what it says, right? This is certainly in line with what the Gentile church has taught for centuries up until very recently. It's at the heart of Replacement Theology. God has cast away the Jews, who are His chosen people. He has rejected us because we rejected Yeshua as the Messiah. He no longer has a plan for us Jewish people or a destiny for us to fulfill. So this translation of this verse has been foundational to Replacement Theology.

But let's just look at the context first. Then we'll look again at the translation. Here's the context. The same author, the same book, the same chapter, just fifteen verses earlier still in the same versions, look at this. This will reveal to you again how steeped the translators were in Replacement Theology:

> Romans 11:1-2 (NKJV) *I say then, has God cast away His people? Certainly not! For I also am an Israelite, of the seed of Abraham, of the tribe of Benjamin. 2 God has not cast away His people whom He foreknew.*

> Romans 11:1 (KJV) *...Hath God cast away his people? God forbid.*

So what's happening here? In these versions what's Paul doing? Do you see the contradiction? In verses 1 and 2, it says God has not cast away His people. In verse 15, it says they've been cast away! Quite a contradiction! Astounding! So let's look at this in the *Complete Jewish Bible*.

> Rom. 11:15 *For if their casting Yeshua aside means reconciliation for the world, what will their accepting him mean? It will be life from the dead!*

Let's do a little analysis of what that is saying. Who has been cast aside or rejected? Yeshua. Who has cast Him aside? The unbelieving Jewish people. And they are still casting Him aside today, right? But when they accept Him, what will happen? Life from the dead!

Okay, so obviously, the KJV and NKJV translators' theology greatly influenced their translations because they didn't even catch the contradiction fifteen verses earlier. Isn't that amazing? In verse 1, God has not cast away His people, but in verse 15 He **has** cast them away, and nobody catches that? The KJV, NKJV, and other translations have greatly influenced the church's theology, which in turn greatly influenced how the church acted toward the Jewish people, which greatly affected world history and Jewish history, as we have noted—all just from the way certain verses were translated.

28. RIGHTLY DIVIDING THE WORD

I recommend and teach from David Stearn's *Complete Jewish Bible* translation for the New Covenant. It is a Jewish friendly translation. It's a paraphrase, not a direct translation, and since it is a paraphrase, he can correct things like this. You might have noticed that Yeshua's Name is not there in that verse, but since Stearn was doing a paraphrase, he could insert it. Then you saw that when you insert Yeshua's Name there to clarify who is being rejected and who is being received, it makes total sense. You can't do that in a literal translation. That's the advantage of David Stearn's paraphrase translation. It enables him to correct the effects of Replacement Theology and other issues that have provoked anti-Semitism.

People liked David Stearn's *Jewish New Testament* so much that they asked him to do the whole Bible, so he did, but he didn't actually translate the Tanakh (Old Testament) himself. What he used for the Tanakh was an old out of copyright translation of the Tanakh that was done by non-Messianic Jewish scholars. The problem with that is it mistranslates Messianic prophesies. So I don't use his version for the Tanakh. I use the *Tree of Life Version* for the Tanakh. I like the way David Stearn did the New Testament because he has the freedom to correct Replacement Theology. The *Tree of Life* New Testament is good too, though, because it is a direct translation done by Messianic Jewish Bible scholars. However, in translating directly, the translators did not have the freedom to do what David Stern does. Here is Romans 11:15 in the *Tree of Life Version*:

> Romans 11:15 (TLV) *For if their rejection leads to the reconciliation of the world, what will their acceptance be but life from the dead?*

Notice the difference there from the *New King James*. This could easily mean "their rejection of Yeshua" rather than God's rejection of them. So that's the third technique: Check out other translations, especially Jewish friendly, non-Replacement Theology translations, when you're reading your Bible.

Technique four: Follow a reading plan. The MJAA has a reading plan that takes you through the whole Bible in a year. I created a reading plan that I can email you a copy of if you contact me through my publisher or through my congregation website, shemayisrael.org. There's also an online chronological reading plan, which means you'll be reading through, let's say, Isaiah, and it will switch you back over to II Kings to read about what was happening when Isaiah was making that prophesy. I've been doing that for the last few years and I find it very helpful.

My recent practice has been, I read the Parashah, which gets you through the Torah, the five books of Moses in a year, and in addition I follow a chronological plan for the rest of the Old Testament. So I'll read one chapter from the Books of Moses. Then I'll read a chapter in the Old Testament from the chronological plan, which goes right into the New Testament, so I'll also read a chapter in the New Testament in David Stearn's version with his commentary. That's what I've been doing for several years, and I love how it ties the whole Bible together for me.

Technique five: Don't just read the Word, study the Word. Certain commentaries are very helpful tools for this. I really like David Stearn's *New Testament Commentary*. I have to confess that most of the theology I know comes from his commentary. I have both his *Jewish New Testament* and his commentary in electronic form, so I can have them side by side on my computer screen. So I read a verse and then I look to see what David Stearn says about that verse.

Now, we need to be cautious about other commentaries and other believing websites. Most of the commentaries out there, especially the older ones, were written by people who were brought up in and trained in Replacement Theology. It became their own theology. So we need to be careful. I refer to them lots of times, but very carefully because of that fact.

There are a lot of Messianic Jewish websites online, but again, be very careful. Some of them have some very strange views. Here's something that I've learned over the years. I try to avoid websites that put down other ministries. You can find plenty of them out there that believe it's their job to expose other Bible teachers, "This person is doing this wrong and this

28. RIGHTLY DIVIDING THE WORD

other person is wrong," on and on. I stay away from those. I'd rather go to the ones that are just teaching what they are getting from God and not putting others down at all.

I believe the internet is an incredibly wonderful blessing for Bible study. One of the greatest values is using it to search for passages. If I'm studying the Bible and I'm looking at one verse, and I have a little bit of a recollection of another verse that applies to it, even if I can only think of one word, I can put that word in a Bible search engine, such as biblestudytools.com, and it will pop up with every verse using that word.

A chain reference Bible is very helpful in this. When you read a verse, you look in the center column to see references for other related verses, and you can go read those verses. I find it fascinating. It takes you all around the Bible, and you see how things connect together. *The Treasury of Scripture Knowledge* is another great chain reference tool, that's also online for free at https://tsk-online.com/TSK/Genesis/1. It brings up all the other Scriptures that have to do with things in the verse you are reading. I find it to be a tremendous help.

Also in some Bible websites, when you're reading one verse, you can click on "compare" and it will show you that verse in tons of other translations. So you can look at just that one verse in all those other translations and see the differences. You can also use the Strong's concordance online instead of a physical hard copy which is a very thick, heavy book that takes time to page through to look something up, which is fine, but it is so much quicker and easier online on websites, such as blueletterbible.org or Biblehub.com. So you can do a **word study.** You can look up any word in the Bible and look at all the different meanings and all the verses it's in and how it is used and from that get the real meaning of the word.

Another very interesting way to study is to follow the career of a character in the Bible of someone like David or Elijah and just read all about that person. Or to do a study on women in the Bible, especially women leaders. Or pick a topic like how to treat widows and orphans and the poor, and see how it is woven throughout Scripture.

If you're trying to learn Hebrew, there are several online Hebrew Bibles, with vowels, without vowels, etc. There are also interlinear Bibles online for Greek and Hebrew. You can read the actual Hebrew and underneath each Hebrew word is an English word in a different color, usually, for each Hebrew word. The great value is that if you just look at parallel translations of Hebrew and English, the word order is all messed up because the Hebrew word order is very different from the English word order. The grammar and syntax are totally different. But when you look at the interlinear, you can see which word means what. Then in some online interlinear Bibles, they put the Strong's Concordance number above the Hebrew word. So you can click on that little number, and it takes you to the Strong's Concordance, and you can find out all the meanings of that word and where else it is used, etc.

I use the interlinear a lot to help me keep learning Hebrew. What I do is I cover up the English and just try to read the Hebrew. When I get to a Hebrew word I don't know yet, I can just peek to read the English word. So without even trying to memorize the Hebrew, after a while, you begin to recognize those Hebrew words because you're seeing them over and over again, and you're associating them with the English meaning. So I highly recommend that if you're trying to learn Hebrew. That's how I have greatly improved my Hebrew by using the interlinear like that in my regular Bible reading.

You can also find the Bible online in other languages. One website has it in 200 languages!

You can also listen to the Bible online. To listen in Hebrew, there is *Serve-A-Verse* at levsoftware.com/SAV/ and *Torah Class* at torahclass.com/audio-bible-in-hebrew/ just to name a couple. To listen in almost any language there's listen.talkingbibles.org/ We live in amazing times when there are so many resources available to us for digging deeper into the Word of God. Hallelujah.

So that is the fifth technique, instead of just reading the Word, study the Word, and using some of the awesome online Bible study tools really helps with that.

Technique six: One very powerful technique is meditating on the Word. I find sometimes, if I don't understand something or I'm trying to see a connection somewhere, I'll just memorize the verse or sort of paraphrase memorize it, and then I'll just think about it over the course of the day, and sleep on it, and pray that God will show me what it's about, and boom, somehow a new thought comes into my mind and I've got a new understanding of it. (We will dig deeper into how to meditate in the next chapter.)

Technique seven: Pray for revelation when you read or study the Bible. Look at this verse again.

John 16:13 ... *when the Spirit of Truth comes, he will guide you into all the truth*....

We all need to understand that what the Lord is saying here is it's the Holy Spirit's role in your life to reveal truth to you, including Biblical truth. So when you read the Word, pray that the Holy Spirit reveals it to you, and He will! He will guide you to all the truth in what you are reading.

Technique eight: Discuss the Word. Discussion actually is one of my favorite ways of learning. Is it yours? We need to talk about things to really understand them. That's the great value of participating in a Bible study. Conversation provokes insight. You see it one way. Somebody else sees it another way. All of a sudden your eyes are opened to that other way of seeing it. That's one of the things I enjoy the most about teaching the Messianic Judaism classes. I get to see things through different people's minds.

But you can actually discuss the Bible with yourself. Did you know that? You can ask yourself questions and answer those questions. Do you do that? Yeah? Okay. But also you can talk with somebody else. It doesn't have to be a heavy thing, like, "Let me tell you what the Bible says. It can be like, "Here's what I saw in the Word. What do you think of it?" Now be ready to listen because if they're really interested they will want to give their opinion and insight. There are also lots of online discussion groups that you can join.

So discussion and even debate is a good Jewish study technique. Have you seen the movie "Yentl"? Remember that movie? Well, that was a picture of this very Jewish way of learning. The scene I'm thinking about is where two students were each given opposite sides of an issue, such as: Should there be capital punishment or not? It didn't matter what their opinion on it was, they had to argue the side of the issue they were given. And they had to debate each other on it. And because they did that, they learned that subject very powerfully.

Technique nine: Learn to teach the Bible. Let me say, the absolute best way to study the Bible is to prepare to teach it. There's an old saying, "You don't really understand something unless you can teach it to someone else." But you might say, "Well, where can I teach it?" Do you have children? Prepare a Bible study for them. That's what I did. First I taught the two-year-olds in Shabbat School because my daughter was two years old, and there was no teacher. And you know what? I learned that it's actually easier to teach adults. If you can get a class of two and three-year-olds to focus their attention for ten minutes, you can do it with adults.

As my kids grew, I taught each class as they got older. Then I started teaching Bible studies at work. That's how I learned to teach and how I learned the Bible better. You learn so much when you're studying it to prepare a lesson on it.

If you are in a Bible study or a small group, I encourage you to try this. If something in your private Bible study time quickens in you, I encourage you to prepare a little study about it. Bring it to the person who is leading the Bible study group and have them critique it. Who knows? They may say, "Well, why don't you share that with the group?" Or you could ask if you could share it. So that could be **another technique—to learn by teaching**. You could also start a Bible study at work or at school or among your friends, and begin to teach.

Let's pray.

Father, we thank You that Your Word is how You feed us, how You refill our tanks. We thank You that You give us Your

Word every day as You also give us our physical food every day. We thank You that You give us Your Word for building Your Kingdom. We thank You that it is one of our weapons for fighting the enemy. And most importantly knowing Your Word is our weapon against being deceived by the enemy.

Help us to know Your Word so well that the enemy cannot trick us with deception. Help us to read every verse in Your Word in context and to be able to easily detect when someone does a false teaching on it from taking it out of context.

Help us to stay clear and to help others to stay clear of Replacement Theology by studying Jewish friendly translations. Help us to remember to take the time to meditate on Your Word, so it can sink deeper into our inner being. Help us to learn to teach Your Word and to remember to pray for revelation from Your Ruakh to help us understand what You are trying to teach us from Your Word.

Help us to find good reading plans that fit our personalities so that we make sure we are reading and studying Your whole Word and not neglecting any part of it. And then bless our times of discussing what we are learning from Your Word so we can be blessed by each other's insights and perspectives. And we pray our discussion times would be guided by Your Spirit, that no spirits of dissension or deception or control or pride or strife and arguing could enter in.

We can never thank You enough for Your Word, Lord. We rejoice every day, and especially on this Simchat Torah day in gratefulness that we have Your life-giving, life-changing, empowering Word! We thank You in Yeshua's Name. Amein.

CHAPTER 29
Biblical Meditation, *Hagah*

In the last chapter, technique number six says that one good way to study the Bible is to meditate on it. So now we are going to dig much deeper into what meditating on the Scripture is and how to actually do it based on this verse:

> Joshua 1:8 *This book of the Torah should not depart from your mouth—you are to **meditate** on it day and night, so that you may be careful to do everything written in it. For then you will make your ways prosperous and then you will be successful.*
>
> Joshua 1:8 (CJB) *Yes, keep this book of the Torah on your lips, and **meditate** on it day and night, so that you will take care to act according to everything written in it. Then your undertakings will prosper, and you will succeed.*

TORAH: So let's start out by making sure we understand what the Lord meant when He told Joshua to meditate on *"the Torah." Torah* the actual word in Hebrew. What Scripture did Joshua have at that point in history? Well, all he had, literally, was just God's instructions to Moses, which Moses had written down. So that's just the first five books of the Bible.

Why meditate? *"So that you may be careful to do everything written in it."* So it's understood that he will be acting on the Word. To have all that in your mind and on your lips, but not act on it would not make any sense at all. So Joshua's success was dependent on his following the instructions given in the Torah.

Now look at the promise God gives. It is a very powerful promise. I mean, look at it! You will have success in all that

29. BIBLICAL MEDITATION

you undertake. You will prosper. In other words, you will accomplish all that God wants you to accomplish. But, it's a conditional promise. Did you notice that? The condition is keeping the instruction of God on Joshua's lips, and meditating on it day and night.

WHAT MEDITATION IS NOT: We must bring out right away what this command does **NOT** mean. Biblical meditation is **NOT** the kind of meditation as defined in yoga or Eastern religions, like Hinduism, or occultic beliefs and practices. Having been involved in those for quite a while before I became a believer, I know exactly what those things are. The technique they use is to focus your thoughts on a sound or a word or a picture, called a mandala. The goal of it is to turn off your conscious thinking and open you up to receive communication from the dark, evil spirit world. I can tell you with surety, you do receive communication from the spirit world, but it is definitely not from God! Especially not in many of the yoga techniques where the word you are taught to focus your thoughts on is actually the name of a Hindu god. So it is evil Hindu gods that then communicate with you.

WORD STUDY ON HAGAH: The Hebrew word for *meditate* in Joshua 1:8 is הָגָה *hagah*. If you look this word up in a Hebrew dictionary, it will tell you it means *mutter, murmur, muse, ponder, imagine, or study*. I did a word study on it. Then I went to a concordance, and I looked it up and found all the places where *hagah* was used. I found that it was translated into the English words, *meditate* or *murmur* or *think on*. So here's a passage I found.

> Psalm 63:5-7 (CJB) *I am as satisfied as with rich food; my mouth praises you with joy on my lips 6 when I remember you on my bed and **meditate** on you in the night watches. 7 For you have been my help; in the shadow of your wings I rejoice;*

So, did you comprehend that? What are we supposed to meditate on? God Himself! His nature, His character.

> Psalm 71:22-24a (CJB) *As for me, I will praise you with a lyre for your faithfulness, my God. I will sing praises to*

you with a lute, Holy One of Isra'el. 23 My lips will shout for joy; I will sing your praise, because you have redeemed me. 24 All day long my tongue will **speak** [hagah] *of your righteousness.*

Now if you just looked at that verse in English only, you would not know it had anything to do meditating, right? But if you notice in verse 24, I put in brackets there that the word translated *speak* is actually the Hebrew word for *meditate, hagah*. So what does it say that we are to meditate on here? His righteousness. Yes. Do you see anything else? His faithfulness, His redemption, His holiness. All of those things. Here's another verse using the Hebrew word *hagah*.

Psalm 77:11-12 (CJB) *So I will remind myself of Yah's doings; yes, I will remember your wonders of old. 12 I will* **meditate** *on your work and think about what you have done.*

Yah is short for *God*. So what are we to meditate on? His works, His doings, His deeds, His miracles, His creation and what He has done. In the Messiah, we meditate on the atonement made by the Messiah. And then finally, this next verse:

Proverbs 8:7 *For my mouth* **speaks** *truth,...*

Again *speaks* is actually the Hebrew word *hagah*. So we meditate on what? Truth.

So there's the list of what we're to meditate on in God's Word. We're to meditate on His righteousness, His wonders, His deeds, His redemption, His faithfulness, His holiness, and His truth. That's how you study the Word in the Hebrew.

So looking back to Joshua 1:8, God promises that when we meditate on these things, we will achieve success, not worldly success, but success in His eyes. In other words, our ability to fulfill our destiny, to fulfill the plan that God has for us, to reach our personal promised land, which is summed up in two little phrases the Lord gave me. Become all He wants us to become in this life, and accomplish all He wants us to accomplish in this life. That's a product of meditating on His Word.

SPEAK IT: Joshua 1:8 *...***should not depart from your mouth***....*

From your mouth. You would think it would be: "should not depart from your mind or your heart," but it's *"should not depart from your mouth!"* That's the *utter* or *speak* part in the meaning of *hagah*. This means you are to **recite it over and over again**. There's another Hebrew word in the Bible for *meditate*, שִׂיחַ *see-akh,* that also means *to talk.* So this is a very Biblical Hebrew concept that speaking is one way to meditate.

So **speaking God's Word out loud**, so your ears can hear it, actually reinforces it in your brain. There's power in actually hearing the Word. This is why Paul particularly exhorts:

> I Timothy 4:13 *Until I come, devote yourself to the public reading of Scripture....*

So hearing the Word of God spoken out loud in person or online is a very important part of meditating on it.

MEMORIZATION::Let's talk more about this Biblical meditation, *hagah*. First of all, God tells Joshua, (CJB) "...*keep it on your lips."* It's important to grasp here that in Joshua's day, the only Torah scroll, besides the one he copied for himself, was in the Tabernacle, so you could only read it there or on the stones where God commanded it to be copied (Deut. 27:8).

In post Babylonian exile days, if you wanted to study the Torah Scroll, you could only do it in the synagogue. If you wanted to do it anywhere else, you basically had to **memorize the Word**, and then repeat it or recite it to yourself because people didn't have a copy of it in their house, or a half a dozen copies like most of us have today. Nor did they have it in their pocket on their phone. They had to memorize it.

Reciting is one way of meditating and **memorizing**. And we're told to do it day and night. So why would that be something that would be important? What does that do?

SCIENTIFIC STUDY ON MEMORY: Well, in 2011, our congregation studied the teachings of Dr. Carolyn Leaf, a neuro-scientist. Her teachings are on how our brain actually works. Part of what we learned was the process by which thoughts go from what's called **short-term memory to long-term memory**. Scientists have actually been able to map what's happening in your brain when you read or hear a statement. They have located a section of the brain where free will actually resides. It's just not nebulously everywhere in our brains. There's actually a part of our brain that makes decisions.

When you're free will experiences whatever that statement or thing that you read is, it passes through your free will section, and it makes a decision whether you should reject it or accept it. So let me give an example. You're in class in school and you're taught that William Henry Harrison was the ninth president of the United States. Okay? So your free will now decides, "Am I going to accept that, or am I going to reject that statement?" Now there's no reason to reject that statement. You're being taught that, so your free will says, "Okay, William Henry Harrison is the ninth president of the United States."

Once you decide to accept it, then it goes into another part of your brain, the short-term memory part. Then you have the option of meditating on it, turning it from that short-term memory to long-term memory. So if you start thinking about this and say, "Well, let's see. Was he the ninth president? Presidents serve about four years each, so that would have put him at about 1840. You might look it up to make sure it's true. And then you might think like I think. I'll find out who his vice president was, what happened while he was in office, etc. All that mental activity is meditating on that statement. So you do that and then tomorrow you won't forget who Harrison was. You'll remember he's the ninth president of the United States. It goes into your long-term memory.

Now here's the really incredible Biblical connection. When it goes into your long-term memory, it's encoded in the neurons, the cells in your brain, and it actually becomes part of you, part of your body. It becomes like it's your flesh. Your brain is like a hard drive on a computer, and that information has now been encoded in there. So there's been a rearrangement of the electrical circuits and the chemicals in your brain to hold that piece of information. A similar thing happens with visual images. If you see something, it just goes right to your short-term memory. But then if you go back and remember it and think about it, "Where was that? Where was this?" ...then it goes into your long term-memory. So if you meditate on God's

Word, on His instructions, that moves them from your short-term memory into your long-term memory.

So for an example, you're in Shabbat service and somebody says, "God loves you." So first of all, your free will says, "Do I accept that or do I reject that?" If you accept it and then begin to think about it, "Well, let's see. How do I know God loves me? Well, He demonstrated His love by coming as the Messiah, sacrificing His life for my sin. Oh that's a lot of demonstration of love!" Then you might think about, "Well, it's really amazing that God could love me and at the same time love 7 billion people. That's a lot of Love that He must have." So you're thinking about that and it goes into your long-term memory. Now you have "God Loves me" as part of God's Word in your long-term memory, and it becomes part of you. It becomes part of your spirit, part of your nature.

The Bible calls this *the renewing of your mind*. It's putting God's Word into your mind, putting it in there so it sticks there. The thing that we all should understand is that your old nature, your flesh, your iniquitous nature knows that it will have less influence once you get God's Word into your mind, so it's going to resist that. It'll say something like, "Well, God doesn't love you because you did such and such." Or you might hear inside your brain, "God *doesn't* love you because you *didn't* do such and such." Well, that's your old nature. That's the enemy trying to stop you from bringing those things in and renewing your mind.

But with our free will, we can decide to believe what we want to. We can decide to say, "I'm going to make that part of my renewed mind." So that's what happens when we meditate on God's Word. It becomes part of us and it changes us.

Eight ways To meditate

So I want to take a few minutes and talk about how we actually do this. How do we practice Biblical meditation? I want to give credit to Rabbi Steve Wyler of Shoresh David Congregation in Tampa who gave just a ten minute talk about this at the rabbi's conference one year. It really has affected me tremendously, and I hope it will do the same for you as I expand on his short talk here.

When I thought about this and prayed about it, I came up with eight ways or techniques or methods, if you will, of meditating on the Word of God.

PRAY: **First**, cover your meditation with **prayer.** You start with saying, "Holy Spirit, enable me to meditate on the Word of God. Help me to put God's Word into my long-term memory."

MEMORIZE: The **second** one is what we just talked about: **memorize the Word**. Memorizing verses and reciting them over and over is a great way to meditate. You might write a verse on an index card and keep it in your pocket or on your refrigerator so you see it over and over. Or you can pull it up on your phone whenever, wherever you are and meditate on it day and night.

PONDER: The **third** one is pretty easy. You **think deeply about it.** You read something in God's Word or you hear it, and you **ponder it**. You **muse on God's Word**. That's one definition of the word *hagah*. Memorizing can help you do that, You might **ponder the meaning,** "What does that really mean?" And ask the Holy Spirit to reveal it to you.

This brings to mind again people not being able to answer simple questions about Bible verses in my Messianic Judaism class. What happens is the question goes through the free will section of their brain, where other questions arise. "What did I learn about this?" "What did this preacher say about it?" What did I hear on the radio or internet about it?" Their mind is doing that rather than actually looking at the verse to see what it says.

IMAGINE: Number **four** is **imagining God's Word.** This is very useful for narrative passages, for all the many stories in the Bible. So let's read the next passage. Then I want you to close your eyes and imagine it. I'll give you little clues as to what you are to imagine. Let's see what you get from this. This is speaking about Yeshua.

> Mark 5:24 *He went with him; and a large crowd followed, pressing all around him.*

Imagine the crowd. Imagine their clothing.

> Mark 5:25-26 *Among them was a woman who had had a hemorrhage for twelve years 26 and had suffered a great deal under many physicians. She had spent her life savings; yet instead of improving, she had grown worse.*

Imagine her shame in having to shout, "Unclean!" wherever she went because she was bleeding.

Mark 5:27 *She had heard about Yeshua, so she came up behind him in the crowd and touched his robe;*

Imagine her pushing people, and because she was wearing distinct clothing because she was bleeding, people maybe seeing who she is and jumping out of the way, so they wouldn't touch her, and her coming up behind Him.

Mark 5:28 *for she said, "If I touch even his clothes, I will be healed."*

Now imagine her grabbing onto the hem of His garment. Actually she grabbed His tzitzit (fringes) because that's what He would have had on the hem.

Mark 5:29 *Instantly the hemorrhaging stopped, and she felt in her body that she had been healed from the disease.*

Imagine the astonishment, the joy!

Mark 5:30-32 *At the same time, Yeshua, aware that power had gone out from him, turned around in the crowd and asked, "Who touched my clothes?" 31 His talmidim responded, "You see the people pressing in on you; and still you ask, `Who touched me?'" 32 But he kept looking around to see who had done it.*

Imagine the power Yeshua felt go out from Him. What did that feel like when power to heal this woman went out from Him?

Mark 5:33 *The woman, frightened and trembling, because she knew what had happened to her, came and fell down in front of him and told him the whole truth.*

Imagine her fear, thinking He was going to rebuke her. She had touched a person she was not supposed to touch because she was unclean. But instead of rebuking her, He said:

Mark 5:34 *"Daughter," he said to her, "your trust has healed you. Go in peace, and be healed of your disease."*

Ah! Imagine that relief! She's healed, and she's not being condemned! She's not being rebuked. Instead she is being commended! Then imagine what happens next. Does she run home to tell her family? Or does she stick close to Yeshua and follow Him closely?

That was imagining. Did you get anything out of that? You can do that yourself. Read a verse, then close your eyes and imagine what it was like. What were the people like? How many were there? What were the surroundings like? This is one of the reasons people like to go to Israel because they can actually see the spots where things happened, and they can imagine it better.

ASK GOD QUESTIONS: The **fifth** way of meditating is to **ask God questions** about His Word. If you don't understand His Word, ask God what it means. It won't necessarily come back to you like, you know, writing in the sky, but He will answer you. I've had this happen so many times, supernaturally. After asking God, someone will say something or I'll read something and all of a sudden a revelation will click in my mind.

Another method that I use for asking God is for those who have the gift of speaking in tongues, which I believe we can all have. Maybe you don't have it because you don't want it, but this is a reason to want it. I will read a Scripture, and if I don't see what God wants to speak to me about it, then I will just start praying in tongues. And as I do that, I'm praying in the Spirit of God, and my brain is shut off, and I get communication from the Spirit world, but it's from the right Spirit. And I often all of a sudden get a revelation of what I should understand about that verse. So **asking God questions and praying in tongues is the fifth one.**

SLEEP ON IT: The **sixth** one is really interesting: **sleep on it.** Seriously! I often will study something, then go to sleep for the night, just like normal, and when I wake up in the morning, I've got the answer! When we watched those video teachings on how the brain works, we were taught that there's a lot going on in your brain at night. It's sorting through everything that went on during your day and kind of filing things away in the right places. It's like rearranging all the things in your brain. So when all that stuff gets rearranged, it makes sense. All of a sudden you know the answer to what you didn't understand. So that's eight ways of meditating on God's Word

SING/CHANT IT: Now I'm going to share the **seventh** way. I think it is going to surprise you even though you are already very familiar with it, but you don't realize that it's actually meditating on the Word. And it's also going to surprise you by its great power and its great ease of implementation. It's to **sing the Word**.

> Psalm 71:23-24 *My lips will shout for joy—when I sing praises to You—and my soul, which You have redeemed. 24 Also my tongue will tell* [hagah] *of Your righteousness all day.*

So as I look at that Psalm, I see a connection there between singing and meditating. Now I want to show you what's called the Chumash. Let me describe it. It's a book that has the total traditional Parashah readings all laid out each week. There are vowels in the Hebrew text, so that you can learn to read with the vowels, but there are also these little marks that are called cantillation marks. When I first started trying to learn Hebrew, it was very confusing because I tried to learn the vowels, and then I saw all these other extra little marks. So I would always get confused about which is which. But finally I learned which were the vowels and which were the cantillation marks, and I could ignore the cantillation marks because they are code for the melody for chanting the verse in Hebrew. Chanting is like what we do with the traditional Hebrew blessings, we chant those. We put them to a melody.

So why would this custom of chanting have developed? Well, here's what I understand. God created our brains to be able to remember words set to melody much more easily and accurately than words without music. Have you noticed that? It's so much easier. In Bible times, after Josiah, Jewish children memorized large portion of Scripture by learning the cantillation melody, and those melodies have been preserved by the little marks, the cantillation marks that are on the scrolls.

Now our brains have not changed. We still remember songs better than text. If I were to hum a familiar melody, most likely you would recall the words immediately, even if you haven't heard it in like 30 years, right?

So here's a test. I can't sing to you from this book, but I can give you the first few words and I bet the melody will come to your mind, and you will know the rest of the words. How about this one? "This land is your land this land is my Land..." Right! Okay a Messianic one. "Awake O Israel..." Right! It goes on: "put off your slumber..."

So there's been a television show and many games based on that ability of the human mind. "Name that tune" is one. I can remember when our kids were little, they could recite dozens of commercials because they remembered the jingles from them. That's why advertisers use music so much. So we can apply the same understanding of how our brains work and the value of setting words to music to help us in meditating on God's words.

Here's the thing that maybe you're aware of or maybe you're not. Many songs that we sing are Scripture songs. Here's a list just going through them alphabetically: Ancient of Days; As the Deer; Awake O Israel; Baruch Adonai; Baruch Haba; Be Unto Your Name; Better Is One Day; Blessed Are You; Burn In Me; Clap Your Hands; Come, Let Us Go Up. Those are all Scripture songs, and I only got to the Cs. They're all exact quotes from Scripture.

So, when we sing these songs, what are we doing? We're meditating on God's Word. You see that? And it helps us to remember the words and the phrases because they are put to melody. But more than that, the songs repeat the words. So you go over them with added melody and harmony, and added rhythm and emotion. So as you're singing it, you're actually kind of getting your feelings involved, which puts it deeper into your brain.

So that is the **great power of music** and the great power of putting Scripture to music.

Now, in addition to many of the Scripture songs, also notice that a lot of the songs are meditations on what God is like. There are meditations on His Name, like this one, "Salvation is Your Name" by Joshua Aaron. Or they're meditations on His righteousness or His protection or His power. Remember we learned we are to meditate on His Word, His nature, and His works. It's all there.

29. BIBLICAL MEDITATION

The value of worship is connecting with God and being connected to the Vine and experiencing His presence, but in addition, worshipping and singing has got to be the most enjoyable, the most easy, and the most powerful way of actually meditating on the Word. It's amazing! And we don't normally think about it that way. I've been led by the Spirit to always start any class or small group I lead with a little bit of worship. Why? Because we're getting into the Spirit by meditating on the Word of God, and connecting with Him.

Now let me also say that with modern technology, it's so easy to do this at other times than just when you're in a meeting. It's so easy to listen to our worship music playlists on our smartphones, i-pads, airpods, etc. In our 21st century technology, you can be meditating on His Word while you're driving, while you're doing the dishes, and while you're taking a walk. Whatever you're doing, you can be meditating on God's Word. And when you sing along, like I do in the car, where nobody can hear me, you're actually adding that singing part of the meditating. So you're putting it in your brain even more. So carry worship music around with you wherever you go, and you have the Word of God being sung to you. So it's something that I just want to encourage you to do because I think it's such an empowering thing.

And finally I want to end with the **eighth way**. If you are musically gifted, not just to play, but musically gifted to **put words to music**, I want to encourage you. Now that you see what I'm talking about here, this is such a powerful gift for the body, to help all the rest of us. I want to encourage you to exercise that **gift of song composition** that you have and **create Scripture songs** or songs about God, about His attributes and things like that. Let the Lord bring forth that gift in you. So if you have that gift and it's dormant maybe, just stand up. Let's pray for that first. Then we'll pray for everything else.

Let's pray.

Father, thank You for this reader who has the gift of music and is able to take words and put them to melody. It's such an awesome thing. I just pray, Father, for You to bring forth that gift, Father, bring it forth. Bring forth the poetic. Bring forth the rhythm. Bring forth the melody. Enable them to put Your Word to music, and to be able to spread it all around.

And Father, I pray for all the rest of us. First of all, we just thank You for Your promise. We thank You that if we meditate on Your Word, You promise great success. We pray, Father, that You would help us with this ancient discipline of meditation. Help us to ponder, to speak, to study, to imagine, to teach, to ask You to reveal, to dream, and to sing Your Word. And we just thank You also, Lord, for the amazing technologies that we have.

[Hold up your device.]

Thank You for this, Lord. Thank You that we can carry around Your Word in our pockets and play it into our ears. And if there's a reader who has not caught up with this technology, Father, I just pray that You would enable them to learn, and that they'd have the resources and the skills to carry worship music around with them. And finally, Lord, I want to thank You for the gift of music. Thank You that You make it easy for us to put Your Word in us through music. In Yeshua's Name. Amein.

CHAPTER 30
Applying Biblical Meditation

In this chapter, I am going to walk you through actually doing some *Hagah* meditating. But first, I want to give you another reason why meditating on God's Word is so valuable.

In my other books, I talk a lot about ridding yourself of ungodly thinking, about having it revealed by the Ruakh HaKodesh, repenting of it, and then to stop thinking in those ways. But in this chapter, I was led to look at the other side of stopping ungodly thinking, and it has a lot to do with meditating. What's the other side? It is how to get your mind to start thinking in Godly ways. So that's what we're going to learn in this chapter. We're going to start with the fruit of the Spirit, which I'm sure you are familiar with. Read this verse aloud:

> Galatians 5:22-23 *But the fruit of the Spirit is love, joy, peace, patience, kindness, goodness, faithfulness, 23 humility, self control. Nothing in the Torah stands against such things.*

Now first of all, this is a very appropriate verse to read today because this is all about fruit, right? And **Sukkot** is a celebration of the harvest, including the harvest of fruit, and also spiritual fruit. Maybe you've never thought of it this way, but the Holy Spirit is a fruit farmer or husbandman. Right? We are His crop. We bring forth fruit. So the reason this is significant is that you can't have the fruit of joy, let's say, if you're thinking negative, doubting, fearful, bitter thoughts. Right? But I've experienced this many times. If I try to stop thinking about something that I don't want to be thinking about, it doesn't work. The way to stop is to think about something else. Have you ever noticed that? Here, don't think about orange monkeys. What just happened? You thought about orange monkeys, and got a picture in your mind of an orange monkey. Right? So, what can we do? Well, we need to do the opposite—the positive, which is to think about good things. Rabbi Sha'ul instructs us to do this in Philippians.

> Philippians 4:8 *In conclusion, brothers, focus your thoughts on what is true, noble, righteous, pure, lovable or admirable, on some virtue or on something praiseworthy.*

Now it's great to read that and say, "Yeah I should do that!" I don't know about you, but for me, it's hard to do because our minds just kind of think about one thing, and then about something else, and then other things pop up, right? Are you with me on that?

So I've come to understand that I can't think only on good things in my own ability. It's not possible. **Only God can enable us to do that.** And I find that He says He will do it, but He will do it **by His Word**. It's by His Word that He does it. So let's look at psalm 119 where David writes about this.

> Psalm 119:11 *I have treasured Your word in my heart, so I might not sin against You.*

It's the Word. So how does the Word get into you, into your innermost being, your heart, or your spirit? Well, Jeremiah, in that wonderful passage about the New Covenant, tells us:

> Jeremiah 31:32 *But this is the covenant I will make with the house of Israel after those days—it is a declaration of A<small>DONAI</small>—I will put my Torah [my instruction] within them. Yes **I will write it on their heart**. I will be their God and they will be My people.*

But the problem is the Ruakh haKodesh **can't put His Word within you** and write it on your heart **unless you are taking in His Word through your eyes and your ears.** There's no way that He can do that unless you are absorbing His Word through those gates. However, it also tells us in the Word that **a casual reading or hearing of God's Word is not enough.** You are most likely familiar with this next passage:

30. APPLYING BIBLICAL MEDITATION

> Joshua 1:7 *Only be very strong, and resolute to **observe diligently** the Torah which Moses My servant commanded you. Do not turn from it to the right or to the left so that you may be successful wherever you go.*

So notice those words "observe diligently." Is that casual reading? No, it's something more than that, and he explains it in verse eight. What is it? Of course you know by now:

> Joshua 1:8 *This book of the Torah should not depart from your mouth—you are to **meditate on it day and night,** so that you may be careful to do everything written in it. For then you will make your ways prosperous and then you will be successful.*

It's *hagah* meditating! And let me say it again. This is not the kind of meditation associated with the occult, Hinduism, or yoga, which I got caught up in, which meditates on Hindu gods and on sounds and meaningless things and opens you up to the wrong spirit world and wrong spirits. This is talking about meditating on what? On the Word of God! Remember the other words used for *hagah?* They are *utter, speak, muse,* and *ponder.* King David confirms this instruction to meditate on God's Word here:

> Psalm 1:2 *But his delight is in the* Torah *of* ADONAI *and on His* Torah *he **meditates day and night.***

And then He gives us a promise similar to the one made to Joshua. It's a wonderful promise:

> Psalm 1:3 *He will be like a planted tree over streams of water, producing its fruit during its season. Its leaf never droops—but in all he does, he succeeds.*

See the parallel there with Joshua? But what's the key action in there? Yes! Meditate on the Word of God! So what I was led to do now is to really get this down to where you understand how to do at least two parts of Biblical, *hagah* meditating, the speaking or uttering part and the pondering or deep thinking part, and hopefully you will begin to practice it. So what we're going to do is take a **couple** different **verses** and meditate on each word or phrase. Okay? This is going to be interactive, so get ready. First we're going to look at this very familiar passage in three different versions. Read each one aloud:

> I John 4:18 *There is no fear in love. On the contrary, love that has achieved its goal gets rid of fear, because fear has to do with punishment; the person who keeps fearing has not been brought to maturity in regard to love.*
>
> I John 4:18 (TLV) **There is no fear in love, but perfect love drives out fear.** *For fear has to do with punishment, and the one who fears has not been made perfect in love.*
>
> I John 4:18 (NKJV) *There is no fear in love; but perfect love casts out fear, because fear involves torment. But he who fears has not been made perfect in love.*

Now before you get scared and think you've got to memorize all of that, we're just going to focus on the first part, *There is no fear in love but perfect love casts out fear.* Can you remember that? Okay. So as we go through this example, please don't just read, but participate in what we're going to do here. Okay? I want you to meditate with me on this passage word by word, phrase by phrase. Okay?

So we're gonna start with **no fear.** So now, say it over to yourself several times. Notice what thoughts come to your mind. Actually take some time right now and do that. .....

Okay. Now this is, by the way, how the Holy Spirit gives me revelation for messages. I read the passage and I think about it and roll it over in my mind. So what I'm going to do is I'm going to share with you what came to my mind when I did this, and then I'm going to let you share what came to your mind. We're going to have several of these.

So here's what came to my mind. Some fears are beneficial. It's good to be afraid when you're about to be hit by a car, right? Fear causes a release of adrenaline to enhance your ability to get out of the way, but that's not the kind of fear that's being referred to here, is it? No, because this fear, notice what it says in the NKJV, *involves torment.* Torment is agonizing, irrational, unfounded fear. Isaiah 41:10 is a verse I remember. God is saying this. Read it aloud:

> Isaiah 41:10 *Fear not, for I am with you, be not dismayed, for I am your God. I will strengthen you. Surely I will help you. I will uphold you with My righteous right hand.*

30. APPLYING BIBLICAL MEDITATION 387

So God commands you to fear not when fear is holding you back from obeying Him and from all kinds of other good things. Then the Bible tells us a little bit more about this kind of tormenting fear in II Timothy:

> II Timothy 1:7 (NKJV) *For God has not given us a spirit of fear, but of power and of love and of a sound mind.*

So what do we learn from this? Fear is a spirit. And it is not given, or sent, by God! Well, who was it sent by then? Ha-satan! Ha-satan sends a spirit of fear to tempt you into being afraid, which, by the way, can cause all kinds of problems: physical, emotional, relational, financial, addictions, all kinds of things.

So now, let's consider many other words that describe all different forms of fear. Read this list. Maybe you'll think of some more, but this is what came to my mind. There's:

worry	terror	dread	apprehension
anxiety	horror	consternation	disquietude
stress	agitation	dismay	foreboding
nervousness	distress	angst	misgiving
panic	trepidation	unease	alarm

Those are all fears! So now let's take a minute. Ask yourself, "Am I now, or have I been, experiencing any of those many forms of fear? Just take a minute to ask yourself that. ....

Now let's pray.

Lord, we take responsibility right now for giving in to the temptation to fear. [The spirit of fear brings temptation.] We ask You to forgive us for giving in to fear because You command us to fear not. We ask You to forgive us for giving in to being afraid or worried or anxious or panicking or dreading, all of those things. We ask Your forgiveness and we receive it because You paid the price for us. We thank You, for Your forgiveness. In Yeshua's Name. Amen.

Okay. Now, how about your thoughts? What did *no fear* bring to your mind when you meditated on it? I did this once for my congregation, and I saw a hand way in the back. It was Denise. She said, "No matter where I go or what I'm doing or whoever taunts me or whatever happens, I will not fear because God is with me." Wonderful.

Now you write your thoughts in your journal or here:

Perfect Love

Great. Okay, now let's go back to the passage. *There is no fear in love ... perfect love...* Let's meditate on **perfect Love.** So let's take a minute and meditate on those words. ....

Okay, here's what came to my mind. The world defines love. Here's the dictionary definition: *an intense feeling of deep affection; to have great interest and pleasure in something; to feel a deep romantic or sexual attachment to someone.* Perfect love is not what the dictionary defines as love. This verse is talking about *perfect* Love. It's God's Love. Its *agape Love.* It's unselfish Love. Here's one description from the Bible. Read it aloud to yourself:

> I Corinthians 13:4-8 *Love is patient and kind, not jealous, not boastful, 5 not proud, rude or selfish, not easily angered, and it keeps no record of wrongs. 6 Love does not gloat over other people's sins but takes its delight in the truth. 7 Love always bears up, always trusts, always hopes, always endures. 8 Love never ends;*

That's perfect Love. Let that sink in for a minute. .....

Now you may have been blessed to have had or now have people in your life who have loved you with near-perfect love like that. I don't think anybody loves with really perfect Love, except the Lord. So think about it, if that's you. Think about how wonderful it has been to be loved that way.

Or you may have loved or now love someone with near-perfect love. But some people have never been loved that way, which is very sad. Maybe you are one of them. My heart goes out to you. Some also have never loved anyone that way.

However, someone really *does* love you with **perfect Love**. Yes, I'm talking about you, the one reading this book. In John chapter 15, Yeshua said this:

30. APPLYING BIBLICAL MEDITATION

John 15:13 *No one has greater love than a person who lays down his life for his friends.*

If you've given your heart to Yeshua, you are what? His friend! And He demonstrated perfect Love by sacrificing His life for you, His friend, enduring unimaginable physical pain, humiliation, separation from God, and death to pay the price to atone for your sins. That's perfect Love.

Now you might say, "Well, that was Yeshua. That was 2000 years ago." But remember, Yeshua is God come in the form of a man. So if He, Yeshua, loves you with perfect Love, who else loves you with perfect Love? God Himself loves you with perfect Love! And how much perfect Love does God love you with? How much? Yeshua told us in a prayer that He prayed to His Father in John17:

John17:23b (NKJV) *...that You [Father] ... have loved them...*
Who's them? His disciples, his friends. He loved them how?

John17:23c (NASB) *... just as You loved Me.*

Can you grasp that? Can you imagine how much the Father Loves Yeshua? I mean He's the Son. He's God Himself! He's always been obedient to God. God's Love for Yeshua is the most perfect Love there could ever be. And Yeshua says that God Loves you the same way He Loves Yeshua! You got that? He Loves you with His perfect Love. That's perfect Love. That's what perfect Love is. Just think on that for a minute. ....

I'm continuing with what happened when we did this in my congregation. Alan said, "God is Love and God is perfect. So God is in us and He's loving us with His perfect Love." Yes.

Okay. Did you get something on perfect Love? Write it down here:

Now let's meditate on that **next phrase**, *perfect love drives out fear*. Take a minute and meditate on that. ......

Here's what came to me. It's from a verse we read earlier.

II Timothy 1:7 (NKJV) *For God has not given us a spirit of fear, but of power and of love and of a sound mind.*

So fear and all it's synonyms, that long list, are evil spirits sent by ha-satan to torment us. So how can Love, which is patient and kind and enduring, **drive out** or **cast out** an evil spirit?

I John 4:8 ... *God is Love.*

So God, who is Love, drives out or casts out fear! Alright, but how does He do it? By it just happening? No, He has delegated the power to those who trust in Yeshua.

Mark 16:17 (TLV) *These signs will accompany those who believe: in My name they will **drive out** demons;*

So we speak in faith because we've been delegated the authority over fear by God who is perfect Love.

I asked for more thoughts. Pastor Tom said, "Because of God's Love, we can always go to Him no matter what has happened or what we have done, and we will be welcomed and forgiven because of God's perfect Love, and will have a place reserved in Heaven." Thank you, Pastor Tom.

What are your thoughts on *perfect love drives out fear*? Write them down.

So let's take a moment now. We already repented of giving in to fear. Right? Remember the process for dealing with spirits is to always humble yourself before God and resist the devil. So we've humbled ourselves before God by repenting of having given in to fear. And I have to say I've given in to fear at times in my life. Have you ever given in to fear? Yeah? Okay, so we've repented of that. Now let's command that fear, worry, anxiety, and tormenting fear to leave.

In the Name of Yeshua, the Name that's above every name, the Name that's above fear, worry, apprehension, terror, horror, in the Name that's above all of those things, we command the spirit of fear, and all its power and all of those sub spirits that go with it, to leave us right now. In the Name of Yeshua, we command them to leave! Any effects of them, we break their power right now, in the Name of Yeshua!

And we ask, Lord, that You would give us the ability to discern when they try to tempt us again, so we can stand against those things in the Name of Yeshua. We thank You for Your power. Hallelujah! Thank You, Lord. Thank You, Lord.

Rejoice

Okay! Ready for **another verse**? Let's meditate together on **joy**. Actually you should have a head start on this because if you just got some deliverance, you should be joyful, right? Victory over fear brings joy!

So this passage immediately precedes what we started with in Philippians 4:8 where Rabbi Sha'ul tells us to focus our thoughts on good things. You most likely know this by heart. Again, read it aloud.

Philippians 4:4 (KJV) *Rejoice in the Lord always: and again I say, Rejoice.*

So let's start with that **first important word, *rejoice***. .....

Here's what came to me. Do you understand that's a command? That was a command, right? *Rejoice in the Lord always: and again I say rejoice.* That's not just a statement or a suggestion, right? Okay, you got that, which means you should be doing what? Rejoicing!

Think about times you have rejoiced. How did you feel when you were rejoicing over something? What other words come to mind when you dwell on *rejoicing*? Singing, happiness, laughing, gratitude, exhilaration, shouting, and dancing.

Now think about times we see people rejoicing. Have you ever watched tennis matches? What happens when the winner finishes the tennis match? They fall on the ground! They can't even stand up, they're rejoicing so much. Right? So what are other occasions that are times of rejoicing? Weddings, baby showers, bar/bat mitzvahs, graduations, homecomings, salvations! Also victory at the end of a war! Election victories, winning contests, whether they're mental contests or athletic contests. Can you remember being present at some of those occasions? Yes? Let that sense of rejoicing enter you now while you think of all Yeshua has done for you and how much He Loves you. ......

One persons thoughts: Mickey said, "David dancing before the Lord." Great. And yes, he had some clothes on.

Now your thoughts. What came to you about rejoice?

Okay. Ready to meditate again? Let's meditate on the phrase, *in the Lord*. *Rejoice in the Lord*. What does that mean to you? Just meditate on it for a while. *Rejoice in the Lord*. .....

Here are my thoughts. Rejoice in what He has done for you, your salvation, forgiveness, putting His Spirit in you, His Love for you, your deliverance, your healing, your restoration, the purpose that He's given you, the wisdom that He's given you. Also rejoice in who He is. In one sermon I did once, I taught from Exodus 33 where God tells us what "His glory" really means. It means His compassion, graciousness, slowness to anger, loving-kindness, truth, mercy, forgiveness and justice, His wisdom and His power and His beauty. Rejoice in those things. Rejoice in the Lord. .....

Our worship leader, Ethel gave her thoughts, "I'm rejoicing in His arms." Wonderful! Awesome! Keep on rejoicing in the Lord.

Your thoughts go in your journal or here:

Okay, **now another word,** *always.* ....

Here are my thoughts. Is right now a part of *always?* Yes, right now is a part of *always!* So rejoice right now! Right now! Okay? Are you rejoicing right now? If not, why not?

Rejoice in who God is and what He's done for you, salvation, His glory. And think about what the word *rejoice* means. Remember, the first part of it, *re-*, means to repeat something; do something again that you did before, like return, renew. *Rejoice* then means to return to the joy you once had. We know that wonderful Psalm that David wrote. Psalm 51:14 *Restore to me* what? ... *the joy of Your salvation!* Can you remember the joy you had when you first gave your heart to the Lord? Yes? I remember smiling. I couldn't quit smiling. Let that joy come to you right now. That's the point. Let it come to you right now. .....

But you might be thinking, "But wait, wait! My circumstances are not good right now. I've got this trial I'm going through. I've got this sickness. I've got this problem. I've got this financial thing." But doesn't *always* include those times too? *Always!* So Yeshua told us this.

> John 16:33a (NKJV) *These things I have spoken to you, that in Me you may have peace. In the world you will have tribulation; ...*

You will have what? *Tribulation*. In Yiddish it's *tsuris, troubles*.

> John 16:33b *...but be of good cheer, I have overcome the world.*

Peace and good cheer in the midst of tribulation is cause for rejoicing? *Rejoice in the Lord always* certainly when your experiencing blessing, but also when you're experiencing trials, when circumstances are good and when circumstances are bad, and when circumstances are neutral. Rabbi Sha'ul says to still rejoice. Now this is important because I heard someone comment that he was rejoicing that he broke his leg. Hey, Rabbi Sha'ul is not saying rejoice because something bad happened or is happening to you or around you right now. He's saying rejoice in the Lord because of what this verse says.

> Romans 8:28a *Furthermore, we know that God causes everything...*

God causes what? *Everything! All things* to do what?

> Romans 8:28b *...to work together for the good of those who love God and are called in accordance with his purpose;*

So when you're going through a trial, when you're anxious about something about to happen, when you're disappointed, when you're offended, you're hurt, you're confused, you're lost, you're angry, you're bitter, or you're tempted, rejoice! Even in the trials, rejoice because God is going to make it work for what? For good for you!

Okay. Sherry had her hand up for five minutes. Your thoughts, Sherry? "We do that with the Mourner's Kaddish." Yes, the Mourner's Kaddish is an example of that! Absolutely, yes! And it comes from the book of Job. When Job's children died. He said, *The Lord gives, and the Lord takes away. Blessed be the name of the Lord.* He praised God. He rejoiced in the midst of terrible tsuris. Your thoughts?

Okay, one other phrase, **and again I say rejoice.** Why did Rabbi Sha'ul repeat this instruction to us? Take some time to think about that. .....

Well, I just have something really simple to say about this. He's repeating it because it's so important! He's saying it over and over again. Listen to what Sha'ul says here:

> Philippians 4:11 *Not that I am saying this to call attention to any need of mine; since, as far as I am concerned, I have learned to be content regardless of circumstances.*

Being content is part of rejoicing regardless of circumstances. Frank had a thought on *again I say rejoice?* "He's still God, so again rejoice." And what are your thoughts on *again I say rejoice?*

Okay are you rejoicing yet? Let's take a minute and meditate on the whole sentence, *Rejoice in the Lord always and again I say rejoice.* Meditate on that for a few minutes. ...

30. APPLYING BIBLICAL MEDITATION 395

Okay, here's what I want to encourage you to do. Try to do this type of meditation for about 15 minutes a day, and you'll find something happening. Once you do it for a while, like in the morning, you will remember the verse you're doing all day long. The verse that you meditate on like that will keep coming to your mind all day, and God will be renewing your mind.

I have been experiencing this since I heard the ten minute talk by Rabbi Steve at the rabbis' conference, when he also had us meditate on the word, *rejoice*, and it's just been lifting me up so much! Whatever I'm doing, whatever is going on, all of a sudden I'll catch myself and realize, I'm not rejoicing. I should be rejoicing! Why shouldn't I rejoice?! And I just start rejoicing! I don't have to do any big theology about it, or you know, any reasoning of, "Well I could rejoice if this were better, or if that were better, or if this would happen." No, it's like, "I can rejoice right now!" And I become joyful! It's amazing! That's renewing your mind. That's how God changes how you think.

Would there be anybody who would not want this fruit of the Spirit? Who would not want this joy? If you don't, we're going to make an appointment with you for a psychiatrist to find out what's wrong with you because we all want joy. Right? Is there anybody who wants fear? No, we all want to have victory over fear.

So I just encourage you to keep doing hagah meditating. Ask the Ruakh to show you what word or Bible passage to meditate on next. I was amazed at how much it affected me in just the first two weeks after I was at that rabbis' conference. It has really made a change in me. Just random times, I'm just joyful and happy. In the middle of working on something or doing something, all of a sudden it's like, "Oh I can be joyful to do this." I can be joyful driving down the street. Somebody cuts me off, I can still be joyful. The snow is coming down, I can still be joyful.

And I believe there's a very strong connection here between when we follow God's written instructions, like rejoicing in Him always, and when He gives us what I call, real-time instructions, when He tells us what we are supposed to do today, not just what is right or wrong, or what our general purpose is to be, but what I am supposed to do today. One is dependent on the other. Those real-time instructions come as they are needed. And remember what the promise is in Joshua 1:8? We will have success and prosper!

    Let's pray.

    Thank You, Lord, for being the great fruit farmer. It's Your plan to grow the fruit of the Spirit in each of our lives, to conform us to the image of Yeshua, to glorify us, to set us apart and make us spotless for You. Help us to understand, Lord, that You are the renewer of our minds, that we can't do it ourselves. And we thank You, Lord, that You tell us that it's Your Word that has the power to renew our minds, to transform us. I just want to thank You, Lord, that Your Word is available to us like never before in history: in books, on computers, on tablets, on phones, on TV, on the radio, on the internet. It's available all over the place.

    So I pray, Father, for all of us. Give us the desire and the discipline to take Your Word in with our eyes and our ears, and fulfill Your Covenant, Your promise to write Your Word on our hearts. We thank You for the promises of the power of meditating on Your Word, that it will bring success, prosperity, fruit, and strength. Teach us, Lord.

    I just gave a little lesson here. Rabbi Steve gave a little lesson. Teach us, Father, how to meditate on Your Word. Others may do it in a different way. But we pray, Father, that You would give us revelation and renew our minds as we meditate on Your Word.

    Enable us to be people who have no fear. Give us the ability to stand against all fear by walking in Your perfect Love. We thank You that we have the power of Your Name, Yeshua, to cast out all fear.

    Enable us, Lord, to be people who rejoice in You always.

    And Lord, we just want to repent. I repent. I can think of how big a proportion of my life I was disobeying that command to rejoice.

[In how much of your life have you not been rejoicing? For me, it was probably like 99 percent before I came to the Lord!]

Lord, forgive us for not obeying Your command to rejoice always.

[We know now that's what it says. It's a commandment. *Rejoice in the Lord always.* There's nobody who's reading this who's done that. In fact, most of us have spent most of our lives not rejoicing.]

So, Father, we ask Your forgiveness. Right now in the Name of Yeshua, we come against every wrong spirit, every spirit of doubt and unbelief, every spirit of fear and distress, every spirit that would cause us to not be able to rejoice. We break the power of those spirits over us, and we thank You, Father, that You are working all things, everything, difficulties included, for our good. So we can rejoice even in the midst of when things are not going well. We can rejoice. Thank You, Lord. Thank You, Lord. In Yeshua's Name! Amein.

[Can You give a rejoicing shout? Remember, we imagined what people look like when they're rejoicing? Remember that? So stand up! Let's do something that would be rejoicing. Go ahead. Do some rejoicing!]

Father, we rejoice in You and in what You've done! And we rejoice in Your Moad, Sukkot!! HALLELUJAH!!!!!

www.ingramcontent.com/pod-product-compliance
Lightning Source LLC
Chambersburg PA
CBHW051047230426
43666CB00012B/2599